ON ECONOMIC THEORY
AND SOCIALISM

by the same author

POLITICAL ECONOMY AND CAPITALISM
STUDIES IN THE DEVELOPMENT OF CAPITALISM
SOVIET ECONOMIC DEVELOPMENT SINCE 1917
WAGES (CAMBRIDGE ECONOMIC HANDBOOK SERIES)
AN ESSAY ON ECONOMIC GROWTH AND PLANNING

ON ECONOMIC THEORY AND SOCIALISM

Collected Papers

by MAURICE DOBB, M.A.
Lecturer and Fellow of Trinity College, Cambridge

LONDON
ROUTLEDGE & KEGAN PAUL LTD

*First published in 1955
by Routledge & Kegan Paul Limited
Broadway House, 68–74 Carter Lane
London, E.C.4
and Printed in Great Britain
by Compton Printing Works
London, N.1
Second impression 1956
Reprinted (with an additional note on p.265) 1965*

PREFACE

WHEN COLLECTED REPRINTS are as much in vogue as they seem to be at present, republication of scattered, and perhaps deservedly forgotten, essays and papers may require less apology than was formerly the case. For the making of such collections, however, no standard criteria seem to exist; and if one were to be quite logical, no line could probably be drawn between including all or including nothing. Once, wisely or unwisely, a start has been made, it is not easy to avoid repetition, or to avoid altogether the ephemeral or what in retrospect may appear trivial, mistaken or outdated. I do not expect to find much agreement that the choice here made has been a reasonable one. The result is admittedly a curiously mixed bag —a mixture of things composed at different dates, in different contexts and for different audiences. I can only hope that readers will appreciate this, and will turn a tolerant if not a blind eye to what is not their particular *pabulum*; and, further, that anything which is read will be looked at with its date as well as its audience in mind.

Articles and essays have been arranged (so far as possible) chronologically within each of the three parts into which the collection has been divided. Part 1 consists chiefly of articles written for academic journals and for specialist readers; Part 2 of lectures or essays intended for a wider and less specialised public; to Part 3 have been relegated such shorter notes and reviews as seemed (rightly or wrongly) to be just worth including. Here again, the line between Parts 1 and 2 has not been at all easy to draw and there may be some overlap between them. A few corrections have been made, and occasional excisions, where it seemed only fair to the reader to do so (e.g. phrasing or argument that was obscure or misleading or references that had become quite obsolete); but apart from these there has been no attempt to revise the imperfect or the out-moded or to rewrite what the author would put differently today.

Explanatory notes have been inserted at the beginning of most items (in one case as prefatory to a group of three essays). Where footnotes have been added in this collection and were not in the original, they have been placed in square brackets and marked in the text with an asterisk

PREFACE

instead of a number. Acknowledgements for permission to reprint are made below in the appropriate places. One article (No. III C), the bulk of one of the two lectures (No. IX) and one short note (No. XVII) have not previously been published.

M.H.D.

Cambridge,
April 1954.

CONTENTS

PREFACE   page v

Part One

I. THE ENTREPRENEUR MYTH [1924]   3
II. A SCEPTICAL VIEW OF THE THEORY OF WAGES [1929]   16
III. THREE ARTICLES ON THE PROBLEM OF ECONOMIC
     CALCULATION IN A SOCIALIST ECONOMY   33
   A. *Economic Theory and the Problems of a Socialist
      Economy* [1933]   34
   B. *A Note on Saving and Investment in a Socialist
      Economy* [1939]   41
   C. *A Review of the Discussion Concerning Economic
      Calculation in a Socialist Economy* [1953]   55
IV. THE ECONOMIC BASIS OF CLASS CONFLICT [1937]   93
V. ON SOME TENDENCIES IN MODERN ECONOMIC THEORY
   [1949]   104
VI. RATES OF GROWTH UNDER THE FIVE-YEAR PLANS [1953]   118
VII. A NOTE ON THE SO-CALLED DEGREE OF CAPITAL-
     INTENSITY OF INVESTMENT IN UNDER-DEVELOPED
     COUNTRIES [1954]   138

Part Two

VIII. A LECTURE ON LENIN [1939]   157
IX. A LECTURE ON MARX [1942]   178
X. BERNARD SHAW AND ECONOMICS [1946]   205
XI. FULL EMPLOYMENT AND CAPITALISM [1950]   215
XII. HISTORICAL MATERIALISM AND THE ROLE OF THE
     ECONOMIC FACTOR [1951]   226

CONTENTS

Part Three

XIII. ECONOMISTS AND THE ECONOMICS OF SOCIALISM 239
XIV. COMMENT ON SOVIET ECONOMIC STATISTICS 247
XV. A NOTE ON THE DISCUSSION OF THE PROBLEM OF CHOICE BETWEEN ALTERNATIVE INVESTMENT PROJECTS 258
XVI. THE ACCUMULATION OF CAPITAL 266
XVII. A NOTE ON THE TRANSFORMATION PROBLEM 273
INDEX 283

Part One

I

THE ENTREPRENEUR MYTH[1]
[1924]

This rather jejune essay in criticism of some traditional notions has been included here since it contains the germ of certain ideas about the origins and growth of capitalism that were developed more fully by the writer twenty years later. Based on a paper read to a Cambridge society the year before, it was published in Economica, *No. 10, February 1924. Acknowledgement is due to the Editorial Board of* Economica *for permission to reprint it.*

IT IS PERHAPS no exaggeration to say that one of the chief reasons why the polemics of socialists and individualists are as a rule so inconclusive is that both tend to regard the period around 1800 as the starting point of everything characteristically modern. The arguments of the two seldom meet. Each emphasises a different point and tends to ignore the particular issue on which his opponent is laying emphasis. When Dr. Marshall patronisingly disposes of the socialist in a footnote, he usually leaves the socialist quite unconvinced; and when Mr. Webb attempts to criticise the social philosophy of the orthodox economists, his criticism often has a peculiar way of missing the mark. One of the reasons for this inconclusiveness is that in general the socialist and the individualist each has only a partial theory of the development of modern capitalism.

To the individualist the Industrial Revolution is important because it introduced the free economic order. The pre-existing 'errors' of the mercantilists were abandoned and the great 'truths' of Adam Smith won the day. Mobility of resources and freedom of enterprise, resulting in a progressive widening of the market, were the two great principles of the

[1] Based on a paper read to the Economics Section of The Heretics, at Cambridge, on May 23rd, 1923.

new era. The keystone was the union of control with risk. These were inventions as important as the more tangible discoveries of Arkwright and Crompton and Cartwright and Watt. Although progress in the future may perfect and develop and perhaps modify those grand principles, it would not be progress by the implicit definition of the word if those principles were abolished. A new economic order must include those principles; it must not supersede them.

To the socialist the Industrial Revolution is important for an opposite reason. It was at this period that society ran upon the wrong lines. The technical changes of this period placed immense power in the hands of the capitalist undertaker. The concentration of workers into factories made of the relation between employer and employed a relation between tyrant and subject—wage-slavery. The principle of *laissez-faire*, which this period introduced, is the charter of the rich and strong to exploit the poor and weak. The socialist condemns the grand principles of the individualist as the conditions of this subjection and exploitation. When the individualist replies, he points out that the industrial autocracy and the inequality of which complaint is made are in part necessary conditions of a system of free enterprise. The union of control with risk may involve evils, but the evils are surely a small price to pay for the blessings it entails? Mitigate those evils by all means, but not at the expense of the good! And when the Fabian endeavours, as on rare occasions he does, to banish the inconclusiveness of the argument and to tackle his opponent on his own ground, he is forced into the position of criticising the efficiency of individualism in particular cases, and of advocating, not its complete supersession, but its modification by a little collectivism in a few *named* cases. The Fabian, if he does this, has accepted the assumptions of the individualist and his difference from the liberal has become merely one of degree.[1]

The more modern and competent presentation of the individualist case derives most of its force from an examination of those origins of modern capitalism which are prior to the Industrial Revolution. This case offers, perhaps for the first time, a scientific refutation of socialist criticism by showing the principles on which individualism is based to be the *necessary* conditions of modern industrial progress. It thus tries to give an historical basis to individualism in place of the metaphysic of 'natural law'. This has

---

[1] Sidgwick supported Socialism as 'a supplementary and subordinate element in a system mainly individualistic' (*Elements of Politics*, 4th edn., p. 146). Von Wieser mentioned that the free economic order 'requires supplementing by suitable interference on the part of governments', but does not require 'complete overturn' (*Natural Value*, p. 56).

THE ENTREPRENEUR MYTH

found, perhaps, its best expression in a post-war work by Professor A. P. Usher.[1]

In the first place Professor Usher criticises what he calls the German Socialist School[2] for ascribing too much importance in social evolution to industrial *forms*. Industrial forms are merely the surface expression of economic development, not its essence. The process of development lies in something more fundamental. In the second place he asserts that this more fundamental factor in social evolution is the division of labour. This forms the groundwork of history. A given degree of intricacy in this economic differentiation will produce the need for a certain kind of integration. Hence, whenever in history there have occurred similar industrial forms, this was because there existed similar degrees of economic differentiation in the two periods. When industrial forms change it is because economic differentiation has become more complex, and a new method of integration is consequently required. The attitude of Professor Usher to modern capitalism is to regard it as the culminating stage in a long series of changes in the economic groundwork—the division of labour. The important departure towards modern industrialism would appear to have been made not in the eighteenth century, but in the fourteenth and fifteenth centuries. At this period the dissolution of Feudalism was well advanced, and the subdivision of the crafts had begun to develop on an extensive scale. Each craft tended to split up into numerous specialised divisions. To prevent this differentiation from dissolving into chaos some new method of integration was needed, which was found in the 'commission' or 'putting out' system. Under this system a large number of small master craftsmen, employing journeymen and apprentices, were dependent on a commercial capitalist undertaker, who marketed the produce and often advanced the raw material. When the division of labour extended further to a splitting up of various parts of a homogeneous process, as in Adam Smith's pin factory, there arose the need for a co-ordinated plan of production and for organised team work. The capitalist undertaker was needed, no longer only as a merchant, but as a disciplinarian, and the factory system was the result.

This interpretation provides an apology for the system of capitalist undertaking by showing it as the necessary condition of the intricate system of specialisation which constitutes modern industrialism. Capitalist undertaking cannot be dispensed with unless the conditions which are

---

[1] *An Introduction to the Industrial History of England.*

[2] Under this head he appears to include Sombart, Bücher, Wagner, Rodbertus, and Marx.

its foundation are dispensed with also. 'A capitalist employer was necessary to prevent specialisation from degenerating into disorder ... (Besides a study of industrial forms) there is need also of a study of conditions that produce this progression from the simpler to the more complex forms. It is peculiarly unfortunate to assume that the main task is completed when certain forms have been arranged in a logical sequence.'[1]

To this view, just as the limitations of nature always impose on mankind a certain element of determinism and necessity, so a certain stage in the division of labour imposes upon society the 'necessity' of the capitalist undertaker. The early economists were, therefore, right in saying that the evils of which the socialists complained were attributable to natural and not to institutional factors.

The economic aspect of individualism as reclad in modern garb is consummately represented in the social philosophy of the Cambridge school of economists, or (as a writer in *The New Republic* recently termed it) of the Cambridge 'Neo-Classicists'. The term Neo-Classicist is not entirely inappropriate; for what the Cambridge school has done is to divest classical political economy of its more obvious crudities, to sever its connection with the philosophy of natural law, and to restate it in terms of the differential calculus. The line of descent is fairly direct from Smith, Malthus, and Ricardo; and Cambridge has remained relatively untouched by the anti-classical doctrines of the German semi-socialists and the Austrian school.

This economic theory regards the *telos* of all economic activity as the maximisation of utilities. This is the economic maxim. Cost represents a deprivation of certain utilities. The economic justification for incurring any cost is that, not only a greater utility is obtained, but the greatest possible utility under the circumstances. Hence, two conditions are necessary to the fulfilment of the economic maxim. First, marginal utility must be greater than marginal cost. Second, economic resources must be so distributed between various uses, that there could be no gain from shifting resources from one use to the other. These conditions imply the existence of an *economic measure* as the regulator of production; and this measure is afforded by the mechanism of price.

From the viewpoint of the economist, therefore, the economic world is a complex of price-relations—of persons striving to satisfy certain wants and coming constantly into conflict with obstacles to that satisfaction. In the centre of this chaos stands the capitalist undertaker. The to-be or not-to-be of a productive enterprise is in his hands; the distribution of re-

[1] Usher, *op. cit.*, pp. 3 and 13.

sources between numerous competing uses is under his control; and he regulates his actions by movements of price, indicative of movements of market demand. The undertaker, therefore, is the nerve-centre of the organism, infinitely delicate. On his state of mind depends the efficiency of the whole. All the technical inventions in the world would avail little if this co-ordinating mechanism ceased to function. Hence, the need for the undertaker is conditioned by the highly complex differentiation of modern society. The payment to evoke this activity is a 'necessary' cost in the sense that it is imposed, not by a particular system of politico-legal relations, but by the division of labour and ultimately by nature. The more clearly the price-index finds expression and the more imperatively the profit principle exacts obedience, the more efficiently is the undertaker likely to fulfil the economic maxim.

It is now generally admitted that the classical economists were too sanguine of the efficient operation of the price and profit principle in the actual world: they were too neglectful of certain divergencies between the ideal economy of their pure theory and the real economy of concrete things. The neo-classicists have repaired this breach in the classical doctrine by the use of the conception of *economic friction*. It is now customary for economists to forestall criticism by indicating that the condition 'other things being equal' must always be carefully remembered in the statement of an economic law. In many cases there is incomplete mobility of resources; in some cases the test of profitability is not completely synonymous with social utility; the price offered by consumers is not always a completely adequate index of need. Nevertheless, the principle of the undertaker's function is paramount. Criticism is wrongly placed when levelled against him. Reforms are ill-advised which hazard his efficient operation.

This all sounds logical enough; moreover, it has great importance, and one must recognise that the Cambridge school has made an invaluable contribution to knowledge. But the Cambridge school is not only a school of pure economic theory. It is a school, too, of *applied* theory, and consequently involves a certain *social philosophy*. The emphasis on this side seems likely to be greater in the future in view of the statement of Mr. Keynes that the future for the economist lies in the obtaining of a 'knowledge of *relevant facts*' and in 'applying economic principles to them'.[1] It is this social philosophy which the writer ventures to criticise—a philosophy which, although not a logical deduction from the pure theory, is nevertheless a reasonable inference from the manner in which that pure

[1] Preface to the first four of the Cambridge Economic Handbooks.

theory is presented, and is clearly the psychological product of that manner of presentation.

What the writer has ventured to call the Entrepreneur Myth forms the pivotal point of this social philosophy. In the historical view it lies in the assumption that, because the capitalist undertaker arose historically as the co-ordinating force in a complex world, therefore in some absolute sense this was the 'necessary' and only possible method by which that integration could have taken place and the complexity of the division of labour was *the* cause of the capitalist undertaker (with the implication that the two are inseparable). True, it may be as futile to ask whether the past could have been other than it was as to ask whether the future will be other than it will be; but speaking theoretically one is justified in maintaining that, if other factors besides the division of labour had not been present, the capitalist undertaker would not have happened. Other social facts, such as class differentiation and private property in land, have equal right to be called 'causes' of the capitalist undertaker; and there is no *prima facie* reason to suppose that the needs of a differentiated society for an integrating force could not have been in the past (and could not be in the future) satisfied in other ways, had social conditions in general been different. Nevertheless this assumption is implicit in a surprisingly large number of works on social philosophy. Maybe, if faced with the issue, Professor Usher would deny that he had made any such assumption. His denial, however, would destroy the historical basis for that individualist philosophy which his work seems to imply. The contrary view, in brief, which the present writer attempts to advance, is that the progression of economic forms is a function *not only of the division of labour, but also of class differentiation.*

The economic aspect of the myth is not involved in the pure theory. It is into *applied economics* that it obtrudes itself. It takes the form of too great a neglect of the exceptions swept aside under 'economic friction', when economic laws are applied to concrete phenomena. We find the too-ready assumption continually being made that the functions performed by the ideal entrepreneur of the pure theory, hedged and guarded with *ceteris paribus*, are the same as those performed by the capitalist undertaker in the actual world. The extent of the divergence of the real from the ideal has not been sufficiently examined; nor has sufficient attention been given to the conditions which may tend to make this divergence so great that any identification of the two becomes, not only unprofitable, but absurd. The conditions arising out of the war, for instance, may be conditions of this kind.

The entrepreneur of the pure theory—the regulator of production according to the economic maxim—is merely an algebraic symbol. It is the formulation of a necessary economic function, for which the fact of economic differentiation creates the need. It is quite wrong to assume, because the same word is used for the function and the person fulfilling it, for the ideal entrepreneur in the world free of economic friction and for the undertaker in the world of very much friction indeed, that therefore the two are identical.[1] This, when stated, appears obvious enough; but the mistake in practice, nevertheless, is not confined to second-rate thinkers.

It would seem that the existence of certain differential advantages was an historical factor of as much influence in the rise of the capitalist undertaker as the complexity of the division of labour, on which Professor Usher lays emphasis. These differential advantages, in part the legacy of feudalism, placed one class of the community in a position where the assumption of risk and the organisation of commerce were relatively easy; while another class, lacking those advantages, was placed in a position of relative dependence. When such advantages were of sufficient scarcity, relative to society's demand for the undertaker, the money return to the activity of the undertaker in consequence was large.

It is, perhaps, in part due to the great emphasis placed on the Industrial Revolution that the strong influence of monopolistic or semi-monopolistic privileges on the rise of the capitalist undertaker has been so much neglected as it has. In general we find monopolistic privileges and the rise of the undertaker connected together in a very significant fashion. The chief effect of these privileges was that they tended to make the supply of resources to fulfil the privileged functions relatively inelastic[2] and so to create a condition of relative scarcity. It will be clear that no comprehensive examination of such privileges could be attempted here. The mention of a few typical cases must suffice.*

Now, it is perfectly true that few of these monopolies were of more than limited duration. It is true that there was always what Dr. Marshall has called 'marginal mobility'. There were always some journeymen

[1] The term *entrepreneur* is, in this paper, confined to the function, and the term *undertaker* to the person fulfilling it in an individualist system.

[2] Inelasticity is intended here to refer to the shape of the most relevant part of the supply curve.

[* Four pages of the original article are omitted here, which gave historical examples of concentration of ownership of land and minerals, of progressive encroachments on early rights of 'free mining' and of gild restrictions and monopolies in pre-capitalist and early-capitalist times.]

rising to be small masters, small masters rising to be big masters, and big masters becoming foreign export merchants. For some reason it seems to have been customary to concentrate attention exclusively on these instances of mobility, and to reject a monopolistic[1] interpretation of the development of class differentiation, because there has always been *some* mobility between grades. But although some mobility existed, and the nature and position of the various barriers were always shifting, it nevertheless remains true that there were sufficient obstructions to mobility, sufficient differential advantages in the hands of certain groups, to make the supply of persons able to assume the various functions associated with capitalist undertaking much less elastic than the supply of persons for manual labour. This enabled the capitalist class to receive a higher range of income and hence to amass more wealth than the less privileged and unprivileged classes. The possession of money and privileges makes easier the acquisition of more money and further privileges, whereas the converse is true of those in a position of dependence. In technical language, the marginal utility of money and time-preference get smaller as a man grows richer; whereas, on the other hand, the marginal utility of money and time preference get larger as a man grows poorer. Once started, therefore, there was a tendency for class differentiation, *ceteris paribus*, to increase.

It was because of this differential advantage that, when society developed the need for the function of integration, the capitalist undertaker had the money, the position, and the political influence to meet the need; and having once absorbed the gains of undertaking of the simplest and most profitable kind, he was in a better position to perform undertaking of a more comprehensive kind. It is characteristic of the habit of assigning the birth of modern capitalism to the Industrial Revolution that the rôle which the mercantilist system of monopoly played in its creation is neglected. Mercantilism, on the contrary to being entirely the senseless and harmful imposition which Adam Smith pilloried, appears to have been a necessary condition of the growth of capitalist undertaking. The view that with its abolition the truly wise, free, and natural economic order had triumphed is purely idyllic. On the contrary, the change merely implied that the differential class advantage had been sufficiently established to be no longer dependent on particular legal privileges. Moreover, mercantilism was opposed by the rising class of industrial undertakers

---

[1] For want of a better term, 'monopoly' is used in this article in the broader sense of a power to create a scarcity of supply whether that power is absolute or not. In some cases the creation of the scarcity may have been due to something other than human volition, e.g., the case of land.

since it tended to put them in a position of disadvantage relative to the merchant undertakers; and not fifty years had elapsed after the triumph of Free Trade before a new mercantilism began to appear—in the shape of the Trusts and modern imperialism. The essential importance of the Industrial Revolution was that it largely dispensed with the numerous intermediate and partially dependent interests of small masters and subcontractors and middlemen merchants, and that it brought about a direct economic relation between the undertaker and his labourers.

The economic theory of capitalist undertaking suffers from a neglect of a somewhat similar kind. Few could quarrel with economists when they show (as does Mr. H. D. Henderson in his *Supply and Demand*) that the more the entrepreneur function is operated efficiently, and the more price and profit as economic *measures* regulate production, the more the economic maxim of greatest economic welfare is fulfilled. But it is wrong to conclude forthwith, as is so frequently done, that because the supremacy of the abstract entrepreneur benefits economic welfare, therefore the supremacy of the concrete undertaker of the real world is a benefit to economic welfare. Between the two there is a gulf fixed.

The most important thing which accounts for this 'gulf' is that the marginal utility of goods measured in money is a function not only of the amount of satisfaction gained by consumers from them, but also of the amount of money possessed by consumers. As Dr. Birck puts it,[1] the 'subjective-price' of a thing is different from the value which it would have if incomes were equal; and in the world as it is everything is a matter of 'subjective-price' relations. Consequently, an economic law stated in terms of a certain value relation can be either of two things: (*a*) it can be regarded as a law which exists in the realm of pure theory, but can only become a law of applied economics where there is economic equality; (*b*) it can be regarded as a law of the real world; but since it is a statement of a 'subjective-price' relation, it must be regarded as entirely relative to a certain distribution of wealth—that existing in modern capitalist communities.

It is, perhaps, no exaggeration to say that most of the theories of the classical economists, like much of liberal political philosophy, would be admirable wisdom in a classless society. It is not applicable, however, to a society based on the kind of differential class advantage which we have just looked at historically. Professor Cannan and Dr. Dalton have indicated one aspect of this when they have said that economists hitherto have developed theories of distribution between abstract *factors* of production,

[1] *The Theory of Marginal Value*, pp. 53 seq.

but not of distribution between *persons* and classes. One could make the criticism more explicit. Economists have thought fit to propound a special theory of exchange between nations, for the reason that mobility of supply of resources is hampered by national boundaries: nations largely constitute 'non-competing groups'. According to this view one nation may obtain an abnormally high level of income because of certain differential advantages in international trade. Economists, as a rule, however, have developed no special theory of exchange between classes; although it is fairly clear that mobility between classes is considerably hampered by social distinctions, unequal educational opportunities, unequal money incomes.[1] Professor Taussig has, in fact, suggested that social classes constitute 'non-competing groups'. If this is so, a considerable part of the superior income of the richer class of society is to be regarded as an *institutional rent* or revenue,[2] due to restriction to a comparative few of the supply of persons performing the functions for which that class receives payment. The restriction is caused by the institutions of a class society. The 'rent' can be regarded either in its scarcity aspect, or in its differential aspect as due to the possession of certain differential class advantages. It was clearly this 'institutional rent' to which Marx was referring when he talked of 'surplus-value'.

The relevance of this to the problem of the entrepreneur is that this inequality of income disturbs the index of utility by which undertaking is regulated. The demand which will be effective in calling forth the production of utilities will be the demand made effective by the command over money. When there are competing demands of rich and poor for luxuries and for necessaries the demand of the rich will triumph under a régime of free enterprise. Consequently, the system of capitalist undertaking is not production in accordance with any true economic maxim of pure theory; it is production regulated by an index which is falsified by that very differential advantage which the system finds necessary to its own efficient working. This evil, moreover, is cumulative. The greater the concession made to the capitalist class as an inducement to them to perform efficiently their functions of undertaking and accumulation, the greater is the falsification of the index of production. Every gain made by an undertaker increases his differential advantage; and by lowering the marginal utility of money to him makes it more easy for him to accumulate capital, to assume risks, to gain access to remunerative posts, and to

[1] Cf. H. Dalton, *Inequality of Incomes*.
[2] This term the writer owes to Mr. H. D. Dickinson. Mr. Dickinson, however, prefers to speak of 'restriction revenue'.

obtain social and political power: the rich tend to get richer, and the poor conversely to get poorer.[1]

These facts are not disputed seriously by economists; although they do not emphasise the implications. But their attitude towards proposals designed to diminish the differential advantage of the capitalist class is a strange one. They will, as a rule, countenance socialistic proposals only so far as the diminution of the differential advantages of the capitalist class does not impair the efficiency of capitalist undertaking and accumulation. In practice, therefore, the economist tends to range himself on the side of the individualist. This is a curious attitude. It defends inequality as necessary to the efficient performance of the entrepreneur function. It admits that because of that inequality the capitalist undertaker fulfils the function badly. It denies that the inequality can be reduced very much, because that would render the system of capitalist undertaking more inefficient still! Here we have a circle from which there is no apparent escape. But surely, it is one of the strongest arguments in favour of collective undertaking and collective accumulation that it will permit of a reduction of inequality and consequently will render possible the regulation of production more in accord with the economic maxim? In weighing the pros and cons, therefore, of any supersession of individualism, it is not sufficient to take into account factors concerned with the operation of one industry alone: there is the additional consideration, relevant to society as a whole, that each extension of collectivism makes possible a reduction of inequality beyond the 'limit' of economic expediency which would otherwise have existed.

But there is, perhaps, a more important case of divergence between the undertaker and the ideal entrepreneur. It is concerned with the phenomenon of the trade cycle and is traceable to the fact that when production is in the hands of a number of individual undertakers, there is introduced an additional element of risk and uncertainty. In the ratio of their competition there is created an immeasurable element, which prevents the economic measure, extolled by pure theory, from regulating production.

An undertaker engaged in supplying a market has to estimate the quantity of supply which it is worth his while to market; and in making this calculation he has two factors to consider. Of these, one is a theoretically calculable one: the state of consumers' demand as expressed in market prices. The other is an incalculable factor: the amount which his com-

---

[1] This point the writer also owes to Mr. H. D. Dickinson. Dr. Dalton has suggested that it is an apparent feature of capitalist society for the relative share of work, as against property, in the national dividend to diminish. *A fortiori*, the relative share of manual labour and lower brain work will tend to decline.

petitors are likely to market. Here there is abundant field for miscalculation; here, where basis for sound calculation is absent, emotional influences (business optimism, etc.) enter in. If this miscalculation is universal and in the same direction, all will be well; for the market for goods afforded by other industries will alter in the same proportion as the miscalculation of supply.* But if the miscalculation is not universal, severe maladjustment and wastage will result—over-capitalisation and over-production in certain industries, leading to a slump.

There are two particular facts in the industrial world which make this a problem of very considerable importance, and not merely a matter of minor fluctuations in limited areas. These are facts concerned with the relation between the constructional trades and the rest of industry.

In the first place, it is clear that the demand for constructional goods will be a very fluctuating one. Constructional goods are probably the most durable of all the products of industry, and the demand for them is likely to be periodic and recurrent, and not steady and continuous. The demand will tend to be very great at particular times, usually during a trade boom, when there is need to replenish existing stocks of constructional goods. Professor Pigou has pointed out that the need on the part of industry for a 10 per cent increase in the *total supply* of machinery may create a demand for an 80 per cent or 100 per cent increase in the *new production* of machinery.[1] At times of industrial expansion, therefore, the constructional trades will receive a very much magnified stimulus. The constructional trades will tend to expand in response. But after the completion of this batch of boom orders, the demand will probably fall off considerably, and the constructional trades will find themselves heavily over-capitalised and over-producing. The rise in price in this case will tend to be a *deceptive* index: it will not be a true index of the state of demand over the *average* of the ensuing years. Undertakers, however, will tend, not only to respond automatically to this index, but to respond in a greater proportion, for the reason we have discussed above. It will be better for *each* undertaker to expand during the boom demand, and to swell the eventual over-production, rather than to have none of the profits of the boom and to suffer just the same the losses of the over-production produced by his rivals' temerity. But what is better for *each* will not be better for *all*.

The conclusion seems fairly clear that for purposes of applied economics

[*This, one can now see with the advantage of hindsight, was a good example of the implicit acceptance of 'Say's Law' by one schooled in economics at that time.]
[1] *Economics of Welfare*, ed. 1920, p. 807.

the implied association of the capitalist undertaker with the entrepreneur function is a source of considerable error. The system of capitalist undertaking is one way of fulfilling this function and it fulfils it with moderate inefficiency. The habit, therefore, should be avoided of attributing the virtues of the abstraction to one particular kind of enterprise—individualism; and economists should cease to sweep aside the inefficient characteristics of the capitalist undertaker under such phrases as 'economic friction'. Where the things included under *ceteris paribus* are relatively unimportant this may be justified. For instance, in discovering the path of a bullet at short range, the facts of gravitation and atmospheric resistance may not be very important. If, however, the law of projectiles stopped short at its first approximation (the case of a vacuum) the result would be seriously wrong in calculating the path of a long-range howitzer shell. Before existing economic theory can be applied, closer approximations must be worked out. At present the entrepreneur of theory is more like the abstract projectile of the first approximation than the real object. The Austrian school, in particular Wieser and Böhm-Bawerk, have at least shown more awareness of this; Wieser, for example, in his *Natural Value*, first formulating his laws of value as laws only fully operative in a classless society. But the English economists are still for the most part firmly set in the traditions of the classical economists.

At any rate, until we cease to pay homage to the holy myth of the entrepreneur, and until we cease to suffer gladly so much because we believe the capitalist undertaker to be indispensable, we shall be incapable of objectively weighing the pros and cons of the various extant proposals for his supersession.

II

A SCEPTICAL VIEW OF THE THEORY OF WAGES
[1929]

It is not uncommon in economic theory to meet with a confusion which, for the sake of a name, may perhaps be called the fallacy of ambiguous status. The marginal productivity theory of distribution, particularly in its application to the theory of wages, seems to be a favourite haunt of this fallacy. We find the theory expounded at two levels (like the familiar example of the Quantity Theory of Money[1]). On the one hand it is capable of a purely formal interpretation as the statement of an equality which carries no causal implication; on the other hand one finds it stated in a more practical form, designed to sustain corollaries as to the way in which wages are determined and as to what events can and what cannot bring about a change in the general wage-level. Not infrequently an exponent fails to make clear which of these two interpretations he intends. Yet this very ambiguity in its statement, so far from proving a handicap, seems to have been an important element in the success which the theory has enjoyed. Most economists (and the overwhelming majority of their students) have treated the theory of wages, apparently, in the second and more practical of these senses: i.e. they have treated it as capable of sustaining the kind of practical corollaries about the efficacy of trade union action which I have quoted on pages 132-3 of my book on *Wages*.[2] Yet when the theory has been criticised in this form, the counter-critics have been apt to fall back upon a defence of it in the

---

[1] See on this Mrs. Joan Robinson's essay in her *Collected Economic Papers* (Oxford, 1951), Part II, pp. 52–8.

[2] 1946 edition (Cambridge Economic Handbooks); the equivalent pages in the 2nd and 3rd editions are 94 and 126 respectively. Cf. also a statement quoted by T. W. Hutchison, *A Review of Economic Doctrines, 1870–1929* (Oxford, 1953), p. 319.

first and more tautological form, and thereby to demonstrate that the theory remains unimpugned.[1]

It is perhaps unnecessary to explain that the following article (which was originally published in the *Economic Journal* of December 1929) was intended as a criticism of the orthodox theory of wages in its second and more practical form—moreover of the orthodox theory as a theory of perfect competition, which is here criticised within its own framework of assumptions. A prefatory word may be called for, however, with regard to certain counter-criticisms which the article itself shortly afterwards received.

Professor J. R. Hicks, in an article in the *Economic Journal* of June 1930, declared that I was mistaken in supposing that the income-position of the wage-earner (*via* its effect on his subjective valuation of money-income) could be an influence upon the wage-level. Hence 'this particular missile' against the accepted theory 'does not reach its mark'. Provided that conditions of competition prevail, 'the terms which were fixed in the first week to the workmen's disadvantage will be subsequently modified by the employers' mutual competition, by some employers endeavouring to take on more men. Wages will thereby be bid up to the normal value of the labourers' marginal net product' (*ibid.*, p. 226). My comment in brief upon this contention of Professor Hicks is that it seems to rest *either* upon the belief that my argument was denying the formal equality of the wage to the marginal net product (an equality which follows directly from the appropriate definitions of perfect competition and of marginal net product), *or* else on the assumption of a quite inelastic supply of labour. The passage which has just been cited is capable of the former interpretation; but in other parts of his article (and in his further Note in the *Economic Journal* of March 1931, pages 145–6) he seems to be using 'normal value' to mean something more than equality with marginal net product (an equality-condition which of itself yields no unique result) and accordingly to be tacitly relying on the assumption of an inelastic supply. If we drop this assumption (which is scarcely realistic), I fail to see any ground for holding that, after the supply-

[1] Cf. on this T. W. Hutchison, *op. cit.*, p. 318: 'As Robertson showed, the marginal productivity analysis can be formulated to take care of the various "dynamic" objections or "grumbles" to the effect that a self-justifying wage-policy over a period of time can force up or force down the initial equilibrium-wage to a new higher or lower equilibrium level by its repercussions on the efficiency or bargaining position of the workers'. At the same time, he points out, 'the fewer possibilities that are inconsistent with the theory, or the less it rules out, the less content and interest it can have. If everything uncontradictory is compatible with them, and anything uncontradictory or conceivable may happen without infringing them, the "laws of distribution" do not forbid anything, and cease to be laws of empirical science.'

curve of labour has been lowered by reason of the workers' poverty, employers' competition will suffice to restore the *previous* level of wages (i.e. the level existing before the supply-curve had been shifted).[1] The most I think one could concede to Professor Hicks's argument is that such a position might be a position of 'neutral equilibrium'.

The notion of a unique long-period equilibrium by 're-contracting' could no doubt be rehabilitated by introducing the assumption of some enduring relationship between the subjective valuation (by workers) of real income and of labour for all levels of real income. But this would have little or no realistic worth—it would be the sort of long-period supply-schedule for labour in general of which Marshall himself was always so wary.

Professor D. H. Robertson, in his well-known essay 'Wage-Grumbles',[2] endorses Professor Hicks's contention that the influence of workers' poverty on the wage-level can be no more than temporary, and goes on to summarise his objections to my own argument under three heads: 'a point of words, a point of analysis, and a point of fact.' Under the first heading he writes: 'I am not persuaded that the present normal level of wages is rightly called "indeterminate" because among the forces determining it is the whole course of past history, including the history of wage-contracts.'[3] Secondly, he claims that in my argument the 'Principle of Joint Demand' is exalted over the 'Principle of Variation' (i.e. the technical substitution of capital for labour as a result of a change in wages) to the extent that the latter 'virtually disappears'. Thirdly, there is the question of fact:

---

[1] Professor Hicks seems to suggest that any reserve of labour will automatically tend to disappear, so that in treating of equilibrium one can speak simply of the labour supply as a given quantity; and he is only willing to concede that there is any substance in my argument when a worker is on piece-rates or is free to vary the hours of work. Professor Hicks also suggests that the current supply-price of labour will only be affected by past wages 'if any of those past wages are carried over or saved, to act as a reserve in the present period' (*Theory of Wages*, p. 102, n. 3). I must confess that I have always failed to understand this contention. If the size of any money-reserve carried over from last week affects the marginal utility of income, then the latter must surely be affected if this reserve is *zero*. Is it not essentially his *lack* of a bank-balance (at times his indebtedness) that makes the worker sell his labour cheaply? However, to say that the marginal utility of income depends upon the *stock* of it possessed is merely a convenient formal mode of stating the matter (adopted by Marshall): it may be more realistic to say that a person's valuation of a shilling depends directly upon the amount of income to which he has recently been accustomed.

[2] In *Economic Fragments* (London, 1931), pp. 42–57; also reprinted in *Readings in the Theory of Income Distribution* (Philadelphia and Toronto, 1946), pp. 221–36.

[3] *Ibid.*, p. 56.

'how much pressure the employing class will stand without growing sulky and refusing to play.'[1] Here Professor Robertson thinks that I am too optimistic.

On the 'point of words': it can be readily agreed that any theory with a claim to realism necessarily includes historical data among its parameters, and that this is no reason of itself to speak of a theory as indeterminate. But, this I submit is not really the question at issue, which is that a theoretical explanation cannot claim to be watertight (or 'determinate') if what it takes as 'data' (i.e. as given magnitudes or the 'independent variables' of the problem) are themselves influenced to any appreciable extent, within the period under consideration, by a change in the quantities which the theory claims to determine (the 'dependent variables' of the problem). In other words you cannot put much trust in forecasts based on any simple causal theory—on a theory which tells you that certain effects are produced by changes in certain causal factors—if 'effects' are likely to react at all appreciably on their 'causes' within the period to which the forecast applies.[2] Of course, to some extent everything in the universe reacts on everything else, and what happens in a particular sector today may be held to be dependent on the whole state of the universe yesterday. But to make a workable causal theory, one always has to assume an *approximate* isolation of the causal factors; and in the degree that this approximation fails, the theory becomes an unreliable instrument of interpretation and of forecast.

On the question of analysis there is little that can be briefly said. My article was not really concerned either to deny or to affirm the so-called 'Principle of Variation': it was concerned rather with stressing the existence of counteracting tendencies to this substitution-effect. Admittedly, this substitution-effect of a wage-change should have been included on page 27 below in stating the grounds for the traditional corollary that a rise in the price of labour will tend to decrease aggregate wage-earnings; and admittedly one's faith in this corollary will be largely influenced by the weight one assigns to this substitution-effect. I would add only this: (*a*) that the substitution-effect, in so far as it is important, is likely to have much importance only as a fairly long-period result—a long-period in which the influence of 'historical' changes in conventional standards and attitudes and in business expectations and practice may well assume a dominant rôle in determining the outcome; (*b*) that Professor Robertson himself

---

[1] *Ibid.*, p. 57.
[2] This is not to say that the theory could not be reconstructed in a more complex form to allow for this interaction; but this could only be done by introducing additional conditions to make a solution possible.

suggests, earlier in his essay, that the modern 'tendency to industrial rationalisation' may leave 'as little room as possible for the operation of the Principle of Variation.'[1]

I should be among the last to deny that 'how much pressure the employing class will stand' is a crucial issue; and that the capitalist class 'growing sulky and refusing to play' may be much more important under capitalism than the more strictly 'economic factors' in the problem of which economists have usually talked. If one is ready to assume with Professor Robertson that the employing class is indispensable, one can no doubt feel safe in laying emphasis upon this type of limit: otherwise to stress it seems likely to carry more revolutionary implications than I think Professor Robertson and those of his school of thought would be willing to entertain. But although capitalist propensity-to-sulk may be a reason for believing that the wage-earners' share of the cake is unlikely to be much increased under capitalism, I fail to see that this is sufficient to imply that trade union or legislative pressure on capitalists can exert *no* beneficial effect upon aggregate (real) wages.

At any rate, recent discussion of the influences which govern investment (both the rate of investment and its forms) have focused attention so largely upon the traditional beliefs and practices, the assumptions and expectations of business men (not to mention the 'degree of monopoly' as an influence upon the level of employment) as to make both my own argument and that of my critics sound, perhaps, today rather old-fashioned.

Acknowledgement is due to the Editors of the *Economic Journal* and to the Council of the Royal Economic Society for permission to reprint this article (which has here been slightly shortened).

A TRADITIONAL EMPIRICISM in Anglo-Saxon countries seems to have given us a bias against those studies of methodology which have held so bold a position among some foreign schools of thought. Usually we are satisfied to put such formal problems behind us with a cursory quotation from Mill, priding ourselves on our faith in common-sense definitions and our devotion to practical results. Our instinct is to be impatient with the critic who says that our theoretical system is 'internally inconsistent', and to reply to him: 'Surely you do not deny that the theory throws light on practical affairs?' Rather sacrifice logical consistency than wreck a fruit-bearing analysis. Rather run the danger that economic quackery may don the guise of political economy than let a chapter of useful 'advice to the Sovereign' pass unnoticed.

[1] *In Economic Fragments* (London, 1931), p. 50.

Such bluff common sense is not without its dangers. It may well be a cloak for laziness of thought which harbours confusion as to what our propositions imply and what our symbols mean. It can often lull us into thinking that we understand the words that we are using when we actually do not—into resting our thought on a number of assumptions which we have not explored and of which we may not even be aware. If, as signs are not altogether lacking, economic science has today reached an important turning-point, this neglect of methodology may be an obstacle to advance. At least, the modern tendency to shift our emphasis to applied economics, to free our definitions from dependence on specific philosophical systems and to bring them into line with the phenomena of the market-place, gives a special urgency to the need to reconsider the actual texture of our generalisations.

This traditional neglect of methodology is particularly exemplified in the somewhat vague notions which seem to prevail among us as to the criterion of *adequacy* when applied to an economic theory. And it lulls rather than clarifies thought to reply that a law is a statement of tendency or that a theory is intended to explain. Nor does the statement that a theory is designed to enable us to make a forecast and that its adequacy should be judged to this end take us very far. A result of this commonsense bias of our textbooks against probing the matter further lies in our inclination to be hoodwinked by a truism under the guise of a pretentious formula, or with an air of finality to explain one unknown quantity in terms of another variable that is equally unknown. And nowhere more than in the sphere of distribution in general, and the problem of wages in particular, does a chaos of theories seem to call for some such criterion of adequacy to clear the field.

The most elementary form of generalisation consists of a statement, based on observation or on logical inference, that two variables are related in some manner, but without the relationship being defined. Second in order comes the statement, in the form of a functional equation, which defines the movement of a particular quantity in terms of other variables to which it is related. Third is a group of generalisations which together enable a certain equilibrium to be postulated.

In the lowest rank of this hierarchy our knowledge is confined to the fact that if one of the factors is changed, the other will change also. In the second case the possible range of associated changes is stated for us and at the same time limited: in the language of practice we are told that change in our original variable can be 'caused' only by a change in one of the stated factors. The factors in question are shown to constitute a system, in which a change at one point will produce change at some other point. But we do not know more than this: we cannot forecast the *degree* of change in x which will result from a given change in y. In the third case we have a higher order of knowledge. Here, on any given set of assumptions, one can postulate a certain 'necessary' equilibrium, and one can postulate the nature and degree of alteration in this equilibrium which a change in the 'given' quantities will achieve. Clearly it is to this third order of knowledge that economic theory seeks to attain and to which all propositions in the theory of value claim to attain. For instance, in so far as the theory of money merely connects the value of money with the related factors on which it depends, it falls within the second rank of the hierarchy. But in so far as it claims to foretell the degree of change in the value of money which will ensue from a given alteration in one of the related factors, e.g. the quantity of money—as did most of the customary pre-war formulations of the theory—then it clearly aspires to the third rank. And the theory of wages, which is here our immediate concern, certainly claims to be judged adequate in its ability to postulate an equilibrium.

About the precise significance of the term 'indeterminate' in economic theory there seems no very settled opinion, and Marshall differs from Edgeworth on the matter, and both of them in turn from Pareto. Less difficulty, however, exists about defining the positive conditions necessary to postulate a determinate equilibrium. Clearly the essential difference which separates cases of our second category from those of the third consists in the fact that the latter consists of statements that can be formulated as a system of differential equations which are capable of *solution*. It is this solution which constitutes the equilibrium, any particular solution depending upon the values assigned to the constants or to the parameters of the system. Where the equations are not capable of solution, no equilibrium can be postulated, and the knowledge which our theory affords is limited to that in our second category. As Pareto has pointed out, the condition for a system of equations to be solvable is that *the number of equations, or independent known conditions, is equal to the number of unknowns*. If the number of equations is less than the number of unknowns, then there are insufficient data to provide a solution. To this end the equations must fulfil an important condition of independence: a change in the value assigned to one independent variable must not affect the form of another equation nor any other of the independent variables. Otherwise there would be some significant relationship left out of account: one of the independent variables indeed would prove not to be independent, but itself an unknown or a dependent variable; and with existing data the equations could not provide a solution.

In the ordinary competitive theory of value the demand and supply curves represent two equations relating demand-price to quantity and supply-price to quantity. In these equations utility and cost respectively figure as independent variables. Thereby a determinate equilibrium is provided, or a single solution which satisfies the conditions for each of the various possible magnitudes to be assigned to utility and cost. The condition of adequacy is fulfilled by virtue of an important assumption—the assumption of the *independence* of the supply and demand curves. General equations of prices for commodities in general, with which Pareto and the Lausanne school are concerned, are likewise rendered determinate on the assumption of the independent existence of two sets of quantities, utilities in consumption and disutilities in production, the pleasures of enjoyment and the pains of effort and sacrifice. Equilibrium is established where the two quantities are equal at the margin of all lines of production. In the theory of distribution an attempt is made to carry over the same method of analysis and to apply it to the price of the factors of production. To take the particular case which interests us here: wages, as the price of labour, are regarded as determined by the conditions of demand and supply, with the condition that in a competitive labour market the demand-price (or marginal net product) and the supply price will coincide. And here again the implicit assumption of the *independence* of the demand and supply curves is required. By 'independence' for this purpose it is necessary to mean that a change in one of them, through its effect on the price of labour or on any other prices, does not thereby produce a change in the other.

An example of where this assumption of independence would not hold in the case of a specific commodity was afforded by Mr. Sraffa in his important article in the *Economic Journal* for December 1926 (to which I am personally indebted for providing this present train of thought):

'If in the production of a particular commodity,' he wrote, 'a considerable part of a factor is employed, the total amount of which is fixed or can be increased only at a more than proportional cost, a small increase in the production of the commodity will necessitate a more intense utilisation of that factor, and this will affect in the same manner the cost of the commodity in question and the cost of the other commodities into the production of which that factor enters; and since commodities into the production of which a common special factor enters are frequently, to a certain extent, substitutes for one another (for example, various kinds of agricultural produce), the modification in their price will not be without appreciable effects upon demand in the industry concerned.'

For instance, if the product in question is wheat in a country where both rye-flour and wheaten-flour are widely consumed, an increased production of wheat, by transferring land to wheat-production, will raise the rent of rye-land and the cost and price of rye, and thereby, since rye is an important substitute for wheat, will affect the demand-curve for wheat. In the majority of cases, however, where a commodity occupies only a small part of the total supply of the factors of production, while the money spent on it represents only a small part of the total income of the consumers who buy it, reactions of this kind are regarded as being sufficiently small as to be negligible. They are relegated to the category of the 'second order of small quantities'. The prices of the factors of production on the one hand, and the marginal utility of income to consumers on the other hand, are regarded as being virtually unaffected by the terms of this particular act of exchange; and the assumption of independence, though not precisely true, is held to be true with a sufficient degree of approximation to satisfy both logic and expediency.

In the classical statement of the wages-fund doctrine wages were assumed to be a simple function of the wages fund, and the labouring population. In this crude form it was subject to the serious objection that an increased supply of labour, cheapening the price of labour, would tend thereby to cause an increase in the wages fund by making the investment of capital in the employment of labour more profitable than it was before. Hence Marshall's dictum that the demand for labour was 'not a fund but a flow.' In the reconstructed form which the theory assumed towards the end of the century the wages fund was itself regarded as a variable which was related to the investor's sacrifice or abstinence in lending his wealth for the employment of labour. This scale of aversions or sacrifices, unlike the wages fund itself, was regarded as unaffected by the dearness or cheapness of labour. Similarly, the supply of labour was related to the disutility involved in work.

Superficially, therefore, the theory of the labour market appears to be as adequate as the theory of a commodity market. Moreover, a particular corollary attaches to the theory of wages which gives to it the most important part of its practical value. This corollary depends on the conception of the wages fund, or the aggregate demand for labour, as being positively correlated with the profit received by the investing class: if profit increases, the supply of capital is likely to increase too. In other words, the wages fund or the demand for labour is regarded as being *elastic*; from which it follows that any increase in the price of labour per unit must *decrease* the earnings of labour *absolutely* (other things being equal), even though it increases them relatively. Conversely, every cheapening of the cost of labour must *increase* aggregate wage-earnings and so benefit capitalists and labourers alike.

But on closer scrutiny the adequacy of this parallel between a labour market and a commodity market proves to be apparent rather than real. Various writers, of course, have pointed out that certain conditions which are assumed as given when the demand for labour is formulated may be affected by changes in wages: for instance, the state of technique and of industrial organisation. But this is not a fundamental difficulty. There exists, however, a more fundamental reason for disputing the assumed independence of the supply and demand curves. In the case of a commodity market, as we have seen, this assumption is justified to the extent that the amount of income spent on the commodity and the amount of the agents of production used in producing it constitute only a small proportion of total income and of the total supply of these agents respectively. In other words, the marginal utility of income both to buyers and sellers can be regarded as unaffected by the price at which exchange takes place and by the volume of such transactions. When labour, however, is being sold, the marginal utility of income, at any rate to the seller, cannot be treated as constant. Since the labourer is propertyless, the sale of his labour will constitute his only source of income, and the terms of the sale will virtually affect his whole position, and will be the principal determinant of the labourer's subjective valuation of his own labour in terms of the income which he secures in return. In other words, a change in the price of labour in either direction is likely to produce a change in the supply-price of labour of a similar kind, thereby creating a tendency for any fall in wages to become cumulative, as in the classic case of sweated trades. If we have here an equilibrium at all, it is unstable rather than stable. The buyer of labour, in so far as he is purchasing a large number of units separately, will not be in the same position. The result of any one transaction concerned with the purchase of a particular unit will not suffice to affect the marginal utility of income to him. But if an employer purchases his labour as a whole by a collective hiring, and to the extent that the employment of labour is his main source of income, every change in the price which he has to pay will suffice materially to affect the marginal utility of income to him.

If this crucial assumption of independence does not hold, then exchange in the labour market ceases to be subject to a determinate equilibrium and is characterised instead by the indeterminateness which is considered to belong to barter transactions. In Marshall's famous 'nuts and apples' example,[1] the actual rate at which the two are bartered cannot be determined, since the initial terms on which exchange takes place will affect the marginal utility of nuts and apples to the respective sellers, and so will affect their respective 'offer curves' representing their future willingness to trade. In these circumstances exchange will continue up to the point where further exchange ceases to afford increased satisfaction to one of the parties—a point lying along a determinate curve which Edgeworth called 'the Contract Curve', and which must lie inside the two zero 'indifference curves' representing the various rates of exchange that yield no net advantage to the two parties. But the final rate of exchange may be at any point along that curve; and, therefore, as Marshall said, while 'equilibrium has been attained, it is not *the* equilibrium, but *an* accidental equilibrium . . . it would be an arbitrary equilibrium'. Marshall points out that this indeterminateness would apply to a hundred people bartering nuts and apples as much as to two, and suggests that it is due simply to the absence of money. If apples were sold against money, they would probably represent so small a proportion of the buyers' purchases that a change in their price would leave the marginal utility of money unaltered, whereas their direct exchange against nuts, of which the buyer has only a limited supply, does not permit the utility of nuts to be treated as a constant as in the former case. Similarly in our case of labour an equilibrium cannot be postulated because labour is not one among many alternative objects of sale and purchase, but is the sole object of exchange in this particular sphere.

But even though the classical conception of a determinate equilibrium of wages may be dethroned, the corollary with regard to aggregate wage-earnings still seems to continue in favour—a corollary now belonging to our second category of knowledge though not to our third and higher category. And this favour it retains for a special and peculiar reason. When with a lowered income the utility of income to the worker increases, he is likely (up to a point at least) to be induced to work harder— to offer more aggregate effort than before. In so far as the changed income he receives reacts on his habits and his conception of conventional necessaries, a secondary effect in the opposite direction will result. A rise of wages may develop new standards and habits which increase his wants and *increase* the utility of income to him; while a fall in wages, by contracting his standards and habits, may decrease his wants and lower the intensity of his desire for income. This secondary effect, however, will probably

[1] *Principles*, App. F.

do little more than retard the operation of the primary effect which we have mentioned. But the case of the capitalists presents an opposite situation. Any change in the bargain between themselves and their labourers, altering the marginal utility of income to them, will affect their willingness to accumulate and invest capital, not in the same, but in the opposite direction. An increase in the marginal utility of income to the worker will *increase* his willingness to work; an increase in the marginal utility of income to the capitalist will *decrease* his willingness to save and invest; and this it will do for the reason that when he invests he is foregoing present wants in return for a future gain, and any increase in the intensity of present wants, by increasing the rate at which he discounts the future, is likely to decrease his willingness to save.

For this reason, the possibility of a change in the labour-bargain reacting on the demand-curve for labour, in the way that it may on the supply-curve, is considered as being very limited. The conception of a demand-curve for labour as independent of the price of labour is still regarded as approximately correct, even though the independence of the supply-curve may be relegated to the limbo of discarded doctrine. And this demand-curve is fairly elastic, so that the amount of labour which the capitalist is willing to purchase will be larger when wages are low than when they are high. Consequently, while the employer may push down the rate of wages and at the same time increase aggregate profit, the labourers on their side, by pushing the terms of the bargain against the employer, cannot increase the aggregate earnings they receive. The dearer the price of labour, other things being equal, the smaller will both aggregate profits and wage-earnings tend to be; the cheaper the price of labour, the larger the income both of capitalists and workers. An extortionate trade union is more likely to do harm to the future than an extortionate employer.

But this view remains insufficient, if not actually false, until we have taken account of the possible effect of changed income on the habits and conventional standards of the investing class. In the case of wage-earners we have suggested that this relation is probably of secondary importance and does not disturb our initial conclusion that the marginal utility of income varies inversely as the amount of income possessed. In the case of the capitalist, however, this relation between income and habit is likely to be of much greater importance, and is probably even of primary importance. This enhanced importance it will have for the reason that the desire for luxuries is much more influenced by habit, custom and conventional standards than is the desire for necessaries. Consequently, desire for income on the part of the propertied class will contain a conventional element to a very much greater extent than will the desire for income on the part of wage-earners, whose chief expenditure is on essential clothes and food. It seems not improbable that the *major* part of the desire for luxuries (or their utility) is conventional—a point which the late Thorstein Veblen has so cogently argued. Our need for afternoon tea is mainly because others drink it; our desire for a tailored suit is chiefly because it is customary and carries a certain social prestige; the zeal for filling bookshelves with first editions and sideboards with hall-marked silver would undoubtedly be much smaller if social prestige did not enter into the matter. If we take all such conventional standards as given parameters in our equations, no formal difficulty arises, and to this extent the conception of an independent demand-curve for labour remains. The question here is one, not of logical consistency, but of consistency with practice. In the case of our previous and more fundamental difficulty it was a case of the logical inconsistency of treating the marginal utility of income to the worker as constant when the income of the worker was implied in any assumption as to what the marginal utility of that income was. Here it is a practical question of whether the assumption of conventional standards as independent of the income of the class in question is consistent or not with the actual facts.

If such an assumption is illegitimate, there is no warrant for concluding that a rise in the price of labour, decreasing the profits of the propertied class, will necessarily cause a shrinkage in savings and hence in the wages fund. It may merely cause a revision of conventional standards, diminishing the intensity of desire for present income on the part of those who have a surplus to invest. True, conventional standards, once acquired, impose a severe resistance against any downward revision. It needed the Great War to weaken the habit of enjoying the drama in the constricting uniform of a high collar and boiled shirt; and even so reasonable a weakening as this lasted scarcely longer than two years. And the history of aristocracies has shown the universal tendency to carry the challenge of privileged standards up to the very point of revolution. But when the national income is expanding, the position is different; and it may well be that if a diminished share accrues to the owners of property, the effect may appear, not in a slackened rate of saving, but merely in privileged standards of consumption, precluded from rapid advancement, remaining on a more modest scale. For instance, there is no warrant for assuming that, if wages had advanced more rapidly over the nineteenth century, our present accumulation of capital would be on a smaller scale. It is at least equally probable that privileged standards of life would have remained more modest and various expenditures, without which our propertied class would today think itself miserable, might never have been invented or acquired.

When we are dealing with sectional wage-changes in a particular industry, the notion of an independent demand-curve for labour will probably still hold good. For a limited period of time the notion of a demand-curve, elastic in character, may hold similarly for the general wage-level. But it is precisely in the short period, probably extending over some years, that the wages fund tends to be fairly inelastic, since it is only through the gradual effect on new savings and on the replacement of old capital that the total stock of capital is affected; and a period of time long enough for a change in labour-cost to react on the supply of capital may be too long for us to treat the conventional standards of the investing class as constants. At any rate when we are considering substantial changes in the wage-level from a long-period view, the conception of an independent demand-curve for labour, equally with that of an independent supply-curve, definitely seems to break down. Neither the 'will to work' nor the 'will to save' are independent of subjective valuations of income by the parties concerned and of conventional standards; and these in turn are not independent of the way in which income has been distributed by the wage-bargains of the immediate past. To postulate an equilibrium level of wages, relative to which any existing rates can be declared to be 'too high' or 'too low', is to stride a system of assumptions which can be made consistent neither with one another nor with the facts. It is to fashion an image of a stable equilibrium that is more remote from an original than the now unfashionable wages fund. As in the barter of apples against nuts, the indeterminateness of the wage-bargain will, of course, be contained within certain limits. The bargain must lie somewhere between the zero indifference-curves of the two parties—the curves representing the various rates of exchange at which no net gain at all results from entering into the bargain. Wages, naturally, cannot fall for long below the level of starvation or exhaustion. Even in a classless society, lacking the adornment of a propertied class, wages could not rise beyond the point where they swallowed the national income minus necessary capital accumulation—however 'necessary' in this case might be defined. But in our present society, if an upper limit to wages exists below this point, it is due, not to some 'natural' law of distribution, but to the existence of leisure-class standards of consumption which brook no interference or revision, and to which society must do homage if the rate of capital accumulation from individualist sources is to be maintained. It is at least significant of the bias of economists that when the wage-level is in question it is the customary standards of the propertied class which are treated as the constant factor and working-class standards of life as adaptable at the behests of a textbook 'equilibrium'. Any payment can be made 'residual' if only sufficient other things are treated as given. Not the least important among the inventions and improvements which affect the wage-level in the future may be a growth of collective saving which, in the character of a 'leisure-class-saving economy', will tend to increase the share of the national income which the wage-earning class can receive. For the burden of supporting the consumption of a *rentier* class at home, from the standpoint of wage-earners, is in essentials no wit different from the burden of paying tribute to holders of an external debt abroad.

A final consideration remains which leads us back from the theory of wages to the theory of value in general. If what has been said about the indeterminate character of distribution be true, this may have a not unimportant bearing on the problem of erecting general equations of prices for all commodities. It may well be that just as a determinate equilibrium for wages can only be postulated for particular sectional wage-rates, so a determinate equilibrium can only be postulated for particular commodities in isolation. In this latter case, as we have mentioned above, the postulate of an equilibrium is rendered adequate on the assumption that any reaction of the price on the marginal utility of income to buyer and seller is so small as to be negligible. The price of one commodity is, therefore, determinate on the assumption that the prices of all other commodities remain constant. As we pass to more important commodities, such as bread in the consumption of the poor, or to larger *groups* of commodities (for instance, the 'two commodities, A and B', which figure in Professor Pigou's *Public Finance*), this assumption progressively breaks down. To surmount this difficulty, one has to introduce *general* equations of prices for all commodities, and for this purpose one has to fall back on the two quantities of utility and disutility. By the aid of these two independent quantities it is possible to conceive of a double set of equations for the *aggregate* of commodities, to which particular demand and supply curves for individual commodities can be related. There will then be a general equilibrium of production where utility and disutility at the margin (measured in money) are everywhere equal.

But this retreat only serves us if we can assume these two quantities, utility and disutility, to be *independent* quantities. Can one in fact do this? Let us imagine that wants generally increase, and with them the possible satisfaction to be obtained in the aggregate is increased. For instance, new tastes may develop for 'talkies' and greyhound racing. If this is so, will not the 'sacrifice' involved in working two hours overtime *also* be increased in some degree—the loss of pleasurable leisure will now be more serious than the mere loss of two hours standing listlessly at the corner of the street? In the 'sacrifice' involved in 'waiting' the point seems even clearer; if the civilised taste for the Riviera had not been developed, the 'sacrifice' involved in buying War Loan instead would not be so great as it is. Conversely, will not every considerable cheapening of production in general encourage and develop new wants and so extend the whole utility-curve to a new position? And do we not even in certain quite important cases adjust our demand-curve for a commodity to the price which we already find on the market and to which we have grown accustomed? Indeed, so long as we define 'disutility' as a psychic 'sacrifice', disutility would seem to be inseparable from 'loss of utility' and therefore correlated with utility; and it is hard to see how this can be treated as an independent magnitude.

The matter appears to be further complicated when we are regarding an economic system in which persons who enjoy utilities in consumption partly constitute a distinct class from the persons who suffer the disutilities of production. Under one set of conditions the worker will equate a loaf of bread to a day's labour, under altered circumstances to the labour of an hour. If one is to speak of a general equilibrium where utility and disutility equate at the margin, one must *assume* a certain relationship between the worker's loaf and his labour, which is itself the result of an indeterminate bargain. Had a different bargain, or a different scale of production, been arrived at previously, a different relation between utility and disutility and a different equilibrium might have been established. And it is in this sense that the solution of the problem of distribution is logically prior to the solution of the problem of value.

It is this kind of criticism at which I believe many of the critics of the modern psychological theory of value have been aiming, if a little darkly. And it is precisely here, I believe, that modern economic theory, so far as it is a consistent system, proves after all to rest upon a hedonistic base. If it can borrow from a hedonistic psychology the conception of two independent quantities of utility and disutility, pleasures and pains, then its system can retain logical consistency (though the difficulty about income-distribution remains). But this implies that 'utility' must mean something more fundamental than 'desire'. and that 'disutility' must mean something more fundamental than 'sacrifice'.

Actually the whole tendency of modern theory is to abandon such psychological conceptions: to make utility and disutility coincident with observed offers on the market; to abandon a 'theory of value' in pursuit of a 'theory of price'. But this is to surrender, not to solve the problem. If he follows this road, the economist may have to abandon his claim to pronounce upon the macroscopic problems of society and to confine himself to the workings of microscopic phenomena; and this would mean that the proud title of *political* economy would come to an end.

III

THREE ARTICLES ON THE PROBLEM OF ECONOMIC CALCULATION IN A SOCIALIST ECONOMY

Of the group of three articles which follow the first two are reprinted from the *Economic Journal* of December 1933 and December 1939, and are contributions to a discussion which occupied a good deal of attention among English economists in the 1930's. One of these is rather general in character, whereas the other is concerned with a more special aspect of the wider discussion—with exploring the implications of a proposed price-mechanism, and in particular its de-stabilising effect on output and investment. (The former is reproduced here in a somewhat abbreviated form and the latter has been slightly shortened by the omission *inter alia* of two unnecessary diagrams.) Since a good deal has been subsequently written both about pricing-policy and about the meaning and implications of economic welfare as a criterion of policy, it has been thought useful to include a fuller reconsideration and restatement, in the shape of a critical review of the discussion to date. This third article has not hitherto been published; although it partly repeats views expressed in two other published articles which are not included in the present collection (articles by the present writer in *Iktisat Fakültesi Mecmuasi* of the University of Istanbul, October 1940, and in the first number of the *Indian Economic Review*, February 1952).

The review-article included below in Part 3 of this collection (pp. 239-46) is concerned with the same theme; and for a reader who is unacquainted with the rather specialised setting and terminology of the economists' discussion this may prove a more palatable introduction to the subject than the trio of articles grouped together under the present heading. Since it is largely repetitive of the latter (though in briefer compass) and is a review of a particular work, it has been placed among the shorter reviews and notes at the end. Another item in Part 3, a short comment on a recent Soviet discussion of investment-criteria, entitled 'A Note on the Discussion of the Problem of Choice between Alternative Investment Projects', is also relevant to the same general topic.

The two articles from the *Economic Journal* are reproduced by kind permission of the Editors and of the Council of the Royal Economic Society.

A. Economic Theory and the Problems of a Socialist Economy [1933]

IT HAS BEEN a common practice for economists to employ the hypothesis of a 'socialist economy' as a term of comparison: a comparison which has generally been used, not to delimit economic concepts and to stress their relevance to some limited historical context, but to assert their universality. As a rule, it has been assumed that in a socialist society the main propositions of economic theory would apply with undiminished force. Obstacles and problems would remain fundamentally the same; and the differences introduced by State investment and an altered distribution of wealth would be of no different order from those which might arise in an individualist system at different times and in different places. To the economist the rise and fall of institutions are a secondary affair. A change of property-rights and of class relationships may profoundly concern the social psychologist or the creator of ethical systems, but they will alter the form of 'the economic problem' hardly at all.[1]

In the past, such statements have generally been assumed unquestioned, rather than analysed and defended; and little attempt has been made to

[1] For instance, Mr. H. D. Henderson speaks of 'the existence in the economic world of an order more profound and more permanent than any of our social schemes, and equally applicable to them all', and of economic laws and relationships which 'seem altogether more fundamental than our present industrial system' (*Supply and Demand*, pp. 11 and 141); while Wieser similarly declares that 'the communistic state must retain the same law in force, or its economy will become chaos' (*Natural Value*, p. 164). Wieser even goes so far as to identify 'natural value' with 'value as it would exist in the communist state'. Pareto asserts that under Socialism 'commodities will be distributed according to the rules which we have discovered in our study of a régime of competition' (*Cours*, Vol. II, p. 364), and Cassel assures us that 'new lines of economic policy, adopted by socialist reformers, which promise anything for the future, tend, so far as prices are concerned, merely to work out the classical ideal of a system of prices' (*Theory of Social Economy*, Vol. I, p. 76).

formulate the detailed corollaries which such statements imply. Yet, clearly, if they are true, such statements have very great significance, not only for practice, but in the very definition of economic concepts. In recent years a more direct practical interest in the matter has caused these propositions to be more concretely framed. The decline of the competitive system, on the one hand, and the achievements of Soviet economy on the other, have given the question a topical interest. As Mr. H. D. Dickinson has reminded us in the June issue of the *Economic Journal*, a virtual school of writers, such as Mises and Brutzkus, has developed, declaring that a socialist economy must fail because the absence of a free market and a price-system would preclude the application of any economic criteria. Against them, others, such as Mr. Dickinson, have proclaimed the possibility of combining a socialist economy with a price-system: a combination which, it is alleged, would provide superior criteria of costs and of demand to those which rule in a capitalist world.[1]

It has become fashionable today to discard the hedonistic basis on which the modern theory of value was formerly supposed to rest, and to treat economics as a non-normative theory of equilibrium. The more formal, of course, that economics is made, the more universal become its propositions; which might seem to imply that the equations of Cassel or Robbins would have more application to a socialist economy than the more homely precepts of Adam Smith. But, in becoming more formal, such propositions have at the same time quite changed their significance. The theory of value, conceived simply as a theory of equilibrium, can postulate that, in a given set of circumstances, prices will conform to a certain pattern; in a different set of circumstances to a different pattern. It can say this, and it can say no more. It may *define* a 'maximum' as consisting in one particular 'pattern'; but the definition will be entirely arbitrary. It is powerless to pass judgment upon any particular arrangement of resources in the real world, and declare one arrangement to be preferable or more 'economic' than another, for the reason that it has specifically excluded any assumption about the ends in view. It is powerless to *prescribe* a maximum for us. A reviewer in this *Journal* recently complained that in a socialist economy the problem would be not that the planning authority '(would) not be

---

[1] Cf. *Economic Journal*, XLIII, 170, pp. 237 *seq.*; also an article by Mr. H. D. Dickinson in *The Political Quarterly*, Vol. I, No. 4. A similar view has been expressed by W. C. Ropner, *The Problem of Pricing in a Socialist State*. The present writer also subscribed to this opinion, devoting a theoretical Excursus of his *Russian Economic Development* (London, 1928), to an exposition of this claim. He now believes this view to be wrong.

able to reach a position of equilibrium, but that it (could) reach too many such positions—precisely an infinite number—and (have) no means of choice between them.'[1] But this is precisely the dilemma of any pure equilibrium theory: it can give no means at all for preferring the 'unique' equilibrium of an individualist economy to any of the n possible alternative equilibria that a planned economy might choose. Economic theory reduced to these dimensions provides absolutely no criterion of judgment at all.

Yet, when it comes to such judgments, the equilibrium theorist, of course, tacitly appeals to a norm. Despite his trumpetings against the welfare-economists, he in fact secretly imports an assumption which at once places him precisely on the same ground as the hedonist whom he has pretended to disown. And in this assumption the whole apparatus of utility and welfare, which it was his pride to dispense with, is implied. But the manœuvre has not been for nothing: it has enabled the scientific dignity of an ethical neutrality to be combined with an undiminished capacity to deliver judgments on practical affairs. The crucial assumption is as simple as it is questionable: it amounts to the sacredness of consumers' preferences (as a general rule, and subject to unimportant exceptions here and there).[2] The virtues of 'economic democracy' which it confers on a free market rest on a similar sacredness of individual choice to the virtues of Parliamentary democracy. Both operate through a convenient franchise system: in the one votes are cast by offers on a market, in the other by crosses at a polling booth. The highest economic good consists in giving the consumer what he thinks he wants, as political good consists in giving the people the government it thinks it deserves. Both conceptions are part of our bourgeois heritage from the nineteenth century. But there is no need to show that there are fallacies in the latter to demonstrate that there are fallacies in the former. The effect of the advertiser on economic choice may be taken as a fair parallel to that of the Press magnate on political opinion: both damage the sacredness of the popular verdict pretty ruthlessly; in both spheres it would seem that bad money drives out good. But in the economic sphere there is not even an approach to universal suffrage: on the contrary, a widely graded system of plural voting is the

[1] N. Kaldor, *Economic Journal*, June 1932, p. 279.

[2] This is the assumption on which Marshall's structure rests. In a footnote he announces that for reasons of practical convenience he will identify 'desire' with 'satisfaction', and 'fall back on the measurement which economics supplies of the motive or moving force to action; and to make it serve, with all its faults, *both* for the desires which prompt activities and for the satisfactions which result from them' (*Principles*, pp. 92–3).

rule. Some men poll each a thousand votes to another's one. Moreover, like the old-fashioned squire, the possessors of many economic 'votes' powerfully influence the verdict of the mass—they 'set the pace', establish the conventions for the multitude and the standards which others strive to imitate and attain.

Mr. Dickinson would have us believe that in a socialist society the objections to the economic democracy of the market, like those to the democracy of the polls, would lose their force. But this is very far from being the case. Unless there were complete equality of reward, 'plural voting' would still remain, if diminished; whereas, if equality of reward prevailed, market valuations would *ipso facto* lose their alleged significance, since money costs would have no meaning. If carpenters are scarcer or more costly to train than scavengers, the market will place a higher value upon their services, and carpenters will derive a higher income and have greater 'voting power' as consumers. On the side of supply the extra 'costliness' of carpenters will receive expression, but only at the expense of giving carpenters a differential 'pull' as consumers, and hence of vitiating the index of demand. On the other hand, if carpenters and scavengers are to be given equal weight as consumers by assuring them equal incomes, then the extra costliness of carpenters will find no expression in costs of production. Here is the central dilemma. Precisely because consumers are also producers, both costs and needs are precluded from receiving simultaneous expression in the same system of market valuations. Precisely to the extent that market valuations are rendered adequate in one direction they lose their significance in the other.* Mr. Dickinson cannot have it both ways.

But this is not all: this is not the only reason why a price-system under socialism might still be far from constituting a perfect automatic regulator of economic affairs. If consumers' choice under capitalism was so malleable by convention and seducible by the advertising agent, what right have we to assume that under socialism it will be supremely wise? If it was so corruptible then, why is it suddenly reliable now? Or if it needed

[* Dr. Lange has declared this statement to be wrong, since, in so far as income-differences are necessary to compensate for different disutilities involved in work, they are quite consistent with the principle of equality (in the sense of equality of welfare as between individuals). This criticism, I agree, is valid in the case he is considering; but it does not apply (as he himself goes on to point out) where income-differences reflect, not differences in disutility of work, but different degrees of scarcity, whether short- or long-term. In such cases, however, he suggests that there is no need for a socialist society to pay wages which include a 'rent element' (*On the Economic Theory of Socialism*, Minnesota, 1938, p. 102).]

to be 'educated' then, why are we to accept the verdict of its untutored state now? If taste is mainly acquired, rather than innate, and shaped by culture and convention, as seems to be the case, there is no reason why, in a socialist order, the State should entirely abrogate the right of creating taste in favour of being its creature. In the creation of new wants, in particular, with which economic progress is so largely concerned, the verdict of a price-system can never give more than a modicum of aid.

Even were it free of these defects, there is a serious limit to the claim of a free market system to provide an automatic index and regulator of economic relationships—a limit which affects one of the fundamental relations in economic society. For this fundamental relation between the production of immediately consumable goods and the production of capital goods it can afford no criterion. This limit, which concerns the very core of the problem of costs, is not only customarily neglected in discussions of the subject, but is even by implication denied. If a price-system prevails, the use of property—of plant, buildings and land—will be priced, whether in a capitalist or a socialist régime. What is to be the basis of this relation between these two categories of cost—the hire of a lathe for a day and of a man's labour for a day? On the answer to this question the whole costing problem turns, and the whole balance between different types of industry depends. But the question receives no answer from any spontaneous verdict of a free market; since the two categories of cost are incurred by dissimilar agencies (or persons).[1] Neither is it answered in a socialist any more than in a capitalist economy. In a capitalist society the two classes of productive agencies are supplied by two distinct social classes; and the pricing of property depends upon the level of wages (i.e. the supply-price of labour) relative to productivity, modified by the rate of saving. In a socialist society property will be in the hands of the State, and this fundamental cost-relation will, of necessity, be determined *a priori* by the decisions of the State as to the proportion of resources to be devoted to the production of consumable goods and of capital goods. That a free market can and must provide the criterion as to what this relation should be is a common illusion—an illusion which seems to lie behind a great deal of the talk about a 'natural' rate of interest, particularly of the 'necessity' of being ruled by this 'natural' rate in a socialist community. In a socialist society there is no excuse for the illusion. Here least of all can any appeal be made to 'economic voting'—an appeal to the time-

[1] In the manner in which equilibrium theory is usually stated there is assumed to be a complete formal parallelism between demand and supply. But this formal treatment neglects this very significant difference of fact

preferences of separate individuals; for, in judgment of the future the 'natural' individual is notoriously unreliable.

But it may be urged: assuming that a given rate of time-preference and a given scale of need are postulated, will there not still remain the question of attaining a maximum relative to these postulated conditions? Will not the 'principle of least cost' require that resources are distributed strictly according to a certain pattern, and anything which does not conform to this pattern be characterised as 'uneconomic'? In other words, must not the principle of equalising the marginal yield of capital in all uses have sway? Mr. Dickinson takes it as axiomatic that equilibrium must be obtained 'by pushing the investment of resources up to the same number of years' purchase in all lines of production.'

*[If such a principle were to rule, this would, of course require that both the priority of different needs and costs (including 'costs' assigned to scarce resources) should be expressed in some common denominator. This could be done without the operation of a free market system to afford the automatic index of economic priority. However, what meaning can be given to the achievement of a 'maximum' of this kind once we abandon the notion of utility, and hence of the maximisation of net utility over time? One would in any case need some objective standard of time-preference to give any precise meaning to the loss suffered over time by failing to apply the principle of equalising marginal yield at each point of time; and such a standard economic theory does not provide. What was lost by failing to attain this 'maximum' might well be smaller than the probable error in any scale of economic priorities established by a free market or in any other way; and there may be circumstances where it would be better to ignore such a principle than to observe it.]

There seems to be one reason in particular why a socialist State should observe, not an equality of net marginal yield, but an alternative rule as the principle of capital investment. This reason (which has been pointed out to me by Mr. Sraffa) is concerned with the fact of obsolescence and of uncertainties arising from technical innovation which waits upon a fall of interest-rates to bring it to birth. It is a commonplace that technical progress does not merely supplement existing equipment, but renders a good deal of it obsolete; and consequently every new phase of capital accumulation, resulting, as it tends to do, in lengthened processes of production, renders obsolete a large part of the older and shorter processes of production. Where the rate of capital accumulation is low and the length

[* The passage in square brackets is a summary of the argument of two pages of the original article which are omitted here.]

of life of material equipment is short, the resulting wastage is not serious. But when periods of very rapid capital accumulation coincide with technical epochs in economic history (as during the Industrial Revolution; in Soviet Russia; and possibly to a smaller extent in the rest of the contemporary world), the wastage which occurs from the scrapping of plant and of the old localised economic units will be abnormally large. In an individualist economy it would seem that the result of a future fall in the rate of interest, as the result of the growth of capital accumulation, is seldom adequately discounted by investors or entrepreneurs (a fact to which recurring crises may well be witness). At least, such discount as is made tends to be based on rule-of-thumb generalisation from the immediate past (e.g. amortisation allowances) which does not allow for any abnormal bursts of obsolescence, such as, for instance, has probably marked the last fifteen years. But to the extent that such changes could be foreseen, as they could with some approximation in a planned economy, it would be economical to invest in the new technical processes in advance of that fall in the interest-rate which would later render them profitable: in other words, to violate the principle of equimarginal returns and apply a *different* time-discount to different sections of an industry and of the economic system, investing part of the available capital resources in ways which yield, not the normal interest-rate of today, but what will be the normal rate, say, ten or twenty years from now. The advantage would consist in the lower obsolescence and the longer term of usefulness of plant. To take a fanciful example: if one did not realise that in five years' time one would be rich enough to build a palace, one might build oneself a house, destined later to become redundant. But if one had been able to forecast the windfall of five years' hence, it would have paid one to forgo the house and live in a bungalow in the interim, and with the difference commence to lay the foundations of the palace.

This can be graphically illustrated in the analogy of the 'pursuit-curve'. A dog is situated at right angles to the path along which his master is bicycling. The dog is running towards his master and, influenced by a simple conditioned reflex, runs always in the direction of his master at the given moment; with the result that his path in pursuit of his master is a curve. But if the dog could have acted on forethought and calculation, he would have taken a straight line to the point along the path which his master would presently reach. A planned economy, it would seem, should take a similar straight line towards a technical level of the future; and the ultimate economising of capital to produce a given result (or, conversely, the more rapid rate of technical advance financed by a given rate of investment) will be the difference in length between the straight line and the curve.

I am conscious that what I have said has been mainly of a negative order. But, as Kant observed, negative may be as significant as positive conclusions in setting thought on to new paths. Yet I do not wish to follow Kant and 'limit knowledge in order to make way for faith'. Planned economy will have its economic laws, as has *laissez-faire* economy; it will have its economic accounting and its calculation. But until we have cleared the site of debris, we cannot commence to dig foundations; and until we have discarded the false analogies which confuse the question, economists and their analyses are likely to shed more obscurity than enlightenment. Interest in the question, moreover, is not solely topical. Because of the light which it throws on the significance of economic concepts, the issue may well be a crucial one, on which the future of economic theory may turn.

B. A Note on Saving and Investment in a Socialist Economy [1939]

1 The purpose of this Note is to point out certain considerations concerning the equilibrium of the system as a whole which seem to have been overlooked in recent discussions of the working of a socialist economy: in particular, to suggest that a rate of interest cannot *simpliciter* provide a stabilising mechanism in such an economy, and that the principle of equating price with marginal cost (as enunciated by several writers) may well run counter to the maintenance of full employment, and in certain circumstances will be impossible of application.

Hitherto discussion of a socialist economy has been pre-occupied with the problem of the allocation of a given quantity of resources between various uses, and little or no attention has been given to problems connected with the rate of investment and its relation to the level of wages and the price-level of consumption-goods, or to the conditions adequate to ensure the full employment of resources. To solve the problem of ideal allocation a number of writers—I refer particularly to Dr. O. Lange, Mr. A. P. Lerner and Mr. R. L. Hall—have agreed in proposing that decisions as to output and investment in a socialist economy should be ruled by the following principles. *First*, all prices, whether in the case of finished goods or of factors of production (in some cases these may be no more than 'accounting-prices', as suggested by Dr. Lange), shall be fixed by a process of trial and error until an 'equilibrium price' is found at which the current supply is equal to the demand. If the commodity or factor in question is in surplus supply (e.g. if unsold stocks are accumulating) the price will be lowered; if it is in deficit-supply, the price will be raised. *Secondly*, decisions as to output and investment shall be taken by each industry on the basis of carrying the utilisation of resources to the point where marginal cost is equated to price: the output of each plant presumably being extended to the point where the short-period (or prime) cost of additional output is equal to the value of that output, and new investment in the industry being undertaken if, and only if, the additional output resulting from the investment, when valued at current prices, equals or exceeds its long-period cost, including the current interest-charge on the capital involved in the construction of the new equipment.[1] The advantage of this mechanism that its sponsors appear to have in mind is that it would facilitate a considerable decentralisation of investment and output decisions. The central planning authority need decide only the *total* amount[2] to be invested in any period: the direction and the form of

[1] Dr. Lange postulates that all managers of industries and plants must be ordered, first to choose 'the combination of factors which minimises the average cost of production', secondly 'to produce as much of each service or commodity as will equalise marginal cost and the price of the product'. With regard to capital he states that 'a price has to be fixed by the Central Planning Board with the provision that these resources can be directed only to industries which are able to "pay", or rather "account for" this price' (*Economic Theory of Socialism*, pp. 75–6, 78, 79). Mr. Lerner has suggested that instructions should be issued 'that the use of every factor is to be extended up to the point where the marginal physical product multiplied by its price is equal to the price of the factor. . . . This value, which has to be equated to the price of the product, we shall call the marginal cost. . . . The guiding principle that we seek is none other than the equation of price to marginal cost' (*Economic Journal*, Vol. XLVII, No. 186, p. 257). Mr. R. L. Hall has written: 'If the rate of interest has been chosen correctly, the total expansions should balance the total contractions . . . if there is a general tendency to expand, the rate must be raised in order to turn some of the apparent profits into losses, and *vice versa*.' 'The aim of the Ministry [of Production] is to equate prices and marginal costs, which is done by varying the amounts of the various goods. . . . Every unit, if properly conducted, will extend its operations to the point where the marginal cost equals the price which is received' (*The Econ. System in a Socialist State*, pp. 92, 119, 129). Professor Pigou has assumed that an accounting price for capital (as for other factors) can be arrived at that 'will exactly clear the market, without shortage or surplus, of that part of money income that is on offer for net investment', but that each industry is told to adjust its production so that 'aggregate costs are equal to aggregate sales proceeds', and its 'average accounting cost is a minimum' (*Socialism and Capitalism*, pp. 112, 115, 129).

[2] I do not recall that it has anywhere been stated how this total is to be valued. As will later appear, it will be a matter of considerable importance whether the total is expressed in terms of wage-units or of the value of final output.

the investment, and *a fortiori* the output of existing plants, could be left to the managements of the various industries to determine according to the second of the above rules. All that the central planning authority would need to do, having decided the total investment for the system as a whole, would be to adjust the aggregate demand for capital to that supply by appropriate shifts of an interest-rate.

Closer inspection reveals the danger that a system controlled in this way may inherit two of the principal vices of capitalism. With a price-mechanism of this kind in operation, the only way of precluding a large measure of chronic unemployment may be to maintain the rate of investment at a given, 'arbitrary' level, which may be quite different from the level that would be dictated by other considerations. Moreover, it is not difficult to show that, unless some stabilising mechanism is introduced, in addition to or as a substitute for this pricing-mechanism, a socialist economy may inherit the instability of capitalism in an even more pronounced form. Perhaps it is a lingering habit of thinking of the 'demand for capital' in terms of the marginal productivity of a given *stock* of capital that is responsible for the apparent readiness to conceive of the rate of interest as a simple mechanism for controlling the rate of investment—to imagine that the 'demand for capital' is a sufficiently stable quantity for the supply and demand for capital to be easily equated by means of appropriate adaptations of an interest-rate. As soon, however, as it is realised that the 'demand for capital' is a function, *inter alia*, of the current *rate of investment*, and that (for reasons to be explained below) this demand will vary directly, and not inversely, with the rate of investment, *ceteris paribus*, the existence of a powerful *de*stabilising influence inherent in this relationship becomes apparent. In other words, the so-called schedule of the marginal efficiency of capital is *not* independent of the rate of investment. If the rate of investment is increased (or decreased), so will be the inducement to invest; and the situation will be one of unstable equilibrium, where the tendency to a Wicksellian cumulative movement, with increased investment 'creating its own draught', can hardly be controlled efficiently by a trial-and-error process of searching for an equilibrium-price for capital. If, moreover, an attempt is made to adhere to the rule of equating price and marginal cost, the volume of output from existing plant, and hence employment, will be determined by the relation between the price-level of finished goods and money-wages, and this relation is also (and for the same reason) a function of the rate of investment. If, therefore, the rate of investment upon which the State happens to have decided is a relatively low one, unemployment may be impossible to avoid, since to intensify the utilisation of existing plant by employing more labour per unit of equipment would cause marginal prime cost to exceed price.[1] On the other hand, if a condition of full employment has already been attained, it will be *impossible* both to increase the rate of investment and at the same time to maintain an equality between price and cost, even between price and short-period marginal cost.[2]

2 To elucidate the reason for these statements let us examine the working of such a mechanism as is proposed by Dr. Lange and Messrs. Lerner and Hall, in a simplified situation and in their own terms. To make the task of analysis easier we will start from the following assumptions. (*a*) We will assume both that the only form of personal income consists of wages,[3] and that wage-earners spend the whole of their income in a given period on consumption goods—that their saving is zero. (*b*) We will assume that prime costs of current output consist exclusively of wages (this is plausible if we imagine that each industry is vertically integrated, and that production in each plant embraces all processes from extraction from the soil to a finished product). We may further assume that each industry undertakes the repair and maintenance of its own plant, employing permanent repair workers as well as process-workers, and counts the wages of the former in its prime or operating costs. (*c*) We will assume that land is a free good and is not priced, so that the only element in total cost other than wages consists of the accounting-price of capital, as currently fixed by the State Bank or Investment Board or Central Planning Council. (*d*) We will assume that there is technical homogeneity between various industries to the extent of making the ratio of capital to labour approximately uniform in them all. (*f*) We will assume that the amount of reserve productive-capacity that exists, at the outset, in the industries producing consumption-goods is small (i.e. short-period costs have a rising tendency).

It will be obvious that there follows from assumptions (*a*) and (*b*) the corollary which can be expressed by saying that:

$$C = W \text{ and } P = \varphi W$$

where C represents the value of output of consumption goods, W repre-

---

[1] This, of course, is to assume that output is at the level at which short-period costs are *rising*.

[2] Cf. below, p. 46 footnote.

[3] This implies that there is no subsidy to consumption in the shape of a money-grant to individuals, i.e. no form of 'social dividend in money'. It is also implied, for the present, that the State levies no taxation, either direct or indirect, on wage-earners.

sents the total wage-bill of the country, P represents total profits of industry, and φ the proportion of the total wage-bill which is expended by the State in new constructional work (i.e. φW is the rate of investment).

It will be convenient to distinguish four classes of decisions that the management of industry will have to take.

1. Given a plant of a particular type and size, how much labour to employ in that plant and how much output to obtain from it? This we will call the intensity of utilisation of a given plant by labour. If the second of the above rules is observed (controlling output in such a way as to attempt to equate price and marginal cost), this will depend on the price of output, the level of wages and the extent to which marginal operating cost (M.O.C.) rises as the intensity of utilisation of the plant is increased. The difference between the price of output and the average operating cost (A.O.C.) multiplied by the output will represent the Profit of that plant.

2. What should be the *size* of each plant? (This is, of course, a decision that will arise only as existing plant wears out, or the construction of new ones is under consideration.) This will be determined by the average *total* cost (A.T.C.) of production in plants of different sizes (including in this the cost of constructing the plant *plus* the accounting-price of the capital involved), according to the rule that, where the plants in the industry are numerous, that size of plant should be chosen which makes A.T.C. a minimum.[1] This can be expressed by Mr. Lerner's envelope U-curve, where the envelope curve represents the A.T.C. under plants of different sizes, and the smaller curves tangential to it represent the cost of producing with a plant of a *given* size.

3. What should be the *number* of plants in an industry? This will generally depend on the profit that each plant is making, as defined under 1. If the profit-rate (i.e. the ratio of profit to the value of the plant when valued at reconstruction-cost) being earned by a typical plant in an industry is greater than the accounting-price of capital, then presumably the number of plants will generally be increased, and *vice versa*. (But there may be exceptions to this rule where economies are to be gained from

[1] The contradiction between this and Mr. Lerner's principle that the size of plant should be chosen which equates M.T.C. and the demand-price (*Economic Journal*, June 1937) is only apparent. Mr. Lerner's principle comes into play where the plants in an industry are sufficiently few to make impossible such a nice adjustment of their *number* as to enable them all to be of optimum size and at the same time to be operated at 'normal' capacity.

enlarging the size of the whole industry, or conversely diseconomies; and these economies or diseconomies may make expansion or contraction desirable even when the profit-rate is equal to the accounting-price of capital.)

4. Which of a variety of technical types of plant (irrespective of their size) to choose to construct? These types will differ, not only in that operating costs under each type of plant will be different, but also in their costs of construction and maintenance. Taking these factors into account, a choice will be made according to a similar rule as in cases of class 3. It will follow that if the accounting-price of capital is low, plant-types which have a relatively high cost of construction, compared to the economies of operating costs that they promise, will be preferred to a greater extent than when the accounting-price is high. Changes of this class represent Mr. Hawtrey's 'deepening process', as distinct from his 'widening process'.

Let us suppose that the State, in order to stimulate an increase of investment, lowers its accounting-price for capital. There will then be a tendency for changes under 3 and 4 to take place. The increased constructional activity will involve either a transfer of labour from making consumption goods to construction jobs (in which case it will necessarily involve some lowering of the intensity of utilisation of plant in the consumption trades), or else the absorption of previously unemployed labour into construction work. The net effect will be a rise in the price of consumption goods (measured either in money or in wage-units);[1] since, as we have seen above, P, which $= C - (W - \varphi W)$, varies with the rate of investment. In other words, if the demand, depending on the total wage-

[1] If there is full employment there will be the difficulty that the rise of price will encourage an increase of output in the consumption trades at the same time as there in an increased demand for labour for construction work. In this case there *must* be some mechanism such as a tax on output of the consumption trades to bridge the gap between M.O.C. and price, and thereby prevent an expansion of output, or even curtail output, so as to release labour for construction work. If, however, there is a reserve of unemployed labour, this difficulty does not arise, and increased investment can occur together with increased output and employment in the consumption trades (M.O.C. and the higher price being equated by an expansion of output, provided that short-period costs are rising for increases of output).

It is to be noted that even if the effect of the increased demand for workers was to raise wages, this would not alter the fact that profits would be raised in step with increased investment. If wages rose, the price of consumption goods would rise correspondingly higher. Similarly, if the increased investment resulted, not in a transfer of labour, but in the employment of some new reserve of labour, the price of consumption goods would be raised by the expenditure of an enhanced total of wages.

bill, rises relatively to the supply of consumption-goods, as will be the consequence of increased investment, the consumption price-level must rise relatively to the wage-level. At a later stage, it is true, as the new plants come into existence, the output of consumption goods will increase and their price will tend to fall again. But for the time being while the investment is taking place, the price-level of finished output will inevitably rise, and with it the profits of industry. This rise will, indeed, measure the community's 'saving'; the profits of industry corresponding to the rate of investment, so that from a budgetary point of view the State investment-programme will be self-financing, creating exactly the amount of profit necessary to finance the investment.[1]

But this very rise of price, by increasing profits, has increased the 'demand for capital', and hence raised the equilibrium-price of capital *above the level at which it originally stood*. If the State delays the raising of its accounting-price (after the initial lowering of it), the inducement to expand constructional activity will not only persist, but will grow cumulatively greater. If, on the other hand, after initially lowering its rate to stimulate investment, it is too quick to raise it again as a check on the inflationary tendency, it may find itself in future in the position where its power to influence investment by a change in its accounting-price is seriously blunted, since industrial managers will never expect such a change in price to last beyond a brief interval, and will take it as heralding an *opposite* change in the near future. In other words, the difficulty which today exists in influencing long-term investment through changes in the short-term rate may reappear, and reappear in an accentuated form.[2]

---

[1] The amount by which the 'employment multiplier' exceeds unity will here depend simply on the gradient of the (rising) short-period cost-curves in existing plants; since this gradient determines the 'shift to profit' as demand increases. But whatever this gradient, equilibrium on the above assumptions requires that output in these plants should be increased to the point where marginal cost has risen sufficiently (relatively to average cost) to yield an aggregate of profit that is equal to the amount of investment.

[2] It will follow that the 'true' accounting-price for capital will be at its lowest when, for any reason, a zero rate of net investment prevails. Profits in this case will be zero, since with a zero rate of investment equilibrium can only be achieved when the price-level of output = A.O.C. of output; wages being, *ex definitione*, the only source of demand for final output, and operating costs consisting solely of wages. It might seem to follow that, since profits are zero, the 'true' accounting-price must also be zero. But this is not the case; since a zero accounting-price for capital might stimulate changes of class 4 above (changes in the technical type of plant), owing to the economy of operating costs that the new type of plant could yield; and to maintain a zero rate of net investment the accounting-price would have to be high enough to

These results will not appear strange to those familiar with the proposition that 'saving equals investment'. Where the State is the investor, its investment decisions will determine and create the communal 'saving' necessary to finance it, as will be the case when investment is done by private entrepreneurs. But when all (or nearly all) personal incomes are spent, this saving must partake of the nature of so-called 'forced saving': the significant effect of the investment will be, not to enhance the money-incomes of individuals, but the income of the State in the shape of industrial profits. The notion that the State 'creates' its own profits by its own investment is, of course, analogous to the contention of Dr. Kalečki in a recent article[1] that, on similar assumptions, capitalists' spending 'creates' capitalists' profits. If, therefore, changes in the price of output, and in the profits to which these give rise, are allowed to influence the investment decisions of industry, a cumulative tendency will be latent in any acceleration or deceleration of investment during the short period (i.e. until the number or the type of plants has had time to be affected. and so influence sufficiently the *rate* of profit in an opposite direction to that in which *total* profit has previously moved).

This characteristic of the situation is more marked in a socialist econ-

---

offset the advantage of any such change. (It will be clear that this corresponds to the marginal productivity of the existing *stock* of capital in traditional capital-theory. It will only be zero when changes of class 4 above have proceeded sufficiently far to reach what has been called the point of 'capital saturation'. Cf. my *Political Economy and Capitalism*, and Lange, *Review of Econ. Studies*, June 1' 36.) On the other hand, if the rule applicable to case 3 above were to be rigidly applied in the sense of reducing the number of plants in an industry if the profit-rate was less than the price of capital, any positive accounting-price for capital would cause changes of this type in the course of time, and the position would be inherently unstable. There would, however, be some level of this accounting-price at which presumably the rate at which changes of type 4 were occurring exactly balanced the rate at which opposite changes of type 3 were taking place; and in this sense what could be defined as zero net investment for the economy as a whole could prevail, even though changes inside the total of existing capital equipment were occurring. It is further to be noted that, if the rule of equating M.O.C. to price is to be observed, the intensive utilisation of existing plant will have to be restricted to a point where A.O.C. = M.O.C., i.e. to a point below that where operating costs begin to rise as output from the plant expands. But this condition can only be fulfilled, either at the expense of some unemployment of existing labour, or else if the number (or size) of plants in each industry has been increased up to the point which corresponds to (and therefore implies the previous existence of) a zero accounting-price for capital.

[1] *Review of Econ. Studies*, February 1937; also in *Essays in the Theory of Economic Fluctuations*. Cf. also Dr. E. C. van Dorp, *A Simple Theory of Capital, Wages, Profit or Loss.*

omy (unless its investment is centrally planned) because, in so far as wages are the only form of personal income and little or nothing is 'saved' out of wages, the demand for finished output is identified with the short-period cost of output unless State expenditure is taking place. In a capitalist society other incomes than wages exist, and to the extent that expenditure from these incomes (measured in real terms) tends to alter inversely with the price of finished output, a stabilising element is introduced; and it is on some such assumption as this that traditional writers seem to have relied when they have pictured the system as tending towards stable equilibrium, and in particular have treated variations in money-wages as an equilibrating influence.

It will further be seen to follow that in this situation, if the rules suggested by Dr. Lange and others are adhered to, the amount of employment will be determined by the rate of investment, given the amount and type of plant already in existence; since the rate of investment, determining as it does the ratio of the price-level of consumption goods to money wages, determines the level of output and hence the employment-capacity of existing plant in the consumption trades. If, therefore, it is desired to maintain full employment, the rate of investment cannot be fixed at the will of the planning authority, except by departing from the rule of equating price with M.O.C. That the State should be under the compulsion in any given situation to maintain a given rate of investment, irrespective of other considerations, as the only alternative to unemployment, on the one hand, or to acute labour-shortage, on the other hand, is clearly irrational.[1]

3 These results do not, of course, follow if we drop our assumption that wages are the only form of personal income and imagine that each individual, over and above his wages, receives a 'social dividend' issued

[1] Only when 'capital saturation' has already been achieved is full employment consistent with a zero rate of net investment on the above assumptions. As the amount of plant and its productivity is increased by successive additions to the stock of capital-equipment, the profit-rate yielded to each industrial plant (and the intensity of utilisation of the plant required to yield this profit) by a given rate of investment will fall. Whether the total amount of labour required to operate the total plant in existence tends to increase or decrease will depend upon whether changes of type 3 are proceeding faster than changes of type 4 in a labour-saving direction, i.e. on the relative rate of changes in the 'widening' process and changes in the 'deepening' process. If no investment were taking place, the capacity of industry to employ labour would be uniquely given by the amount of plant in existence and its productivity, i.e. by the employment-giving capacity of existing plant (given the above rule of equating M.O.C. to price)

directly by the State.[1] But it is not merely the presence of this additional income, but appropriate variations in it, that will exercise a stabilising influence. If therefore the cumulative tendencies latent in the situation are to be counteracted, this social dividend must be made to vary inversely with the rate of investment; while its absolute amount must be fixed so that, together with the rate of investment, it is able to secure full employment. Again, an excise or turnover tax, varying directly with the rate of investment, could be employed as a stabilising mechanism. In this case, marginal cost *plus* the tax would presumably be equated to price;[2] and when the rate of investment was increased in a condition of full employment, the inevitable gap between M.O.C. and price would be bridged by the tax, profits in the consumption trades would be prevented from expanding, and output in these trades would be restricted and labour released for transfer to constructional work.[3] Where the rate of investment was relatively high a tax would be the appropriate mechanism; where the rate of investment was below a certain critical level, a social dividend. Provided that such a mechanism, centrally controlled, were in operation, the kind of pricing-system suggested by Dr. Lange would not be impracticable.

But it may well seem to many a somewhat strange and cumbrous procedure to have to create a specialised device of variable social dividends or taxes in order to 'neutralise' money sufficiently for a system of accounting-prices to operate smoothly; and one may be tempted to think that it has little to recommend it except as an ingenious proposal for reproducing

[1] As Dr. Lange himself suggests where he refers to part of income being paid in this way. Mr. H. D. Dickinson has also hinted at something of the same kind. But these writers apparently regard this as an optional, and not as a *necessary*, arrangement, and the amount of any such income as being 'arbitrary'. Dr. Lange, indeed, refers to this dividend as being 'determined by the total yield of capital and natural resources' minus investment (*op. cit.*, p. 75). But this seems to be to put the cart before the horse, since it is the size of this dividend *plus* investment that will determine both the profits of State industry (i.e. 'the total yield of capital', presumably) and the level of employment, and unless the dividend is made to fall as investment rises (or *vice versa*) total profits will rise (or fall).

[2] Marginal cost, although no longer equal, would still be *proportional* to price; and this, as Mr. Kahn has pointed out (*Economic Journal*, Vol. XLV, No. 177), is all that is required to secure the 'ideal' allocation of resources.

[3] It seems clear that this is the primary function performed by the very high turnover taxes in U.S.S.R. under the very high rates of investment of the Five Year Plans. Without them the symptoms of labour scarcity would grow more acute and the queues and goods-shortages of the early '30's would recur. At the same time, these turnover taxes are used to differentiate between different kinds of consumption goods, e.g. luxuries and necessaries.

in a socialist economy the 'ideal capitalism' of economists' imagination. If the absolute level of prices (whether of finished or intermediate products) is irrelevant and the significant consideration is the *comparative* productivity of economic resources, it is not clear why economic decisions could not be as wisely and more simply taken by a direct inspection of these comparative productivities, rather than by an elaborate attempt to equate two sets of prices—that of products and of all resources used. The former method would require that all investment decisions (at any rate in their general outline) should be centralised in the hands of the central planning authorities, and only wages (and not the price of capital) included in the calculation of costs. This would mean that control over questions of class 2, 3 and 4 above was centralised: in deciding *how much* of the community's resources to invest the planning authority would simultaneously decide (on the basis of data and advice provided by each industry) how and where investment should take place. For this method there seems to be much more to be said than has generally been admitted. In taking such decisions the planning authority would apply the rule of the maximum directly, instead of through the mediation of an accounting-price for capital: i.e. it would direct each type of resources to that use where its productivity (at the margin), valued in terms of final output, was estimated to be a maximum. Since the decision would be concerned directly with the comparative productivities of different uses (and not with the difference between value of output and an accounting-price) changes in the *absolute* level of price of final output would be irrelevant to the decision, so that the difficulties we have mentioned connected with changes in this level would not arise. The planning authorities would simply have to know which direction was up-hill on the productivity slope, and always shift resources up-hill until they could climb no further. It has been objected that the centralising of such investment-decisions might prove unduly cumbersome for them to be wisely taken. But it would, surely, be possible for each industrial management to submit its own draft sectional plan on the basis of precisely the same data as are available to them under Dr. Lange's scheme (plans drafted, perhaps on the basis of an accounting-price, or else simply on provisional data about quantity of resources available to that industry),[1] and for the central

[1] It is quite possible that Dr. Lange's proposal would prove serviceable as part of the technique of planning, even though it ceased to play a rôle as an automatic regulator of the actual decisions ultimately taken. In other words a preliminary accounting-price might be issued to industrial units as a basis on which to construct the first draft plans, this price being issued simply as a 'feeler' during the process of drafting, but not necessarily playing any decisive rôle subsequently.

authority to confine itself to subsequent pruning and integration of these draft sectional plans? The difference would be that the process of trial and error and adjustment and readjustment would take place *before* any plans were finally sanctioned and embodied in concrete acts of investment, instead of after.

Would the planning authority, nevertheless, operate ('on paper') with ratios analogous to the traditional concept of a rate of interest, even though it did not *charge* an interest-rate even for accounting purposes? In taking decisions of any of types 2, 3 and 4 above, the planning authority would presumably be confronted with data that could be expressed in terms of a ratio of net productivity (after allowing for the cost of depreciation or maintenance as well as ordinary operating costs) to construction cost. If all projects were expressed in terms of such a ratio, a priority-list of projects could be drawn up, and the allocation of resources be simply decided by moving down this priority-list. Here it is clear that the comparative, and not the absolute, size of these ratios would be the dominant consideration. The important thing would be that an investment-use which showed a higher net productivity-ratio should always be satisfied before an investment-use with a lower net productivity-ratio. Thus, decisions of type 2 would be made by giving priority to the construction of that size of plant which yielded the highest net productivity in relation to construction cost. With regard to the choice between changes of types 3 and 4: it would probably happen that some technical methods with a small construction cost figured higher in the list even though their current cost of operation and maintenance was relatively high; and consequently their construction would at first be preferred. As, however, the number of plants of this type was increased, the price of their products would tend to fall, thereby lowering their productivity-ratio *proportionately more*[1] than that of technical methods with lower costs of operation and maintenance but higher initial construction-costs; and as this occurred the latter would climb in the priority-list and investment in the new method would begin. When the new method had come into use, it would then pay to transfer labour previously employed on the repair and maintenance of the old plant to maintenance-work on the new, since the net productivity of maintenance-work on the latter would now be the greater. In this way

[1] This for the reason that if x is the product, y the cost of the product, $x - y$ the profit, and $\frac{a}{b}$ the ratio of the new price-level to the old, then $\dfrac{\frac{a}{b}x - y}{x - y}$ will be larger, the *smaller* is y.

the new plant would gradually replace the old; and the process of successive transition to more complicated projects would continue, until the possibilities of economies in operating and maintenance costs by changes of type 4 had been exhausted.[1]

4 But there is a consideration which is to my mind conclusive in rendering centrally planned investment superior to a decentralised system operating under the control of an accounting-price or interest-rate. It is that by the former method investment could be more wisely and consistently planned through time, since investment decisions could be taken in the light of fuller knowledge of the data on which the rightness or wrongness of such decisions must depend.* This would seem to be so crucial an element in the superiority of a socialist over a capitalist economy as to render it an essential keystone of a planning system. If, on the other hand, questions of plant-construction were left to be decided decentrally, according to rule-of-thumb responses to accounting-prices, the industrial managers who decided these things would be largely in blinkers with regard to developments elsewhere and to future developments, upon which their decisions ought to depend. It follows from the situation in which they are placed that these managers could not have all the relevant data before them; and this is the crucial difficulty.[2] It is an over-simplification to imagine that all that is necessary, either in a capitalist or a socialist economy, is to know the *present* loan-price and the present price of products. Since investment represents a locking-up of resources over time, the *future* price of capital and the future price of products would be relevant to any of the decisions of types 2, 3 and 4 referred to above. The capitalist entrepreneur takes his decision on the basis of *expectations* as to

---

[1] I have elsewhere suggested that there may be situations where it would be desirable *immediately* to invest in the most productive methods, even where these were relatively slow-yielding and involved a large initial construction cost. The example above is intended to show how the calculation of comparative productivity ratios could take place where more gradual progression from simple to complex technical methods was appropriate.

[* On this question see the further remarks on *ex ante* co-ordination of investment-decisions below, pp. 76-7; also above, pp. 40-1.]

[2] That this is a matter of the objective situation and not of subjective factors (the efficiency of managers and their powers of vision, etc.), does not seem always to have been appreciated; e.g. Pigou, *Economics in Practice*, pp. 114-15, and T. W. Hutchison, *Basic Postulates of Economic Theory*, pp. 186-7, where this argument is cited as though it depended on the personal qualities of administrators who take the decisions, and not on their situation.

the future trend of these factors, and because these expectations are necessarily mere guesses, mistakes and subsequent jerks in development and fluctuations develop. On what is the industrial manager in a socialist economy to base his decision? If on similar guesses, then similar mistakes and jerks and possibly fluctuations (if not quickly corrected) will result. In order to estimate the future trend of interest-rates and the price of his product, he will have to guess, not only what the State policy with regard to investment is going to be (of this, as Dr. Lange points out, he may have a pretty fair idea), but what the current reaction of industrial-managements is going to be to the current interest-rate—how much current construction-work is being undertaken in the economy at large, and its results. In other words, the future trend will itself be affected by his own decision and that of all his fellow-industrialists; and his decision will have to depend, in part, on what he guesses the response of his fellow-managers will be, this including a guess as to what *they* will guess *his* decision will be. It seems inconceivable that this guessing-game can be reduced to any simple set of rules. Nor is this something that can be remedied by a grading of the accounting-price of capital according to the period of the investment; since the central planning board can, in turn, only fix a long-term rate on the basis of a guess as to what the reaction of industrial managers will be both to it and to current short-term rates, and this reaction will partly depend on guesses as to how this long-term rate is going to *change*. Indeed, it is difficult to see how Dr. Lange's accounting-price for capital, if it is to be a long-term rate, can be a 'trial and error' rate in any significant sense of the term, since the process of trial and error that is to test it and adjust it necessarily lies in the future, and is itself being influenced by current happenings which, under a régime of decentralised investment decisions, are outside the planning authority's immediate control. It would seem as though the only accounting-price for capital that can properly be said to be subject to trial and error, and hence have any tendency to be a 'true rate', is a short-term rate.

Where decisions cannot be quickly revised, as is the case with long-term investment, it would seem to be rational that a series of decisions, each of which affects the others, should be co-ordinated in a unified decision instead of being separated into a number of autonomous decisions. But even if all questions of investment were decided (or had to be finally sanctioned) centrally, questions of class 1 above (the volume of output from a *given* plant) might still be settled according to Dr. Lange's and Mr. Lerner's rule; i.e. of equating M.O.C. with price. This would mean that 'short period' questions could be decentralised; i.e. day-to-day decisions about the intensity of utilisation of plant, and as much adaptation to meet unforeseen circumstances as would be possible within a given set of investment-decisions recently taken. But here again some of the difficulties discussed in the first half of this article would obtrude and the wisdom of even this amount of decentralised autonomy might be questioned. Where there was a reserve of unemployed labour, it would be preferable as we have seen to extend output and employment beyond the point where price= marginal prime cost.[1] On the other hand, in a condition of full employment the problem of acute labour shortage would emerge if the rate of investment were to be increased; and to meet it, control over the output programmes of individual plants would have to revert to the central planning authority, or output be limited by means of an output-tax levied on each plant. With sufficient foresight, however, this difficulty could be partly prevented; which is a particular witness to the importance of taking investment-decisions in the light of knowledge of future investment trends. The situation just described implies that there are (at the moment) too many plants in each industry. If in the past investment had taken the form of appropriate changes of class 4, instead of changes of class 3—if there had been an extension of the 'deepening process' faster than the 'widening process'—this situation need not have arisen. To prevent such a situation from *ever* arising would, of course, require a length of vision that is beyond the bounds of reasonable hope. But with a moderate degree of planning ahead its possibility could be considerably reduced.

C. A Review of the Discussion concerning Economic Calculation in a Socialist Economy
[1953]

1 Since the Second World War the debate among academic economists about the so-called pricing-problem under socialism (alternatively referred to as the problem of economic calculation or as the allocation-problem) has largely become, on this side of the Atlantic at any rate, a discussion about the price-policy for nationalised industries and the mechanism of economic planning. The debate was started, however, more

[1] In a situation where unemployment prevails the principle of marginal cost is generally inappropriate, since increase of output involves the transfer of workers not from alternative employment, but from idleness. Hence there is no social cost involved in their employment.

than thirty years ago, on the broader issue of the possibility or impossibility of any rational calculation in a socialist economy—as those who have followed the economic literature of the past three decades hardly need reminding. In the form in which Professor Mises launched the debate in 1920, the problem of economic calculation was asserted to be incapable of solution in a socialist economy; and the existence of this problem was accordingly stressed as a crucial objection to socialism. The argument was, in brief, that without a market for 'production goods' and factors of production the value of these things could not be objectively determined. Without such determination by a market-process costs would have no meaning, and significant economic calculation would be impossible. Said Mises: 'Just because no production good will ever become the object of exchange, it will be impossible to determine its monetary value.... Money could never fill in a socialist state the rôle it fills in a competitive society in determining the value of production goods. Calculation in terms of money will here be impossible.... There would be no means of determining what was rational, and hence it is obvious that production could never be directed by economic considerations.... In place of the economy of the "anarchic" method of production, recourse will be had to the senseless output of an absurd apparatus. The wheels will turn, but will run to no effect.'[1] There will only be 'groping in the dark'.

Little doubt, I think, remains today that the debate which followed the Mises-challenge has gone against those who started the polemic: at least to the extent of demonstrating that there is no fundamental inconsistency between social ownership of the means of production and rational economic calculation, as the Mises-school assumed there to be and tried to demonstrate by a simple *a priori* argument. As Professor Bergson has said: 'By now it seems generally agreed that the argument on these questions advanced by Mises himself, at least according to one interpretation, is without much force'.[2] Indeed, in the course of the 1930's the argument of the disciples of Mises shifted its ground; and as Professor Oskar Lange

---

[1] Ludwig von Mises, 'Die Wirtschaftsrechnung im sozialistischen Gemeinwesen', in *Archiv für Sozialwissenschaft*, Vol. 47, April 1920; reprinted in *Collectivist Economic Planning*, ed. Hayek (London, 1935), pp. 92, 105–6. A closely similar argument had been advanced prior to this by Professor N. G. Pierson in an article in *De Economist* in 1902, but little notice seems to have been taken of this at the time. Max Weber declared in his *Wirtschaft und Gesellschaft*, which was published in 1921, that 'it is certainly impossible to talk of a *rationally* "planned economy" ' (pp. 55–6; *cit.* Hayek, *op. cit.*, p. 34).

[2] On 'Socialist Economics' in *A Survey of Contemporary Economics* (American Econ. Association, ed. Howard S. Ellis; Philadelphia, 1948), p. 412.

has pointed out, in this 'more refined form' anti-socialists of the Mises-Hayek persuasion 'do not deny the *theoretical* possibility of a rational allocation of resources in a socialist economy; they only doubt the possibility of a satisfactory *practical* solution of the problem'.[1]

This result has been largely due to the detailed demonstration by a number of participants in the debate of the manner in which values could be assigned to producers' goods and factors of production in a socialist economy. Their solution took two forms. Firstly, according to the well-known solution of Professor H. D. Dickinson, there was nothing inconsistent with socialism in having actual market prices for such things. Industrial managers could compete with one another for land, labour and capital, and for plant and equipment, fuel and power and raw materials, by a process of market bidding, in such a way that the prices at which these were supplied 'found their own level'—a level at which the demand for them was equated with the available supply. According to the second version (usually associated with the name of Professor Lange), there need be no actual markets and actual prices, other than the retail market for final consumer goods: it would be sufficient if there were accounting prices, established by a process of 'trial and error'; industrial managers taking their decisions about output and investment on the basis of these accounting-prices, and these accounting-prices being moved up or down at intervals until there was no longer any excess demand or unused supply.[2]

Owing to the very formal setting of the discussion as started by Mises (and carried on by most of the subsequent participants), it does not seem to have been always clear that the solutions which these writers propounded (in terms of competitive bidding either on actual markets or in some quasi-market setting), placed severe limitations on the type of economic mechanism which a socialist economy could employ if it was to remain 'rational'. In particular, it implied a system of decentralised decisions about output and investment—decentralised to the level of managers of economic enterprises—as opposed to centrally planned decisions on these matters. Professor Dickinson's article, it is true, on a careful reading can be seen to be open to the interpretation of either playing at competition on actual markets or (so far at any rate as investment-decisions are concerned) of working out successive approximations inside

---

[1] Oskar Lange and F. M. Taylor, *On the Economic Theory of Socialism* (Minnesota, 1938), p. 62.

[2] H. D. Dickinson, 'Price Formation in a Socialist Community', in *Economic Journal*, June 1933, pp. 237-50; Oskar Lange, *op. cit.*, pp. 72-90.

a planning office. (This ambiguity was no doubt because the writer's preoccupation was with propounding a theoretical answer to the Mises-challenge rather than with advocating any particular solution.) However, in his subsequent book, *The Economics of Socialism*, he makes plain that what he is suggesting (for his 'Sector of Individual Consumption') is a particular mechanism of decentralised decisions (of his other 'Sector of Communal Consumption' we shall have something to say below). It is not altogether impossible to think of the 'trial and error' or 'accounting prices' solution as a purely planning technique. But, in the form in which it was outlined by Professor Lange, it was clearly intended to operate as a decentralised mechanism, with one set of rules for managers of enterprises or industries[1] and another set for the central economic authorities.[2] As such, at any rate, it has now become customary to interpret this proposal;[3] and as such the anti-planners in the social-democratic camp have come in recent years to welcome it as a theoretical demonstration of the necessity for what they have emotively termed 'democratic planning' and of the inferior character of so-called 'totalitarian planning', which is alleged to sacrifice the welfare of consumers to the arbitrary value-judgments of economic dictators.[4] To this matter of the mechanism of economic decision we shall return.

As for the general course of the debate, it is some measure of the extent to which the balance had been tilted by the end of the 'thirties that opinion should have come to regard the analysis of optimum welfare-conditions as holding a *tendenz* in favour of socialism, rather than against

[1] I.e., extend output or investment to the point of equality of selling price with marginal cost measured in accounting prices, and choose that method of production which minimises average cost in accounting prices.

[2] I.e., vary the accounting-prices for producers' goods (e.g. machinery, raw materials, fuel and power) and factors of production until demand is equated with supply; raising the price if there is an excess-demand, lowering them if there is an excess-supply.

[3] Cf.: 'Perhaps the most striking feature of Lange's model is that the function of the Central Planning Board is virtually confined to providing a substitute for the market as the coordinator of the activities of the various plants and industries. The truth is that Lange's Board is not a *planning* agency at all but rather a *price-fixing* agency: in his model production decisions are left to a myriad of essentially independent units.' (P. Sweezy, *Socialism*, New York, 1949, p. 233.)

[4] Already before the war there was a school of socialist thought which held that: 'The various kinds of planning, or interference with the price system ... are possible rather than necessary elements of socialism. ... It is a mistake to suppose that any interference with the price system as such is good or bad. Such interferences may be either progressive or regressive or neutral ... planning has its limits and its dangers.' (Douglas Jay, *The Socialist Case*, London, 1937, pp. 349, 351.)

it. This change of climate, surprising enough at first sight, was largely due to the renewed attention paid by economists in the 'twenties and early 'thirties to cases of so-called 'decreasing cost' lines of production (where marginal cost is below average cost, *ex definitione*); since analysis of these cases carried the implication that only under socialism (where the making of profit was no object and industries could be run, if need be, at a loss) could the principle of equating price with marginal cost be rigorously and uniformly applied. Perhaps the fear that Mises had loosed a Frankenstein-monster which might live to turn against its creator may have influenced some of those who later sought to reconsider the foundations of the whole discussion. However, the corollaries of the Mises-theorem could still be used none the less as an argument against centralised planning of the Soviet type (and were so used very freely in the post-war years, as we have just seen). Directed against this particular foe the Mises-challenge was deemed to have lost none of its sting.

There by the time of the Second World War the debate seemed to rest. As an incidental product on the formal side there had been considerable refinement in the way of stating the 'optimum conditions' for allocating 'resources.'[1] Neither here nor in the elaboration of the actual price-

[1] *Optimum*, i.e., from the point of view of maximising welfare; cf. especially A. Birk (Bergson), 'A Reformulation of Certain Aspects of Welfare Economics', in *Quarterly Journal of Economics*, February, 1938, pp. 310 *seq*. The essentials of this theory can be summed up in three conditions. (1) That the ratios of the marginal utilities of various commodities (or their marginal rates of substitution to consumers) should be equal to the ratios of their prices. (2) That the ratios of the marginal productivities of various factors (or their rates of substitution), expressed in each case in terms of the product in question, should be the same in all industries (and plants). (3) That the marginal productivity of each factor, expressed in value-terms (i.e. at current product-prices), should be equal in all industries (and plants).

The first of these conditions is usually considered as being fulfilled if consumers have freedom in distributing their expenditure between commodities so as to get the most for their money. By itself, this condition has little significance: it could, for instance, be fulfilled at any set of relative prices. But it is the pivot upon which the significance of condition (3) depends. The significance of (2) as a separate condition will be referred to below (p. 61 n.). (3) is taken to imply that no gain in value is possible (and hence, combined with (1), no gain in utility to consumers) from shifting productive resources from one industry to another.

It is to be noted that these conditions as stated do not require the introduction of factor-prices—they are stated purely in terms of product-prices (and (2) is independent even of these). Once factor-prices have been introduced, (2) and (3) can be expressed in the form that the ratios of marginal costs of the various products should be equal to the ratios of product-prices. There are, however, purists who are not content with this latter version, but insist that there must be, not merely proportionality, but *equality* of marginal costs and prices: otherwise disutility of work, and of mechanisms did it look as though much more remained to be said. There is good reason to suppose that most of the participants in the debate regarded the matter as talked out—and justifiably, so far as discussion within its previous limits was concerned. The time had come, it seemed, to turn to other things.

Yet in retrospect it now seems clear that the more realistic kernel of the matter—an examination of the discussion's relevance to actual situations facing policy-makers and planners—had scarcely even been disclosed to view. Even on the rather formal plane at which most of the debate had been conducted certain complications had been ignored and a false impression of precision and certainty conveyed. If only because the discussion which flared-up anew after the war has led to some re-examination of fundamentals, it is perhaps not altogether otiose to try and review how the question now stands.

2 Confining ourselves for the present to the question as to how 'optimum conditions' for maximising welfare are defined, we are immediately confronted with a crucial difficulty. How to handle the matter of income-distribution has always proved to be an awkward obstacle in the path of the debate; and what has made the economists' discussion so unreal to most laymen has been its abstraction of the problem of allocation of resources from that of the distribution of income. Evidently, there were two ways in which this embarrassing question of income-distribution could be handled. One was to include some statement about distribution among the optimum conditions themselves. This was the course adopted, for example, by Professor A. P. Lerner, who posited that 'the probable value of total satisfactions is maximised by dividing income *evenly*'.[1] To most economists, however, this course was unacceptable, on the curiously solipsistic view[2] that so-called 'interpersonal comparisons of utility' have no scientific basis, and that accordingly one can postulate nothing about

different kinds of occupation, to producers is not optimally balanced against gain to consumers (see Bergson, *loc. cit.*, p. 314; A. Lerner, *Economics of Control*, pp. 100–3). It is difficult, however, to see what meaning can be given to this equality-version in the case of factors other than labour.

[1] *Economics of Control* (New York, 1944), p. 29. Professor Lerner's argument as it stands, however, rests on the questionable assumption of the equi-probability of the unknown.

[2] Cf. Little: 'It is clear that if one accepts behaviour as evidence for other minds, then one must admit that one can compare other minds on the basis of such evidence. Therefore those who "deny" interpersonal comparisons must deny the existence of other minds.' (*Critique of Welfare Economics*, Oxford, 1950, p. 57.)

income-distribution without introducing an ethical value-judgment. They have accordingly adopted the alternative course of taking the distribution of income as *given* and enunciating propositions about the optimum allocation of resources on this assumption (which looks like a modern example of that separation of the problems of production and of distribution that Marx criticised a century ago in the case of J. S. Mill). This method led to some odd results when it came to drawing practical inferences from the theorem. To the plain man it has always seemed absurd, even disingenuous, to enunciate certain propositions about the conditions for maximising welfare when it was clear to all that, with the existing distribution of income, welfare could be increased by deliberately violating these conditions (e.g. by rationing scarce commodities and subsidising food and house-building while taxing luxuries). Economists have defended themselves by saying that they were merely dealing with one question at a time; that in the interests of clear thinking they were handling separately two distinct problems in maximising economic welfare, one involving a 'value judgment' and the other not; and that it was only sensible to show how the best could be made (from the production-angle) of whatever distribution of money-income one happened to have (or had decided it was best to have). The plain man, probably still puzzled and only half-convinced, has had to content himself with the retort that, while such a separation may be all very well as an analytical and a classroom technique, the economist has no right to imply that a 'free price-system' is always good policy or that inequalities between individuals and classes must *only* be remedied by money-income changes or transfers.

Even as an analytical technique this separating of the definition of a welfare maximum from income-distribution proves more questionable the more closely one examines it. The positivists have proudly proclaimed that their definition affords an entirely objective criterion for policy. But as soon as one tries to give real content to the definition, its essential barrenness appears. It amounts to defining a position as a maximum if it is one in which no individual can be made better off without making anyone else worse off.[1] But this is a curiously limited way of defining a maximum;

---

[1] This is the significance, in the usual form in which the optimum conditions are stated, of the condition about the ratio of the marginal productivities of factors (or their marginal rates of substitution) being equalised in all industries (and firms); since, if this ratio is not equal, it will be possible by swapping resources between industries to increase the output of one product without decreasing that of others. The other conditions (into the statement of which prices enter) are concerned, however, with uni-directional shifts in the quantity of *all* factors between industries, and hence with increasing some products at the expense of others.

according to it there is no unique position, but a very large number of possible 'maxima'; and as a criterion for policy it is inevitably silent about the majority of changes which come up for judgment—changes which involve gain to some and loss to others.[1] To break out of the narrow limits within which such a criterion can claim to have validity, another definition has been suggested, in terms of the so-called 'compensation principle'.[2] This postulates that a welfare-maximum has been reached if no change is possible which can bring enough gain to beneficiaries from the change to enable them to compensate, *if they should wish to do so*, the losers from the change so as to leave the latter no worse off than they were before the change occurred.[3] The field of application of such a criterion is

[1] Cf. Samuelson's statement that a maximum so defined 'is not a unique point' (*Foundations of Economic Analysis*, p. 214), and Lange on the 'arbitrary parameters' contained in the solution of any such set of maximising equations ('The Foundations of Welfare Economics', in *Econometrica*, Vol. X, Nos. 3-4, July–October, 1942, pp. 216-18). This definition was originally advanced by Pareto, and was summarily dismissed by Wicksell with the words: 'Pareto's doctrine contributes nothing' (*Lectures*, Vol. I, p. 83). What it amounts to, in terms of the familiar (to economists) indifference-curve technique, is that from any point which is not on the so-called 'contract-curve' (defined as the locus of points of tangency of indifference-curves) a movement is always possible which yields gain to *both* parties—movement *onto* the contract-curve. The latter is thus a maximum relative to certain neighbouring points. But *all* points on the contract-curve are maxima in this sense; and a point A on this contract-curve can only be said to be 'superior' to a point B that is *off* the curve if it lies within the area bounded by the two indifference-curves which intersect at B. One cannot say whether B is superior or inferior to any other point C that is off the contract-curve (and outside the area just mentioned); one can make no pronouncement about the relative merits of points A' and A which are both on the contract-curve (the movement from one to the other representing a change of income-distribution); and one cannot even say whether points C or C' which are *off* the curve are severally inferior or not to point A which is *on* the curve (but outside the areas bounded by the two pairs of indifference-curves which intersect respectively at C and C').

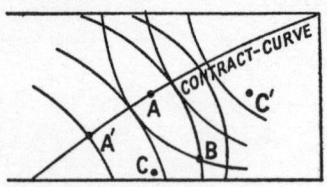

[2] Mr. Kaldor originally introduced this as a criterion of an *increase of real income*, and to justify thereby 'dividing "welfare economics" into two parts'—production and distribution (*Economic Journal*, September, 1939, pp. 549-52). But it has been widely treated as affording an independent criterion of increase in social welfare (and he himself evidently regarded it as *a* criterion).

[3] And/or (according to an alternative definition) if it would not have been worth while for the prospective losers to give a bribe to the prospective beneficiaries sufficiently large to persuade the latter not to make (or advocate) the change. It has been

certainly wider than that of the previous one. Its defect lies in assuming as between different individuals that an equal gain and loss of money income represents an equal gain or loss of welfare; and in this defect is concealed a similar bias to that of the earlier 'positivist' definition. It is equivalent to stating that a course of action is socially desirable if the resulting gain, measured in money, to those benefited exceeds the loss, measured in money, suffered by the losers. And such a criterion, as Professor Baumol has well said, has 'a predilection for the distributive *status quo*, in that it is weighted by the "compensating power" of the individuals involved.'[1]

Apart from the incompleteness of such criteria, maturer reflection has shown that the plain man's intuition in regarding this whole approach as suspect was right after all; and that even for formal purposes the problem of allocating productive resources and the question of income-distribution cannot be treated separately. In Mr. Little's words, 'the question of income distribution is logically prior to the question of the ideal output'.[2] The reason is that any distribution of money income between individuals and classes only acquires significance (from the standpoint discussed, namely social welfare) to the extent that it gives rise to a certain distribution of *real* income; and most changes[3] in the allocation of resources, and hence in the proportions in which different commodities are supplied (and in the prices of these commodities), inevitably alter the distribution of *real* income between different groups of consumers.[4] The most obvious

shown that these two criteria (commonly known as the Hicks-Kaldor and the Scitovsky criteria respectively) do not necessarily yield identical results.

[1] W. J. Baumol, on 'Community Indifference', in *Review of Economic Studies*, Vol. XIV (1946–7), p. 46. Its 'predilection for the distributive *status quo*' is not, however, because the income-position of the individuals concerned affects their *ability* to compensate (this depends simply on the result of the change in question): it is because the balancing of the gain and loss from the change takes no account of the difference to welfare which a given gain or loss of income may make to individuals having different incomes (e.g. representing a *smaller* gain or loss to a rich man than to a poor man). Thus a given gain of income to the rich may be sufficient to enable them to compensate poorer losers sufficiently to leave the latter at the same income-level as before; but it does not follow from this that, if compensation is in fact not paid, the gain of welfare to the rich is greater than the loss of welfare by the poorer losers.

[2] *Op. cit.*, p. 182.

[3] I.e. all changes that are not 'neutral' as between different consumers, in the sense that they affect the cost of living of different consumers differently, since the commodities in question are consumed in different proportions by different people.

[4] Conversely, any change in income-*distribution* must be regarded as altering the size of total income, unless one has some independent measure for real income on the side of production, e.g. labour. As Dr. Arrow has said with regard to the 'compensation principle': 'there is no meaning to total output independent of distribution'

example of this (in a society of unequal incomes) is a transfer of resources from producing expensive luxuries to producing necessities, with a smaller supply of the former and a larger supply (and a fall in price) of the latter in consequence. This shift of production of itself, and independently of any change in the relative money-incomes of individuals, modifies the distribution of real income in favour of poorer consumers.[1] Indeed, *real income* can only be given a meaning in terms of welfare (or some such), and welfare is admittedly affected by distribution.

The force of this rather obvious conclusion seems to have been impressed upon economists as a result of re-examining the implications of applying rigorously the so-called 'marginalist principle'—the principle that resources should be so allocated between different lines of production as to make prices everywhere equal to (or at least equi-proportional to) marginal costs. The application of this principle will result in running at a loss those industries that are subject to decreasing cost[2] as output expands, since in these cases marginal cost (and hence price) will necessarily be below average cost; and conversely with industries subject to increasing cost, where marginal cost is above average cost. The question immediately arises as to the source of the subsidies payable to the industries which are to be run at a loss. If, for example, railways or electricity-production were to be deliberately run at a loss, they would presumably have to be subsidised at the expense of non-railway-users or non-electricity-users. Expressing the matter in real terms: if an application of the marginal prin-

(K. J. Arrow, *Social Choice and Individual Values*, New York, 1951, p. 40). Cf. also G. Myrdal, *The Political Element in the Development of Economic Theory* (Eng. trans. P. Streeten, London, 1953), pp. 132-3, who anticipated this criticism already in 1928. Were it not for this crucial difficulty, one would be tempted to say that the 'compensation principle', while unsatisfactory as a criterion for welfare, provided a definition of maximum *output*, and hence a means of drawing a logical line between problems of production and problems of distribution.

[1] Cf. P. Samuelson, *Foundations of Economic Analysis*, p. 225, who puts the same point in a different form, as a criticism of equality of money-income (or for that matter of any postulated distribution of *money*-income) as *optimum*: 'at different relative prices between vegetables and non-vegetables an equal distribution of income [between vegetarians and non-vegetarians] can no longer be optimal.' Cf. also Nancy Ruggles in 'The Theory of Marginal Cost Pricing' in *Review of Economic Studies*, No. 43 (1949-50), p. 123: 'No such separation of the problem is possible. Every pricing system results in some sort of income distribution and no substantial redistribution of income is possible without changing that pricing system.'

[2] Or industries which are subject to decreasing cost to a greater extent than the average of industries (and hence marginal cost abnormally low compared to average cost), in the case of the more lenient version of the principle (that prices should be everywhere in the same proportional relationship to marginal cost).

ciple involves an expansion of output in some lines of production and a transfer of productive resources thereto from other lines of production, consumers of the former will be benefited and consumers of the latter adversely affected. Only if the expenditure-patterns of all consumers were uniform would there be no such distribution-effect to be taken into account. The net effect of such changes in distribution may be beneficial or harmful; but it cannot be omitted from the reckoning. In other words, there is a logical inconsistency in speaking of the application of certain allocation-principles in face of a given distribution of *real* income, since the very application (or non-application) of such principles will help to determine what this distribution is; whereas, if one refers to the distribution of *money* income (instead of real income) as being given, one achieves no more than a verbal evasion of the difficulty, since the effect of different allocations of resources on the relative positions of different individuals still has to be evaluated and included in the reckoning.

The significance of this for the wider debate on the pricing problem may not seem at first sight to be very great. It implies apparently that the case for 'a free price system' or talk of optimum conditions for allocating resources are only relevant when the distribution of income is 'ideal', or nearly so; and since it can be shown (to the satisfaction of a very wide body of opinion, at least) that, if 'ideal' does not imply equality of money incomes, it must imply a much greater approximation to equality than exists, or is practicable, in capitalist society, this means that the argument can have relevance only to a socialist society. The Mises-boot turns out to be on the other leg from that on which Mises supposed it to be.

There is, however, a more fundamental implication. It is one that affects the 'limits' or 'tolerances' within which one can expect precision of any solution to the allocation-problem. This is not merely a matter of the degree of refinement which one can reasonably expect to find *in practice*, i.e. in application of a principle (although there is a good deal that could be said on this aspect of the matter also). It is a matter of the degree of refinement with which a solution can be propounded even in general terms. If one sets out a series of precisely formulated conditions under which something will be maximised, one implies that this something can be fairly precisely known and compared. But when it comes to including among these maximum conditions the way in which income is to be distributed between different individuals, this precision vanishes.[1] One may

---

[1] For the reasons already mentioned, this distribution-condition is not capable of any formulation that is both simple and precise. To define it in money-income terms will be no more than a rough and approximate mode of statement, since a given dis-

hold that comparison of the economic welfare of different people can be derived empirically; but it is hard to believe that anyone seriously holds that an empirical basis exists for anything more than a rather rough-and-ready comparison. One may be able to judge, for example, that the difference made to A's welfare by having a house to live in instead of a Nissen-hut is greater than the difference made to B's by having a motor-car to ride in where previously he had none. But at the same time there may be many cases, involving no such striking difference of situation, where a comparison of this kind is difficult, if not impossible to make. Alternatively one may believe that all such statements involve a value-judgment and in this case the value-judgments involved can hardly be endowed with any high degree of precision. (Even Professor Lerner's postulate of absolute equality as the optimum is only intended to represent the 'most probable' position of the maximum, and there will be a considerable range of positions on either side of it where the alleged probability will be very nearly as great, and where in fact the optimum may well lie.)

This is equivalent to saying that the optimum cannot be defined as a unique position, but must be treated as an area or range of positions within which no decisive choice can be made. One can postulate that any position within this range is superior to any position outside it; but one cannot be more exact than this and postulate anything about the relative heights of positions inside it. The summit of the welfare-hill can only be approximately estimated. As Mr. Little has concluded: 'It is a mistake to suppose that anything except a very rough approximation to the "ideal", even when it is theoretically determinate, can be confidently held to be beneficial'; and again, 'any divergence from "optimum" conditions must be large before one could have any reasonable degree of confidence that an improvement would result from trying to satisfy them.'[1] Or to quote

---

tribution of money-income will yield a different distribution of welfare for each (different) price-structure (if tastes are not uniform) and for each different pattern of comparative individual tastes. To define it as such a distribution of real income as will equalise the marginal utility of income to all persons gives an *appearance* of precision; but although this may be the clearest way of summing-up what one means (or at least a possible meaning) by treating everyone equally, no one, I think, would suggest that the practical verification of this criterion could be anything more than very rough and approximate. Cf. in this connection Dr. Arrow's question in reviewing Mr. Little: 'How do we describe distribution of real income? . . . How do we even formulate such judgements?' (*American Economic Review*, December, 1951, p. 927).

[1] *Op. cit.*, pp. 194, 271.

Professor Baumol: 'The desires of the individual are often nebulous, so there is likely to be no unique ideal output, but rather a considerable range of possible output combinations, which for practical purposes are equally preferable.... Where there are many substitutes for most commodities... only extreme deviations from the ideal output are then likely to be of any substantial importance.'[1]

When we come to the practical corollaries of any maximising theorem, it is clear that what we have just been saying may make a substantial, even a crucial, difference. It will make a difference to the weight we attach to *this* particular type of efficiency-problem, concerned with the general allocation-pattern of resources, compared with others (and there *are* other types of efficiency-problem, as we shall presently see). It will affect our judgment as to the worth-whileness of the cost involved in having a particular mechanism to handle this problem (that the price-system may itself involve costs does not always seem to have been recognised by its devotees). Finally it may crucially affect our choice of mechanism itself. A great deal, of course, will depend on how much lack of precision is involved in the considerations discussed in the last paragraph. But in the degree to which our optimum has to be defined, for realistic purposes, as a range of possible positions, not as a single position—as an area rather than as a point on a map—it will follow that 'errors' of allocation which fall below a certain magnitude are not significant for our problem—in fact will not be detectable or even definable as errors at all. To involve a clear loss of welfare, mistakes of economic policy will have to be large mistakes, not just small ones. And as we all know, large sins are easier to correct, if not always to avoid, than small ones. Changing the metaphor: to the extent that the target at which we are aiming is vague and not precise—to the extent that the problem becomes one of avoiding wide misses rather than concentrating upon some imaginary bull's-eye—it becomes pointless to devote time and ingenuity to the invention of perfect telescopic sights, since anything that is sufficiently wide of the mark to matter will be capable of detection by the naked eye.

It has always been taken for granted, apparently, by the Mises-school that there is nothing intermediate between rationality, achievable by a streamlined pricing-system, and the irrationality of planners who grope blindly in the dark. Even those writers who demonstrated in reply to Mises that once consumers' demand-schedules, production-functions and

[1] W. J. Baumol, *Welfare Economics and the Theory of the State* (London, 1952), p. 61.

the resources available are known 'the problem of choice is soluble'[1] seem to have accepted the necessity for some form of pricing of producers' goods, owing to the complexities involved in reaching a solution in any other way. It might seem to be common sense, if the essence of the theory is that the marginal productivity of homogeneous resources should be equalised in all uses, to realise this equality by direct inspection of the results of movements at the margin, instead of resorting to the Heath-Robinson device of pricing these resources first in order to compare input-prices with the values of output, and to allocate resources in the light of this comparison. Professor Robbins's reference to the 'thousands of equations' which a planning office would need in practice to solve in order to handle the problem by direct inspection seems to have frightened economists away from the (at first glance) common-sense solution. What makes the practical problem of calculating and directly comparing 'net productivities' more complex than might at first appear is the *heterogeneity* of economic resources in the real world. This is specially true of that textbook-category 'capital', which in actuality is composed of a very numerous and heterogeneous collection of capital goods (machine-tools, building materials and prime-movers, not to mention fuel and power and raw materials generally), which can only be reduced to a common unit, and hence aggregated, in terms either of labour or of money-value—it cannot be measured in units of itself. We will not discuss here whether with modern mechanical calculating devices the solving of 'thousands of equations' would be quite such an insuperable task for a planning office as Professor Robbins and his audience assumed it would be; nor whether or not simplified models in terms of labour (e.g. of the Leontief type) have too restrictive assumptions to be usable as adequate approximations. But clearly the degree of approximation to which one expects precision in the result will be highly relevant to the answering of such questions, and will make all the difference to the complexity of the calculations referred to. If a low degree of approximation will suffice—if correction of substantial departures from an 'ideal' position is all that is required, and not the persistent maintenance of a precise equilibrium position[2]—then a theoretically imperfect device, if cheap in practice, may have marked advantages over the more elaborate but more theoretically perfect instrument.

[1] Lange, *op. cit.*, p. 60. Cf. also H. D. Dickinson in *Economic Journal*, June, 1933, p. 242, and A. C. Pigou, *Socialism versus Capitalism* (London, 1937), p. 118.
[2] Cf. Professor Baumol: 'The ability to *correct* rather than *avoid* errors is the best that can be claimed for the responsiveness to consumers' desires of any economy' (*op. cit.*, p. 159).

3 If the conditions for maximising welfare are stated in a sufficiently general way (e.g. Professor Bergson's 'social welfare function') they can be held to embrace any act of social choice, in whatever manner it is made, provided only that this choice obeys certain canons of rationality. At this level of abstraction the theory can be said to be supra-institutional and to be applicable to any type of economic system. But then it is doubtful whether such theorems get much beyond the realm of tautology; and if they do not they can imply no imperatives about actual economic mechanisms. (Do they do more than tell us what is implied in any choice between alternatives which is consistently motivated by the desire to maximise something?) The gist of the discussion in the last section was that, however such theorems of social choice are formulated, they must include (implicitly or explicitly) some statement about the relative real-income-positions of the individuals composing the community; and this we saw to be a crucial qualification. We must now turn to consider the theory as formulated in more realistic terms; since only in this form can it be held to sustain corollaries about the necessity for a particular kind of pricing-system.

In this form the theory is a close cousin to the Subjective Theory of Value; and as the latter starts from the desires or behaviour-reactions of consumers, so the theory of social choice generally treats the economic welfare which it seeks to maximise as composed of the satisfactions of the desires of individual consumers—moreover (an important qualification as we shall see) of those desires which are capable of expression on a market. Total welfare is a summation of individual satisfactions; the distribution of income determining the 'weight' to be attached to various individuals in the process of this summation. The common-sense case for a so-called 'free price-system' is that this provides a system of voting by consumers as to how they would prefer productive resources to be allocated—a form of voting, moreover, which allows minority desires to be satisfied. It is customary to add that where the alternatives are numerous and finely graded this is the only form of voting which is capable of yielding correct results. Such is the doctrine of so-called 'consumers' sovereignty'—at least one form of it, and I believe the most common form.

To avoid misunderstanding, it is apparently necessary to start by saying that no one (so far as the present writer is aware) claims that the desires of individual consumers are irrelevant to social choice. Everyone admits that, in varying degrees, individual preferences must come into the picture. Accordingly, in the remarks which follow the writer must not be thought to be denying that consumers' demands are an important factor to be taken into account by any planners or policy-makers, and that a retail consumers' market is a very serviceable, even essential, way of registering these demands. What is in question is whether these individual desires, as registered on a market, are the exclusive, or even preponderant, factor to be taken into account; and whether accordingly a mechanism whereby production is automatically steered by market indices will necessarily produce 'correct' results. Since propaganda has succeeded in creating a widespread belief that Marxism, at any rate, represents a complete negation of consumers' wishes as an influence upon production, one should perhaps quote in this context the statement of Marx (apparently intended to refer to any type of exchange society, if not to any type of economy) that 'consumption furnishes the impulse of production as well as its object, which plays in production the part of its guiding aim',[1] as well as the recent declaration of Stalin that 'the basic economic law of socialism' presupposes 'the maximum satisfaction of the constantly rising material and cultural requirements of the whole of society'.[2]

To emphasise this might seem superfluous, were it not that, not only Professors Mises and Hayek, but also less extreme devotees of consumers' sovereignty seem to have assumed that there are but two alternatives—an automatic price-system as the embodiment of 100 per cent consumers' sovereignty and the regimentation of consumers by economic dictatorship—with nothing intermediate between them.[3] The political analogy of election-voting should have sufficed to throw doubt on so *simpliste* a view; since the representative system is very far from submitting every choice to a general vote of all individuals, delegating most decisions as 'expert' matters to parliamentary representatives or in turn to Ministers or to committees appointed by these representatives; and yet it is usually classed as 'democratic'. It would be an odd use of language to say that one was submitting oneself to dictatorship over consumption because one left the choice of an optimum diet to a doctor or accepted the verdict of a *maître d'hôtel* or *restaurateur* on the best dish or wine to choose. The assumption that there is no intermediate position between 100 per cent

[1] *Critique of Political Economy* (Chicago, 1904), p. 279.
[2] *Economic Problems of Socialism in U.S.S.R.* (Moscow, 1952), p. 45.
[3] Only such an assumption seems capable of lending relevance to Professor Hayek's charge of advocating a barrack-room régime once levelled at the present writer (*Collectivist Economic Planning*, London, 1935, p. 215), or to some of the remarks of Professor Lerner (e.g. his references to 'contempt for the masses', ignoring the popular verdict, 'authoritarianism', in *Review of Economic Studies*, October, 1934, pp. 54–5).

consumers' sovereignty and dictatorial choice would only be justified if it could be shown that there is no practicable method whereby planners could take decisions about production, on the basis of data provided by a retail market, with even a low degree of approximation to the 'ideal' result. This is something which the Mises-school and those influenced by them have taken for granted but not demonstrated. How low a degree of approximation one is willing to regard as permissible is a matter for discussion; and clearly one's verdict on this will be influenced by one's estimate of how complete and reliable an index of social welfare consumers' market-behaviour provides—as well as by the type of consideration discussed in the last section.

About the adequacy of consumers' market-behaviour as indices it is possible to have a number of substantial doubts without wishing to see the consumer 'regimented' or to see one's own particular scale of values uniformly imposed on everyone else (as one can doubt the wisdom of putting every decision of foreign or domestic policy to a referendum without qualifying as an advocate of dictatorship).[1] Firstly, there may be doubt as to the rationality of consumers' market behaviour. Secondly, there is the matter of 'collective wants', which cannot be satisfied by individuals as separate units and which accordingly are not represented (at any rate not adequately) in the demands of individual consumers as expressed on a market. These Professor H. D. Dickinson appears to distinguish as being of two kinds: things which cannot be individually appropriated (save by the rich), like a park or picture-gallery or museum; and things which 'must be enjoyed to some extent by all or none', like football or a banquet.[2] Thirdly, there are those cases where the satisfaction an individual derives from a thing is dependent partly or wholly upon the consumption of it (or of other things) by other people—a category which may overlap with the previous one and which has been christened by Professor Meade 'external economies and diseconomies in private consumption'.[3] Among the examples used to illustrate them are cases in which social convention or custom shape the want for a thing: for instance, if one has a grander car or television set or can give larger parties than one's neighbours one is happy, but if a neighbour should eclipse one in such expenditures happi-

[1] Put in more formal language: it is obviously quite possible to hold the view that social welfare is not exclusively a function of individual tastes as expressed in market-behaviour, while still holding that the choice proper for society as a whole should usually respond positively to any change in individual tastes, *ceteris paribus*.

[2] H. D. Dickinson, *Economics of Socialism*, p. 53.

[3] J. E. Meade, in *Economic Journal*, April, 1945, p. 53. Cf. also Samuelson, *Foundations*, p. 224.

ness may give place to discomfort and misery. Even apart from such Veblenesque cases there are numerous ways in which one may be benefited, or the reverse, by the expenditure or habits of one's fellows—by the sort of house he builds and the colour he paints it, by musical instruments in the flat next door and by whether social intercourse with one's neighbours is enriched or not by common tastes for books and music, or possibly for cricket and the pools.

It is common in discussions of consumers' choice to define rationality in terms of some criterion of consistency (e.g. that if one chooses A in preference to B and B in preference to C, one must also choose A rather than C)—a consistency which, although it need not apply for all time (since tastes are allowed to alter), must presumably operate over an appreciable stretch of time. If one is a behaviourist, this is presumably the most that one can make rationality mean. I am using 'rationality', however, in a fuller sense than this; and while consistency is no doubt a necessary condition of it, consistency is not, I think, a sufficient condition in the non-behaviourist sense of which I am speaking. The latter is related to the distinction which Marshall made between 'desires' and 'satisfactions', and bears analogy with (though not, I believe, identical with) the Kantian distinction between pragmatic and moral imperatives.[1] It is rationality in the familiar sense of people 'not knowing what is good for them', and in pursuit of certain ends adopting means which are ill-adapted to achieving those ends. Clearly children cannot be relied on to be rational in this sense; since experience is needed to convince that fire burns and that some things eaten, though sweet in the mouth, are bitter in the belly. Some people take a long time to learn, even when they are grown up; and it would be rash to assume that the process of learning is complete in the majority of adults of any age (in fact, there is plenty of evidence to the contrary, not only in the sphere of patent medicines and narcotics). The reasons why even adult desires for things may bear no very close relation to the welfare derived from them are numerous: in some cases because consumers lack the knowledge to discriminate; because their experience of alternatives is a limited one (e.g. in the cases of alternative diets or of forms of entertainment); because they are unreflective and easily moved by immediate or superficial stimuli (e.g. by the name or wrapping on the outside or the shine of gilt on a bauble;) or simply because they are gullible. Moreover, human wants may lie at different levels of consciousness, and people may be only dimly aware of some of them.[2] If one's hedonistic calculus admits of *qualitative* differences of satisfaction, in the sense of

[1] Cf. K. Arrow, *op. cit.*, pp. 82 and 84.   [2] *Ibid.*, p. 86.

higher satisfaction (good music) and lower satisfactions (American crooners), then one will regard the satisfaction of desires as welfare-yielding only in the degree that desires are educated, and one will detect a 'Gresham's law' of taste at work in the so-called consumers' sovereignty of a commercialised society. (Few, surely, could seriously maintain that the amount and sort of music to be played by the B.B.C. should be decided by a market mechanism?)[1] When it comes to choices extending over time, individual preferences are notoriously irrational[2] and exhibit a tendency to myopic underestimation of the future, due to what Professor Pigou has aptly termed 'deficiency of the telescopic faculty' in individuals —a consideration which is relevant not only to the choice between present consumption and saving, but also to the choice between durable and non-durable goods.

The answer commonly made to this sort of criticism is that it implies the existence of some transcendental scale of values as a criterion of the 'rightness' or 'wrongness' of consumers' desires, and that the only alternative to relying on the verdict of consumers as to what they *think* they want is to enthrone a dictator to impose his own scale of values upon society. There is no doubt, to my mind, that this is a false antithesis, as has already been said, and that to judge that housewives and shoppers are fallible—the sort of judgment everyone makes at some time and someone makes every day—is not necessarily to aspire to be a dictator over housewives (for one thing, one may include oneself in the judgment of fallibility). To revert once more to the political analogy: discussion of the machinery of democratic government is full of implicit judgments of this kind and of suggested devices for diminishing the chance of 'false' decisions. (One may cite as a parallel the Webbs' statement regarding the referendum in trade union government, that 'few trade unions have actually desired bankruptcy, but many trade unions have voted for policies which involved it'.) Unless Welfare is *defined* exclusively in terms of consumers' market-behaviour (which would be a quite arbitrary definition), one cannot avoid this type of question and this sort of judgment. And even if Welfare were to be so defined, this would still leave open the question of whether it represented a desirable or sufficient goal of social policy.

However, one need not dwell here on the philosophic basis of such verdicts on consumers' behaviour, or stay to argue whether there is any less fallible way of making economic choices; since in our present context this is not really the point. The point is how much value to attach to

---

[1] This was written before the campaign for commercial television.
[2] See above, pp. 38-9.

an 'ideal' defined in terms of a maximum satisfaction of consumers' *desires* and to mechanisms designed in service thereto. In the degree to which we doubt the rationality of consumers' market behaviour—even if we cannot define what rational behaviour is—we shall attach smaller importance to the attainment of this 'ideal', and we shall think that little is likely to be lost by adopting an economic mechanism which is only capable of adjusting production to consumers' demand at a lower level of approximation than would an automatic price-system.[1]

The mere mention of 'collective wants' serves to indicate that not all human wants are registered on a market; and that as social ends these compete with the ends which a market system serves. As for the fact that wants are not purely individual, but are socially moulded and contain strong conventional elements—this matter is better left to be dealt with in the following section, in the setting of economic movement and change.

4 The debate of which we have been speaking was concerned essentially with positions of equilibrium, and with the choice of one among many possible equilibrium positions as the optimum. As such it was conducted in terms of the theory of static equilibrium; and although attempts were made to treat certain dynamic problems in analogous terms (e.g. investment treated as distribution of resources over time, instead of between various uses at a single moment of time), the most important considerations affecting economic development were excluded. Yet when we turn to enquire as to the *relevance* of the sort of issues with which the Mises-debate has been occupied, it is its relevance to problems of planning and policy-making in a context of economic development with which we must be concerned. One way, I think, of putting sharply this question of relevance is to ask how far anyone can argue seriously that any exact realistic content could be given to the notion of the social marginal productivity (in terms of the addition to consumers' welfare which it will some day make possible) of a given investment today in expanding British steel capacity by a small amount; and, if it can, how far the manager of an individual steel plant, either in a capitalist or a socialist economy, could be regarded as capable of thinking and calculating in terms of it.

In what essential respects, then, does the economic problem differ as soon as we put it in a context of economic change?

---

[1] It is fallacious to assume as is so commonly done that the absence of any certain criterion of welfare is an argument for leaving decisions to the market: the element of doubt attaches as much to the market's verdict as to any alternative mode of decision.

The relevant differences, I would suggest, can be grouped under three main heads. Firstly, there are those interdependencies between events in different industries and different economic sectors which figure in the ordinary theory of equilibrium in the shape of 'external economies', and which acquire crucial importance in the theory of development since they represent the dependence of change at one point upon simultaneous changes at other points—for example, the growth of a certain industry on appropriate transport facilities or upon the growth of certain subsidiary or complementary industries. Secondly, there is the question of how the course of change is affected by imperfect knowledge or by foresight. Thirdly, there is the fact that things which figure as 'data' in the static problem are converted into variables, and dependent variables. On the one hand, the system's endowment of productive resources (qualitatively as well as quantitatively), and hence the cost-structure of production, are moulded by historical change; on the other hand, the pattern of human wants—the consumers' 'indifference map' to which productive resources are adapted in the static allocation-problem—itself undergoes change and development.

The first of these differences might at first glance be dismissed as something which introduced no novel element into the problem. Do such interdependencies between events differ essentially from the 'external economies' which figure in the familiar theory; and if not why should they not be taken account of in a similar way?[1] The essential difference, however, becomes clear when one sees this factor acting in conjunction with the second. It then becomes evident that the occurrence of some change at any one point will depend (to the extent of any such relation of interdependence) upon the expectation of changes occurring elsewhere. If there be little ground for such an expectation—in some cases if the probability that the other changes will happen falls much short of certainty—no one of an interrelated set of changes may ever take place. This situation is familiar enough in the case of underdeveloped countries: an industry fails to develop in a certain region because transport and other facilities are not available there, and transport facilities or subsidiary industries or power-plants do not develop in that region because of the absence of the main industry. Or again, an engineering industry may fail to grow because of uncertainty about the development of other industries

[1] External economies (and diseconomies) are a cause of divergence between individual and social interest; but so far as they have a monetary expression and take a price-form, it has been held that their existence would not be a cause of such divergence if the marginal-cost-pricing rule were adopted universally.

whose growth would provide a demand for engineering products, while at the same time these other industries may be retarded by the scarcity or non-availability of engineering products. Such examples are a commonplace today except to the most doctrinaire exponents of *laissez-faire*. They have indeed had their place in economic literature in the guise of the 'infant industries' argument—rather grudgingly relegated in most textbooks to the category of 'exceptional cases' and pushed into an obscure corner.

The importance of such cases in our present context is that certain kinds of development may only come upon the agenda if development is centrally planned as an organic whole; whereas, if the mechanism of economic decision is that of a decentralised pricing system (with industrial managers taking their output and investment-decisions on the basis of the present pattern of market-prices or accounting-prices, modified by guesses as to future price-movements), these types of development may not happen at all. Even if they should start, under the impulse of a unanimous mood of optimism among the takers of economic decisions, the several parts of the pattern of development will lack co-ordination and will accordingly tend to be such as to involve subsequent maladjustments, frustrations and distortions, probably of a serious and costly character.

In other words, the type of mechanism whereby economic decisions are taken may be the crucial factor in determining the form and direction of development. Not merely is it the case that an automatic price-system cannot be relied on to produce the socially desirable result, but there is reason to suppose that it may be itself an obstacle to the desirable development occurring—i.e. occurring at all, or if it does so of occurring in the most desirable (e.g. least costly) way. One may express the crux of the matter by saying that the quintessential function of planning as an economic mechanism is that it is a means of substituting *ex ante* co-ordination of the constituent elements in a scheme of development—i.e. *before* decisions have been embodied in action and in actual commitments—for the co-ordination *ex post* which a decentralised pricing-system provides (*via* the 'revising' effect of price-movements which are the subsequent, and generally delayed, effect of previous decisions, when the latter have borne fruit in actual input- or output-changes).[1] Only if economic processes were timeless, so that the process of revision-via-price-changes could be treated as instantaneous, would the two types of co-ordination amount to the same thing. As we know, most economic processes, especi-

[1] On this question of co-ordinating investment-decisions over time, see also above, pp. 40-1 and pp. 53-4.

ally those concerned with investment in fixed capital, involve substantial time-lags in adjustment—time-lags which have figured prominently in recent theoretical studies of economic fluctuations. Of course, the co-ordination which centralised planning attempts to provide *ex ante* may for various reasons fall far short of ideal co-ordination. To the extent that an element of uncertainty must remain from the objective nature of things, it is inevitable that such co-ordination will in some degree fall short of perfect co-ordination. But in so far as it eliminates what may be called 'subjective uncertainty'—the uncertainty of each separate decision-taker as to the actions, present and future, of other decision-takers—it has evidently a much greater potentiality as a co-ordinating mechanism than any decentralised system, and can reasonably be expected to yield a quite different result.

If we try to form a realistic picture of the kind of decisions which confront planners and policy-makers under conditions of economic change, it immediately becomes plain that the key decisions affecting development could not be left under socialism to the automatic adjudication of any market or pricing-system. Firstly, there is the decision as to the amount of labour and other resources to be devoted to investment—to constructional work designed to increase the productivity of labour in the future. For the reason mentioned above (p. 73) there is no valid ground for expecting the result to be an optimum one if this decision were left to be determined by any kind of market-process (e.g. by attracting savings through a market in government loans); and most writers on the subject (at any rate Professor Lange,[1] Mr. R. L. Hall[2] and Professor Pigou[3]) concede that it would have to be taken as a policy-decision by the State on behalf of the community as a whole. Secondly, there is the decision as to how this total of investible resources is to be distributed between Marx's two main departments of industry—industries producing capital goods and industries producing consumer goods. As we have noted elsewhere,[4] this is a crucial decision, governing as it does simultaneously the relative rates of growth of consumption and investment in the near future and also the rate of growth of output as a whole. Even less can one conceive of this being left to the automatic verdict of any imaginable market (or quasi-market) mechanism; if only because in any unplanned system investment in the expansion of capital goods industries always represents an act of faith *par excellence*—faith that investment will be maintained in the

---

[1] *Economic Theory of Socialism*, p. 85.
[2] *The Economic System in a Socialist State* (London, 1937), p. 125.
[3] *Op. cit.*, pp. 131-3.   [4] Pages 130-1.

economic system at large of a size and a form to keep the new productive capacity of the capital goods industries in activity. The faith of those who initiate the expansion may be dim or it may be over-zealous, according to circumstances; but there is no reason at all to expect that the chance decisions of an unco-ordinated series of managers (or boards) will be 'ideal', however hard they study market-indices—the presumption, indeed, is the contrary. Thirdly, there are decisions concerning the location of industry, which as we have seen will need to be closely geared with decisions about transport- and power-developments—also with decisions affecting the labour supply, such as urban development and housing policy and training facilities. No unique meaning can be given to 'least-cost location' for an industry unless it is specified which of these interdependent factors are to be treated as variables in the problem and which are to be taken as constant—whether the optimum siting of a new plant or industry has to be chosen on the basis of the transport-map or the power-map as these exist at the moment, or whether consequential adaptations in these factors are to be assumed, and a choice made by a simultaneous adjustment of all of them. Clearly all that an automatic pricing-mechanism can do is to interpret 'least cost' in the former of these senses: on the basis of other surrounding factors being what they are at the moment. It is incapable of registering the shadows cast by coming events that have still to be realised. Yet it is evidently the second of these senses of 'least cost' that is relevant to any social decision about location of industry. In so far as industrial managers in a decentralised system departed from a strict interpretation of the Lange-Lerner pricing-rules and took the future into account, this would be by means of precisely the same guesses and expectations as those which actuate capitalist entrepreneurs, and subject to similar limitations and defects.

Key decisions of this type will constitute the framework of economic development, defining its general shape and direction; and only within this general framework can decisions affecting the adaptation of production to consumers' wants have play. But in a context of change and development it can no longer be assumed that consumers' wants form the given data of the allocation-problem (and here we come to the third of the crucial differences, mentioned at the outset of this section, between conditions of change and conditions of static equilibrium). One cannot imagine a process of economic change without a changing pattern of human wants, if only as a direct by-product of changing income and the appearance of new products. It would be fantastic to suppose that the wants for these new commodities had somehow been latent in the consumer before they had ever entered his experience—that they had been written somewhere on his so-called 'indifference-map' under the label of 'wants unsupplied'—or even to suppose that the want for the new can be treated by simple analogy with a want for something already familiar (the 'newness' being thereby reduced, as it were, to the second order of small quantities, and neglected). When we abandon the myth of the consumer as an isolated individual, an economists' child of nature, and take account of the strong element of social convention in all human wants (at least in all those above the level of the bare necessities of living), we realise that the consumer and his wants are a social product, moulded both by the commodities which enter into his experience and by the social standards and customs among which he has been reared. Thus economic policy, in shaping the course of development, inevitably shapes with it the changing pattern of consumers' wants; and as little with television sets or refrigerators as with narcotics or children's 'comics' can the policy-maker resign the responsibility for deciding whether society would be the worse or the better for putting them into production. A verdict of the market before they have become part of the accepted 'way of life' would yield one result, and afterwards another; on which verdict is the planner to rely? Indeed, the former verdict may really be no indicator at all—like a Gallup Poll which asked whether people would vote for a party which they had never seen or heard; while the latter will largely reflect the change in social habits for which past decisions about production have been responsible. The setting of new and higher social standards will undoubtedly be one of the central preoccupations of a socialist society, and one that is inseparable from the promotion of a higher standard of life. And as Professor Cairncross has said: 'To substitute one assortment of goods and services for another may do far less for the people's welfare than the setting of new social standards or the direction of their energies into new and more acceptable channels. . . . Many of our wants are shaped by the very system of production which exists to supply them.'[1]

Few of those who have discussed the allocation problem would deny that there are other types of efficiency problem which are not looked after by the marginal adjustments of which their theory speaks. What most of them, however, seem to have ignored is that the importance of their own efficiency problem may in practice be overshadowed by that of others. This, indeed, seems likely to be the case at times when economic development is at all rapid. The sort of efficiency with which

[1] A. Cairncross, *Introduction to Economics* (1st edn., London, 1944), p. 213.

the allocation-problem is concerned is the increased effectiveness of resources to be derived from marginal adjustments; this increased effectiveness being confined to those units of resources at the margin which are subject to transfer in the process of moving from an 'imperfect' towards a 'perfect' allocation. The sort of efficiency, by contrast, which comes in the wake of economic development is connected with a rise in the overall effectiveness with which resources in general are used, particularly with a rise in the productivity of labour in consequence of improved organisation, improved technique or more abundant capital equipment (or a conjunction of all three). This is not to say that a rise in the effectiveness of resources at the margin (by a more appropriate distribution of them) does not express itself as a rise in the average effectiveness with which *all* resources are used. It is to say what is obvious enough once it is stated, that the rise in average productivity will be of a considerably smaller magnitude than the increase in productivity of those marginal units which are subjected to adjustment and transfer—smaller in the degree that the latter form a small proportion of the whole. Too much preoccupation with what is happening at the margin may accordingly lead one to exaggerate the proportional effect on efficiency of marginal adjustments. Thus, let us suppose that the application of some 'marginal rule' would involve a transfer of resources at the margin amounting to one-tenth of all resources in use, and that this transfer from less to more productive uses would increase the productivity of the units transferred by x per cent. Averaged out over *all* resources this marginal gain in productivity would, of course, amount to no more than $\frac{x}{10}$ per cent. Thus a gain from the application of this kind of efficiency-criterion may have less importance in the total picture than at first sight appears, and less importance than an apparently less impressive increase in the overall effectiveness with which resources are used. In practice the latter seems likely to be of a considerably higher order of importance in a period of rapid development such as the period of the Soviet Five-Year Plans; and in such circumstances economic policy-makers and planners may be quite justified in treating it, rather than the economists' type of efficiency-problem, as their main preoccupation.[1]

[1] Thus even Mr. P. J. D. Wiles, after a scornful tirade against the 'choicelessness' of Soviet economy, concludes by saying: 'There is substance in the charge that "scarcity" economics is finicky and academic. . . . The loss of "welfare" or "efficiency" through an incorrect micro-economic allocation of resources is surely less than that brought about by unemployment, restrictive labour practices, the refusal to share

5 We have seen that an influential argument used in favour of a decentralised mechanism of decision, based on some kind of automatic price-system, is its alleged simplicity, by contrast with an arrangement whereby a complex of choices have to be made by a central authority in face of a highly complex series of alternatives. The force of the argument turns on the actual complexity of the situation with which any group of economic planners is likely to be confronted. Here again it would look as though the abstract model which economists have built has biased their view of reality—in this case the refinement of the model making the problems of economic decision appear actually more cumbrous than they are in cruder reality.

The assumptions most suitable—even essential—for handling by accepted marginal techniques are such as make the number of possible positions between which choice has to be made indefinitely large. These assumptions can be summed up as continuous variation of the relevant coefficients and variables, leading to the smooth curves familiar in the geometry of economic textbooks. To the extent that discontinuity, instead of continuity, prevails, the number of alternative positions, or allocation-patterns, which the planner can choose between is reduced. In the extreme case of what is known as 'fixed technical coefficients' combined with a high degree of 'complementarity' in consumers' wants little or no choice would be possible at all.[1] (This implies that the proportions in which different productive factors—labour, mechanical equipment, raw materials—in each industry can be combined are fixed, and that consumers are such creatures of habit that they desire things in rigidly fixed proportions.) Clearly both extremes—continuous variation and fixed proportions—are highly unrealistic; the actual situation is likely to lie somewhere in between. The nearer it approximates to the former, the more will it correspond to the picture familiar to the modern economist's

trade secrets or the suppression of workable patents, could any of these losses ever be measured. Thus in the Soviet economy there are, as it were, always too few hairbrushes and too many nailbrushes in view of the resources available, while in a "capitalist" economy this proportion is always more nearly right. But the production of both these articles is growing at about 10 per cent per annum in U.S.S.R. and at about 2 per cent per annum in "capitalist" countries. In the end the Soviet citizen will be supplied better even with hairbrushes.' ('Scarcity, Marxism and Gosplan', in *Oxford Economic Papers*, October 1953, pp. 315-16.)

[1] Theoretically there might be no solution consistent with the employment of all available resources (total output of the given assortment of commodities required by consumers being governed by the productive factor most limited in supply).

special world. In the degree that it approximates to the latter, it will have a very different, and in one respect simpler, configuration.

On such a question it would be absurd to dogmatise. To pronounce with any assurance which of various hypotheses is the more realistic would require both a much closer and a more extensive acquaintance with the actual shape of problems confronting planning bodies than the present writer can claim to have. It may not be absurd, however, to put forward the suggestion that actual situations may be a good deal nearer to the extreme of rigid proportions than economists have generally assumed. That economists should have acquired a bias from their own formalism is not altogether surprising, if only because this formal world lends itself to elegant solutions and to streamlined answers to a number of questions. Professor Paul Baran expresses a still-heterodox view when he writes of conditions of development: 'The problem facing the [Planning] Board would be not slow adjustments to small changes—the main prerequisite for the applicability of the rules derives from static analysis—but choice among few technological alternatives involving large indivisibilities and "fixed coefficients".'[1]

The most familiar element of discontinuity, widely discussed in recent economic literature, is the so-called indivisibility of capital equipment: a characteristic of much capital equipment is that it can only be supplied in units of a certain minimum size (e.g. a railway track between London and Edinburgh, a blast furnace or a rolling mill). The significance of this is that where the indivisible unit is large relatively to the scale on which production is carried on, there is no conceivable pricing-rule (at least, of a simple character)[2] which could afford a 'correct' investment-criterion. Whether or not the equipment may be made to 'pay' (by selling output at a price which covers both prime costs and also a charge for the cost of the capital equipment) is no criterion: there may be cases where the equipment does not pay although its existence is socially desirable; again, there may be cases where it can pay its way and yet investment in it is not socially advantageous. The criterion, as in the classic example of Dupuit's bridge,[3] is the total social benefit to be derived from its existence, com-

[1] In *Survey of Contemporary Economics*, Vol. II (ed. for American Economic Association by B. F. Haley), p. 385.

[2] In theory 'perfect discrimination' (i.e. a different price to each buyer, proportional to the strength of his demand) could afford a criterion; but it would have significant distribution-effects.

[3] Dupuit took as an example a bridge across a river: if a toll were charged sufficient to cover the capital cost of the bridge, this would involve an undesirable restriction of its use (in terms of Dupuit's example a halving of its use and a reduction of the

pared with the potential total benefit if the investment (of the same total value) had been made elsewhere. True, it can be argued that to require an investment to cover its 'average cost' is not entirely irrelevant as a criterion, even if an insufficient one, and that it may at least prevent a number of constructional 'white elephants' from being brought into existence or preserved. Such a requirement of covering total cost might possibly be useful as a first approximation; but there seems to be no ground for thinking that the cases of insufficient social benefit which it could warn against would be as numerous or important as the cases where it would yield the wrong answer or would result in unnecessary restriction of use.

It is to be noted that the problem here indicated is not confined to cases of one-plant lines of production, but applies also to cases where the number of indivisible units in use, though more than one, is very small; since in such cases it will only be by accident that the demand at a price equal to the average total cost suffices to employ these units to full capacity, no more and no less.[1] As the number of units concerned increases, however, the divergence between the 'covering total cost' criterion and the 'social benefit' criterion gets smaller. In a socialist economy it seems likely that industrial plants will be fairly highly specialised; and that as the plants in an industry grow more numerous, the new plants will be devoted (perhaps more often than not) to the production of some new product-variety rather than to duplicating the work of some existing plant. It will be in this way in a developing economy, as the stock of capital grows, that variety in production and consumption will be progressively extended. Hence, if one treats each product-variety as a separate commodity, the number of cases where technical indivisibility is significantly large rela-

utility derived from it of one-fifth). Since its use involved a zero marginal cost, he concluded that the bridge should be free, and thus the benefit derived from it maximised. (This article of J. Dupuit, 'De la Mesure de l'Utilité des Travaux Publics', first appeared in *Annales des Ponts et Chaussées*, 2e serie, Vol: VIII, in 1844; it has been translated into English in *International Economic Papers*, International Economic Association, London and New York, 1952, No. 2, pp. 83–110.)

[1] Only when this condition is fulfilled will the two criteria yield the same answer. When it is not fulfilled two cases may arise: investment in the last unit may be justified by the social benefit criterion, but there exists no practicable combination of price and output at which total cost can be covered (short of adopting the price-policy of discriminating monopoly); or there is a possible price at which total cost can be covered, but only at the expense of creating excess capacity, and leaving one or all of the units less fully used than they might otherwise have been. If at full-capacity output a price could be charged which *more* than covers total cost, then the question arises as to whether investment in a further unit is justified or not.

tively to the demand for the commodity seems likely to be greater than is commonly supposed. To the extent that this is so, investment decisions will be concerned with the question of new wants—each new investment will involve *extending* the number of alternatives available to the consumer, rather than with choosing between an addition to the output of this or that existing commodity within a given and existing range of commodities.

Secondly, as regards technical coefficients of production, the opportunity for at least some variation exists in nearly all cases. But such variation often seems to be of a strictly limited character, and sometimes only to be possible in discontinuous 'jumps'. With given technical equipment there is generally *some* possibility of varying the labour force, given minor technical adjustments, as war experience seems to show. But this possibility is not necessarily very extensive without serious disturbance of the production process (e.g. the number employed on an assembly-line process); and in numerous cases is non-existent (e.g. in staffing railway locomotives or a fleet of buses, in the manning of most machine-tools, in the number of charge-hands per blast-furnace). When it comes to changing the technical process itself, the available alternatives are unlikely to constitute a continuous series, but will more probably be few in number; the transition from one to another (e.g. from hand-operated to automatic looms, or from traditional building methods to the method of site-assembly of prefabricated parts) involving a considerable change both in productivity and in capital cost.

The third element of rigidity in the situation consists of the various joint-supply and joint-demand relationships in production, which are the extreme form of those interrelationships mentioned in the previous section, and which are specially characteristic of certain leading branches of modern heavy industry.

Fourthly, there is the influence of analogous relations of complementarity in consumers' demand. While these are probably of insufficient importance to have much significance by themselves, they may none the less acquire importance in our present context when they act in conjunction with factors of rigidity on the side of production. What may cause them to bulk larger than we think is the strong influence of custom and convention on wants, of which we have already spoken—an influence which, although no doubt exceptionally prominent in a society characterised by 'conspicuous consumption' and 'honorific waste' and other such Veblenesque traits, is not entirely confined thereto. Social or class convention, in moulding consumption to set patterns and 'ways of life', can act as a potent cement to complementary relations in consumers' expenditure.

There is a peculiar demand situation which under socialism may be characteristic of the majority of durable consumer goods and which seems worth mentioning in this connection. Where there are no large inequalities of income, the market-demand for a thing is likely to be negligible above a certain price-level and then highly elastic within the neighbourhood of that price. As long as the cost of production of, say, a refrigerator, television set or a people's motor-car is above a certain critical level, there will be very few buyers for it; as soon as its cost can be brought down to this level, it will probably be at once in demand by the great majority of consumers. One may describe this situation, if one likes, by saying that at this critical level the market-demand-curve will have a kink or a sharp change of direction. The practical consequence will be that no intermediate position may be practicable for planning between not putting the commodity into mass production at all and producing it on a very large scale indeed.

Finally there is a consideration of a rather different kind which indicates that the choices open to any planning body may be subject to narrower limits than is generally assumed. The fact that economic planning, as we have suggested, is able to achieve a smooth process of development does not imply that it can act without constraint and adopt any path it pleases.[1] Within a single quinquennium the proportions in which different things can be produced will be determined within fairly strict limits by decisions taken in the past—decisions which have fixed the amount of productive capacity available in different industries. Investment-decisions will be subject to the constraint of existing steel-producing capacity; decisions about the level of consumption to the existing size of consumer goods industries. As the horizon of planning extends, the range of practicable decision—the degree of freedom—increases, until in a sufficiently long period all eggs can be unscrambled; the existing stock of accumulated capital equipment can be remade to any shape and use, as well as enlarged by new investment. In practice, however, no planning, however ambitious, can have more than a fairly limited time-horizon, since the number of incalculables in the situation will increase progressively as the perspective of any plan

---

[1] It is to be noted that this was the burden of an important part of the argument of Stalin in his recent *Economic Problems of Socialism in the U.S.S.R.*, as against those who 'imagine that Soviet government can "do anything", that "nothing is beyond it"' (p. 13). He was mainly concerned, however, to emphasise the limitation of production-possibilities by existing 'social relations of production'.

is extended into the future. It may well be that this practicable time-horizon is considerably shorter than the economists' abstract long-period in which productive resources become indefinitely mobile and adaptable. To the extent that it is shorter, the constraints upon planning agenda will be more numerous: the element of determinism in policy-decisions will be more prominent and the patterns to be woven of the future will be fewer.

6 With what conclusion are we then left? Is it the purely negative one: that there is no easy or precise way of defining a welfare optimum as a goal of social policy, and that to pursue such a goal must be anyhow a rough-and-ready affair of guesswork and approximation? If so, the claims to precision of any pricing-system as an automatic optimum-finder falls to the ground. I think we are inevitably led to some such conclusion as this; and that the upshot of the long-drawn-out, often subtly contrived, economists' discussion is to lay a number of ideological ghosts rather than to provide positive advice for policy-makers in a socialist economy. It seems to me quite clear that the major decisions controlling economic development, and hence human welfare, must be taken as policy-decisions by some organ of central government, and that the principles which govern them cannot be reduced to any simple formula. Among these decisions are the rate of investment and the distribution of investment between the capital goods and consumer goods industries; the relative rates of growth of transport, fuel and power, agriculture in relation to industry, and the regional distribution of production; the rate of introduction of new products and their character, and the degree of standardisation or variety in production that the economy at any stage of its development feels able to afford. Such decisions will have to be taken by some similar process, and on the basis of similar data, as are a number of crucial decisions today which affect human welfare in no small degree: for example, the proportion of national income devoted to armament and other military expenditures, the size of the building programme, the character of urban development and national monetary policy.

Yet there are many of an impatient temper who may think that it should be possible for economists to say more than this. If they suppose that there can be easy short-cuts to an answer to such questions as those we have just mentioned, then I suggest that they are dwelling in a land of illusions—a land only a little less thickly clouded with illusions than that inhabited by the Mises-school, who suppose that these matters are all optimally settled in the market, 'as by an unseen hand', in that economists' Land of Cathay, 'a freely competitive capitalism'. But once purged of such illusions, the impatient may well be right in their dislike of a nihilistic conclusion—in their belief that some general criteria *are* possible, for some types of economic decision at any rate, and that all need not be empirical guesswork and groping in the dark.

In the first place, if we take decisions concerning the relative outputs of different consumer goods, there are certain things about which there can be little doubt as to the correct proportions and orders of priority—where it should be possible to find fairly widespread agreement in a given community as to what is most conducive to welfare. This, I think, applies to most of the basic necessities of life, such as housing, primary foodstuffs and a modicum of clothing, the care of children and the requirements of public health (let us say, up to a Rowntree 'Human Needs Standard' for all). These are either things where there is a fair amount of uniformity in the needs of different households (apart from the varying size of the family), or where the prescriptions of dieticians or public health experts would be accepted by most people as the soundest available criteria of what is conducive to welfare. These constitute, indeed, a leading category of Professor Dickinson's 'Sector of Communal Consumption', which he thinks might not unsuitably be supplied free[1] (or at a low charge, enough to discourage waste). If the demand for any of them should prove to be more elastic than was expected, they might be supplied either at some low charge or else free only up to a maximum amount, until such time as they could be produced in sufficient quantities to meet all demands.

Secondly, as regards other types of consumer goods, fairly simple criteria will be available to a planning authority—criteria both simple and adequate enough if we have in mind the correction of serious departures from an 'ideal' allocation and not the attainment of a unique optimum. (As we have seen above, the former is all that one could reasonably aim at; and to seek the latter is to follow a will o' the wisp.) If retail prices for consumer goods are the (approximate) expression of existing supply-demand relationships of various goods (as they are bound to be unless there is rationing or unless there are to be either shop-shortages or queues), then the ratios of these to the prime cost of their production would provide an index of the degree of short-supply of various commodities. Data would presumably be available as to the capital cost of increasing output by a given amount in each case, expressible in some

---

[1] 'There seems to be no reason why bread, milk, simply cooked meals, clothing of a plain standardised type, and many other things, should not be provided as free unrationed issues, leaving the more luxurious and varied qualities to be provided in response to market demand.' (H. D. Dickinson, *op. cit.*, p. 53.)

form as a capital-output ratio; and the combination of this kind of ratio with the former one could be made the basis for a priority-list of projects for expanding the supplies of various consumer goods. The fact that the takers of economic decisions refused to be slaves to such indices—declined to promote them to an automatic mechanism and often allowed other more imponderable considerations to have weight in the final choice—would not mean that planners would fail to use them at all, or to take serious account of them in all cases where the discrepancies in the relevant ratios were of a sufficient order of magnitude to make a significant difference to consumers' welfare.

The first of the two ratios we have just mentioned is in the Soviet example approximately equivalent to the rate of turnover tax, which is used to divert directly into the budget the margin between prime cost of production (and of wholesale and retail distribution) and the retail price, instead of allowing this to accrue as profits to industrial or distributive enterprises. There is some conflict of evidence as to whether this turnover tax (and hence the retail prices of various commodities) is in fact adjusted at frequent intervals to the changing situation of the retail market, or whether it is kept constant over fairly long periods; short period changes in the state of excess demand being left to show itself in a running-down of stocks or in shop-shortages and queues. In a period of general expansion of supplies the latter may be regarded as inconveniences which, since they are no more than transitory, can be treated as of minor concern; while the rate of stock depletion or the length of the order-book may be regarded as affording in most cases as reliable an index of short-supply or excess-demand as does the ratio of short-period price to costs. In the course of the successive price-reductions of recent years, the reductions have varied quite widely for different commodities; these reductions being governed presumably either by cuts in the turnover tax rate—cuts being largest in those commodities that were in relatively plentiful supply—or else by reductions in cost of production as a result of rising productivity. Practice may well be a compromise between the two alternatives; prices generally being maintained in some constant relation to costs unless the change in the supply-demand situation of a commodity exceeds a certain order of magnitude. After all, it comes to much the same thing in the long run[1] whether price is kept in some normal relation to cost and excess demand in the short period is taken as a reason for increasing output until the excess demand disappears, or price itself is adjusted to demand-changes in the short-period, and output is then adapted until price falls again to a

[1] Subject, however, to a qualification to be mentioned below, p. 90.

'normal' level. Whatever the practice may be, it is clear that the situation furnishes indices which are sufficiently sensitive to register any serious failure to adapt supply to consumer preferences, and there seems to be not much doubt that the production-plans for various types of consumer goods are in practice influenced by indices of the relative strength of consumers' demand for these various things.

In Soviet practice there is apparently not a great deal of latitude for short-period variations in output of a given plant. Once a plant has been constructed and is in production, the Plan seems generally to provide at least for output at full capacity with one shift working; such variation as there is taking the form of varying the number of shifts. As regards the technical type of plant to be constructed, various indices have been used (most commonly in the past some kind of 'period of recoupment' or 'ratio of effectiveness' of the investment) and have been the subject of discussion in Soviet literature—a matter which is touched on elsewhere in the present collection (below, pp. 258-65). This seems to have been the leading instance (especially in railway transport and electricity generation) where a problem akin to that discussed by Western economists has cropped up as a live issue in Soviet economic administration.[1]

So far as the substance behind the technicalities of the Dupuit-Hotelling-Lerner case for the marginal cost rule is concerned, this is something which should not be too difficult to apply by plain common-sense rule-of-thumb. Indeed, its chief virtue seems to be the negative one of warning us not to be hamstrung by adherence to faulty principles: in particular, not to permit excess capacity to go unused simply in order to make capital equipment 'pay'[2]. This no socialist administrator or planner seems likely to do unless he has been too well educated in the precepts and practice of a capitalist economy. The opposite case is perhaps more difficult, where equipment is operated so intensively (in view of existing demand) as to involve steeply rising expenses, out of relation to the social value of the additional output. But again is it not common-sense judgment that is

---

[1] Since this was written a decision has been reached as a result of further discussions between academic and practical economists that 'a uniform ratio of effectiveness of investment' (e.g. relating investment in capital equipment to consequential economy in current operating expenses) should be used as a criterion in the choice between alternative technical variants of a given investment-project (i.e. to decide questions of so-called 'capital intensity' of investment): *Voprosi Ekonomiki*. 1954, No. 3, pp. 99-103.

[2] As we have seen, the 'external economies' case, except where these do not take a price-form (e.g. smoke nuisance, river-pollution, etc.), has generally been held to be reducible to the existence of excess capacity elsewhere in the system.

needed rather than subtle calculating mechanisms? This is certainly a case where restricting excess-demand by price-raising is called for, and for raising it by as much as the additional (short-period) cost of supplying marginal consumers. The price-rise may or may not have a substantial effect in pruning the demand: in either case the question will then arise as to whether to instal additional equipment, so that the overloading of existing equipment can be avoided and the surplus demand be satisfied more economically. It seems likely that the bias of industrial managers towards expansion of their own enterprises will make investment in new equipment the most probable answer. But while this may well be the right answer in the sufficiently long run (unless the increase of demand is temporary), it may not be the right answer in the immediate future when investment of resources (e.g. of steel or other scarce constructional materials) in this use competes with investments in many other uses. Accordingly, what seems to be needed in this case is some index to which the planning authorities (or industrial ministries) can appeal to reject proposals for expansion where expansion is *not* immediately called for. If there are significantly-large 'indivisibilities' in the problem, then as we have seen no precise criterion is possible, and to make a rough-and-ready judgment of the comparative social benefits is the best that anyone can do. However, for all cases where this is relevant, data will be readily available to permit a comparison to be made of the 'surplus proceeds' with existing equipment (or alternatively the additional prime costs incurred by overloading) and the cost of new equipment; and thus enable the planning authority to veto proposals for expansion if the ratio of the former to the latter is below a certain critical figure (e.g. below that prevailing in the case of other and rival expansion-projects).[1]

What Soviet planning has in fact done with regard to investment policy

---

[1] On this question there is some confusion of thought. It is sometimes suggested that such a criterion for deciding about new investment will be absent if capital-costs are not included in the price charged to consumers. But what is necessary is merely that short-period price should reflect the existing level of demand (i.e., in the case we are considering, be raised as a method of restricting excess demand), and the result of this price-situation *compared* with the capital cost of expansion. Recent criticism of electricity price-policy in this country has been put in the form that so-called 'capacity costs' of generating plant ought to be included in the price charged to 'peak' demand, since it is to meet the pressure of demand at peak periods that the cost of constructing new generating plant is being incurred. But the essential point is that the price for supply at peak-periods should be sufficiently high to restrict demand to existing capacity (i.e. eliminate the need for power-cuts) and a *comparison* be made between receipts at these prices and the cost of installing new plant.

is to decide all questions centrally,[1] but to require each industrial enterprise to cover its prime costs (including amortisation allowances); these enterprises being persuaded to keep prime costs to the minimum and to expand output up to the limit of steeply-rising prime costs (or to the full capacity level) by the fact that the selling-price of their output is fixed in advance by the planning authorities.[2] This emphasis in Soviet planning practice on perfecting a system of interlaced control and financial inducements for harnessing the individual enterprise to the Plan illustrates its preoccupation with that other type of efficiency problem of which we have spoken above—that of increasing the average effectiveness with which productive resources are used. So also does the collateral emphasis on elaborating an interconnected system of input-output coefficients through the so-called 'method of balances', which has been regarded as the central core of Soviet planning methodology. The 'balanced' or 'proportioned development' of which Soviet planners speak is, of course, a different matter from the optimum proportions to which Western economists refer. The latter are concerned with final positions of equilibrium, to which an optimum value is attached; the former with the preservation of certain relations within a process of movement so that maladjustments, crises or fluctuations may be avoided. When it is appreciated that the Western discussion of optimum conditions ignores the process of adjustment by which equilibria are reached[3] (or else tacitly assumes that ideal equilibria can be reached instantaneously, or once reached constantly maintained), even an uncritical believer in the value of such optima may be ready to concede that 'balanced development' in the

---

[1] At the same time much pre-digestion of data (and in particular provisional decisions between alternative technical projects and methods) is done at the level of the several industries (being distinguished in current terminology as the province of industrial 'project-makers' rather than of 'planners'); and it is with reference to this work, in selecting and 'putting-up a case' for particular projects, that the indices just mentioned, relating capital cost to expected economies, have apparently been used.

[2] This selling-price is based upon the 'planned costs' (*plus* a small planned profit mark-up) of the output programme as laid down for the enterprise in the annual plan. It is to be noted that the enterprise would not be able to increase its profits (which are partially at its own disposal) by expanding output beyond the point where prime costs at the margin were equal to the pre-fixed selling-price (wholesale price *sans* turnover tax); but until that point was reached it would lose, not gain, by curtailing output.

[3] Cf. on this point M. W. Reder, *Studies in the Theory of Welfare Economics* (New York, 1947), pp. 103, 176-7: 'we must deal with the welfare properties of the paths to, and between, equilibrium positions before we can do more than take enlightened guesses as to what is the "best" policy from the welfare point of view.'

Soviet sense is at least of equal consequence for social welfare as is the attainment of a 'correct' equilibrium in his own sense of the term.

In a developing economy, at any rate, there would seem to be little room for doubt that the practical difference between a rapid and a slow rate of increase of productivity, or between a smooth compared with a fluctuating process of growth, can make a difference to welfare that quite dwarfs any claims which an ideal price-mechanism can reasonably make to put the consumer 'further up the hill' of his indifference-map. If the result of our discussion is a shift of focus from the latter type of problem to the former, this does not mean that we have reached a barren and negative result.

IV

THE ECONOMIC BASIS OF CLASS CONFLICT [1937]

This was a paper contributed to a Conference held under the auspices of the Institute of Sociology at King's College of Household and Social Science, London, September 24th-26th, 1937. It was published in 1938 by the Le Play House Press in the Report of the Conference, entitled *Class Conflict and Social Stratification*, ed. T. H. Marshall; and is reprinted here by kind permission of the Institute of Sociology.

IT IS A STRANGE COINCIDENCE that the unfinished manuscript of Marx's *magnum opus*—of the man who has been most responsible for developing the notion of class conflict—should have ended where he was entering on a definition of a class and of its distinction from other social groups. The concept of class has, however, been by no means the peculiar child of one thinker or of one school of thought. While some have denied that there is such an entity, and some have even denounced it as a misbegotten conception,[1] it was a notion which increasingly forced itself upon the thought of social thinkers and of social historians during the nineteenth century under the influence of the facts which they sought to handle; just as today it is forcing its attention upon the political theorist and the moralist as the key to understanding of the major political, and even the ideal, conflicts in the world today. That the notion corresponds both to something actual and to something fundamental in contemporary society

---

[1] Professor Carr-Saunders and D. C. Jones, in their *Social Structure of England and Wales* (pp. 71-2) appear to deny that it is statistically discoverable as a social grouping. Mr. Keynes tells of the late Professor Foxwell that he once declined to deliver a Presidential Address to the Royal Economic Society about Ricardo on the ground that 'his onslaught on the author of the dreadful heresy of a conflict of interest between capital and labour would have been too provocative.'

becomes, I think, increasingly evident as research into social history deepens and as contemporary history unfolds.

It seems to have been during the period of the French Revolution that the notion of class conflict took a place in the realm of ideas; its appearance following the emergence of the Third Estate as a social force and the first open and sharply defined contest of this Estate with the aristocracy which history had seen on an extensive scale. Earlier writers had, of course, referred to classes and class-differences; but the notions of conflict and of changing relationships between classes seem to have had little or no place in their thought. As the writer of the article on 'Class Struggle' in the *Encyclopaedia of the Social Sciences* has observed, the notion made its appearance in the works of Mignet, Augustin Thierry, Adolphe Thiers, de Tocqueville and Macaulay; but it was in 1848 (in *The Communist Manifesto*), after the proletariat had entered the scene as a separate social movement (in England in Owenism and Chartism and on the Continent in the events preceding 1848), that the concept of class struggle as a dominant form of historical movement was developed. In classical Political Economy in England the notion of class, and to some extent of class conflict, occupied a prominent place. The 'mean and malignant system' of colonial exploitation (as Adam Smith termed it), that 'vast system of outdoor relief for the upper classes' (as James Mill called it), or the limitations on the import of corn, were attributable to the influence of class interest—a common interest in a category of income which transcended individuals. It was clearly no accident, nor was it for reasons simply of formal convenience, that the Political Economists cast their theory of how the income of society was distributed in terms of 'the three classes of the community which concur in its formation'. As to the basis of this grouping and of its origins they may have had no very clear ideas. For them it was simply one of the forms which the division of labour assumed in a civilised society. But the fact that it appeared to them so natural to group the problem in this way, without reason or argument, suggests that the three-fold division was generally regarded as something actual and fundamental, and that it was not a peculiar creation of economists.

Amid the complex and changing constellation of social tendencies it would be a particularly vain task to look for a precise, logically neat, definition of a class; and those who have thought that the notion must be so defined to be real have had small difficulty in demonstrating that it cannot exist. When an industry, a commodity, or capital and land are difficult to define, the frontiers of classes are still harder; and as Alfred Marshall was fond of emphasising, one must not look for sharp dividing-lines in the real world and thought must not seek to impose them on reality. Clearly, definition here needs to be, not by delimitation, but by type; and the reference of the term must be a 'substantial' reference. While an industry is defined in terms of the species of commodity it yields, a trade or profession in terms of the material handled or some homogeneous service performed, a class is to be defined in terms of a common source of income,[1] which lays the basis of a common interest and probably also a common mode of life and common psychological traits. In a society of private property, where this property is not widely diffused, but is concentrated for the most part in a few hands, a basis is clearly laid for significant differences in the source of income of different sections of society.

If, however, there is to be a reason for treating the common characteristic which defines a class as transcending other social groupings—as something more than one form of classification among many others—the definition must imply an element of antagonism with another class or classes, the contrast with which is part of its definition; and such an antagonism must be of a sufficient order of importance for it to unite the various individuals and groups which are tied by this common interest, and so to give rise to actual conflict along class lines. Except in the case of an exclusive caste, or in a society where social differences are permanently riveted by law, there will be some movement of individuals from one camp to the other, and the boundaries between the camps will be ill-defined, the intermediate territory being characterised by overlapping and by hybrid-types. A condition of any opposition between them developing will be that movement between them, while it may occur, is *limited* in some significant degree and is not free. Otherwise one would have the picture which certain nineteenth-century economists tried to draw (and to pass off as a true portrait) of a society which has sufficient mobility of individuals between its various parts that no conflict of interest (the rent of natural scarcities apart) can prevail over the essential harmony of its co-operating members (since, if any individual feels that he is at a relative disadvantage, he can move to where the advantage is greater, and in doing

---

[1] For reasons outlined below it is the *source* rather than the *amount* of income that is significant here. This is not to say that differences in amount of income will have no importance; it is merely to say that of themselves, they are unlikely to give rise to *class* groupings. It is true, of course, that they may be the origin of other more significant differences (as has been the case in the historical evolution of classes). At any rate in contemporary society the influence of income-differences is generally to reinforce the influence of differences in the source of income. When individuals derive income from more than one source, it will clearly be the source on which they predominantly rely which will usually determine their social alignment.

so aid in equalising net advantages). In other words, inequality of opportunity is an essential ingredient of the situation from which class conflict is born.

On the other hand, while unequal opportunity is a necessary ingredient, it is not a sufficient ingredient to introduce that novel qualitative element into the situation to which we presumably refer when we speak of class interests as dividing society on an extensive scale. As Mr. T. H. Marshall has already pointed out, it is not at all a necessary condition that no minor antagonisms should exist inside a class-group. Nor is it even necessary that the common class interest should at all times prevail over these sectional interests: it seems enough that they should prevail, and hence become a dominant social conflict, in circumstances which fairly frequently happen, or are likely to happen, and to recur. A professional group may impose restrictions on entry which render the opportunities of following that profession very unequal for different individuals. This will not necessarily create a class interest in the sense which we mean, since, although the clients of that profession or excluded entrants to it may have an interest in scrapping these restrictions, this will not necessarily affect their attitude to that larger complex of institutions which forms what we call the economic system of the epoch and which determines the size of the national income and the general shape of its distribution. It is the association of unequal opportunity, and of the rival interests which this creates, with what Marx called the prevailing mode of production (a term which included the social relations between men which hinge upon the form of ownership of the means of production) that creates the possibility of the wider and more deeply rooted social conflict that we clearly mean when we speak of the struggle of classes.

It is hardly necessary for me to attempt (even if I were competent to do so) to define the common element in the various situations which have created conflicts of this kind at various periods of history. Classification depends less on formal precision of definition than on practical judgment applied to particular cases; and in modern society there can be little doubt about what we refer to when we speak of class conflict. The private ownership of economic property is clearly the crux of the system of production which we know as capitalism, and of the social relations which depend upon it; and the concentration of property-ownership which is characteristic of our age creates both a divergence in the source of income between different sections of society and an inequality of opportunity of a sufficiently pronounced and comprehensive character to create sharply rival poles of interest—those who stand to gain by perpetuating and extending the rights of private property in land and capital, on the one hand, and those who would gain by their abolition or modification, on the other hand. The problem of multiple sources of income of course exists. But with property distributed as it is in capitalist society this question of social hybrids is not a very serious one; and for practical purposes classification along class lines is clear enough and can be (and customarily is) made for at least three-quarters of the population. Professor Pigou has pointed out that for that two-thirds of the population which is dependent on wages 'probably little more than one-thirty-fifth of (their) total income' is accounted for by income from any form of property, 'all the rest being received as wages of labour.'[1] Even for that 14 per cent of the occupied population who constitute the salary-group, income from property can hardly account for more than one-tenth of their income, and probably for less. At the other extreme of those $1\frac{1}{2}$ per cent who have four-figure incomes and account for 23 per cent of total income, the amount of their income which is derived from paid employment must be insignificant. Of the 17 million odd persons who own less than £100 of capital the average holding has been estimated as being no more than £30 to £50 per person, and the total of such small holding, as amounting to no more than 5 per cent of total capital. On the other hand, 80 per cent of total capital is owned by 5 per cent of the population (aged twenty-five and over); one-half of it being in individual holdings of more than £5,000, and nearly half of this in holdings of over £100,000[2] It must be remembered that in this country, unlike countries which have a large peasantry, those listed as 'independent workers' form only 6 per cent of all occupied persons. Even if we include with them all small farmers who employ labour and small shopkeepers, the figure can hardly come to more than 8 per cent.

The more we study the world today, and the more we penetrate behind the reasons for which people *say* they act, or consciously think they are acting, to find the real motive forces which impel them, the less doubt, one might think, there could be about the importance of class conflict as a dominant feature of contemporary history. But it is a familiar fact that ruling classes always strive to conceal the existence of precisely those forms of social conflict which are most dangerous to their own hegemony; and to emphasise, even at critical periods to stimulate, other and subordinate forms of group conflict. Such concealment, by emphasis on social unity, is a principal function of a dominant ideology,

[1] *Economics of Welfare*, 3rd edn., p. 655.
[2] Daniels and Campion, *The Distribution of the National Capital*.

as Professor Mannheim has indicated; and it is accordingly not surprising that there should be many who deny the importance of class interest as a social force and that plausible reasons should exist to which they can appeal. The whole notion comes as something offensive to the presuppositions of traditional thought. The reasons for which the significance of class conflict is usually denied are of two main kinds. On the one hand, it is denied that divergences of interest between capital and labour, while they may occur, are of much importance; on the other hand, attention is drawn to the other types of social grouping, such as professional groups, trades and industries, or nations, which give rise, it is claimed, to more significant conflicts than does the more vaguely defined division of society into classes.

The former of these contentions has been a special theme of economic writings for a century. So impressed have modern economists been with what they have conceived to be the essential harmony of interest between the factors of production as to deny any meaning to that relationship between capital and labour which Marx termed 'exploitation'—in other words, to deny any sense in which the relation between capitalist employers and their labourers could have any major analogy with the relation between masters and slaves or serf-owners and serfs. This denial seems largely to depend on a demonstration that cases where the income of capitalists can increase without a corresponding increase in the income of labour, and *vice versa*, are rare and unimportant.[1] To discuss this contention at all adequately would, of course, require more attention than can be given to it here. It must suffice merely to say this. I believe that the demonstration depends on a series of special assumptions which today are being seriously laid open to question: in particular, assumptions as to the nature of the equilibrating forces in the labour market which seem to be very far from those that are found in reality (and which recent doctrines about 'imperfect competition' are calling in question); an assumption that a condition of full employment (or some close approximation to it) is a normal condition of the system; and the assumption that the causes of industrial fluctuations and recurrent economic stagnation are due to external influences (e.g. defects in the monetary system) rather than to anything inherent in capitalism as a system of production. If such assump-

---

[1] Cf. particularly A. Marshall, *Principles*, p. 540; Pigou, *Economics of Welfare*, pp. 656–62. It does not, of course, follow, even though the incomes of labour and capital rise and fall together, that income *per head*, and still less the welfare, of the two classes are so associated. An increase in the supply of labour may increase the total income both of capital and of labour, but it may well lower labour incomes *per head*.

tions do not hold, then it seems to follow that economic events quite frequently occur which are motivated by the desire to maintain or to increase the return on capital, and which result in damage to the income of labour (e.g. through wage-reduction or unemployment). In this monopolistic age, at any rate, the contention that one factor of production can only gain by methods which yield a simultaneous gain to other factors clearly rests on a more slender foundation than formerly. Even so, this contention does not suffice of itself to demonstrate an essential harmony of interest: even if it were true that a gain to labour and a gain to capital were generally associated, it might still be the case that the gain to labour is made smaller, and any increase of income retarded, by the institution of private ownership of capital. Some further contention is, therefore, required: namely, that the rate of capital accumulation and of technical progress is rendered greater under this system than is conceivable under any other. All that can be briefly said of such a statement is: firstly, that this, again, in a monopolistic age seems to have increasingly meagre evidence to support it; secondly, that there is a growing body of economic opinion which not only questions whether the process of capital investment is not unnaturally retarded under the present system (by the high consumption-standards of a leisured class and by the various resistances which such a society imposes to any sharp fall in the return on capital), but is also inclined to believe that the under-employment of existing resources, both of equipment and of manpower, is a chronic, and not merely an abnormal, condition of the system. To this must be added certain considerations which do not directly relate to the income-position of the classes (although they may affect it indirectly in no negligible degree), but which may be of prime importance in promoting social conflict. I refer to the power which the possession of property gives to its possessors as against those who have for livelihood only the sale of their own hands: the fact that this power may be sufficient to force men to join a company union for which they have no use, to break the law regarding hours of work or safety for fear of dismissal and victimisation, or even (as I have heard told of certain colliery villages) to prevent employees from joining W.E.A. classes. Such an influence of some over the lives and actions of others is additional to the ability to exercise political influence or powerfully to influence social values and customs (in the ways, for example, that Veblen so forcefully described), which the possession of property gives and of which the lack of property deprives.

Emphasis on the significance of other forms of social grouping probably has greater plausibility for most people than the contention that divergence of class interest rarely occurs. In the nineteenth century it might have been said that craft interests were more important in dividing the working class than a class interest as wage-earners was in uniting them. But craft restrictions have since been on the decline, and today are relatively unimportant. Even in the case of the professions, where entrance qualifications are generally more effective, Professor Carr-Saunders and Mr. Wilson have told us that there is little evidence of any considerable influence on the incomes of professional workers exerted by monopolistic entrance restrictions *per se*.[1] With regard to division along industrial lines: it has often been asserted that workpeople in a particular industry stand to gain more by combining with their employer to share the profits of monopoly at the expense of some third party than they do by pressing their claims at the expense of their own employer's profits. To this I think it can be said that there is little evidence from the actions of workpeople and employers that this is today at all frequent; and where it is found, there seems generally to be some special circumstance which accounts for this co-operation. Moreover, there is this general consideration which is relevant here. When an industry establishes any form of monopolistic organisation, this is controlled and operated by and for the capitalist owners of the industry; and as soon as such an organisation has become strong and comprehensive, its influence is as likely to be exerted against the wage-earners in the industry or industries concerned (in monopolistically reducing the price of labour) as against consumers (by monopolistically raising prices). This likelihood would only cease if labour were to be given the place of joint partners (real and not merely nominal) with capital in controlling such organisations and their policy; and of the willingness of capital to concede such rights of joint control in any significant degree there is no present evidence.

More convincing is the emphasis frequently placed on the interests of the national group, or of the imperial unit, as transcending the interests of class; and evidence in support of this is adduced by pointing to the experience of the Great War of 1914–18 and to the phenomenon of Fascism. But when we examine these examples, we find that there are circumstances which severely qualify the conclusions which these examples are held to support: qualifications which are to my mind decisive. It must be remembered that the national unity of belligerent countries from 1914 onwards—a unity which was at least as much the creation of a concerted and highly organised campaign of official propaganda as of spontaneous feeling—gave way before the war was ended to revolutions in two

[1] A. M. Carr-Saunders and P. A. Wilson, *The Professions*.

countries which ranged society along class lines, and on the conclusion of the war to an accentuation of class conflicts, in victor and vanquished nations alike, on a scale which had not been witnessed for decades. Fascism, it is true, represents an attempt to suppress class conflict by treating it as an illusion, born of a wicked or a false ideology, and to substitute for class-consciousness the worship of the ideal of the nation-State and of imperial and racial aggrandisement. But are not the very methods which it has found necessary to use to further this aim the strongest witness to the deep-rooted reality of what it has tried to suppress—extraordinary methods of terrorism, the scrapping of Parliamentary democracy and the forcible elimination of independent mass organisations? Can anyone yet say that this suppression of class-sentiment has been successful; and does any serious sociologist really believe that it is Fascist ideology that is broad-based in realism and its Marxist opponent who traffics in pure illusion?

There is the further consideration that national conflict itself may partially derive its particular forms and its force from the nature of class conflict. Professor Robbins has elsewhere argued that even in a world of classless states the most important differences of interest between nations would persist and would even reveal themselves in a more open form.[1] Conflict would arise from the divergent interests of regions possessing divergent standards of life, especially in relation to the movement of capital between them. This argument seems to neglect an important distinction. In present-day society the gain to the capitalist class from exporting capital (as from acquiring colonies to provide a protected outlet for such investment) is a double one: the higher profit to be reaped abroad and also the higher profit (and cheaper labour supply) to be secured at home as the result of the relaxation of pressure on the investment market, and through it on the demand for labour. In a classless society the latter motive would be absent; and such a society might be as reluctant to lend its capital abroad, in preference to using it for internal

---

[1] *Economic Planning and International Order.* I think that one need not take very seriously that part of Professor Robbins's argument which implies that a crucial contradiction would exist if standards of life were not all levelled to equality. I see no inherent reason for this necessity. I can imagine differences arising over immigration; though much less than today if unemployment and the fear of undercutting wages were abolished. The principal difference of interest would seem to be as to how far richer countries should suffer 'forced saving' to help their poorer neighbours. It is, of course, conceivable that this might provoke a war of the poorer nations against the richer. But, as a cause of conflict this would surely be of a very much smaller order of magnitude than the economic causes of war which exist today?

development, as capitalist states are eager to find foreign outlets for it. The crucial distinction which Professor Robbins's argument seems to me to miss is that, whereas conflicts today arise from competitive keenness to invest abroad, and to annex privileged investment-fields, the divergent interests of which he speaks would arise from a *reluctance* to do so—a quite different, and I should have thought (whatever its effect on national standards of life might be) a much less combustible, state of affairs.

There remain two distinctions which it is, perhaps, important to mention, even if nothing adequate can be said about them in so short a space. When one speaks of an economic interest as a basis of conflict, is it of a real or of an imagined interest that it is proper to speak; is it the short-period or the long-period interest which one is to regard as decisive? Of the first distinction I will say only this as a confession of opinion. I believe that in economic affairs—in respect to the things which men do in vital matters connected with a livelihood—imagined interests may sway some people some of the time but seldom sway most people most of the time. There would seem to be a process of selection in which real interest, through the pressure of experience, selects the dominant strain. At any rate, a common interest which is to be strong enough to transcend individual and sectional interests must, I think, rest on reality and not illusion. This is not to say that individuals and groups may not be short-sighted in pursuit of their own advantage. It would be absurd not to suppose that their vision and their calculation are limited. This brings me to the second distinction. When one speaks of class interest, I think one necessarily refers to long-period rather than to short-period interest, at the same time implying such limits on the length of vision as are to be expected in the circumstances of the time. (The nature of any historical epoch, and the perspective from which a particular class views events, must of necessity impose definite horizons to the field of vision.) The contrast between the sectional interest and the more fundamental class interest which transcends it would generally seem to coincide with this distinction between a shorter and a longer interest. It may be in the short-period interest of a group of workers to combine with a trust or a cartel to exploit consumers (or of workers in general to combine with their rulers to control India or annex Abyssinia), while their long-period interest is to combine with other workers against that same trust or cartel. But I would suggest this as a necessary condition for the triumph of the latter over the former: that for at least some of the track immediate interest and ultimate interest must run along parallel lines—must lead in the same direction and result in substantially similar alignments (for example, the immediate interest of workers to co-operate with other workers to secure a wage advance at the expense of their employers and an ultimate interest in expropriating the employing class). It is when this fusion occurs of what is closest to the vision with what makes a more indirect and long-distance appeal that the combined influence of the two can exert its supremacy over interests which at other times may exclusively occupy the field of vision, and being embodied in institutions, ideas, moral standards, can come to exert a permanent influence. It is largely out of such circumstances that class consciousness is apparently born; it is then that a class from being an economic potentiality becomes a political actuality (becomes what Marx called a 'class for itself');[1] and it is largely to the occurrence of such situations that I believe one must look as the basis for actual class conflict.

[1] Cf. Marx in his 18th *Brumaire*, where he discusses the position of the peasantry and concludes that, while they have the economic potentialities for being a class, for a variety of reasons they seldom become a class in political actuality; using this analysis to interpret the social roots of Bonapartism. Cf. also some remarks of Georges Sorel in *Matériaux d'une Théorie d'un Prolétariat*, pp. 182 seq.

V

ON SOME TENDENCIES IN MODERN ECONOMIC THEORY [1949]

This essay appeared in Philosophy for the Future, *edited by R. W. Sellars, V. J. McGill and Martin Farber, and published by The Macmillan Company of New York in 1949. It is here reproduced by kind permission of the editors and the publishers of that volume.*

THERE IS CERTAINLY no easy way of summarising the present state of economic theory. Recent tendencies have been so numerous and so varied. All one can briefly say is that controversy, which twenty years ago was commonly thought to have been stilled (in those agreed 'general principles of thought' in the elements of which 'important improvements are becoming rare', to which Lord Keynes referred in the early 'twenties), has broken out afresh in the past two decades and has developed on a number of fronts. Hitherto an orthodoxy had fastened upon the world of academic economics as rigorous as the J. S. Mill orthodoxy which ruled England in the decades before the so-called 'Jevonian revolution'. It can hardly be a coincidence that this rebirth of controversy should have followed the economic crisis of the early 'thirties. Involved in this quickening of debate has been a requestioning of fundamentals: requestioning of assumptions which previously had been taken for granted or had passed unnoticed. By some this has been regarded as an opportunity for repair and reconstruction of the foundations with more lasting material and to a more modern design. Others have treated it as a veritable crisis of economic theory, from which the firm and rounded limbs of the traditional structure of doctrine are unlikely to emerge again as a consistent whole.

Prominent among recent novelties in the world of economic analysis have been the recasting of price theory in terms of monopoly, in place of the traditional assumptions about perfect competition, and a concentration upon a theory of the forces which determine the level of economic activity of the economic system as a whole (as distinct from the theory of relative prices), with the corollary that equilibrium is possible at various levels of employment or of plant-capacity. In close affinity to the latter have marched a variety of studies in economic fluctuations (macrodynamic studies, as they have been called), according to varying assumptions about time-lags and about the movements of various series of economic quantities. Prototype of many of these studies was the so-called 'cobweb theorem', which was concerned with the conditions under which price and output, instead of converging rapidly upon a position of stable equilibrium, might fluctuate extensively around such a position. In other words, the notion of stable economic equilibrium was itself called in question.

It is evident that the general effect of these recent developments has been to jettison the traditional basis upon which economic theory in the nineteenth century was built as an elaborate apologetic of capitalism, which was pictured as a self-adjusting economic mechanism tending (with a few exceptions) constantly to maintain an optimum allocation of resources among various productive uses. Where competition is imperfect or monopoly enters, none of the equilibrium positions of traditional doctrine apply. Firms are not of the most economical size, and even where prices conform to costs the latter are not minimised. The distribution of factors of production among various uses is distorted, and a new type of unproductive expense is created, and generalised—selling expenses designed to cajole the consumer and shift demand. Profit is seen as the creature of, and the motive for, restriction and uneconomic practices. Moreover the possibility was demonstrated both of extensive fluctuations of economic activity—resulting not simply from 'accidental' influences but from factors inherent in the system—and of a chronic state of under-utilised resources which the system had no tendency to remedy. Such a chronic state of economic stagnation might well become accentuated as the productivity of the system grew. These conclusions derived largely, of course, from a shift of assumptions—and a shift in the theoretical model which unquestionably brought it nearer to the real world—but also to some extent from logical critique of the older theory which revealed that accepted conclusions did not necessarily follow from the premises of this theory, or only followed by virtue of certain further and previously hidden premises which, once brought to light, could not be seriously maintained.

The more advertised controversies around these shifts of doctrine have tended to conceal some questionings which go deeper into fundamental issues of economic method: issues not unrelated to recent controversy, but comparatively little noted. I refer particularly to the questioning of the scope and nature of the subject of economics itself, and of the nature of the theory of value which forms the very texture of economic analysis. Most economists have supposed that controversy over both these issues had long ago been laid to rest. A tradition of accepted doctrine had reigned for nearly half a century which few cared, still fewer dared, to call in question. In recent years there can be detected an undercurrent of doubt (if no more) as to whether these basic matters are as settled as has come to be supposed. At any rate the times seem propitious for reopening them.

The problem of the scope and nature of the subject and the problem of the proper basis for its theory of value are more closely connected than might at first seem to be the case. The connection will perhaps be apparent if we start by considering what is involved in the former. The methodology of modern economics (unlike that of classical political economy) has tended to make economics essentially a theory of exchange—a determinate theory of price relationships between things which appear on a market as objects of sale and purchase. True, a department of the subject still appears in economic textbooks under the label of 'the theory of production'. But this is concerned with little more than determining the size of the firm, as the exchange unit, and hence the number of firms; which is a matter incidental to determining the prices of products in a market (since the number of firms is relevant to the nature and extent of competition in this market and to the effect on price of changes in demand). Of a separate theory of distribution modern economic theory contains even less, whatever label may be used. What is customarily called distribution is nothing more than an extension of the general theory of price relations from products to factors of production, the latter being treated—in complete abstraction from the individuals which supply them, and the social relations of those individuals —simply as productive services which enter the market because there is a demand for them derived from the demand for the final product.[1] In this

[1] In other words, the pricing of factors of production is treated as a constituent part of the general theory of price determination—determination simultaneously of factor prices and product prices. In a recent collection entitled *Readings in the Theory of Income Distribution*, scarcely any attention is paid to influences affecting the supply of different productive agents, still less to their social and institutional roots, or to income distribution between individuals and social classes. 'Distribution' is virtually identified with the theory of marginal productivity, which is simply the theory of price in a particular application. So far as profits are concerned, as Mrs. Joan Robinson has shown, modern economics contains no satisfactory theory of profits at all.

character as a theory of exchange, economic analysis has been regarded as furnishing principles which hold true of *any* type of exchange society. As such they have a universal significance fashioned from the common substance of which all exchange societies are made. For economists who stand in the neo-Kantian tradition and derive their methodology from Max Weber, economic laws have the force of 'synthetic *a priori* propositions': as Professor Hayek has declared,[1] they are built up from, 'not physical facts', but wholes 'constituted' out of 'familiar categories of our minds', which apply to all economic experience. They are not contingent on historically relative, institutional factors: on the contrary, they embody certain 'necessities' which are alleged to constrain the working of any type of economic system. In a phrase of Professor Robbins which has come to enjoy wide currency among English-speaking economists, the economic problem is defined as essentially consisting in 'the relationship between given ends and scarce means which have alternative uses'.

An inevitable result of this refinement of the scope of economic theory has been to exclude a large tract of economic territory which to any realistic view is of great importance for understanding the economic shape, and especially the larger movement, of society. Excluded are such considerations as the ownership of the means of production and the class relations contingent thereon. Excluded is any notion of a distinction between cost payments and a surplus, which formed the crux of the classical approach to questions of distribution. Excluded also is any notion of capitalism as an economic system with specific *differentiae*, since such *differentiae* can be given no meaning within the narrowed circle of economic notions. If meaning can be given at all to a notion such as capitalism (which is more often than not denied), this is said to be a job for the sociologist, not for the economist. The only 'system' which can occupy an economist's attention is the market system—the form of price determination.

It is not, of course, denied that so-called historically relative elements enter into economics. But they do not make their appearance until the second storey of the building is reached. They admittedly enter into the particular as distinct from the general theory of price determination. But in doing so they play a very special and subordinate role: they have the character of 'data' which fix the particular values of the variables, but do not substantially affect the main equations, defining essential relationships, of which economic theory consists. Such a conception evidently implies that the sphere of exchange is capable of being isolated, so far as its main causal sequences are concerned. It can be treated as constituting in

[1] *Ethics*, October 1943, pp. 11 *seq*.

the main causally autonomous territory. In so far as he introduces 'sociological' factors as 'data', the economist justifies his method of handling them by the assumption that they are independently determined from an outside sphere, and that any interaction between that sphere and the circle of economic relations proper is too small to impugn the postulated independence of the latter, and can accordingly be ignored.

Reflection soon indicates that such a conception can be sustained only at the cost of a drastic departure from reality. Most obvious of the difficulties under which it has always laboured is that it has virtually to take the distribution of income as given, since this affects not only the supply of different productive agents but also the pattern of demand. Yet the prices of factors of production, and hence the incomes of those who supply them, are among the dependent variables of the pricing problem. It is hardly surprising in the circumstances that modern economic theory should have abandoned the attempt to provide a theory of distribution: a problem which Ricardo had regarded as central to economic enquiry. The omission has been justified on the ground that the assumption of income distribution as an independently determined datum is no more drastic than the assumptions which any alternative type of theory would have to make; and that all abstraction which cuts off a slice or aspect of the real world for the purpose of analysis must ignore certain types of interaction. Whether this particular simplification is more or less drastic than others depends of course on the view one takes as to what is important, and what is relatively unimportant, in the genesis of economic processes. When we look further, however, it becomes increasingly doubtful whether any propositions of substantial importance can be made about exchange relations without introducing 'social' or 'institutional' data.[1]

The pretence that market relations constitute a 'system' for which general principles can be enunciated seems to derive from a particular view as to where the main determinants of exchange relations are to be found. It apparently derives from the notion that these determinants are to be found in the mental attitudes of consumers: in other words from some version of the Subjective Theory of Value, according to which 'the economic constants depend upon human consciousness' (as Pigou has expressed it—with the added admission that such constants 'change under the influence of environment'). The supply of agents of production (land, labour, capital) is independently given by social factors outside the market;

---

[1] Cf. some remarks of the present writer in his *Studies in the Development of Capitalism* (London, 1946), pp. 29–31.

while the conditions governing their combination and productivity are similarly given by technical factors. In a formal sense, these can be regarded as the essential determinants of price equilibrium equally with the desires of individual consumers. Yet the whole emphasis of the theory, by virtue of the form in which it is cast, is upon the latter. It is certain uniform characteristics of the relation between individual consumers and the objects of consumption that give to the principles of price determination their alleged generality: justify the claim that general laws of exchange can exist in their own right. When the formal theory of price determination comes to be translated into practical terms, there seems to lie at the heart of the matter some notion of consumers' sovereignty (in one of its variants): that, wherever exchange is free, desires of consumers control the pattern both of prices and of allocation of productive resources to minister to those desires in an optimum fashion (with the implied corollary that the mechanism of a free market is necessary in any economic system if consumers' welfare is to sway production).

How, then, does this differ from the classical approach? The methodology of classical political economy was far from clearly formulated, if it was formulated at all. But the picture which it presented was of a quite opposite order of determination. Exchange relationships were regarded as being essentially determined by facts of production; and any claim of universality in economic laws was based on the persistence of certain features of production over large tracts of economic history (in particular, the mobility of labour). In other words, the explanation of exchange relations was sought neither within the circle of those relations nor in the attitudes and behaviour of any of the participants in exchange, but in certain real cost relationships between factors of production and the product which emerged therefrom. Thus Marx laid emphasis on the fact that value was a *social* relation and not merely a relation of exchange. In this approach demand was not ignored. But, whereas it was held to be a determinant of the *amounts produced* of different things, and hence of the distribution of labour and other resources among various productive uses, it was regarded as being irrelevant to the *exchange ratios* between commodities. Thus, if the demand for commodity A increased relatively to the demand for commodity B, this would cause more of A to be produced and more labour to be employed in the industry producing it as compared with the labour devoted to the production of B. But the normal exchange value of A in terms of B would remain unaffected because this was determined by the comparative cost relation (i.e. the amount of labour required per unit of product) prevailing in the two cases. Thus abstraction could be made from demand in formulating essential economic principles. It was not the individual wills and attitudes of participants in the market, whether they were buyers or sellers, but objective ratios of production that determined the value relations constituting the warp and weft of economic law. It was this notion of the *objectivity* of economic laws that attracted the attention of Marx to classical political economy. Whatever mystical interpretation may have been given to Adam Smith's metaphor of 'the unseen hand', it is clear that the notion of economic law which we find in Smith and Ricardo and their immediate followers has close kinship with Hegel's notion that 'out of the actions of men comes something quite different from what they intend and directly know and will'. Moreover, the notion had been expressly used by Smith to rebut the previous obsession of economic writers (those of the Mercantilist school) with an autonomous sphere of exchange, and to reveal exchange as the sphere of the apparent and the phenomenal and production as the sphere of the essential and the substantial. This emphasis, again, accorded closely with the conception of historical materialism that the fundamental order of determination was from the 'mode of production' (in which were included the 'social relations of production') to other levels in the structure of economic relations of society as a whole. Moreover, in defining the three main revenues into which 'the whole annual produce of the labour of every country must resolve itself', they rested their definition on actual social classes. The factors of production, land, labour, and capital, were intended explicitly to correspond to the classes of landlords, capitalists, and workers; and the questions which their theory of distribution sought to answer were concerned with the different characters and modes of determination of the revenues of these classes.

The formal requirement which a theory of value must fulfil has been expressed by E. Heimann in his *History of Economic Doctrines* as follows: 'The crux of the problem of value in economics consists in this. No sum total of cost factors (land, capital, and the various kinds of labour) can be arrived at unless they are reduced to a common denominator.' The classical theory reduced all cost to terms of labour: labour conceived as the expenditure of quanta of human energy. The only two value theories which can lay claim to fulfil the condition that has just been mentioned are this classical Labour Value Theory of Ricardo and Marx and the modern Utility Theory.[1] They are the only real contestants in the field.

[1] In the Utility Theory all cost factors are equated in terms of their *values*; and the latter are treated as derived (on the marginal productivity principle) from the values of final products, which in turn are derived from utility.

Since the so-called 'Jevonian revolution' in economic thought, which followed so close upon the heels of the work with which Marx crowned the classical edifice, the second of these claimants has been accepted almost universally as having unquestioned superiority, by reason of its greater generality and its ability to furnish a theory of price determination both at the macroscopic and at the microscopic level. The classical labour theory (which was admittedly interested primarily in answering questions at the macroscopic level) has been held to fail at either level for two main reasons: firstly, because it cannot deal with situations where capital is used in differing amounts relatively to labour in different lines of production; secondly, because the cost at which a thing can be produced cannot be given independently of demand, but varies with the scale on which the thing is produced, the quantity produced depending on the demand. The cost of production of a commodity, accordingly, is not capable of being given a unique meaning.

The first of these objections really rests on a misconception of the classical theory. This stated, not that exchange ratios (or prices) were *equal* to the ratios of embodied labour (save in special conditions). It stated that exchange ratios were in the last analysis *determined* by the relative quantities of embodied labour in various commodities. The statement which was implied in Ricardo and developed by Marx in his famous theory of 'prices of production' was that, where the proportions of capital to labour in different lines of production were different, the price of each commodity depended *both* on the amount of labour required to produce it *and* on the profit which had to be paid on the amount of capital advanced; and that this profit depended on the rate of profit, which was itself determined by the proportion of the labour force of society which was engaged in producing what is nowadays spoken of as 'wage-goods' (or in classical terms, 'workers' subsistence').[1] In Marx's words, 'prices of production' represent deviations from 'values' determined by the extent to which in any industry the 'composition of capital' is above or below the average and by the rate of profit; but this rate of profit, on which the size of these 'deviations' depends, is itself determined in terms of the labour principle of value.*

[1] This can be seen to be given by the productivity of labour in terms of wage goods and of commodities in general and the level of wages. It is the same thing as saying that the amount of profit (and given the stock of capital, the rate of profit) depends upon the ratio of the amount of labour time required on the average to produce a worker's subsistence (i.e. to produce the equivalent of his real wage) over a given period and the labour time worked by the worker over that period.

[* On this see further below, 'A Note on the Transformation Problem', p. 273.]

The other objection at first looks more formidable. Is it not a commonplace of elementary economic textbooks that production in nearly all industries is subject to either 'increasing returns' or 'diminishing returns' as output increases (and sometimes to one at some levels of output and to the other at higher levels of output); and that the condition of 'constant returns', where cost is independent of output (and hence of demand), is a rare and special case—a case where opposing tendencies happen to cancel out, or all factors of production, including capital equipment, are supplied in relatively small divisible units? On this whole subject there was a good deal of recondite discussion among economists in the late 'twenties and early 'thirties. One conclusion emerging from this discussion, to which surprisingly little attention has been paid, was that a condition of 'constant costs' *in the relevant sense* was probably to be regarded as the general rule in many-firm industries under competitive conditions, rather than the exception. Accordingly, the classical assumption that cost had a meaning independently of demand was belatedly justified. This conclusion was explicitly stated in the much-quoted article by Mr. P. Sraffa in the *Economic Journal* of December 1926, which started the discussion; but to the statement and its implications most economists seem to have turned a blind eye. Mr. Sraffa's categorical statement was as follows: 'In normal cases the cost of production of commodities produced competitively must be regarded as constant in respect of small variations in the quantity produced. And so, as a simple way of approaching the problem of competitive value, the old and now obsolete theory which makes it dependent on the cost of production alone, appears to hold its own as the best available.'

The reason for this statement, so paradoxical to the ear of the modern economist, is as follows. For costs in a many-firm competitive industry to change by reason of a change in scale of that industry (and hence for costs to be a function of the demand for the industry's product), the industry must represent a very substantial part of the use for some particular agent of production which is limited in supply or alternatively indivisible (like many types of industrial plant and equipment). It is only as a result of a change in the demand for this agent of production (e.g. land in the case of agriculture, or some subsidiary product in the case of a manufacturing industry), and hence in its price and/or the intensity with which it is used, that the costs of the industry in question are likely to be affected. Such a case is, however, likely to be rare, rather than typical, and to be more rare the more narrowly an industry is defined.[1]

[1] So far as economies arising from division of labour and specialisation are concerned: those internal to a firm will (according to a familiar principle of the modern

What, then, can be said of the rival claims of the Subjective Theory, which have for so long been accepted as impeccably superior? Here, again, certain recent tendencies in economic theory have not been without an influence, even if this implication has for the most part passed unnoticed. So long as the Subjective Theory was rooted in the notion of Utility (in the sense of satisfaction), it could pass at least the formal test for fulfilling the requirements of a theory of value (subject to an exception which will be mentioned below). If one was willing to believe in such an entity as Utility (with the description of human psychology implied therein), and if one was further willing, by an assumption of human rationality, to postulate a fairly close identity between this quantity and human desires (and hence consumers' demand on a market), the theory was at least plausible. In the present century the latter postulate has become difficult, if not impossible, to square with the observed facts of an advertising age: the malleability of consumers' demand, and the dependence of demand on selling expenditure incurred by sellers and on the whole complex of sales devices and sales propaganda. Moreover, the tendency of economists in the present century has been increasingly to drop the notion of Utility altogether as an untenable or at least a needless hypothesis. Instead price determination is made to rest on preferences of consumers as registered by the observed behaviour of consumers on a market.

After this drastic operation with Occam's razor, one may well ask whether anything substantial is left on which to erect a theory of price determination. The structure of theory looks impressive; and its elevation is elegant enough with its mathematical streamlining. But what exactly is the base on which it all rests? If one analyses the propositions about demand which it employs as central determinants, one may well ask whether anything more is being stated than that things sell at certain prices because consumers buy them at those prices. At first sight this may seem a grotesque parody. But further examination will show, I think, that nothing of substantial meaning is really being said by modern price theory beyond this. The Utility theory *was* definitely saying something more substantial (whether one believes such an entity as Utility to exist or to be related to demand is another matter). It was saying some-

---

theory of the firm) have been eliminated before the equilibrium size of the firm has been reached (provided that the industry remains a many-firm and competitive industry); and specialisation dependent on the multiplication of products or of product-types has properly to be treated as part of the general development of industry, and is expressible as a function of economic development in general and not of the size of a single industry alone.

thing about what lay *behind* consumers' market behaviour and independently of the latter; and it was this something that was held to *determine* consumers' demand and, through demand, market prices. But now that this something-behind-demand has been jettisoned, what have we left other than a description of an exchange ratio itself—the act of exchange in its aspect of a purchase?

True, modern price theory gives an *appearance* of saying something more: of explaining an exchange ratio in terms of something outside the exchange transaction itself—namely, a demand curve, or schedule of demand prices. This looks very satisfying on paper. But how many of those who manipulate the geometry and algebra of demand functions have ever given a satisfactory explanation of what the entity represented by a demand curve really is? Is it observed uniformities in consumers' market behaviour in varying price situations? Of these there exists no sufficient empirical evidence. Is it an instinctive behaviour mechanism in the psychological make-up of individuals, of such a kind as to define their potential reactions to every kind of price situation on the market, whether these situations have ever been directly experienced or not? Can one really believe in anything of the kind, even as an unverified but plausible hypothesis? And if a demand curve is none of these things, what are we left with? Can causal statement go beyond the tautological statement that in any given case a commodity is sold at a certain price because someone has bought it at that price?

If we translate the issue into practical terms, it seems to amount to this. Have we any warrant for saying that market prices are determined by the attitudes and actions of consumers, rather than that consumers' attitudes are conditioned by the market prices with which they are confronted? When we take account of the part played by conventional elements in moulding demand and of the fact that demand for any particular thing depends upon the nature and range of the alternatives which are offered (in the determination of which initiative must come in the main from producers), not to mention the malleability of demand in face of advertising pressure which we have mentioned, there would seem to be at least as much ground for thinking that consumers' actions adapt themselves to the market[1] as for thinking the converse. We seem to be left with the

---

[1] We are speaking here, of course, of adaptation in a more fundamental sense than the mere fact that each individual consumer takes the market price as given and adapts his purchases accordingly. This fact is allowed for in the ordinary theory, and indeed occupies an important place in it: what Professor Oskar Lange has called the 'parametric function of prices' in this theory. But the point is that here the adapta-

conclusion that modern economic theory has really no theory of value at all.

There is one crucial respect in which the Subjective Theory, in any of its variants, has signally failed to fulfil an essential condition of formal completeness. One might even speak here of a crucial contradiction lying close to the heart of the modern theory. This theory has provided no satisfactory method of measuring capital as a separate factor of production. In the Labour theory capital (in its quantitative aspect) is regarded as consisting of the labour embodied in the actual products (machines, structures, materials, etc.) of which it is composed. But in the modern theory capital appears merely in the guise of a set of values. Its price (the return on capital) is regarded as being determined by the value of its marginal product. Yet the marginal product (from which its own valuation and measurement are treated as being in some way derived) has to be expressed in relation to a *unit* of capital, and hence can be given no meaning until such a unit has been independently defined. Here is a special point of difficulty which cannot receive adequate discussion within the limits of this essay. It must suffice to state the opinion that no satisfactory solution of this difficulty has been provided by modern theories of capital, including those which have sought to represent capital as a quantity measurable in two dimensions, compounded of labour and time.

What, then, of the theory of monopoly price, to which some of the most notable contributions of economists in the past fifteen years have been made? To the determination of monopoly price the classical Labour theory admittedly affords no clue: such prices appear as 'deviations' due to factors of which the general theory takes no account, and which have to be explained in terms of the special circumstances of particular situations. The fact that modern price theory can explain the monopoly case as well as the competitive case has been regarded as one of its outstanding merits. There can be no doubt that modern theories of monopoly and of 'monopolistic' or 'imperfect' competition have carried generalisation about various kinds of monopoly situation further than it has ever been carried before: possibly as far as it can be made to go. At the same time, I think it can scarcely be questioned that no *general* theory of price determination under monopoly has been yielded, in the sense of a determinate theory of the *total* price situation. As Dr. Paul Sweezy has well said:

tions which each consumer makes are regarded as being circumscribed by his individual 'demand schedule', so that in the final analysis the totality of these schedules (and the individual actions conditioned by them) is held to determine the structure of market prices.

'When the power of limiting supply is in the hands of producers, so also is the power of setting prices, and to determine theoretically, and with a useful degree of generality, at what point prices will be set is impossible; too many diverse factors enter into the determination of a given price to permit the construction of a precise theory with any but the most limited applicability. This is fully proved by the attempts of orthodox economic theory in recent years to establish objective laws of price under conditions of total or partial monopoly. Aside from a few empty propositions such as that price will be set where profit is maximised, monopolistic price theory rapidly turns into a catalogue of special cases, each with its own particular solution. No reasonably general laws of monopoly price have been discovered because none exist.'[1]

Admittedly a theory of value expressed in terms of cost relations (i.e. in terms of labour) can afford an explanation of actual price phenomena only with a degree of approximation sufficient to interpret the larger movements of economic society and to focus attention upon the most important influences governing the prices of individual commodities. This needs to be supplemented by special studies of particular situations: studies which are likely to yield little unless they are inspired more richly than hitherto by empirical investigation (e.g. as to how output decisions are taken and profit margins determined in actual cases). If such studies, and generalisations emerging from them, were set within the wider framework of a value theory of the classical type, the whole would have the advantage of a perspective which is lacking in academic economics today. Study of market phenomena would be reintegrated with those factors (for so long dismissed as extra-economic, 'sociological' factors) which constitute the material basis of society: its property institutions, its production relations and productive forces. For questions of economic development —an aspect of their subject about which economists, with rare exceptions, have said little—such reintegration is of outstanding importance. In all questions of this type a notion of the proper *order of determination*—of the true causal-genetic sequence of events—can at once be seen to be of crucial importance. It is true that an important lesson of any study in economic and social interpretation is that oversimplification can be the foe of understanding, and that the complexity of mutual interaction must not be obscured by a too schematic and mechanical view of causal determination. At the same time it must be recognised that the study of economic change, whether in the past or in the present, is increasingly demonstrating the primacy of what Marx termed the 'mode of production' of the

[1] *The Theory of Capitalist Development* (New York, 1942), pp. 270-1.

epoch; and if this is so, theoretical 'models' of the economic system which conceal, instead of illuminating, the fact are in essence obscurantist.

In conclusion, to avoid misunderstanding, one should, perhaps, add this comment about economic method. The significance of a theory of value has to be looked at, I believe, not as a premise from which all else in economics is deducible *a priori*, but rather as a *method* of analysis: a conceptual framework for focusing our attention upon causal sequences and economic mechanisms which are the important ones for understanding the real world and for acting upon it. Any theory of value is, of course, making a general statement about the real world—about the way it is constructed. This is to say that it makes a qualitative statement about the world in the act of postulating a quantitative relationship. It is true, presumably, that the notion of property income as surplus-value (requiring special explanation to account for its emergence and the specific form of its appropriation) is implicit in the Labour theory of value; just as the notion that consumers' welfare is maximised and that all factor groups get paid their value contribution (marginal) is deducible from the Utility theory of value, once the postulate of free competition has been added to it and appropriately defined. But is this not because in each case a language is provided in which such questions can be discussed (while other questions at the same time are excluded as meaningless), rather than because one is enabled to deduce a series of categories from an initial one, within which, like Chinese boxes, all the rest are contained? Is not the proper way of regarding the matter that a constructional principle is provided for building a model of the economic system in which questions such as this (and also answers to them) are implied in the *modus operandi* of the model? The crucial consideration is: Which type of model gives the truer representation of economic actuality, especially in its change and movement?

VI

RATES OF GROWTH UNDER THE FIVE-YEAR PLANS [1953]

This appeared as an article in *Soviet Studies* (University of Glasgow), Vol. IV, No. 4, April 1953, and is reprinted here by kind permission of the editors of that journal.

1 THE DISCUSSION that has taken place concerning the valuation of industrial output in terms of 1926–7 prices is well known, and the writer of the present article has no intention of entering again upon this discussion here. Suffice to say that it appears to have left many in a state of doubt whether any statement at all can be made about the rate of growth of Soviet production since 1928[1]—and this despite the fact that the extent of the alleged 'upward bias' of valuation in 1926–7 prices, according to what is claimed by the most authoritative critics of the output-index, is of the order of 25 to 30 per cent at the outside.[2] Since, however, there are

---

[1] Cf. the statement in D. McCord Wright's *Capitalism* (Harvard Economic Handbook Series, 1951) p. 99, that 'the available Russian statistics do not, I believe, furnish a reliable basis of comparison' of the rates of growth of production in U.S.S.R. and in other countries.

[2] See A. Gerschenkron, 'The Rate of Industrial Growth in Russia since 1885' in *Journal of Economic History*, Suppl. VII, 1947, pp. 167–8; Paul Baran in *Review of Economic Statistics*, November 1947, pp. 233–4. True, Mr. Naum Jasny's estimates imply a larger difference (*The Soviet Price System*, pp. 113–14); but he assumes without any sufficient reason that all new types of producers' goods were introduced into the index at the prices of the year of their introduction into production, instead of being adjusted to a '1926–7 level' by means of a price-index of comparable products (cf. here the present writer's *Soviet Economic Development since 1917*, pp. 261–2). Indeed, he misreads a citation (on p. 112) from a recent Soviet writer (Joffe) who speaks of new machinery production of which the 'prices are established on the basis of the cost of production of the present year *with a correction*' [italics mine]: when that writer speaks of these 'corrected prices' as differing little 'in the majority of cases' from current prices, he evidently does *not* mean to imply that current prices (and hence

RATES OF GROWTH UNDER THE FIVE-YEAR PLANS

quantity-figures (i.e. in terms of real output) for a number of basic products such as steel and fuel and power, we can if we like by-pass this discussion about the valuation-problem, in order to obtain an idea of the order of magnitude of industrial growth during the period of the Soviet Five-Year Plans. These basic products for which quantity figures are available can be regarded, with good reason, as crucial indices of industrial development and are frequently quoted as such. Their rate of growth seems to lag behind as often as it exceeds the rate of increase of output in general, as measured by the usual indices, so that the picture of growth which they yield does not seem likely in the normal case to exaggerate the trend of industrial output as a whole. In U.S.A., for example, between 1899 and 1929, blast-furnace products increased about three times and coal about two-and-a-half times, while the output index for manufacturing industry in general increased by between three and three-and-a-half times, although the increase for steel was above the latter (namely, an increase of more than four times).[1] True, under the Soviet Five-Year Plans such products shared in the investment-priority assigned to heavy

'corrected prices') are much higher than the 1926-7 level, but that current prices of machinery products are very much the same as 1926-7. This quite accords with a comparison of the valuation of the production of medium, general and electrical engineering (a) in 1926-7 prices, (b) in current prices, in the two tables of the 1941 Plan (referred to by Mr. Seton in *Soviet Studies* for April 1952, esp. Table I on p. 354), which yields something very close to a 1 : 1 relationship between (a) and (b). That pre-war costs should have remained close to the level of the 1920's despite substantial increases of money-wages in the interim is not, on reflection, surprising in the case of industries which had undergone an extensive technical revolution during the '30's and in which labour cost is not a very high proportion of total cost (to a less extent the same was true of iron and steel where the ratio was only 1 : 2, and of chemicals and building materials where it was around 1 : 1.8). What is more surprising is that even Mr. Gerschenkron should assume that such ratios are to be explained, not by real-cost reductions in these industries, but by a wholesale 'cooking' of the 1926-7 index in the case of new products (cf. his *A Dollar Index of Soviet Machinery Output, 1927-8 to 1937*, Rand Corporation, California, 1951, pp. 5-8).

[1] Cf. the present writer in *Review of Economics and Statistics*, February 1948, p. 36; *Historical Statistics of the U.S. 1789-1945*; Nourse, etc., *America's Capacity to Produce*. Petroleum and electricity registered much higher rates of growth over these three decades; so that an average for coal, rolled iron and steel, petrol and electricity works out at as much as eleven or twelve times (with 1899 = 100; or some eight times with 1917 = 100 for each item), whereas for coal, rolled iron and steel, steel ingots and castings it is under four. (For these calculations I am indebted to Miss S. Y. Mallett, of the Faculty of Economics and Politics, Cambridge.) But these were the decades of phenomenal growth in petrol and electricity following the technical revolution associated with the internal combustion engine and electricity. As we shall see below, there is no such extreme disparity as this between the metal-fuel-power items in the Soviet case.

industry—indeed, figured high on the list of such priorities. It is a well-known fact, however, that, when one introduces value-considerations, the output-growth of basic metals and fuel and power is usually much smaller than that of heavy industry products in general, since the latter include highly-fabricated products of the engineering industry and in the course of industrial development the 'coefficient of fabrication' (expressing the ratio of value-added by engineering processes to the value of basic materials) tends to rise.[1] In the Soviet case emphasis on development of various branches of engineering was unusually great.

If we take steel, coal, oil and electricity as our four indicators, we find that the rate of growth of this metal-fuel-power group, as measured by the unweighted average of the output-changes of the four, has been remarkably constant over the periods of the first two Five-Year Plans (i.e. the decade of 1928-37) and of the post-war fourth Plan: namely an annual (compound) rate of growth of approximately 15 per cent, or a doubling of output each quinquennium. During the period of the First Plan the output of these products increased by rather less than twice (but the period over which plan-fulfilment was officially measured was less than the full five years); and during the Second Plan they increased by rather more than twice. Since we have no official output-data for individual products in 1945, we must measure the post-war quinquennial rate of growth by the increase between 1946 and 1951, which gives a percentage of 103 per cent.[2] Estimates have been made, however, for 1945, and if we take one of these and compare it with the output figures for 1950, we get the closely similar percentage of 109 per cent.[3] We can accordingly take this trend (15 per cent annual growth or a doubling each quinquennium) as typical of the period since 1928,[4] other than the war years and the

[1] For example, in U.S.A. between 1899 and 1929 the ratio of the increase of value-added by the machinery industry to the increase of blast-furnace products was of the order of magnitude of 8 : 3 (*Review of Economics and Statistics*, February 1948, p. 36).

[2] Cf. *Economic Survey of Europe for 1951* (U.N. Econ. Commission for Europe, Geneva, 1952), p. 127; annual reports on the Plan by Gosplan and Ts.S.U. If we were to include non-ferrous metals such as copper, zinc and lead, this would raise the index of growth rather than lower it.

[3] A. Bergson, J. H. Blackman, A. Erlich, 'Postwar Economic Reconstruction and Development in the U.S.S.R.', in *Annals of the American Academy of Political and Social Science*, May 1949, p. 56; Communiqué of Gosplan and Ts.S.U. 'On the Results of the Fulfilment of the Fourth Five-Year Plan of the U.S.S.R. for 1946-50', in *Planovoye Khozyaistvo*, 1951, No. 2, pp. 3-5.

[4] It may be of some interest to note that this growth-rate is identical with the so-called 'adjusted rate' for all industry suggested by Mr. Gerschenkron for the period 1928-38 ('The Rate of Industrial Growth in Russia since 1885', *loc. cit.*, p. 168).

RATES OF GROWTH UNDER THE FIVE-YEAR PLANS

three-and-a-half years of intensive rearmament from 1938 to 1941. (During this latter period the growth-rate of our four indicators seems to have fallen to a third of the 'normal' and to less than half of the target-rate for the Third Plan[1]).

While the overall growth-rate of this metal-fuel-power group has been fairly constant, there has been considerable variation in the growth-rates of the individual items, especially oil and steel. In the case of the latter, however, it is to be noted that the very low rate of growth of the First Plan was the result, in a sense, of an accident in the end-dating of this period: the completion of new steel plants constructed under the Plan tended to 'bunch' at the end of the period, and delays in getting them into full production (combined with the advancing of the terminal date of the Plan under the 'Five-Year Plan in Four Years' slogan) prevented increase in capacity from expressing itself in the 1932 output-figures. Correspondingly the abnormally high rate of increase during the Second Plan is explained by the carry-over into that period of output-increases attributable to capacity-increases carried out under the First Plan. The low rate of increase of oil during the Second Plan seems likely to have been due mainly to concentration during those years on development work in the 'Second Baku' and other easterly areas. The details can be seen at a glance from the following table:

ACTUAL INCREASE OF OUTPUT IN QUANTITY TERMS DURING THREE QUINQUENNIA

	1928–32	1933–37	1947–51
Coal	84 per cent	98 per cent	75 per cent
Oil	90 ,,	37 ,,	92 ,,
Steel	37 ,,	200 ,,	135 ,,
Electricity	168 ,,	171 ,,	110 ,,
UNWEIGHTED AVERAGE	94 ,,	126 ,,	103 ,,

These rates of growth may be compared with those shown by the *value*-index (at 1926–7 prices) of total industrial output—namely an annual growth of approximately 20 per cent during the first quinquennium and of 17 per cent during the second, or an average of 18·3 over the decade 1928–38. The three years of the uncompleted Third Plan, however, showed a much lower annual rate of 13 per cent; and for the whole period 1928–40 the average annual rate works out at 17·5 per cent.[2] If we measure

[1] If we include the three years of the Third Plan, we get an annual growth-rate for the whole period 1928–40 of about 14 per cent—just under 13 per cent for steel, just under 14 for coal, just under 21 per cent for electricity and 8½ per cent for oil.
[2] Cf. Gerschenkron, *loc. cit.*, p. 165.

the post-war growth by comparing 1946 and 1951, we get an annual rate of increase intermediate between those just mentioned—namely, 18 to 19 per cent. But if we measure it over the Five-Year Plan period proper (the first year of which, 1946, was a year of reconversion which showed a consequent drop in the production index[1]) we get a lower figure of between 13 and 14 per cent.

As is well-known, however, there was a large disparity between the rates of growth of different sectors of industry; and in the pre-war period from 1928 to 1940 the output of capital goods registered more than double the rate of increase of that of consumer goods.[2] According to the Third Five-Year Plan, the disparity between the two sectors was to be reduced: an average annual rate of growth of 15 per cent being set as the target for capital goods and 12 per cent for consumers' goods; with rates of about 14 and 10 per cent respectively as the actual recorded performance during the three operative years of the Plan. Over the period of the Fourth Plan proper (1946–50) the increase of consumers' goods was actually higher than that of capital goods; but this was because the output of consumers' goods had fallen during the war by much more than had the output of the metal, engineering and chemical industries.[3] After 1946, however, the 'normal' relationship between the growth-rates of the two main sectors of industry was resumed. It is of interest to note at this point that in the new (Fifth) Plan for 1951–5 the disparity between the two has been further reduced, although the growth of capital goods continues to lead.

The main indices of growth for the four Five-Year Plans, distinguished in each case (where the information is available) between plan and actual fulfilment, are summarised in the following table; the equivalent increases provided for by the recently-issued Fifth Plan being included for comparison.

[1] G. Malenkov in his Report to the 19th Party Congress on October 5th, 1952, gave the indices for 1945 and 1946 as 92 and 77 respectively (1940=100), and for 1950 and 1951 as 173 and 202 (page 53 of Eng. reprint pubd. by the Foreign Languages Publishing House, Moscow, 1952).

[2] For the five commodities in the consumers' goods group for which there are quantity-figures for the period 1928–40 (paper, sugar, cotton fabrics, woollens and leather shoes) the unweighted average of their increases amounts to 177 per cent over the whole period—a good deal less than the value-index for all consumers' goods.

[3] Malenkov (*loc. cit.*, p. 53) gives the indices for 'production of consumer goods' for 1945 and 1946 as 59 and 67 (1940=100) and for 'production of means of production' as 112 and 82. The figures for 1950 and 1951 are 123 and 143 respectively for consumers' goods and 205 and 239 for means of production.

RATES OF GROWTH UNDER THE FIVE-YEAR PLANS

PERCENTAGE QUINQUENNIAL INCREASES UNDER THE FIVE-YEAR PLANS[1]

	1st Plan 1928–32		2nd Plan 1933–7		3rd Plan 1938–42		4th Plan 1946–50			5th Plan 1951–55
	Plan	Actual	Plan	Actual	Plan	Actual (3 years)	Plan	Actual 1946–50	Actual 1947–51	
Increase of Total Industrial Output	133	118	114	121	92	45	61	88	162	70
Increase of Capital Goods	148	158	97	150	107	53	—	82	192	80
Increase of Consumers' Goods	120	87	133	100	72	31	—	108	113	65
Unweighted Average of Quantity-Increases of Metal-Fuel-Power Group	173	94	152	126	82	17	—	—	103	70

2 How does this growth-rate for our metal-fuel-power group compare with the growth-rates characteristic of other periods and other countries? If we take such comparative indices of industrial growth as are available, we find that they tend to be grouped around three magnitudes: (a) that found among countries at an early stage of industrial development (and expressing the vigour of initial impetus or the 'large percentage increase of small numbers'); (b) that to be found in all (or most) capitalist countries in special (and short-lived) boom periods; (c) that to be found

[1] Cf. Gosplan, *Summary of the Fulfilment of the First Plan* (Moscow, 1933); Gosplan, *The Second Five-Year Plan* (Moscow, 1936); V. Molotov, *The Third Five-Year Plan* (Moscow, 1939); *Law on the Fourth Five-Year Plan* (Moscow, 1946); 'Directives of the 19th Party Congress for the 5th Five-Year Plan' in *Planovoye Khozyaistvo*, 1952, No. 4; A. Baykov, *Devt. of the Soviet Econ. System, passim*. The figures of total output and of capital goods and consumers' goods for the First Plan refer to 'Census Industry' (enterprises having 16 and more workers where there is mechanical power or 30 and more workers where there is no mechanical power); those for the Second Plan and after are for all industry.

as a longer-term trend in older industrial countries at a relatively late stage in their development.

Characteristic of (*a*) was Tsarist Russia between 1885 and 1913, with an annual (compound) growth-rate of 5·7 per cent (or a doubling every 12½ years), or Sweden over the same period with an annual growth-rate of 6·17. The appropriate U.S.A. figure for the same period was 5·26, and the German 4·49. In all these countries industrial output approximately quadrupled between 1885 and 1913. As characteristic of (*b*) we may take the exceptional decade of the 1890's in Russia, which showed an annual growth-rate of slightly more than 8 per cent, or U.S.A. in the second half of the 1880's with 8·7 per cent, Japan between 1907 and 1913 with a rate of 8·6 per cent and the United Kingdom in the post-war years of 1946–50 with a rate of 7 or 8 per cent.[1] As regards (*c*), the Swedish economist Gustav Cassel once estimated the average rate of growth in Western Europe during six decades prior to 1914 as just over 4 per cent per annum (basing his estimate on pig-iron production). This is only a little below the League of Nations figure for world manufacturing production during the three decades prior to 1900, when the index showed a three-fold increase, increasing again by rather less than three times between 1900 and 1929. While the equivalent American figure was rather higher than this, for the later period 1899–1937 the average annual rate was no more than 3½ per cent (or 5 per cent if we measure up to 1929 only and omit the last eight depression-years). For the U.K. between 1885 and 1913 it was under 3 per cent (industrial output taking from 1875 to 1913 to double itself).[2]

It accordingly seems reasonable to take a figure of 5 to 6 per cent as applicable to capitalist countries developing under fairly favourable conditions, rising to 8 per cent or slightly more in exceptional boom periods, lasting for about a quinquennium; and we may conclude that the Soviet growth-rate for metal-fuel-power over the period since 1928 (omitting

---

[1] The expansion of industrial production in U.S.A. between 1939 and 1943 was comparable with the Soviet rate; but the former case was a rather special one in that it represented the utilisation of an exceptionally large amount of reserve capacity, especially in the steel industry, under pressure of war demands. The bringing into play of reserve capacity is also, of course, a large factor in most cases of (*b*) above.

[2] Cf. League of Nations, *Industrialization and Foreign Trade*, 1945, p. 130; A. Gerschenkron, *loc. cit.*, pp. 155–6; S. Fabricant, *Output of Manufacturing Industries 1899–1937* (New York, 1940), pp. 7, 44–5; London and Cambridge Economic Service Index of Industrial Production. As we have seen above, the U.S.A. increase in the metal-fuel-power items was substantially higher than the above rates owing to exceptional increases in oil and electricity between 1900 and 1929 (above page 119 n.).

the war years) was nearly three times the former and rather less than double the latter. Taking as terms of comparison the three magnitudes distinguished in the last paragraph, it seems clear that the Soviet growth-rate for metal-fuel-power was nearly three times (*a*), more than three times (*c*), and not quite double (*b*).

It is well known that the basis of this high rate of growth in the U.S.S.R. was an ambitious investment programme; moreover, an investment programme giving priority to expansion of the productive capacity of industries producing means of production (or capital goods). It has been officially estimated that the proportion of the national income devoted to investment was more than 25 per cent on the average of the period 1928-40, and about the same proportion in the post-war quinquennium.[1] It is obvious that such proportions will be affected by the relative values of capital goods and consumers' goods (and by changes in these values), and that comparisons between different countries may be affected thereby. There seems little doubt, however, that whatever relative valuation be taken the order of magnitude involved is considerably higher in the case of the Soviet Five-Year Plans than in the case of other countries—probably twice as great. The interesting question which arises (since it may affect the probability of past growth-rates continuing in the future) is whether this investment, and the consequential increase in output, was accompanied by an enlargement of the total labour-force employed in industry or by increased productivity per head of a constant labour-force—and if by both, in what proportions were the two factors of expansion mixed?

The answer is that both factors have played a part, and their order of

---

[1] A. Petrov, *Planovoye Khozyaistvo*, 1947, No. 2, p. 64. The equivalent proportion for Great Britain in 1947-9 was 11 per cent (and 8 per cent in 1938); for France an average of 12 per cent in 1948-9 and for Sweden 12 per cent in 1938-9 and an average of 13 per cent for 1947-9 (*Econ. Survey of Europe in 1949*, Research Dept. of E.C.E., Geneva, p. 23). Professor A. Bergson's estimate for net investment in U.S.S.R. in 1937 is rather lower than the official figure, namely, 20-23 per cent of net national product. As regards *gross* investment, he suggests 25 per cent as the proportion of gross product going as gross investment, against 15 per cent in U.S.A. One might here expect the difference between U.S.S.R. and other countries to be smaller than in the case of net investment, since the replacement-demand for capital goods will be larger, the larger the existing stock of capital equipment, and hence (if it be the case that the ratio of capital to output is higher in more developed countries) will probably be larger relatively to gross production and to net investment in a more advanced country. However, Professor Bergson suggests that in U.S.A. in the decade 1869-78 the proportion of the gross product devoted to gross investment may have been as high as 19 per cent (A. Bergson, 'Soviet National Income and Product in 1937', Part II, *Quarterly Journal of Economics*, August 1950, pp. 435, 438-40).

importance has varied at different periods, with a tendency for the second to take the lead since the middle 'thirties. Between 1928 and 1940 growth of output seems to have derived in about equal degree from both. But during the First Five-Year Plan increase in the labour-force (which approximately doubled) evidently played a more important part than increase of labour productivity (which grew by 36 per cent), while in the latter half of the pre-war period their rôles were reversed, the increase in the total employed labour-force (i.e. all those persons employed at a wage or a salary) proceeding more slowly from 22 million at the end of 1932 to 30 million by 1940.[1] Between 1928 and 1940 the annual rate of increase of productivity (per man-year) was about 11 per cent; being under 10 per cent between 1928 and 1935 and rising to 13 per cent between 1936 and 1940.[2] In the post-war period it was apparently again derived more from growth in productivity than from increased employment. In the final years of the quinquennium labour-productivity was growing by approximately 12 per cent per annum (close to the pre-war figure), and was announced as being in 1950 higher than 1940 by 37 per

---

[1] Employment in *industry* grew at approximately the same rate as the total labour-force—if anything, by rather more during the later part of the period: namely, from some 3 million in 1928 to 6·5 million in 1932 and to 11 million in 1941. The number employed in construction actually fell after 1932.

[2] *Trud v S.S.S.R.* 1936; W. Galenson, 'Russian Labour Productivity Statistics', *Industrial and Labor Relations Review*, July 1951, p. 500. Dr. Rostas's figure of increase in productivity per man-hour in American industry between 1929 and 1950 is 2 per cent per annum; for both Britain and U.S.A. from 1946–50 about 5 to 6 per cent (*Econ. Journal*, March 1952, pp. 20, 22). The British Government's *Economic Survey for 1950*, referring to manufacturing, mining, building and public utilities combined, spoke of productivity having 'increased by an average of 7 per cent a year during the last 3 years' (p. 17).

Productivity in Soviet industry at the end of the '30's was commonly estimated at about 40 per cent of the U.S. level (or close to the British level). It is interesting to note that growth of industrial output in U.S.A. between 1899 and 1937 was derived in roughly equal proportions from increased employment and increased productivity, each of which about doubled over the period as a whole; but the increase in employment was confined to the period up to 1919, while most of the increase in productivity came between 1919 and 1937 (S. Fabricant, *Employment in Manufacturing, 1899–1939*, New York, 1942, pp. 6–9, 331).

It has been suggested that the pre-war Soviet index of productivity may have exaggerated the increase somewhat because it used gross value of output as weights, thus giving greater weight to industries concerned with more highly fabricated products (or end-stages of production). Since 1943, however, another index has apparently been used in which the weighting of various industries has been according to the number of workers employed (W. Galenson, *loc. cit.*, pp. 497–8).

cent.[1] Meanwhile the total labour-force had grown by rather less than a third—in the last few years of the Plan by nearly 2 million a year, or by about 4 per cent.[2] Malenkov, speaking of 1951 compared with 1940, claims that increased productivity accounted for two-thirds or more of the rise of industrial output.[3]

An annual increase of 4 per cent in those employed at a wage or salary is more than twice the natural rate of growth of the population (which according to pre-war census data was under 2 per cent per annum). To the extent of a half to two-thirds, accordingly, the increased labour-force for industry, transport, construction, etc., has come, and apparently continues to come, from transfer of farm population to the towns.[4] The question arises as to whether transfers of similar magnitude can be expected in the coming decade or decades, and whether or not this factor in industrial growth can be relied on to continue. In the past the rapid increase in the industrial population has been met from the pre-existing 'rural overpopulation' (conservatively estimated to have amounted on the eve of the First Five-Year Plan to between 8 and 9 million);[5] and, as this came to be absorbed, the increase was met by the labour-saving effects of mechanisation in agriculture, creating a reserve of labour on collective farms which could be drawn into industrial employment without any adverse effect on agricultural output. Can the creation of this reserve be expected in the future to match the growing requirements of industry, transport, and construction and other urban employments for manpower?

[1] Regarding the economists' distinction between 'widening' and 'deepening', it is of interest to note that the Fourth Five-Year Plan spoke of an increase in 'the amount of capital equipment per worker by approximately 50 per cent' between 1940 and 1950.

[2] The increase of employment in the national economy as a whole in 1951 was 1.6 million (L. Volodarsky in *Planovoye Khozyaistvo*, 1952, No. 1, p. 31).

[3] *Loc. cit.*, p. 61. He spoke of the rise between 1940 and 1951 as being 50 per cent. It is to be noted that he was speaking here of industry proper. Figures for employment in industry alone are not available; but it seems probable that the proportional increase here was less than for employment as a whole. That some of the increase in the latter came from an unplanned increase in the labour-force in building and construction is suggested by the fact that productivity in building and construction rose by only 23 per cent (i.e. 1950 over 1940) instead of 40 per cent as planned.

[4] According to Mr. Lorimer's estimate, the farm population of the U.S.S.R. decreased by 15-20 per cent between 1928 and 1940, while the urban population doubled. The decline in the farm population in relation to arable area was as large as 30 per cent or more (Frank Lorimer, *The Population of the Soviet Union*, League of Nations, Geneva, 1946, p. 110).

[5] Strumilin's estimate: see the present writer's *Soviet Economic Development since 1917*, p. 189.

This is a question to which no more than a very tentative answer is possible. If, however, we can take as an approximate index of mechanisation the number of tractors in proportion to arable area, it would look as though there still remains plenty of room for extension. Despite the rapid strides made in mechanisation over the past two decades, the fact remains that with 18 per cent of the world's arable area the U.S.S.R. (with a tractor park of just over half a million) has only 9 per cent of the world's tractors. Accordingly, the ratio of tractors to hectares of arable area in U.S.S.R. remained (in 1951) at 1 : 400, compared with a ratio of 1 : 171 as the average for Europe as a whole (excluding the U.S.S.R.) and 1 : 53 for North America.[1] Even when allowance has been made for the considerably higher degree of tractor-utilisation in the U.S.S.R. than in other countries (owing to their concentration in Machine Tractor Stations), there does not seem to be much sign of an early limit being reached to labour-saving improvement in agriculture. It is possible, however, that some slackening in the proportional (as distinct from the absolute) growth of the industrial labour-force may have to be allowed for inside the present decade.

3 So far we have been talking mainly of comparative trends; but trends have an interest largely in relation to comparative levels. If we were to project the rate of growth of which we have been speaking into the future, what kind of picture should we get of the 'catching-up and overtaking in economic and technical levels' of western countries? Already by the end of 1951 the U.S.S.R. was producing (to quote Mr. Beria) 'about as much steel as Great Britain, France, Belgium and Sweden combined', and more electricity than Great Britain and France combined.[2] If we were to assume that the growth-rate of our metal-fuel-power group at 15 per cent per annum would continue for the next two or three quinquennia

[1] *The European Tractor Industry in the Setting of the World Market*, United Nations, E.C.E., Geneva, February 1952, pp. 3-4 and Tables 1 and 48. It should be noticed, however, that the new Plan hopes to achieve the mechanisation of ploughing and sowing of grain, industrial and fodder crops by 1955 to the extent of 90–95 per cent, and of harvesting of grain to the extent of 80–90 per cent, of beet to the extent of 90–95 per cent and of cotton to the extent of 60–67 per cent. ('Directive for the 5th Plan', Part II, Section 9; *Planovoye Khozyaistvo*, 1952, No. 4, pp. 15–16.)

[2] L. P. Beria's Report to a celebration-session of the Moscow Soviet on November 6th, 1951, in *Planovoye Khozyaistvo*, 1951, No. 6, p. 5. The annual increase in recent years of steel was mentioned as 'about 4 million tons', of coal an average of 24 million tons, of oil 4½ million tons, and electricity 'more than 13 milliard kilowatt-hours'.

(a not unreasonable assumption in the absence of raw material shortages, of which there is no immediate sign), at what dates would Soviet production of these things surpass that of Western Europe and of U.S.A.?

The picture we obtain from such extrapolation is that the U.S.A. 1948-outputs would be comfortably surpassed in everything but oil by 1960, and the 1949-outputs of Western Europe (defined so as to include Sweden, Norway, Denmark, Austria, Italy, Spain, Western Germany, as well as U.K., France and Benelux) would be surpassed by about 1956. If we make what may well be rather optimistic assumptions about American and Western European rates of growth, such as have been current in recent years, we reach the conclusion that Soviet output of this metal-fuel-power group will surpass that of Western Europe thus projected during the second half of the 'fifties, and that of U.S.A. thus projected during the first half of the 'sixties. This is to speak in terms of *absolute* output: if we speak of output *per capita* of population, then equality would be reached a year or two earlier with Western Europe *per capita* (since the population of U.S.S.R. is smaller than that of Western Europe, as defined, by nearly a quarter), and a few years later with U.S.A. (since the population of U.S.S.R. is larger than that of U.S.A. by approximately a third).[1] It must be noted, however, that the rates of growth here assumed for U.S.S.R. are much higher than (about double) those implied in the oft-quoted statement of Stalin in February 1946, concerning possible long-term targets: these implied that by the first half of the 'sixties Soviet steel output would have surpassed the *1929* U.S.A. level.

Comparative consumption, both absolute and *per capita*, would tend to reach equality more slowly than this, to the extent that investment-priority continued to be given to the capital goods industries and the output of consumption goods continued to grow more slowly than the average. Moreover, if we speak of the standard of life, this is a matter of agricultural production and its increase (especially the increase of higher-quality foodstuffs), of house-building and communal facilities and services as well as of industrial consumers' goods. In this connection the recent statement of Stalin in his pre-Congress communication is significant, in which he asserts that one of three 'main preliminary conditions' for the

[1] For these calculations I am indebted to a hitherto unpublished paper by Mr. Walter H. Pawley on 'Industrial Development in Russia'. For future production trends in U.S.A. and W. Europe Mr. Pawley bases himself on estimates made in 1948 by the U.S. President's Council of Economic Advisers and of the Twentieth Century Fund concerning trends in national income and gross national product in U.S.A., and on the *Economic Survey of Europe for 1949* of the Research Division of the E.C.E. regarding potential increase in industrial production in W. Europe.

transition from socialism to communism is 'a continuous expansion of all social production, with a relatively higher rate of expansion of the production of means of production'.[1] At the same time he emphasises that 'the basic law of socialism' is 'the maximum satisfaction of the constantly rising material and cultural requirements of the whole of society'.[2] The future seems likely, accordingly, to see (given the maintenance of peace) a narrowing of the disparity between the growth-rates of the two sectors or departments of industry and an approximation of the growth of consumers' goods to the average rate (as is evident in the new Five-Year Plan). Moreover, at some stage in the maturing of this transition there will presumably be a shift in the growth-rates of the two departments in favour of consumers' goods production; the output of steel and engineering, instead of being ploughed back to further their own expansion, being increasingly directed to expanding the equipment of the consumers' goods industries. This was, indeed, the original intention of the Second Plan, as we have seen, although in this respect fulfilment did not coincide with intention (due to those 'major corrections' introduced into the Plan owing to the 'international situation' of which Mr. Molotov spoke in his report on the Third Five-Year Plan).[3]

Evidently there are three phases which have to be distinguished in a process of economic development of the Soviet type. In distinguishing them we have to start from the premise that investment in the two main departments of industry has this significant difference. A given amount of investment in the industries making consumers' goods (Group B industries, equivalent to Marx's Department II) enlarges the productive capacity of such industry, and hence the level of annual consumption, by an equivalent amount. In this sense its effect on the level of consumption is a once-for-all effect. But investment in industries making capital goods (Group A industries, roughly equivalent[4] to Marx's Department I), in augmenting capacity for turning out capital equipment, raises not merely the potential level but the potential *increase* in the consumption-level each year in the future (since that increase is dependent on the output of new

[1] *Economic Problems of Socialism in the U.S.S.R.* (Moscow, 1952), p. 74.

[2] *Ibid.*, p. 45. Cf. also Mikoyan's assertion in his Congress speech of October 9th: 'The needs and interests of the Soviet consumer should become law for industry.'

[3] V. Molotov, *The Third Five-Year Plan for the National-Economic Development of the U.S.S.R.* (Moscow, 1939), p. 11. The following annual rates of increase for 1933–7 were set in the original Plan: industry as a whole 16·5 per cent, means of production 14·5, articles of consumption 18·5 per cent. (*Second Five-Year Plan*, Moscow, 1936, p. 121.)

[4] Marx's Dept. I also included the production of raw materials for all industries.

productive equipment for the industries making consumers' goods). Its effect in raising (eventually) the level of consumption is, therefore, a *continuing* effect; and this kind of investment, expressed in terms of economic growth, has to be treated as a dynamic factor of a higher power.

It can also be shown to follow from what has just been said that the general growth-rate of output as a whole (Group A plus Group B) will tend, *ceteris paribus*, to be an increasing, a constant or a decreasing one, according to the proportions in which new investment is distributed between the two departments of industry;[1] and as the proportionate share of consumers' goods industries in new investment rises above a certain critical level the general growth-rate of output as a whole will tend to fall.

This distinction between investment in the two departments of industry can be said to be the essential *rationale* of the investment-priority in favour of heavy industry which has been the keynote of Soviet policy hitherto, and which looks like continuing to be so over the coming decade, if in modified form. Every enlargement of the output-capacity of steel or power or machine-making is, therefore, creating the possibility of a rapid rise in the growth-rate of consumers' goods industries at some future date, and the high growth-rates of heavy industry in past Plans can be said to have laid the basis for an unprecedented buoyancy in the growth-rate of consumers' goods industries in future Plans—for this growth-rate to rise considerably above the quinquennial doubling of which we have been speaking. This second phase of the industrialisation process, when consumers' goods industries take the lead, may be regarded as constituting the objective basis of the much-discussed 'transition to communism'. Yet in the degree that this buoyancy reveals itself and is accompanied by a reduced share of investment for the capital goods industries, this rapid rise in the level of consumption must presage a slackening of the growth-rate of consumption at some subsequent date—this for the simple reason that the *absolute* increase of productive capacity in consumers' goods industries is set, in the limit, by the size of the industries producing capital goods, and when the latter are no longer growing (or are growing at a relatively low rate) the constant absolute increase must represent a diminishing *proportional* increase. But this third phase of development is,

[1] Given a constant ratio of capital to net output and of net output to investment, the growth-rate will tend to maintain itself at a constant rate if new investment is distributed between the two departments in the same proportions as the existing stock of capital equipment in the two departments; but it will tend to rise over time if a larger proportion of investment than this is directed to Group A or Department I, and conversely if a larger proportion is directed to Group B or Department II.

of course, one which still lies a good distance ahead. What one could reasonably expect in the more immediate future is some such buoyancy-phase as that of which we have spoken, with the growth-rate of consumption tracing a steeply-rising curve, in the degree to which the investment-priority hitherto assigned to capital goods industries is relaxed in favour of Group B industries. If this is taken into account, the 'catching up and overtaking' of Western standards of life may be much nearer (given peace) than is commonly supposed.

4 The new (Fifth) Five-Year Plan for 1951–5 is characterised by two main features: (a) a slower general rate of growth than in previous quinquennial plans, (b) a narrowing of the divergence between the rates of growth of the two main departments of industry. Industrial production as a whole is to increase at an annual rate of 12 per cent; the output of Group A industries, producing means of production, is to increase at an annual rate of 13 per cent, and that of Group B industries, producing consumers' goods, at an annual rate of 11 per cent. The metal-fuel-power group which we have used above as an indicator is to expand at the same rate as production in general—namely at 12 per cent, which represents a doubling of output about every seven years instead of the quinquennial doubling of which we were speaking in §2, and is slightly below even the target set for this group in the Third Plan. National income over the quinquennium is planned to grow by 'not less than 60 per cent'.[1]

There are several possible explanations of this somewhat slackened growth-rate of industry about which it may be of interest to say a few words.

In introducing the Plan at the XIXth Party Congress on October 8th, 1952, the chairman of Gosplan (M. Z. Saburov) explained the 'somewhat lower rate of increase in industrial output during the Fifth Five-Year Plan . . . by the fact that we have finished rehabilitating industry—the rapid increase in output having been due to the putting into operation of restored plants—and, on the other hand, to the fact that we must secure a further considerable improvement in quality and increase the variety of output in the course of the new Five-Year Plan'. What makes one hesitate to accept this as the whole story is that the first half of this explanation does not explain the difference from the pre-war growth-rate (being relevant only to comparison with the post-war quinquennium); and as regards the second half, with its emphasis on the effect of raising quality,

[1] Directives for the Fifth Plan, Part I, Sections 1, 2; Part IV, Section 1; in *Planovoye Khozyaistvo*, 1952, No. 4, pp. 4–5, 20.

while this might affect figures of quantity-increase, one would not expect it necessarily to affect total *value*-figures (in so far as higher qualities were higher-valued). However, probably not all quality-improvements find a value-expression; while increased variety in production is very likely to be purchased at the expense of some reduction in the output-rate, in so far as it reduces the weight of mass-produced standard lines in the total. This may well account, therefore, for some slackening of the growth-rate of output in consumer goods industries and in engineering; but it would seem much less likely to be a factor in the case of metal-fuel-power.

Secondly, the difference from previous Plans might be held to be purely 'statistical': the result of abandoning (since 1950) calculation in the old '1926-7 constant prices' and transferring to a new system of constant prices based on current wholesale prices.[1] In terms of present-day prices most heavy industry products will evidently have a much smaller weight than they did in terms of '1926-7 prices', and this would tend to reduce the weight attaching to the relatively high rates of increase of these products in composing the average. This, however, affords a much less convincing explanation when the growth-rates of heavy and light industry are fairly close together, as they are in the new Plan, than it would if these growth-rates showed a wide disparity and the average had moved markedly nearer to the lower of the two than formerly. Moreover, it does not explain the smaller rate of increase of our metal-fuel-power group, which is in *quantity* terms, not values, and remains to be explained apart from any change in the basis of valuation. At first sight it is tempting to explain the matter in terms of a lower weight attaching to certain engineering products *within* the capital goods group—say, machine-tools and electrical equipment and vehicles with abnormally high rates of growth. A lower weight for such products would lower the rate of increase for this group as a whole and both move it nearer to the average and lower the overall average. Few, however, of the individual products in this group for which details are separately given show rates of growth

---

[1] For the present quinquennium all output is to be calculated in terms of wholesale (*optovie*) prices (*sans* turnover tax) prevailing on January 1st, 1952; new products of subsequent years and 'that part of production which is not reckoned in natural units' being reduced to the basis of January 1st, 1952, by an index of the (1952-weighted) average of price-changes of the remaining output of the enterprise or industry in question. Reduction to the same basis will be retrospectively made for the output each month of 1950 and 1951 (all output that is reckoned in natural units being valued at prices of January 1st, 1952, and the remainder reduced to this price-level by an index of average price-change of the former type of output for the enterprise or industry in question). See *Planovoye Khozyaistvo*, 1952, No. 1, pp. 77–9.

much above the average; the exceptions being hydro-turbines, oil equipment and chemical equipment, large metal-cutting lathes, steam boilers shipbuilding, heavy forging and punching machines and 'control instruments and automatic and remote-control instruments'. On the other hand the increase for motors and tractors is no more than 20 per cent. Among non-ferrous metals lead, zinc and aluminium are assigned increases of 150 to 170 per cent, while the increases for copper and tin are not much above the average and nickel below it. The increase mentioned for 'the engineering and metal-processing industries' as a whole is approximately 100 per cent, or 15 per cent per annum. Such a statistical factor may possibly contribute some part of the explanation, but it hardly seems capable of explaining the whole or even the major part of it.

Thirdly, the suggestion might be made that the slackened rate of increase is due to a slackened rate of investment as a whole. The official statement that investment under the new Plan is nearly double that in the previous quinquennium[1] does not lend plausibility to this suggestion. And when we inquire as to what the motive for such a slackening could be, doubt about such an explanation increases; for it is a fallacy to suppose that a fall in investment must *ipso facto* involve a rise in consumption—in any fairly short period of time it is unlikely to do so, unless there is some bottleneck-factor (e.g. some scarce material or skilled labour) that is shared by both of the main departments of industry and can be transferred from one department of industry to the other if the demand for capital goods or constructional activity slackens. Otherwise, the output of consumers' goods will be dependent upon the productive forces and resources specialised to them, in particular upon the capacity of plant and equipment in these industries, which may take several years to expand; and a fall in the rate of investment may have no other immediate effect than to lay idle some productive capacity in the capital goods industries. A *shift* of investment from heavy to light industry (as we have seen in the previous section) will tend to retard the general growth-rate. But it cannot reduce this general growth-rate until the shift has gone far enough to raise the rate of increase of consumers' goods *above* that of capital goods;[2] and since

---

[1] Directives for the Fifth Plan, Part I, Section 3, and Conclusion (a); *Planovoye Khozyaistvo*, 1952, No. 4, pp. 5, 23.

[2] In so far as this occurs, then of course investment as a proportion of total production must fall (and in *this* sense—as a proportion of a growing total income—the rate of investment can be said to have fallen). But then both this *and* the declining growth-rate are joint-effects of the shift in investment between the two Departments, and it would be misleading to speak of one of two effects of a common cause as though it were the cause of the other.

the shift has not yet, apparently, gone so far as this, it cannot be a factor in explaining the growth-rate of the present quinquennium.

There remain, however, two further possibilities regarding investment. There is some reason to expect that, as the level of technique rises, the ratio of capital to net output will rise, measured in physical terms (if that can be given a precise meaning, e.g. in terms of the quantity of steel embodied in plant and equipment of given output-capacity). Available evidence on this point is too slender to make any dogmatic statement possible.[1] But such a tendency seems likely to operate at least in some sectors of industry. If this be the case, then a slackened growth-rate will be the probable concomitant, *ceteris paribus*, of progress from lower to higher levels of technique; since a capital goods industry of given size (measured, e.g. by the amount of machinery and equipment that it produces) will be capable now of begetting only a smaller increment of output in industry in general than previously. As regards technical change, it is clear that Soviet industry has undergone an important qualitative change over the past fifteen years, and especially since the war.

The other possibility is that, although investment has not fallen, more of it may go in directions which do not result in a rise of output in any simple or direct way, at any rate within the quinquennium. One form this may take is investment in armament industries (e.g. aircraft factories or atom-piles), in response to the high level of American armament expenditures of recent years;[2] the object of this investment probably being more to bring into being productive capacity capable of rapid mobilisation in an emergency than to augment current output. Railway and canal building would also come into this category as regards early effects ('the five years are to see the opening . . . of about 150 per cent more new railways than during the period of the Fourth Plan'[3]); as would also some of the long-term electrification projects like the Kama, Irtysh

---

[1] Cf. on this point *Industrialization and Foreign Trade* (League of Nations, 1945), pp. 49–50.

[2] Those who for propaganda reasons have been emphasising rearmament as a major factor in Soviet economy should reflect upon the contrast between present trends in metal-fuel-power and the virtual halting of growth (especially in steel) from 1938 to 1940, and between tractor production in recent years and its abrupt fall from the 1936-peak to the very low 1940 level. If rearmament were occurring on anything like the post-Munich scale, the slackening of the growth-rate in other industries would be considerably greater than the fall that is in question.

[3] M. Z. Saburov, speech of October 8th, 1952 (reprinted as *Doklad o Direktivakh XIX Siezda Partii po Piatomu Planu*, Moscow, 1952, pp. 29–30), and Directives for the Plan, Part III, Section 3(b), in *Plan. Khoz.*, 1952, No. 4, p. 18.

and Angara river schemes, while the Kuibyshev power station on the Volga, of two million kilowatt capacity, to be connected with Moscow by a 400,000-volt transmission line, will begin to function in the last year of the Plan but not before. It is a special feature of the present quinquennium that ambitious constructional projects of this kind, which in earlier Plans failed to qualify for inclusion as being too costly or too long-term and slow-yielding or both, are now promoted on to the agenda. The number of constructional schemes directed towards improving agricultural production rather than industry is also a feature of these years ('capital investments in irrigation and melioration increasing approximately fourfold'[1]). There is, indeed, explicit mention in the Directives for the Plan, in Part I, Section 3 (relating to investment) of creating 'reserves in building metallurgical enterprises, power stations, oil refineries, and coal mines to ensure the necessary development of these branches of industry in subsequent years'.[2] Finally, there is house-building, which is, apparently, absorbing an even larger slice of investment than it did in the post-war years of reconstruction (capital investment in house-building by the State being doubled as compared with the preceding quinquennium—which itself witnessed an impressive volume of housebuilding;[3] and the output of building materials such as bricks and slates being increased by about twice the average increase for industry in general and cement by rather less than twice the average increase).

In view of what has been said, many readers may feel it wiser to suspend

[1] *Plan Khoz.*, 1952, No. 4, p. 17.   [2] *Ibid.*, p. 5.

[3] Malenkov mentions 'over 3,800,000 houses in rural areas' and '155 million square metres of floor space' in urban building as the achievement of 'the post-war years' (*op. cit.*, p. 94). He is presumably speaking of the period up to, and including, 1952, since the figures are higher than those given in the official report on the Results of the Fourth Plan, which were 2,700,000 rural houses and more than 100 million square metres of floor space built by 'State enterprises, institutions and local Soviets, and also by the population of towns and workers' settlements with the aid of State credits' (*Plan. Khoz.*, 1951, No. 2, p. 13). This figure of urban floor-space during the Fourth Plan is roughly equivalent to 2·5 million small flat-dwellings of 2 rooms *plus* kitchen and bathroom (or some 1½ million 3-room flats as mentioned by Professor Madge in the last issue of *Soviet Studies*, p. 231). It is not clear whether the doubling of investment under the new Plan represents a doubling in real, or only in money, terms; at any rate (since much of it may go in expansion and new equipment) it does not necessarily imply a doubling of actual completed building. The target for rural house building has not been stated: that for urban building by the State is given in the Plan as 105 million square metres (*Plan. Khoz.*, 1952, No. 4, p. 21); and if we assume that other building is the same proportion of the whole as previously, this would make total urban building greater by some 20 per cent than in the previous quinquennium (when it was above the Plan).

judgment as to the reasons for the somewhat lower rate of growth in the new Plan. If some guess is to be hazarded, the writer can only conclude by suggesting that in his own tentative opinion the last two possibilities mentioned, in combination with the first (the emphasis on quality and variety mentioned by Mr. Saburov), seem to have most to recommend them.*

[*The concluding paragraphs of this article, dealing in greater detail with several aspects of the new Plan, have been omitted.]

VII

A NOTE ON THE SO-CALLED DEGREE OF CAPITAL-INTENSITY OF INVESTMENT IN UNDER-DEVELOPED COUNTRIES[1] [1954]

This article is reproduced from *Économie Appliquée* (Institut de Science Économique Appliquée, Paris), 1954, No. 3, by kind permission of the editor of that journal.

1 THE DEFECTS OF TREATING 'CAPITAL' as a factor of production (on a par with land and labour) are well-known. It has encouraged a formalism in the treatment of distribution as a special case of the general theory of price-equilibrium which has obscured the distinction between technical instruments of production and titles or property-rights in them, and has consequently left no room for crucial characteristics of income-distribution (e.g. Marx's relation of exploitation or Professor Perroux's relation of dominance). It has also been associated in the past with considerable confusion between the stock of capital in existence and the rate of flow of new investment in additions to that stock (especially in connection with the notion of marginal productivity; the marginal productivity of a stock of capital being commonly confused until quite recently with what has now come to be called the marginal efficiency of investment, and the 'equilibrium-return' on capital erroneously identified with the former even when positive net investment was assumed). Moreover, there has always been the more fundamental difficulty that, if capital is regarded as concrete instruments of production, heterogeneity is an essential characteristic even more than in the case of land; whereas if capital is regarded as paper titles to ownership it cannot be independently valued,

[1] The writer is indebted to Professor Paul Baran and Mr. H. G. Johnson for comments and suggestions made on an early draft of this article, and to Mr. Johnson in particular for drawing the writer's attention to the importance of the 'compounding effect' where production-periods differ.

except in terms of its *yield* (capitalised at some assumed rate of interest). In other words, it is not something which can be measured in units of itself, and any measurement of it in money-values inevitably involves circularity so far as an explanation of the return or yield on capital is concerned.[1] The only unit in which it can be measured, apart from money, is labour; and there have been those who have wondered why, if this be the case, capital should not be treated simply as a particular form of application of labour (Ricardo's labour employed for a certain duration of time, or Marx's 'stored-up labour', or Wicksell's 'saved-up labour and land'), rather than as a distinct factor of production in its own right.

It is not the intention of this Note to explore methodological questions such as these; they have been touched on here merely as issues in the background which are related, indirectly at least, to the particular point about the principles governing investment-policy with which this Note is concerned. In mentioning them I do not wish to imply that there is any *necessary* connection between any of these general notions about capital and the particular corollaries to which I am about to refer; but that there is some *de facto* connection between them seems to be evident enough. The effect of a theoretical model's shape in predisposing one to a certain emphasis (by throwing some factors into bold relief and others into obscurity) is often as important as the logical connection between premises and conclusions.

The special question with which I wish to deal is of central importance for the economic policies of under-developed countries at the present time. Discussion of such policies among economists has been governed by a dogma, which has come to have the status of a first principle. This usually appears in some such form as this: that, since a scarcity of capital relatively to labour is a usual characteristic of under-developed countries, capital investment needs there to take the form of projects of 'low capital-intensity' (or relatively labour-using and capital-saving technical methods).[2]

[1] This is what Wicksell referred to as a 'theoretical anomaly', only resolvable in his opinion by reducing all capital goods into labour and land (cf. *Lectures on Political Economy*, London, 1934, Vol. I, pp. 149-50). But he never explained how the land and labour to which it was reduced could be expressed in a common unit (Petty's ancient problem of finding 'a par between labour and land').

[2] E.g.: 'The densely populated countries in process of development do not need tools and machines of the same degree of capital intensity as those used in the advanced economies where labour is relatively scarce. Some of the equipment and hence also the techniques of production imported from more developed countries are likely to be highly capital-intensive and therefore not well adapted to countries where capital is scarce and labour abundant.' (R. Nurkse, *Problems of Capital Formation in Underdeveloped Countries*, p. 45.)

In other words, investment in agriculture[1] and light industry (or even in the development of handicrafts) is to be preferred to investment in heavy industry; relatively primitive technical methods should be preferred initially to highly mechanised forms of production which use relatively much fixed capital and relatively little labour. Anything else is regarded as irrational and uneconomic. Sometimes one meets the principle expressed in a different way: that undeveloped countries are apt to be ones with a large labour-surplus (actual unemployed or what has come to be called in Mrs. Joan Robinson's phrase 'disguised unemployment'); and accordingly investment in labour-using, and not in labour-saving, forms will make the biggest contribution to the reduction of unemployment. On this has been erected something of a theory of stages through which an economy in the course of its development should pass, each stage being dependent upon a particular ratio of capital to labour as factors of production; and in discussions of the so-called 'Soviet way of industrialisation', the latter's emphasis on the growth of heavy industry is commonly dismissed as an uneconomic 'skipping of stages' by contrast with the more cautious progress through successive stages traditionally advocated by economists in the West.

The first form in which the above principle is stated rests on the assumption of a given *stock* of capital equipment in existence as the country's heritage from the past. Hence, assuming potential variation of technical forms, and assuming that the supplies of labour and land are also given, there will be one technical form (a relatively capital-saving and labour-using one if capital is scarce relatively to labour) that will secure the full employment of all the factors. This has usually been taken to imply that new investment should take the same (or a closely similar) form to that appropriate to the existing capital stock; although it is not obvious why this should be so when new investment is concerned with *changing* the size of the existing stock of capital. (Clearly, the traditional implication is only plausible if the rate of investment is assumed to be very small compared with the existing capital stock, so that the ratio of the latter to other factors is much the same at time t_2 as it was at time t_1). If, however, labour is so plentiful as to cause much of it to be unemployed, this would appear to be a situation in which a rapid increase in the existing stock of capital (i.e. an unusually high rate of investment) is called for.

[1] Some agricultural investments are, of course, of a highly capital-intensive kind (e.g. some of the irrigation, afforestation and 'nature-transforming' projects in U.S.S.R.). The reference here is to the equipping of agriculture with relatively inexpensive instruments, manures, well-sinking facilities, buildings, etc.

The second version of the principle seems to rest implicitly on the same assumption as the first and/or the assumption that the rate of new investment is given.

My main intention here is not to discuss how far such arguments are relevant to the actual conditions of under-developed countries, but rather to make explicit the assumptions upon which the traditional dogma is based and to show that a change in the assumptions can make a radical difference to the conclusion. It does not follow from what I am going to say that the traditional principle will have no application to particular cases; but it does follow, I think, that this principle has much less generality than it is usually assumed to have.

Let us take a highly simplified case, in which investment is treated as consisting essentially in the application of labour to a particular form of production, namely the manufacture of capital goods, and the only limit on the amount of investment which can be undertaken consists of the surplus of consumer goods over some given standard of needs which the consumer goods industries can produce. For simplicity we shall follow the Ricardian tradition of treating essential consumer goods (or subsistence) as a homogeneous commodity, corn, and shall refer to the industry producing it as agriculture. It will follow that the capital goods in this simplified economy will consist of things which serve the needs of agriculture directly or indirectly, such as tractors, fertilisers, fuel and power: again for simplicity we shall refer to them as a homogeneous product, tractors. (The complication of introducing capital goods which serve the needs of capital goods production will be considered later on.)

If the level of wages (measured in corn) is written as w, the amount of labour employed in producing corn as L_c and the amount of corn produced per worker (in agriculture) in a given period as P_c, then it will follow that the practicable amount of investment will be a function of w, L_c and P_c, such that $I = (P_c - w)L_c$. In other words, investment will equal the total corn-surplus in agriculture. Measured in terms of the labour employed in the tractor industry (or L_i) investment will $= \dfrac{(P_c - w) L_c}{w}$

We can if we like regard L_c as governed at any time by the stock of tractors in agriculture (e.g. to every tractor a tractor-driver, and that is all). Hence L_c will grow from year to year at a rate governed by L_i and by P_i (the productivity of labour in the tractor industry measured in tractor-units). The increase in total corn-output will $= L_i \times P_i \times P_c$; but, given L_i, a given corn-output will involve a larger total employment the lower is P_c relative to P_i, and *vice versa*.

If in the production of tractors there are two alternative types of tractor which can be manufactured, one costing twice as much labour (in man-hours) to produce (hence halving P_i) but promising an increase of P_c when used in agriculture of more than twice, compared with its rival, there would seem to be no doubt at all which alternative to choose. The form of investment which yields the larger P_c, since it raises P_c by more than it lowers P_i, will yield the larger corn-output (governed by P_cP_i given L_i) after an interval of time equal to the production-period of the tractor-type in question (ignoring for the moment possible differences in the production-periods of alternative types). Since this will also yield the larger corn-surplus ($= (P_c - w) L_c$), it will from thenceforth[1] make possible a larger (and cumulative) expansion of investment, and hence will maximise both total output and total employment at an early date.

If the substitution of more costly capital goods with labour-saving effect for less costly and more labour-using ones, and a consequential rise in the ratio of L_i to L_c, is regarded as constituting an increase in capital-intensity, then we have apparently reached the conclusion that the more capital-intensive form of investment should be chosen, since this will permit the more rapid increase of the rate of investment in the near future. By dropping the assumption that the rate of investment is fixed (e.g. independently determined by some factor such as 'finance'), and assuming instead that this will vary with the surplus of corn produced, one has arrived at a quite opposite result to the traditional theorem. In common-sense terms what this amounts to is that a country with a surplus of labour, instead of having less capital-intensive forms of investment, will have a proportionately larger capital goods industry than will other countries.

Is there a flaw in this reasoning? Building models to yield the conclusion one wishes can be, of course, an all-too-easy game.

Does the flaw consist in the assumption that an increase in corn-productivity of the improved type of tractor is in greater proportion than the increase in its cost (in labour)? The answer is 'no', since forms of investment of higher capital-intensity which do not result in any increase in corn-production are not likely to come upon the agenda of a development plan—from a social point of view they would seem to have nothing to recommend them by comparison with projects of lower capital-intensity. And as we have seen, if they do not yield an increase in corn-

[1] To be quite accurate one should speak here of the production-period of tractors *plus* that of corn—if extra labour can only begin to be employed *after* the extra subsistence for it has been harvested.

productivity that is in greater proportion than their increased cost (i.e. an increase of $P_i P_c$) their introduction will not yield a larger corn-production than alternative investment-projects. Thus, unless they fulfil this condition, they are not likely to be seriously discussed as alternatives in any circumstances, either in an undeveloped or an advanced economy. True, even if this condition is not fulfilled, the corn-*surplus*, and hence the future growth of I, may nevertheless be greater as a result of the labour-saving (and hence w-saving) effect of the improved type of tractor.[1] Judged by the criterion we have adopted here—the effect on employment and output of the subsequent expansion of investment—a choice in favour of the improved type would even in this case be justified. We could, therefore, have adopted a more lenient condition[2] than we have done in our example, and our argument would still stand. But the form in which the argument was presented would have been rather more complicated.

Nor is our conclusion necessarily affected by our assumption that w is constant. We could substitute for this the assumption that w rises with an increase of P_c; and unless the increase of w, relatively to the changes in P_c and P_i, is above a certain critical magnitude, it will still follow that both the corn-surplus and I will increase with an increase of P_c. If, however, the rise of w reaches this critical magnitude, it will place a ceiling upon the degree of capital-intensity of investment. How then is this critical magnitude to be defined? We have seen that in comparing two forms of investment it was necessary to take account of the difference made to corn-production and the corn-surplus *both* by the difference of P_c in the two cases *and* by the difference in P_i. For the corn-surplus to increase (as a result of choosing one form in preference to the other) when w also increases, the rise of P_c must be sufficient to offset the *combined* effect on the corn-surplus of the fall in P_i and of the rise in w.[3] Nor is this all. If the rise of w applies also to the tractor industry, this rise will affect the amount of labour in the tractor industry which a given corn-surplus can maintain (i.e. it will deflate I measured in terms of labour). Accordingly,

---

[1] The analogy will be noticed here with Ricardo's well-known argument that machinery may increase the *net* product even though it decreases the *gross* product.

[2] The condition for the corn-surplus to be increased can be written as follows. If x is the proportional fall of P_i, and σ is the proportional share of the total corn-product which is surplus under the less capital-intensive method that forms the term of comparison (i.e., $\sigma = \dfrac{P_c - w}{P_c}$); then the proportional increase of P_c must exceed $\dfrac{x}{1-x} \times \sigma$.

[3] That is, the magnitude referred to in the previous footnote as the condition for the corn-surplus to be increased would need to be multiplied by the proportional rise of w.

for I measured in labour to increase (or δL_i to be positive), the corn-surplus itself must increase proportionately more than the increase in w. When the rise of P_c is no longer sufficient, relatively to the fall of P_i and rise of w, to fulfil this condition, an increase in the degree of capital-intensity w ll cease to be worth-while. The height of the ceiling will accordingly be dependent primarily on the wage-policy adopted; i.e. on the rate of growth of w relatively to the changes in P_c and P_i.[1]

Does the flaw consist, then, in our failing to take account of the existing stock of capital as a limiting factor on the amount of employment and output? In agriculture this has been explicitly allowed for in the condition that an increase of L_c is governed by the output of the tractor industry measured in tractors as units (irrespective of their type); this condition implying a certain 'technical coefficient' governing the joint employment of tractors and men. It is true that no such condition has been explicitly introduced for the tractor industry. However, the omission could be repaired without any damage to the essential argument by regarding any labour newly recruited into this industry as first having to spend a period of time in making machines with which to work before it could turn out tractors, and expressing this as a lengthening of the production-period of tractors (a change in the average production-period which would be a function of the *rate of increase* of L_i and would operate only over the period when I was rising). But is this assumption (it may be asked) at all a plausible one? Can we imagine the equipment of capital goods industries being enlarged without, not only more labour, but also the diversion of some existing capital equipment to its manufacture—in other words, in terms of our example, without some fall in the output of tractors (due to this diversion of manufacturing equipment), if only a temporary fall? I would not wish to deny that there is force in this objection. Yet even if we admit it, the implication is not, I think, damaging to our main conclusion: namely, that if the more capital-intensive type of investment is chosen, both corn-surplus and potential investment will be greater by the end of

[1] A crucial constant (as we have seen above) is σ, the share of the total corn-product that is surplus in the method with the lower P_c which is being used as the term of comparison. As P_c grows, and with it σ (if P_c grows faster than w), the qualifying ratio of the change in P_c to the change in P_i will increase, and the condition which higher capital-intensity has to fulfil in order to qualify by our criterion becomes equivalently more severe. This condition when w is rising can be expressed as follows. If x is the proportional fall of P_i, y the proportional rise of w, and σ is the share of the product which is corn-surplus in the case which is being used as the term of comparison, then the increase of P_c must exceed $\dfrac{x}{1-x} \times \sigma$ by $y + y(1+y)$.

a production-period. The retardation of tractor-output will apply, in our example, to the *second* production-period, when investment has been stepped-up as a result of the rise of corn-surplus consequent on the production of a new tractor-type in the first period.[1] But this retardation would not, save in rather special circumstances, represent a *fall* in the existing stock of tractors in agriculture (and consequently a subsequent fall in corn-output and surplus)—merely a slackening in the rate of increase in that stock. In other words, it would be a partial but not a complete offset to the rise of P_c, and the retardation would be a *once-for-all* not a continuing one, operating only so long as the new equipment for the tractor-industry was being made in order to permit the intake of new labour into this industry.

2   Mention of the period of production brings us, however, to a more difficult problem, and one which many will regard as the heart of the matter. Some, I think, will treat an increase in this period as a crucial element in any increase in capital-intensity. As soon as we introduce into our example the condition that the tractor-type with the higher P_c costs not only more labour to produce but also more time,[2] doubt is cast on our conclusion that corn-output will be maximised at the end of its (longer) period of production by the adoption of this type. For periods of time shorter than this it is clear that output may well be larger if the tractor with the lower P_c is adopted, since the latter can be finished more quickly and the supply of new tractors to agriculture take place at an earlier date. During the intervening years between the finishing-date of the simpler

[1] It is, of course, possible to think of this being anticipated, and equipment being diverted during the *first* period to the making of new equipment ready for the intake of more labour into the tractor-industry during the *second* period. In this case the output of tractors *would* be affected during the first period. But since the amount of such diversion would depend on how much I was expected to increase in the second period, it could not affect the comparison between the two tractor-types: whichever promised the larger increase of corn-surplus would involve the larger diversion. In the limiting case it could nullify the advantage of the method yielding the higher P_c; but it could not tilt the balance of advantage in favour of the alternative method.

[2] It is, of course, usually the case that the period of production can be shortened if more labour is employed per unit of time; and in this sense the period might seem to be arbitrary. But the flexibility is presumably in most cases (with possible exceptions in a few cases like road-making) limited, the shortening of the period being only possible by increasing the total expenditure of labour. In any short-period this is likely to be the case in view of the fixity of technical equipment. Hence it may not be unreasonable to assume that a certain period of time is associated with a given cost in labour in the existing circumstances of an industry.

and quicker-to-make type and the finishing-date of the more complex and slower-to-make type, corn-output and corn-surplus will be higher if investment takes the less capital-intensive form. Accordingly, we seem to be confronted by a choice to be depicted as something like this:

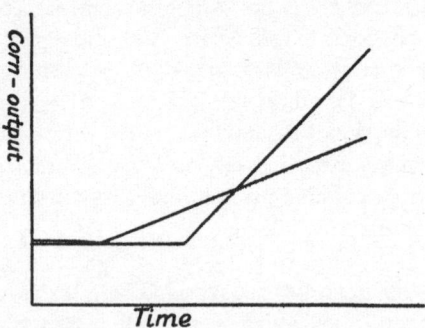

But this is not all. When the two alternatives differ in their production-periods as well as in their costs it no longer necessarily follows that the type with the higher P_c will show the larger corn-surplus even by the end of its (longer) production-period. In the case of the tractor-type with the shorter production-period, the chance of reinvesting an additional corn-surplus in a further expansion of L_i at an *earlier date* (and subsequently at more frequent intervals) introduces an important compounding-effect of the initial and earlier increase; and this compounding-effect may suffice to make total output greater even after the completion-date of the tractor-type with the higher P_c. The crucial question is whether there is any reason to expect the method with the higher P_c to result *eventually* in a higher level of output.

The answer depends on the size of the compounding-effect and on the degree of superiority in $P_i P_c$ of the more capital-intensive method. It will no longer follow in all cases that a superiority in $P_i P_c$ will make for the more rapid expansion of output and surplus and consequently of investment even in the long run; since the existence of the compounding-effect that we have just mentioned may give the method with the shorter production-period a countervailing advantage. But it will remain true that superiority in $P_i P_c$ will yield the more rapid expansion in those cases where the superiority in $P_i P_c$ is sufficiently great to outweigh this compounding-effect.

The importance of the compounding-effect can be measured by the extent to which a given increase of corn-surplus can produce a further increase of corn-surplus within each production-period (via the expanded investment in tractors which it occasions). This crucial magnitude can be seen, on reflection, to be equal to the following:

$$\frac{\frac{s}{w} \times P_i \times P_c \left(1 - \frac{w}{P_c}\right)}{s}$$

where s is the initial ncrement of surplus. It will be noted that the last term of the numerator is synonymous with the crucial proportion σ referred to above on page 143 footnote 2, and the footnote to page 144. It is also to be noted that this Expansion-Factor (as we may call it) is greater the *smaller* is w relatively to P_c. It can, therefore, be written more simply:

$$\frac{\frac{s}{w} \cdot P_i P_c \sigma}{s}$$

The larger is this Expansion-Factor, the larger will the superiority in P_c need to be for a method with a longer production-period to yield superior results to the method with a lower P_c but a quicker production-turnover. In other words, the increase in P_c resulting from the more capital-intensive method must be sufficient, not merely to offset the fall of P_i (and hence make $P_i P_c$ greater), but also by its labour-saving-in-agriculture effect to enhance the corn-surplus sufficiently to offset the advantage enjoyed by less time-consuming methods from an earlier (and more frequent) reinvestment of their (initially smaller) corn-surplus. When w is high relatively to P_c (and σ accordingly small as a proportion of corn-output) a relatively small growth of P_c will suffice to bring about a large increase in the Expansion-Factor (by occasioning a proportionately large rise of σ). But as the ratio of P_c to w rises (and with it σ), a larger growth of P_c will be required in order to raise the Expansion-Factor by a given amount.

Thus, just as we have seen that a *rise* in w will place a ceiling on the degree of capital-intensity of investment, so also will the existing *level* of w relatively to P_c. A relatively low level of w, since it enhances the magnitude of the 'compounding-effect', in which the advantage of shorter production-periods consists, will require a large superiority in P_c for the more capital-intensive method to qualify as economic (i.e. a large superiority in P_c compared to the greater length of its production-period); and methods which lack sufficient superiority in P_c to offset the compounding-effect of methods with smaller P_c but shorter production-periods will fail to qualify. For most values of the variables which seem likely to be met with in practice the modification introduced into the argument, if important, does not seem likely to be of major importance.[1]

Moreover, it is to be noted that, although in under-developed countries w is likely to be low, so also is productivity, and that accordingly there is no strong reason to suppose that the crucial proportion σ will be higher in under-developed than in developed countries (indeed, there may well be reason to expect the contrary).

If we exclude those cases where the rise of P_c is insufficient to offset the disadvantage of a longer production-period, the crucial issue is reducible to a choice between having more corn-output in earlier years and more corn-output (and its more rapid expansion) in later years. The choice will depend on the relative weight to be attached to additional income in the near future and in the more distant future. The traditional view treats the decision as being made by the instrument of an interest-rate expressive either of the relative 'scarcity' of capital or of a time-discount (the latter being due either to 'pure time-preference' or to the difference in marginal utility of present and of expected future income). An interest-charge for the time for which capital (in our example the wage-cost of the labour employed in making tractors) is advanced is included in the respective costs of the alternative investment projects, and choice between any pair of alternatives is made in favour of that which yields the highest ratio of net return to cost. It follows that the higher the interest-rate, the larger will be the number of capital-intensive projects to be ruled off the agenda as giving inferior results, and *vice versa*. In the actual practice of a capitalist economy uncertainty of the future is probably a much more potent factor in the decision than is the interest-factor; uncertainty generally operating in favour of the less capital-intensive and more cautious path of development. But that is not directly germane to the question we are considering.

According to our present model the traditional view could perhaps be expressed in terms of a postulated rate of change of w. Thus if either a constant rate of change over time or some relation between a rising w and a rising P_c were to be postulated (e.g. as being most calculated to maximise consumers' welfare through time), this would as we have seen set a ceiling to the capital-intensity of projects to be chosen at any one time—a ceiling which would be lower the lower the initial level of w

[1] It would appear that only where the ratio of consumption to net output is around one-half, or less than one-half, does this consideration begin to cause serious trouble, and then only if the difference of production-period in the cases compared is considerable, e.g. is more than 50 per cent.

relatively to P_c and the more rapidly in the immediate future w was postulated to rise with any rise in P_c. In terms of the diagram on page 146, a rising w could be represented as making the slope of the curve of rising corn-output less steep, and in the extreme case (where w absorbed the whole of any increase of output) flattening the curve out after its initial step-up to a higher level.

Are we, then, back after all at the point where we started: that in under-developed countries this ceiling will generally be so low as to rehabilitate the traditional corollary? I think not, since the upshot of our argument is that the choice between more or less capital-intensive forms of investment has nothing to do with existing factor-proportions, which are commonly asserted to govern such a choice. It depends, not on the existing ratio of available labour to capital (treated as a stock), but on precisely the same considerations as those which determine the choice between a high and a low rate of investment (or rate of increase in the existing stock of capital-goods)—namely the importance to be attached to raising consumption in the immediate future compared with the potential increase of consumption in the more distant future which a particular rate of investment and form of investment will make possible. In other words, the same grounds which would justify a high rate of investment (high, e.g., compared with *per capita* income) would justify also a high degree of capital intensity in the choice of investment-forms; and *vice versa*. I cannot see that there is any *a priori* reason to suppose that an undeveloped country should always choose a lower rate of investment than a more developed one—if anything the converse, since, although the lowness of existing consumption per head may put a high premium upon raising it in the near future, the effect upon productivity (and hence upon potential consumption in the more distant future) of a given increase in the (relatively small) stock of capital is likely also to be abnormally large.

There is one further qualification that should be introduced to the conclusions we drew from our simplified example of tractors and corn. We have said nothing about replacement of the existing stock of tractors in agriculture, and have talked as though capital equipment once brought into existence would last indefinitely if currently maintained. If, however, we assume that a certain proportion of this stock comes up for renewal each year, then the choice in favour of the more productive type of tractor will apply to this annual replacement as well as to *new* investment. Since the new type of tractor costs more labour to produce, it follows that a given annual rate of replacement (whether measured in labour or in productive power) will represent a smaller number of tractor-units than before (each tractor-unit being of higher productive-power). Since we have assumed that in agriculture the tractor-labour coefficient is unaltered, the result will be a fall in the employment afforded to labour in agriculture by the existing stock of capital equipment (including the part of it replaced). This will involve a net reduction in employment in agriculture if (but only if) replacement exceeds new investment. In this case the choice of the more capital-intensive method will mean an absolute fall in employment in agriculture to be offset against the rise in employment in the tractor-industry which (after an interval) it makes possible.

In conclusion one may ask whether anything has been gained by the mode of presentation adopted in this Note. Or does it in the end arrive at the same results as can be reached by using the more conventional approach? There can be no doubt, I think, that its emphasis and perspective are quite different. In the first place it focuses attention on the result to be achieved after an initial interval of time; while the conventional approach devotes more attention to what occurs in the immediate future. The former emphasis will be regarded as the more useful, the shorter the initial period and the smaller the weight to be attached to a rise of consumption in the early years. Secondly, it has the (to my mind very important) advantage of throwing into relief the cumulative influence of investment in more productive methods in making possible further investment (i.e. 'deepening' promoting 'widening')—of emphasising that one is dealing with the slope of *a curve of growth* and not just with a once-for-all rise. In our simplified example of tractors and corn we treated investment and employment as dependent on the supply of consumer goods (corn). There is some reason to regard this as characteristic of the situation in under-developed countries at an early stage of industrialisation. But the essentials of the analysis could be applied, *mutatis mutandis*, to a situation where the rate of investment was primarily dependent, not on the current supply of subsistence (or 'wage-goods'), but on the existing stock of fixed capital. In such a situation a similar multiplier-effect to that of which we have spoken attaches to any enlargement of the capital goods industries; an outstanding feature of investment devoted to expanding the productive capacity of the capital goods industry being its effect in enlarging the *rate of growth* of output at future dates. Investment which takes place in, say, the textile industry or food industry will expand the potential output of these industries by a given amount, and hence will raise the *level* of consumption by a given amount; whereas investment in the steel or engineering industry, in expanding the potential output of steel and machinery, will *ipso facto* expand the potential rate of expansion of other industries and hence the *rate of increase* of consumption.¹ The one form of investment has a once-for-all effect, the other a continuing effect on the level of income and consumption.* This crucial difference is obscured by theories which treat investment simply in terms of the foregoing of present consumption in return for a future increase in consumption: here investment is always treated as though it was direct investment in the consumption goods industries. Moreover, notions of the marginal productivity of capital or of investment (so far as I am aware) are always expressed in terms of a once-for-all effect on the income-stream, and do not include the specific multiplier-influence on future income-levels of investment in the capital goods industries, or in what Marx (who made so much of the distinction between the two departments of industry) called Department I.

Thirdly, the fact that our model enables us to treat wages (= consumption) as an independent variable, and wage-policy as playing a crucial rôle in setting a ceiling to the capital intensity of investment projects, seems to the present writer to have an important advantage if one is viewing development in the context of a planned economy. Under such circumstances the rate at which real wages are planned to rise over time is a policy-question for decision by the State; it is in these terms that questions of time-comparison will in practice arise; and it seems to be clear that for any plan or long-term perspective this will in fact play a crucial rôle.

3 Since the purpose of this Note has been to question the pretensions to generality of a current dogma—to show its dependence on certain static assumptions—the degree of realism of the simplified model here adopted has not been discussed: no more has been claimed for it than that it has at least an equal claim to realism as more conventional types of model. As we introduce qualifications from the complexities of the real world, the lines of our simplified drawing begin to get blurred and altered. Yet I cannot see that this modification is so great as to render the original

---

[1] A further (and completing) act of investment will of course be needed to bring to maturity this subsequent increase of consumption—investment in the actual building of, say, clothing factories with the steel which the new steel plants can now produce. But the primary half of the investment has already been done; and can be conceived as constituting a joint demand for a *series* of secondary and completing acts of investment in all subsequent years.

[*See above, pp. 130-1.]

sketch unrecognisable as a free-hand portrait. Of these qualifications I will mention only three most obvious ones.[1]

In the first place there is reason to suppose that it will be the *marketed* surplus of agriculture which plays the crucial rôle in under-developed countries in setting the limits to the possible rate of industrialisation, and that this marketed surplus does not rise automatically as a result of an increase in productivity. With an individualist peasant-economy peasants may take advantage of a rise of P_c to consume more themselves or they may reduce the amount of their own labour. The former possibility can be treated, in terms of our example, as a rise in w. Unless the ratio of increase of w to increase of P_c is equal to or above the critical magnitude mentioned above, it will not upset our main conclusion—though it will mean that to this extent the rise of w can no longer be regarded as a policy-matter, but has to be regarded as an objective factor in the situation, to be estimated and treated as part of the data of the problem. The second possible reaction—a reduction of L_c for every increase in P_c—may be more serious, since if it is sufficiently large to cause $P_c L_c$ to *fall* when P_c increases (and to fall in such a way as to involve no reduction in the total of corn consumed by the agricultural population), then the choice of the more productive form of investment will be positively harmful. But so in this case would any type of improvement designed to raise agricultural productivity.

The second qualification is that in practice it may well be neither labour in general nor the fund of subsistence goods available for its support that is the limiting factor on the rate of investment, but the supply of *trained* labour capable of handling modern machinery. The precise significance of introducing this qualification is not at first sight easy to gauge. Its introduction into the analysis seems to have this rather curious effect. If the supply of trained labour is very restricted, this fact would seem to restore the assumption of a fixed rate of investment, and by making the investment-ceiling a low one to remove the chief advantage (according to our argument) of investing in the more productive methods. On the other hand, if we focus our attention upon factory industry and

[1] A further qualification is introduced by considering the *social* investment involved in industrial development, as has been pointed out to me by Professor Baran. Social investment (e.g. in housing and urban development), which the argument of this Note ignores, may in practice have a decisive influence in favour of labour-saving forms of investment. Such social investment will be a function of the number of workers employed in industry, and the additional cost of this may outweigh the saving in industrial investment of choosing less capital-intensive (but more labour-using) technique.

the technical methods of production appropriate thereto, it is labour that now becomes the scarce factor (since it is here *trained* labour that alone counts), and the main prop of the orthodox argument in favour of labour-intensive forms of investment (that labour is plentiful relatively to capital) is removed.

Undoubtedly the introduction of this qualification makes a good deal of difference to the *a priori* argument. Admittedly it introduces a different ceiling to investment (at any rate to investment in factory industry) from that which our argument has supposed, and a ceiling which in most undeveloped countries is probably a fairly low one. To this extent the cumulative effect of an increase of P_e in permitting a rise in investment in ensuing production-periods is diminished. If handicraft skills are widely diffused, whereas factory skill is confined to relatively few, this may well be a reason for giving a large place in the initial stages of a development plan to handicraft production and adapting the expansion of factory production to the maximum rate at which it is practicable to train-up new supplies of factory-skill. But unless the existing supply of the latter is exceptionally scarce and the possibilities of expanding it by training schemes are very narrow, I do not see that the introduction of this qualification suffices to restore the orthodox corollary. The very scarcity of factory-skill would, indeed, seem to imply that such investment as was made in factory industry should be in highly labour-saving forms of production there, parallel with a considerable expansion of handicraft.[1] Moreover, there is this important practical consideration: that the acquisition of factory skill is as much a matter of experience as of training, and that an essential condition for developing such skill is to develop industry itself and with it the number of those directly acquainted with modern technical processes.

Lastly there is the question of foreign trade. Hitherto we have been talking in terms of a closed economy. In actual practice most under-developed countries will rely to some extent, in the early stages at least, on importing capital goods from abroad. From one point of view this makes an initial expansion of the capital goods industries easier than in our example, in so far as the mechanical equipment for these industries could

---

[1] Factory-skill and handicraft skills being here treated theoretically as 'non-competing groups', and investments of quite different capital-intensity as appropriate to the factory and handicraft sectors. In terms of our simplified model, this is equivalent to saying that the simpler type of tractor should be supplied to agriculture, but at the same time in the tractor industry itself capital-intensive methods of production should be used.

be imported, whereas we were assuming that the equipment to make more tractors would have to be made by this industry's own labour before additional labour could be employed in tractor-production. On the other hand, if the possibilities of importing it are very restricted and the country in question is very deficient in equipment for the capital goods industries, this import-bottleneck may be the crucial factor in setting the ceiling to investment; and the fact that this is the crucial bottleneck will put a premium on production methods which are saving of technical equipment. This I believe is *the* case where the traditional corollary about labour-intensive forms of investment comes into its own—where expansion of the capital goods industry is retarded by the lack of certain specialised (and unsubstitutable) equipment which cannot yet be manufactured at home. But it has to be remembered that for this case to hold at all strictly rather special conditions must characterise the foreign-trade relations of the country in question: these must be such that any expansion of trade has sharply disadvantageous effects on the *terms* of trade. Otherwise, an increased import of machinery, etc., from abroad could be acquired by employing surplus labour on production for export: in our simplified example, equipment for the tractor-industry (as a prior condition of an increased rate of investment) could be acquired by exporting part of the larger corn-surplus (consequent on a higher P_c).

Part Two

VIII

A LECTURE ON LENIN
[1939]

Delivered at the School of Slavonic and East European Studies in the University of London on May 22nd, 1939, and published in *The Slavonic Year-Book* for 1939-40, it is here reproduced by kind permission of the Editor of the *Slavonic Review*.

I THINK IT CAN BE SAID without fear of much dispute that Lenin was one of the most successful of great historical figures. Admittedly success is capable of varying interpretations. But if we include in success both the boldness of design as well as the magnitude of achievement, there can be little doubt of his outstanding importance. Some figures in history may be able to show a more precise correspondence of hope and achievement, but their hope was usually less ambitious, their design more limited. Few, if any, can have designed so revolutionary a transformation of the basis of society as the expropriation of the propertied class of a great nation and the construction of a totally new economic order and lived to see it being carried into effect. Yet how many successful men have seemed to the world at large so obscure as Lenin did for all but seven years of his life; or at times so very far from success as he was in the days when he rented cheap lodgings at 30 Holford Square between King's Cross and Sadler's Wells, or when, only four months before he was in the Kremlin, he was saved the fate that was later to befall Karl Liebknecht and Rosa Luxemburg by hiding for weeks in a hayloft in the marshes near the Finnish border and escaping across the frontier on the cab of an engine disguised as a fireman?

Such a surprising measure of coincidence between design and achievement can hardly be treated just as a sport of history, and least of all in the case of Lenin can it be attributed primarily to personal qualities. That

A LECTURE ON LENIN

the qualities he possessed played an important part in the achievement we shall presently make clear; but they were not the qualities usually associated with great historical figures that impose their will upon the world. They were attributes of greatness of a unique kind. Few leaders of a movement can have been so lacking in affectation and relied for their effect so little on appearing as towering above their fellows; probably none has treated his mission so completely as a collective and not a personal endeavour; and his capacity for leadership lay as much in his ability to listen as in his ability to speak. In the dark days of famine and civil war H. G. Wells, in his well-known phrase, dubbed him 'dreamer in the Kremlin'. Dream he could, and dream he continued to do in years of bleak hopelessness when others would have despaired and changed their course. But few dreamers can have tuned their dreams so soberly to reality, or been so quick to sense the need to tack their course when the weather changed while still keeping their bearings. Lenin's peculiar quality of greatness was that he knew how to keep his ear close to the ground. The secret of his influence was not that he could subordinate the mass to himself, but that he could be a part of the mass and lead at the same time. It was not a pose with him, but of his nature, to be the leader of a State of 160 millions who wore a cloth cap. The reasons for his success are to be sought, not in any of the traditional attributes of personal greatness, but in the ideas which he embodied, in their quality of realism, in the extent to which they ran with the stream of contemporary history.

Lenin was born in April 1870 at Simbirsk in the middle Volga, his family name being Ulyanov (whence the subsequent rechristening of Simbirsk as Ulyanovsk), his christian name Vladimir, his patronymic Ilyich. His father had been senior Physics Master at the Penza College of Gentry, with a *penchant* for scientific research, and was later appointed an inspector of schools and then director of education for the district. Towards the end of his life he was awarded the title of State Councillor which ranked him as belonging to the gentry. His mother came of a local doctor's family, and was well if rather narrowly educated at home in the style of provincial middle-class families. Vladimir entered the *gymnasium* or secondary school at the age of nine, and was a successful schoolboy, to judge by the complimentary reports of his headmaster, who by a strange coincidence was the father of Kerensky. The event which seems to have been the turning point of his life occurred during his last year at the *gymnasium* and in the year following the death of his father. His elder brother Alexander while a student at the capital had become associated with the revolutionary organisation known as Narodnaya Volya, a body which organised terroristic activity against the Tsar and his leading officials. In 1887 this elder brother was executed for complicity in a plot to assassinate Tsar Alexander III. Profoundly moved by this event, Vladimir began to study the books left by the brother whom he had so much admired. Among them were the works of Marx. The same year he entered the University of Kazan, only to be arrested by the police in December, expelled from the University and banished for a year to his maternal grandmother's estate in the village of Kokushkino—whether because he bore the damning name of Ulyanov, or because he had taken part in a political meeting of students is not perfectly clear. But his career as a rebel against the old order had begun. His academic studies had to be continued outside the walls of the University as an external student; and after four years that were shared between intensive study and participation in secret Marxist study circles in Samara and Kazan (where he first met the writer Gorky, then a worker in an underground bakery), he took the law examination at St. Petersburg, which enabled him to practise as a junior barrister. This was in 1891 when he was at the age of twenty-one. The story is told that the police officer who took him to Kokushkino after his arrest ventured on a word of paternal advice: 'What's the use of rebelling, young man? You're knocking your head against a brick wall.' 'But it is a rotting wall,' Lenin replied. 'Kick it hard and it will crumble.'

Pondering over his brother's death had led him, however, to the conclusion that his brother's way was not the right way of knocking down that brick wall. His sister tells how he met the news of the execution. With set face he muttered: 'No, we shall not go along that road. We need not go along that road.' For the heroism and asceticism of these early revolutionaries of the Narodnaya Volya persuasion (Narodniks as they came to be called) he always held a deep admiration. But their method of 'propaganda by deed'—individual acts of violence—was a product of romantic, not of realistic thinking, and represented a primitive stage of opposition unsuited to the real problems of the age. Not dramatic gestures of individual rebels, but a mass movement was required. When, accordingly, he moved to Petersburg in 1893, he was drawn, not to his brother's party, but to the groups of the Marxist Emancipation of Labour, whose theoretical leader was Plekhanov. These were at that time no more than small privately meeting groups of students and middle-class people and not a party in the proper sense; but the personnel of these social-democratic groups which he joined was symbolic of the gap between his road and that which his brother had taken. His associates in these groups were not high-souled *littérateurs* and *philosophes*; they were engineers like the brothers Krassin or Krzhyzhanovsky, who was to be the architect thirty years later of Lenin's electrification plan, Krupskaya his future wife, who organised night-school classes in political economy for working men, and later industrial workers from the metal works of St. Petersburg. It is significant that during these years he not only gave lectures and wrote a pamphlet against the Narodniks—the revolutionaries of his brother's persuasion—but he also wrote a pamphlet about factory fines: a subject of grievance and dispute in the local factories at that time. The latter he did with characteristic thoroughness; and a worker with whom he talked to secure information about factory problems at the end of their talk wiped his brow and said: 'I would rather work overtime than answer your questions.' At the same time he wrote articles criticising the so-called 'legal Marxists'—well-known figures like Struve and Tugan-Baranovsky and Bulgakov—on the ground that they were tending to make the movement against the autocracy predominantly a middle-class one, and that they were neglecting the essential rôle of the working class and hence were seducing social-democrats from the vitally urgent task of striking their roots deep in the factory proletariat. These three aspects of his work were all for him part of an integral whole. Theoretical discussion about whether Russian development could avoid capitalism necessarily for him went hand in hand with the study of questions of detail like factory fines, because these were matters of immediate moment to the workers. Propaganda about general aims must be joined with education over concrete immediate questions. He was fond of Plekhanov's phrase: 'Propaganda gives many ideas to a small circle; agitation a single idea to the masses.' In 1895 Lenin made his first journey abroad to Switzerland, Paris and Berlin, and made his first personal contact with Plekhanov and his group. He came back to organise the loose circles and study groups into the nucleus of a political party. The winter of 1895 was one of hardship and discontent in the working-class district of Vassili Ostrov; and there were a number of strikes, including one at the English-owned Thornton mills, where Krupskaya penetrated to make contact with women workers. The police were not slow to strike back, and in December Lenin (along with most of his colleagues) was arrested and later was exiled to the edge of the Siberian *taiga*. Here a year later he was joined by Krupskaya. They were married, and proceeded to spend their exile honeymoon laboriously translating from the English *Industrial Democracy* by Sidney and Beatrice Webb. Here he hunted and skated and played chess, finished his study on the *Development of Capitalism in Russia*, and read not only Marx and the philosophers Hegel and Kant but the Russian classics such as Pushkin, Lermontov, Turgenev and Tolstoy; keeping as much as possible apart from the personal feuds and squabbles that are the inevitable accompaniment of prison or exile. On their release in 1900 they went abroad, at first to Zurich and Munich and then to London.

During his Petersburg years of 1893-5 when he had disputed with the Narodniks and during his years of prison and exile Lenin's essential ideas about socialism and capitalism were taking shape in his mind. What then was the contribution that he made to socialist theory? Prior to 1900, except for the doubts of Bernstein and the 'Revisionists', socialists had generally held the view that capitalism, with its growing concentration of capital and the growing numbers and consolidation of an industrial proletariat, was driving inevitably towards socialism. This transition to socialism would be precipitated by the progressive breakdown of the old order, due to its inability to control and organise the productive forces it had unleashed. But as to the form that this transition to socialism would take, and the precise rôle to be played in it by the factory proletariat, ideas were pretty vague. The implication certainly was that capitalism would totter first in the older and most developed industrial countries of the west; and certainly not in a semi-industrialised country such as Russia. It was in giving concreteness to what had previously been no more than a roughly-sketched historical perspective that the novelty of Lenin's contribution lay. It is a mistake to imply, as some have done, that in the realm of theory he did little more than take over ready-made the ideas of Marx, and that his essential interest lay in political strategy and tactics. To questions of strategy and tactics he certainly devoted more attention than had leading figures in the socialist movement before him. But what is of equal interest to his ideas on strategy, and in many ways more important, was the interpretation of current history in terms of which his strategy was moulded. This was entirely his own, and opened quite new perspectives to socialist thought. This interpretation started with an analysis of the stage of economic and social development reached by Russia at the turn of the century, which was later to be broadened into an analysis of twentieth-century developments in the capitalist world at large in his study on *Imperialism*. His interpretation of the position in Russia led to a quite novel view of the relation between the socialist revolution and a liberal or bourgeois-democratic revolution, and the relation of the working class to each as well as to other classes in society. This led him to a more precise definition of the attitude of the socialist movement toward the State, and of the political and economic forms through which the transition from capitalism to socialism would take place. Incidental to this was his conception of a political party of an entirely new type and his view that it was objectively possible for the social revolution to come in a relatively backward country like Russia before it came in more developed countries of the West.

The Narodniks held that industrial capitalism in Russia was mainly a foreign importation, and that Russia's path of development lay in a direct transition to socialism, without passing through the epoch of industrialisation. The germ of this future socialism lay in the old village commune; whence it followed that socialism was to be an essentially rural, rather than urban, product; and its harbingers were to be the peasantry and not an industrial proletariat. Lenin replied to this with facts and figures to show that industrial capitalism, and with it an industrial proletariat, had already reached a stage of considerable development, that the village commune was a decaying relic, and that the village economy itself was already showing signs of class stratification, with the formation of a *kulak*-class of traders and usurers on the one hand and a landless proletariat on the other.

But just as in his Petersburg days he had criticised the Narodniks on the one hand and the 'legal Marxists' on the other for ignoring the historical rôle of the proletariat, his new concern in his early years abroad was to denounce another tendency, which degraded that historical rôle in a more subtle way. This tendency, which found adherents within the ranks of the Marxists themselves, came to be known as 'Economism'. 'Economism' could be termed a Russian cousin to French syndicalism; its spokesmen, who ran a paper of their own, called *Rabochee Delo*, declared that the exclusive task of socialists must be to help the working class to develop factory groups and trade unions, and through them to agitate for industrial and economic demands. Political questions—the struggle for democracy against the Tsardom—were not the concern of the proletariat; these were middle-class questions that could be left for the middle class to handle. In his booklet *What Is To Be Done?* Lenin vigorously attacked this conception. As we have seen, Lenin himself believed that the movement must be based primarily on the working class; that it must have its roots in the factories, and always join propaganda closely with day-to-day agitation. But he was opposed to any rigid line of separation being drawn between the workers and revolutionary intellectuals, and still more to any fencing off of 'economic' questions to be the province of factory workers and 'political' questions which were no proper concern of theirs. The grounds for his vehemence against the 'Economists' at this particular time seem to have been twofold. First, such a policy would have excluded any possibility of the working class playing a leading rôle in the contest with Tsardom, i.e. in the first or bourgeois-democratic revolution. In such purely liberal questions as free speech and democracy the working class could have no interest (according to the 'Economists'): their duty was to stand aside until such time as they could carry through the socialisation of the means of production. But as we shall see presently, the view that the working class must be in the van even of a purely bourgeois-democratic movement was both a cardinal and a novel principle in Lenin's theory. Moreover, to isolate the workers in this way would be to cut them off from potential allies, particularly from the peasantry. Secondly, Lenin saw the danger that 'Economism' would serve to keep alive the 'primitive' backwardness of political organisation which he was so anxious to overcome—the primitive ineffectiveness of small groups and circles, loosely co-ordinated and incapable of providing an effective leadership to a mass political movement. Moreover, he saw the danger that it would merely confuse the broad organisation and the narrow, and simultaneously preclude the building of a really broad trade union and factory movement and the crystallisation of an effective and homogeneous socialist party, whose function was to give political leadership to the larger mass movement—provide its eyes, as it were, and its general staff. In *What Is To Be Done?* he spoke of the need for trade union organisation to be 'as wide as possible' and 'as public as conditions will allow', and of the need for the masses 'not only to advance concrete demands, but also to advance an increasing number of leaders from their own ranks'. 'On the other hand, the organisation of revolutionaries must be comprised first and foremost of people whose profession is that of revolutionaries. As this is the common feature of the members of such an organisation, all distinctions between workers and intellectuals, and certainly distinctions between trades and professions, must be dropped. . . . Without the "dozen" of tried and talented leaders, professionally trained, schooled by long experience and working in perfect harmony, no class in modern society is capable of conducting a determined struggle.' Citing the early chapters of the Webbs' *Industrial Democracy*, he criticised two naïve and primitive interpretations of democracy that sought to exalt the 'crowd' at the expense of 'leaders' and to preclude centralised organisation and staff work. 'Specialisation requires centralisation', he declared. Returning to the relationship between this new type of leadership and the wider mass movement to which it must appeal, he added: 'It is not our business to grow wheat in flower-pots. While the old-fashioned folk are tending their flower-pot crops, we must prepare reapers to reap the wheat of tomorrow.'

It was to overcome such primitiveness and to build the kind of party he envisaged inside Russia that Lenin formed the idea of an all-Russian newspaper, to be edited abroad and smuggled illegally into Russia. It was this project that took shape in the famous *Iskra*, which was controlled by an editorial board of which Lenin was a member. Publication was decided on, however, only after some strained disagreements between 'the elders', grouped round Plekhanov—exiles who had been away from Russia for more than a decade—and the younger generation. In a few years' time this disagreement was to widen into that split between Mensheviks and Bolsheviks which lasted down to and through the Civil War of 1918-20. In the active editorial work of *Iskra* Lenin played the most prominent rôle, first in Munich and then in London, where the paper was printed at the press of the Social-Democratic Federation on the site of the present Marx House and Library in Clerkenwell Green. His stay in London lasted for twelve months; and here he divided his time between lodgings off Tottenham Court Road or King's Cross, the Reading Room of the British Museum, visits to the Zoo or fascinated journeys on tops of 'buses, or taking sandwiches on walks into the country on Sundays, 'intoxicated with the air like children' (as he wrote to his mother). But no period of his life was destined to follow an uninterrupted routine for very long. In July of 1903 the Second Congress of the Social-Democratic Party of Russia opened in Brussels (it was later transferred to London). This was really the foundation congress of the party, the first in 1898 consisting of only nine delegates; and here Lenin sought to carry a stage further his campaign to build a centralised party, as a general staff of a popular movement, from the mosaic of loosely co-ordinated groups and circles. The crucial disagreement that was to widen into a split came over what has seemed to most commentators a trivial phrase. To Lenin these few words represented the parting of the ways between the traditional party and the political party of a new type. His chief antagonist in the dispute was his colleague Martov, for whom he had a considerable personal affection. Martov proposed that all persons should be admitted as members of the party who 'work under the control of the party and contribute to it financially'. This, clearly, would have allowed of a broad and rather loosely knit, largely inactive membership. Lenin moved that the statute should read: 'a member of the party is one who *participates* in an *organisation* of the party'. 'It is far better', he said in supporting his viewpoint, 'that ten persons who do real work should not call themselves members than that one person who is a mere chatterbox should have the right and opportunity to be a party member.' Lenin succeeded in carrying the majority of the conference with him; whence the title of Bolshevik, or Majority, Faction, as his section came to be known, by contrast with Menshevik, or Minority, Faction. When it came to the election of the new editorial board of *Iskra*, Lenin, Martov and Plekhanov were proposed; but Martov declined to serve, and the split was complete. For a few months after the congress Lenin continued to work in harness with Plekhanov, who at this stage adhered to the Majority side. But the alliance was not to be for long. When Martov arranged a Congress of Russian Social-Democrats Abroad (i.e. of the exiles) where he had a majority and used it as an organisational focus for the Mensheviks to combat the influence of the Lenin-policy, Plekhanov sought a compromise with him, proposing to accept most of the demands that the Minority had presented to the central committee, and to co-opt all the old Martov-group back on to the editorial board of *Iskra*. Lenin, feeling out-manœuvred and isolated, resigned from the editorial board. It must have been for him a bitter decision: to sever himself from the paper of which he had dreamed and for which he had schemed in his years of exile. Distraught and exhausted, he and his wife shouldered rucksacks and retired into the Swiss Alps, choosing always 'the wildest paths far away from human beings', as Krupskaya relates. When he returned into the valleys, calmer and refreshed, a month later, it was to study books on military tactics in the secluded library of the Reading Society of Geneva, and to prepare for the issue of a new paper, to be the organ of the Bolshevik group and rival to the new Menshevik *Iskra*. This appeared under the title of *Vpered* in December 1904.

Close on the heels of this split came the revolutionary events of 1905, by which the rival views of Menshevik and Bolshevik were to be more concretely defined. The tactics which the Mensheviks had proposed consisted in bringing pressure on the middle class by presenting demands to the Zemstva, or provincial councils, and later to the Duma. Since the coming revolution would be no more than a bourgeois liberal revolution, the socialists must stand in the background and remain in opposition as a 'pressure group', since to participate in a provisional government would be to carry out, not a working class programme, but a liberal middle-class programme. To this attitude Lenin was sharply opposed. In his view it was essential that the working class should participate in the popular movement to the full, and if possible secure the leadership in it; firstly, because the workers were the most consistent and best organised opponents of the old régime, secondly because in doing so they could pave the way for an early transition to the full socialist revolution. Hence it was the task of socialists to participate even in a Provisional Government, not in order to carry out their 'maximum programme' (socialism), but in order to carry out a purely democratic programme. 'The proletariat alone is capable', he wrote, 'of proceeding reliably to the end, for its goal lies far beyond the democratic revolution. For this reason the proletariat must fight in the front rank for a republic and must contemptuously reject the advice that is given to it to take care not to scare the bourgeoisie.'

This theory of the rôle of the working class in the liberal revolution was closely connected with his theory of the relation between the working class and its allies. While he was concerned to stress the rôle of the proletariat as the principal driving-force of the popular movement, he was far removed from the notion of a narrow 'one-class' movement. A large part of the reason why he had fought 'Economism' and now sponsored the view that the organised workers must be in the forefront of the popular movement was that only in this way could it cement its alliance with the urban petite-bourgeoisie and the peasantry. On alliance with the peasantry he always laid special stress; and neglect of the peasantry was a recurring ground of his criticism both of the Mensheviks and of Trotsky. 'The proletariat', he wrote in these days, 'must carry out to the end the democratic revolution, and thus unite to itself the mass of the peasantry in order to crush the resistance of the autocracy, and to counteract the vacillation of the bourgeoisie.' Earlier, in his polemic against the 'Economists', he had spoken of the need for socialist organisers, to 'go among all classes of the population and not *only* to the factories'; adding, with characteristic breadth of vision, that 'services, each of them small in itself, but incalculable taken together, could be rendered to our cause by office employees and officials, not only in the factories, but in the postal service, on the railways, in the Customs, among the clergy, and in *every other* walk of life including even the police service and the Court.'

Krupskaya tells how the first news of the events of 1905 reached the small colony of Bolshevik exiles in Geneva; how Lenin and she on their way to the Library met Lunacharsky's wife, 'so excited that she could not speak, but only helplessly wave her muff'; and how the small colony as a whole drifted spontaneously to the Lepeshinsky *émigrés* restaurant, 'hardly spoke to one another' but 'with tense faces sang the Revolutionary Funeral March'. Lenin's every thought, she tells us, was now centred on Russia: he began feverishly to think in terms of military preparation and an armed uprising against the Tsardom; made plans with Krassin and with Father Gapon (who apparently bungled his share of the business) for the secret import of arms into Russia; and wrote to the Bolshevik committee in Petersburg that 'in an affair of this kind there should be less smooth schemes and discussions: it is frantic energy, and yet more energy that is required'. In the autumn of the year he returned in disguise to Petersburg and then to Moscow. But by the winter of 1905 the revolutionary movement had already passed its zenith, and the general strike and the rising in Moscow and Petersburg and other industrial centres in December were successfully crushed by the Tsar's troops. Lenin held on, in the belief that with the coming of spring the peasant movement would rise again and spread its infection to the troops; and in the meantime he counselled the workers to bide their time and not to be provoked into premature and unconcerted action. While advocating 'guerrilla tactics' against the government in the proper circumstances and subject to proper discipline and organisation, he vigorously attacked the anarchists, who advocated continuous and indiscriminate acts of violence and looting, and opposed their admission to the Soviets. At this time he advocated the boycott first of the Bulygin and then of the Witte Duma, which the Tsar had called as a concession to the popular movement. On May 9th, white-faced and nervous, he was addressing a public meeting in Petersburg for the first time. But at the beginning of July the Duma was dissolved by the authorities, social-democratic newspapers were shut down and a wave of arrests took place. Lenin for a time evaded arrest, despite the activity of police spies who had penetrated near to the heart of the Bolshevik organisation. But in 1907 he was forced to cross into Finland. Being tracked down there by the police, he eventually escaped to Sweden after a perilous journey across two miles of cracking ice, with two tipsy Finnish peasants as escort. Later he and his wife went back to Geneva; as they trudged from the station to their old exiles' lodgings, he muttered: 'I feel just as though we had come back here to be buried.'

Long years of reaction were to follow. Despondency set in, particularly among the *émigrés*; and Lenin wrote to F. A. Rothstein in London: 'The falling away of the intelligentsia is enormous.' Yet in this period of the declining wave his realism perhaps showed itself even more resolutely than in the days of hope. Quick to appreciate the changed situation, he urged that strategy must take a sharp turn: every attempt must be made to develop legal forms of propaganda and organisation. In this new situation he advocated participation in the Duma; and he criticised the boycott-group among the Bolsheviks, who wanted to concentrate on the intensive development of instructor schools and groups by contrast with the extensive development of the wider movement; criticising them as vigorously as he did the so-called 'Liquidators' among the Mensheviks, who advocated the liquidation of the illegal party organisation. It was in these years of his second exile in Western Europe that he carried on a philosophic controversy with those fellow-Bolsheviks who had become converts to the fashionable philosophy of Ernst Mach. The advocates of this view, who included Lunacharsky and Bogdanov, formed a distinct group within the Bolshevik party, largely coinciding with the section that had advocated the boycott of the Third Duma, and organising a political school of its own under Gorky's auspices on the island of Capri. It was against the views of this group, and against similar neo-Kantian tendencies, that Lenin in 1908 published his book of philosophical criticism, *Materialism and Empirio-Criticism*. For Lenin all reality was knowable through human activity, and to erect any final distinction between the 'thing in itself' and the 'thing for us' was to open the door to scepticism and to set limits to the efficacy of rationally guided human action.

It is Lenin's views on the war and on the revolution of March 1917 that are perhaps of chief interest to people in this country; yet, since they are also the most familiar, it may be unnecessary to dwell upon them at length. The basis of his attitude to these questions is to be found in the study of *Imperialism: the final stage of Capitalism*, which was published early in the war years. In this study he characterised the present stage of world capitalism as being one in which, inside each country, large monopolistic groups of finance-capital had risen to positions of dominance, and consolidating their influence over the State had launched out on campaigns of economic and political expansion which inevitably resulted in an armed struggle to partition the globe. One result of these new developments was that the 'inequality of economic development' between different countries, which in the nineteenth century had apparently been growing less, was now accentuated. Those Powers that had been first and most successful in the game of colonial acquisition—and these were generally the most advanced capitalist countries—were able to acquire a new lease of life. The colonial tribute which countries like Britain enjoyed created not only a swollen *rentier* middle class, but also a privileged aristocracy of labour—pampered 'palace slaves' who lived in part at the expense of the sweated 'plantation slaves' at the periphery of Empire. Hence there emerged the objective possibility that the class struggle might reach its acute stage, and the old régime totter, in a semi-industrialised country like Russia (which Lenin later dubbed the 'weakest

A LECTURE ON LENIN

link' in the chain of capitalist states), instead of in more highly industrialised countries like Britain or U.S.A. Moreover, the colonial policy of Imperialism would quickly prove to have sown dragon's teeth: before long the rise of a native bourgeoisie and proletariat in the colonies, and with them the rise of colonial nationalism, would provide vast stretches of flaming frontiers in revolt against the Empires of capitalist Imperialism, and vast new reserves of allies for the labour movements of the West.

The attitude of continental socialism on the question of war had been to some extent a changing one: this had always been recognised as a matter, not of rigid principle, but of the particular situation in which the question arose. In the nineteenth century 'wars of national defence', particularly if against autocratic powers, were recognised as 'progressive wars' which socialists could support: a precedent which the pro-war socialists of 1914 in Germany, Russia and France alike invoked in support of the line they took. The novel contribution that Lenin made to this question was to postulate that in this new epoch of Imperialism wars between large capitalist Powers altogether ceased to come within the category of 'defensive wars': all were robber-wars, part of a giant struggle of the epoch to partition the globe. Hence it was the duty of socialists to adopt a standpoint of uncompromising opposition to their own government in wartime, and to take advantage of the weakness and embarrassment of their own ruling class to rally the workers to take power into their own hands at the earliest opportunity. In this epoch, he said, colonial wars of liberation from the imperialist yoke were the only 'progressive wars' that it was permissible for socialists to support. Had he lived to see the growth of Fascist Imperialism, there can be small doubt that he would have extended this statement to include the defence of a democratic country like Czechoslovakia against totalitarian attack.

True to this standpoint, Lenin during the war years preached the doctrine that came to be known as 'revolutionary defeatism', and after the breakdown of the pre-war Second International he sought to draw together the anti-war sections of the movements in the various countries, first at the Zimmerwald Conference in 1915 and then at Kienthal in 1916: gatherings which formed a prelude to the convocation two years later of the first congress of the Third International in Moscow.

When the first revolution of March 1917 which overthrew the Tsar took place, Lenin was in Zurich. A few days after the news reached them, a meeting of *émigré* groups in Switzerland was held to consider ways and means of securing their return to Russia. Approaches were made to the Provisional Government in Petrograd for permission to return. These approaches at first proved unsuccessful; and meantime Lenin had seized upon a plan proposed by Martov for permission to be sought in Berlin to pass through Germany in exchange for German and Austrian prisoners in Russia. Negotiations were set on foot through the intervention of the Swiss socialist Platten (aided, I believe, by Parvus in Berlin). Permission was eventually granted; and Lenin, who impatiently insisted on leaving at a few hours' notice by the first available train, travelled through Germany with some thirty other *émigrés* from Switzerland in the famous 'sealed train' (which became the basis of the later charge that he was a German agent). This time his return to the city that was later to bear his name was very different from his return twelve years before: a guard of honour of Kronstadt sailors at the Finland station to greet him, a bouquet of flowers, speeches of welcome from the Petrograd Soviet of Workers and Soldiers Deputies, Lenin hoisted onto an armoured car and searchlights illuminating the road from the station to the Kseshinskaya Mansion, the party headquarters.

The policy that he proceeded to outline in his famous April Theses was in substance the same as the policy he had advocated in 1905. Some members even of his own party held that, as this was the period of the bourgeois-democratic revolution, the Bolsheviks must remain in the background as a 'ginger group' in opposition. Since the objective situation was not ripe for a transition to socialism, the question of a seizure of power by the working class could not arise at the present stage. To Lenin, however, the situation had changed in important respects since 1905: capitalism, and with it the industrial proletariat, had developed to a significant extent since then; while peasant revolt against the landlord class had reached the stage of spontaneous seizure of estates in a number of districts. Moreover, the war situation made the crucial difference that the capitalist class of Russia were now irretrievably tied to monopoly-capital in Britain and France, so that their influence was definitely a reactionary one. Having taken power from the Tsarist bureaucracy with the help of the popular movement, they would inevitably turn and suppress the popular movement. Hence the urgent need for power to pass into the hands of the working class and the peasantry, not in order to make an immediate transition to socialism, but to complete the democratic revolution and 'secure the rights of the people as a whole'. (It is a common misapprehension that he was urging the immediate introduction of full socialism: this he explicitly repudiated.) By doing this the transition to socialism would also be accelerated and this transition when it came would be rendered 'as painless as possible'. The Bolsheviks, he urged, must fight 'for a more democratic workers' and peasants' republic, wherein the police and the standing army would be replaced by a general army of the people, a universal militia; and representative parliamentary institutions would gradually give place to Soviets of people's representatives (from classes and professions or from localities) functioning both as legislative and executive bodies'.

For a time it seems clear that he thought that this transition to Soviet power could be achieved peaceably by an ending of the existing system of Dual Power through a gradual transfer of functions from the Provisional Government to the Soviet; and at first he did not call for the overthrow of the Provisional Government. Kerensky, on the other hand, apparently told Buchanan that 'the Soviets will die a natural death'. In the course of July, however, discontent reached the point where a spontaneous demonstration, led by a machine-gun regiment and joined by sailors from Kronstadt, was organised in the streets of the capital against the Provisional Government, calling for the downfall of the Government and 'all power to the Soviets'. Faced with this situation, there was hesitation among the Bolsheviks as to the attitude that they should adopt. It was eventually decided that the Bolsheviks, since they could not prevent it, should support the demonstration, but at the same time confine it to a peaceful demonstration and discourage any use of force. Although Lenin addressed the demonstrators from the balcony of the Bolshevik headquarters, urging restraint, the demonstration did not remain a peaceful one; some shots were fired, sporadic fighting occurred, and the Government brought up troops to disperse the demonstration. The Bolsheviks were blamed for what had occurred. The charge was published that Lenin was a spy in the pay of Germany. The offices of *Pravda* were raided by a group of young officers and smashed. Arrests of Bolsheviks followed; and Lenin with some difficulty was persuaded by his colleagues to go into hiding in Finland. If he had not done so, he would certainly have been arrested; and he might have met the fate of Karl Liebknecht.

By the autumn the situation had changed. The summer offensive on the Eastern Front had failed. Disorganisation in the rear had grown, desertions from the army and discontent with the war were spreading like a forest fire. Behind the backs of the Provisional Government plans were on foot for a counter-revolution to suppress the Soviets and to 'restore discipline': plans which, it is now clear, had the support of certain representatives of the Allies, and which culminated in the *coup* of General Kornilov. Lenin now felt assured that a peaceful solution of the *impasse* was no longer possible: the revolution was faced with the grim alternative between counter-revolution, with the suppression of the Soviets, and the forcible transfer of power to the Soviets. In October the Bolsheviks secured a majority both in the Moscow and the Petrograd Soviet. They had the allegiance of the Kronstadt sailors and a number of regiments in the capital. Lenin was insistent that the hour to strike had come, and that to delay and even to wait for the Constituent Assembly would be to court defeat. Under the slogan of 'Peace and Bread', the Bolsheviks issued the call for 'All Power to the Soviets', and sent Red Guard detachments to seize the key points in the city and to enforce the resignation of the Provisional Government in the Winter Palace.

There was some fighting in Moscow, less in Petrograd; but it was soon over. The real armed struggle did not come till eight months later with the outbreak of civil war and foreign intervention. Among the first acts of the new Government were the Land Decree, empowering the village committees to divide the land of the old estates among the peasantry, and an appeal to all the belligerent governments to attend a peace conference to conclude a peace on the basis of the principle: 'No annexations and no indemnities'. While the banks were nationalised and an extensive system of State controls over trade and industry was inaugurated, there was not in the initial months of the revolution any general socialisation of industry. The wholesale nationalisation that took place eight months later was an act of military improvisation after civil war and foreign invasion had started, and after most enterprises had either been closed by their owners or seized on their own initiative by local factory committees.

The story of the next few years is now too familiar to need retelling: of the German invasion and the imposed Treaty of Brest-Litovsk; of the rising of the Left Social Revolutionaries in the streets of Moscow; of the plot, in which the English spy Captain Reilly had a hand, to arrest Lenin and instal a new government; of the shooting of Lenin by Dora Kaplan, a Left Social Revolutionary, as he left a meeting of workers in a Petrograd factory; of the grim years of civil war and famine, with fighting on seven fronts against the combined forces of English, French, Japanese and Americans; of the return, in 1920, to the task of economic reconstruction under the so-called New Economic Policy, which was of Lenin's piloting if not entirely of his creation. What is less understood about these years is Lenin's attitude to the question of dictatorship and democracy. In his booklet, *State and Revolution*, written during the events of 1917, Lenin had expounded the theory that the existing State, despite its democratic trappings, was in the last analysis an instrument of the capitalist class for preserving its own hegemony. Hence, the working class could not assume power through the machinery of the existing State, but only by building up its own institutions and forcibly transferring power to them from the existing State. During the transition period, however, between the old order and the new, the new workers' State must be as centralised and as coercive as the old State had been: the political form of this transition period must consist of the Dictatorship of the Proletariat, which he defined as a form of class alliance between the working class and the peasantry, with the former as senior partner. But because he had criticised so severely the limitations of bourgeois democracy, it is quite incorrect to depict him, as so many have done, as being in principle anti-democratic. On the contrary, the Dictatorship of the Proletariat itself was, in his eyes, a 'higher form of democracy' than what had preceded it, since it represented the interests of 'the vast majority of the people', while at the same time being no more than transitional in character, laying the foundation for the free democracy of a classless society, where 'every kitchen-maid shall have learned to take a hand in the conduct of the State'.

With what picture are we left of the personality of the man who was to be the founder and the inspirer of the first socialist state in the world? Certainly with the picture of a complex personality, very different from that which was current in the outside world during the seven hurried years of his life when he was 'front page news'. For like Buonaparte in early nineteenth-century England, Lenin became a bogy-man, used to frighten children of all ages in the post-war years when Europe stood at the crossroads. But even when we lay caricature aside, there remains much in the picture of his character as it is commonly drawn that seems to correspond ill with the facts as we see them at a closer view. Of Lenin the politician, the revolutionary, the world today knows, of course, a good deal. Of the Lenin that appears in his tender and affectionate letters to his mother the world naturally has little idea: it has little knowledge of the man who liked to sit in *cafés chantants* in Paris and applaud the political jokes; who could sit enthralled at a show of Tolstoy's *Living Corpse* in a Berne theatre; who once was so moved by a story of Chekhov that he could not sleep; who could be absorbed by a concert of Beethoven or Chaikovski, and whose advice to modernist young communists, despising all poets except Mayakovsky, was to read Pushkin and the classics. Of the Lenin who joked with fishermen at Capri, gazed at the expanse of London from Primrose Hill, bicycled dangerously about the streets of Geneva, and climbed for weeks on end in the Swiss mountains we know very little. Of the man who could sway a conference without tricks of rhetoric or emotion, who lived with ascetic simplicity even in his Kremlin days; who so seldom had the limelight and was embarrassed when he did; who could be ruthless in controversy even with friends, like Martov, of whom he was fond; who as an administrator believed in tidiness and efficiency and inveighed against the soullessness of bureaucratic methods—of these sides of the man we now know rather more.

Lenin has been pictured by some writers as a man of irascible temperament who could not work with others, and the splits and controversies among Russian socialists have been attributed to this cause. Certainly he did not mince words when he felt deeply. But there seems little doubt that the sharpness of controversy in which he indulged was due, not to personal ill-will, but to his sense of the overwhelming importance of the issues involved. For him controversy was the forge of truth. It is clear that he parted from such colleagues as Plekhanov and Martov only with personal distress; and when a comrade, in the dark days of 1908, chided him for isolating himself by his strictness of principle, he replied simply: 'There are occasions when a leader must stand alone to preserve the purity of his flag.' When, after the 1903 conference, a delegate complained of the depressing atmosphere of controversy which pervaded the conference, Lenin is said to have replied: 'What a fine thing our congress is. Opportunity for open fighting. Opinions expressed. Tendencies revealed. Groups defined. Hands raised. A decision taken. A stage passed through. That's what I like. That's life. It's something different from the endless wearying intellectual discussions which finish, not because people have solved the problem, but simply because they have got tired of talking.' Krupskaya comments: 'That quotation sums up Ilyich to a "T".'

It has often been said of him that as regards theory he was a dogmatist, who took over the ideas of Marx uncritically. Yet this view is hard to square with his own insistence on the falsity of abstract schematism, on the need continually to readjust one's generalisations in face of concrete study of ever-changing situations, and on his own estimate of the significance of Marx. In 1899 he wrote: 'We do not regard Marx's theory as something final and inviolable; on the contrary we are convinced that it has only laid the cornerstone of the science which socialists *must* advance in all directions if they do not want to lag behind the march of life. We think that an *independent* elaboration of Marx's theory is especially necessary for Russian socialists since this theory provides only general *guiding* principles, which in *particular* are to be applied differently to England and to France, differently to France and to Germany, differently to Germany and to Russia.'

And what of Lenin's alleged cruelty—the legend of the modern Genghis Khan, ruthless to sacrifice the lives of thousands to his aims? Ruthless he certainly was, both to suppress sentiment in himself and to enforce measures that he deemed were necessary if socialism was to be achieved. With sentiment that spelt hesitation or weakness in face of a crucial decision he clearly had no patience either in himself or others. But it is also clear that this ruthlessness came from a sense of historical necessity, not from personal temperament; it was because he felt that the cruelties of the old régime were greater than the cruelties of revolution, and not because he was a man without feeling. A story that Maxim Gorky tells of him mates oddly with the common legend. He had been listening to a concert of Beethoven in a Moscow flat. His first reaction was plain enthusiasm. 'I know nothing greater than the Appassionata; I would like to listen to it every day. It is marvellous superhuman music; what marvellous things human beings can do.' Then after a pause he added sadly: 'But one can't listen to music too often. It affects the nerves; makes you want to stroke the heads of people who could create such beauty while living in this vile hell. And just now you mustn't stroke anyone's head—you might get your hand bitten off. Our duty is infernally hard.' Again in his later years, playing with children in Gorki village: 'These will have happier lives than we had,' he remarked. 'There will not be so much cruelty in their lives.' Then, growing pensive and gazing at the distant hills, 'And yet I do not altogether envy them; our generation achieved something of amazing significance for history. The cruelty which the conditions of our life made necessary will be understood and vindicated. Everything will be understood, everything.' Gorky goes on to tell of how in the civil war days he used to come to Lenin in the Kremlin and plead with him for individual 'hard cases'; that while he found Lenin always stern and unsentimental he never found him inconsiderate where there was anything possible that he could do; and as evidence that Lenin had not lightly dismissed such personal considerations from his mind, Gorky tells how afterwards he often learned of small acts of consideration even to enemies for which Lenin had spared time from other pressing duties.

Gorky gives us another picture of him: 'He loved fun, and when he laughed it was with his whole body. Stocky and thick set, with his socratic head and quick eyes, he would often adopt a strange and rather comical posture—he would throw his head back, inclining it somehow on to his shoulder, thrust his fingers under his armpits, in his waistcoat armholes. There was something deliciously funny in this pose, something of a triumphant fighting cock; and at such moments he beamed all over with joy, a grown-up child in this accursed world.'

In May 1922, at the time of the Genoa Conference, sclerosis of the brain developed. He suffered a severe haemorrhage which left him paralysed and dumb. One of the three bullets Dora Kaplan had fired at him still lodged close to his spine. They operated to extract the bullet. But the strain of years of exile and the night vigils of the civil war years had told on his frame. After a temporary recovery, sufficient to enable him to return to Moscow to direct the arrangements for Russia's participation in the Genoa Conference and to speak before the Comintern and the Moscow Soviet, he had a relapse. In December came the second stroke which paralysed an arm and a leg. He had strength only to dictate a few letters each day to his secretary, and with dogged persistence to prepare a few articles. On March 9th, 1923, came a third stroke which deprived him of speech. They took him back to his beloved village of Gorki, where Krupskaya tended him as faithfully as she had done since their Siberian days. Again he rallied, took motor drives and could walk a little, and in October even visited Moscow again for a few hours. On January 21st, 1924, with a fourth stroke, came the end.

They brought him from Gorki by special train; and for four days he lay in state in the pillared Hall of the Trade Unions (the former Noblemen's Club) in Moscow, while an endless procession of people day and night passed through. Persons of all kinds, but mostly humble ordinary folk from town and village, waited hours in long queues in the snow, with the temperature thirty degrees below zero. It was an unusually severe winter, and great fires were lit in the Moscow streets to warm the waiting crowds. There can be no doubt of the deep affection of ordinary people: he was so little the great man and so much one of themselves. There was no stage-management about this simple devotion of thousands; few leaders of a great State could ever have received a more sincere popular tribute. On the fourth day his chief colleagues carried his coffin through the Red Square on their shoulders, and buried him beneath the Kremlin wall.

He lived to see the dawn of what he had dreamed; he lived at least to see the clouds of civil war recede. But in the early 'twenties, when the 'scissors crisis' of 1923 was scarcely surmounted, that dawn was still pale; and his last thoughts must still have contained anxieties and doubts. Yet to look upon the dawn was no doubt the only reward for his stubbornness in years of exile that he would have asked for. While the world will remember him in the brief years of his triumph, his qualities that are most memorable were perhaps those he showed in the days when the world did not know his name.

> 'It is easy to sing when the streets
> Themselves are alive with singing, when the drum beats
> The rhythm we want in us all . . .
> It is easy enough to speak the words that move
> When the crowd is aroused and wants what you wish to prove.
> What's not so easy is to lead in the dark
> From moment to moment knowing just where the spark
> And just how strong, may be struck. For the real work
> Is the work that no one sees and earns no remark.'

These words of Randall Swingler, dedicated to a communist, might have been a fitting epitaph. The capacity to 'lead in the dark', 'to feel the rhythm grow when there's hardly a sound': this was the quality which made him outstanding and was the ground of his immortal achievement.

IX

A LECTURE ON MARX
[1942]

This was a lecture delivered on November 14th, 1942, as one of a series of seven open Lectures on Eminent Economists arranged by the Faculty of Economics and Politics at Cambridge during the Michaelmas Term of that year. In the latter part of section 2 some paragraphs have been included which are extensions of the original lecture; these paragraphs being taken from a pamphlet by the present writer, entitled *Marx as an Economist, an essay* (Lawrence and Wishart, London, 1943), by kind permission of the publishers. For most of its biographical data, especially in the early life of Marx, this lecture has drawn heavily upon the standard biography of Marx by Franz Mehring, *Karl Marx: the Story of his Life* (trans. Edward Fitzgerald, London, 1936.)

WHEN WE TRY TO UNDERSTAND the writings and the mind of some social thinker of the past, we may approach the matter in two ways. We may start by enquiring what answers he gave to the sort of questions that thinkers of our own day are accustomed to pose: to confront him, as it were, with a questionnaire couched in terms of the fashions of today. On the other hand, we may start by trying to find out the sort of questions he was really seeking to answer—to make out what shape the problem had which formed the background of his thinking. Having done this, we may then ask ourselves whether some of these questions he was asking may not be ones that we should be asking today. Since he stood at a different place in history, it is probable that some of the questions he was asking were different from those which occupy us today. Not all of them may be relevant to our present-day world. But if he was of outstanding stature as a thinker, the chances are that many of them will be.

It is the second of these approaches that I shall try and adopt today in considering one of the least understood of economists and social thinkers. I am going to ask you to stand in his shoes, historically speaking, and to look out upon the world with his eyes.

The problem confronting a thinker has two aspects. There is the problem presented by the ideas of his predecessors: the picture they have drawn of the world, the interpretations they have propounded, and the riddles they have left unsolved. Then there are the questions which the society around him is presenting—the practical problems of the hour. A social thinker of any importance is bound to be occupied, in some degree, with both these aspects. At any rate for Marx they were intimately combined. Few thinkers can have been more seriously concerned with critical assessment of the thought of his predecessors—with finding out where it illuminated and where it obscured reality. Very few thinkers can have been more acutely aware of the problems of his age: the torments of contemporary society which cried in his ears for treatment only less urgently than do those of our own world in our own ears today.

1   Karl Heinrich Marx was born in 1818 in an imposing baroque house in Trier (or Trèves), a city of the Mosel valley in the Rhineland: a part of Germany that had been affected most fully by the liberal ideas which flowed in the wake of Napoleon's occupation, and an area where the industrial revolution was already making its appearance. But 1818, three years after the Battle of Waterloo, was only eleven years after the Prussian emancipation of the serfs; and Germany for the most part still bore the imprint of an essentially feudal society, and was ruled by an autocratic government to which the ideas of the French Revolution were anathema. German towns at the time were still (as Dr. Clapham has described them) 'the quiet little places of the fairy books, with huddled roofs and spires, from which the view over the ploughlands and orchards was so easy'. Marx came of a middle-class Jewish family; but while his paternal grandfather was a Rabbi and his mother came of a century-long line of Rabbis in Holland, his father was a barrister (later becoming a *Justizrat*) who adopted the Christian religion six years after Karl Heinrich was born. The father was an enlightened but traditional thinker, faithful to the Prussian State, an admirer of Frederick the Great and a hater of Napoleon. The son, however, was to enter the University just at the time when a strong revolt against the Prussian State was setting in among the keener minds of the younger generation. At the age of seventeen Karl Marx went for a year to the University of Bonn, where he studied law. But, if we are to believe the admonishing letters of his father, much of his

time was spent in running up bills and in 'wild frolics'. He joined, not only what was called the Poets' Club, but also one of the student tavern clubs; he once fought a duel; and according to the university records he suffered 'one day's confinement for nocturnal drunkenness and disturbance of the peace'. Perhaps this exuberance was not unconnected with the fact that he was busy getting engaged to his sister's intimate friend who lived next door to them at Trier: the daughter of a senior civil servant and Privy Councillor. In his future father-in-law, the half-German half-Scotch Baron von Westphalen, the young Karl was to find a second father after his own heart: not a narrow-minded 'cabbage-junker', but a West German gentleman of liberal ideas and catholic tastes, who gave him the run of his library and took him for long walks in the surrounding hills, reciting to him whole passages of Homer or of Shakespeare, much of which he knew by heart in English. No doubt Karl Marx's warm affection for Shakespeare dated from these walks.

It was when Marx moved to the University of Berlin, a year later, that his serious studies began. Referring to this university at the time, Ludwig Feuerbach wrote: 'other universities are positively bacchanalian compared with this workhouse'—which may have been a reason why Karl Marx's father sent him there from the frivolities of Bonn. Here he filled a number of exercise-books with rather clumsy lyrical verse dedicated to his betrothed (two examples of which were actually published in a Berlin journal called *Atenäum*); went to the minimum number of lectures on law; but began a wide reading in German history and literature and the classics. Here were laid the foundations of that many-sided erudition and keen historical sense which his works display. The father, however, who had designed for his son an orderly academic career, was still apparently ill-pleased. Perhaps because the onset of his fatal illness made him irritable, he wrote reproachful letters to his son complaining of 'lack of order and repellent unsociability, a brooding prowling around in all the fields of science, a stuffy brooding under a dismal oil lamp', and of 'going to seed in a scholastic dressing-gown with unkempt hair as a change from going to seed with a beer-mug in hand'.

But it was to philosophy that the intellectual passion of Marx's university years was to be mainly directed; and the subject of the dissertation which he finally presented for his doctorate in 1841 was a comparison of the philosophies of Democritus and Epicurus. This interest was not unconnected with his study of law: it seems to have originated in a search for a philosophy of law, and thence to have developed into a search for a philosophy of history. The philosopher Hegel had been dead just

A LECTURE ON MARX

ten years when Marx entered the university, and the influence of his philosophy in German university circles was in full tide. But the school that Hegel had founded had already divided into two wings: a Right and a Left. The older generation in their professorial chairs interpreted this philosophy as a justification of the Prussian State, of the established Church and of rigid conformity to tradition, both in thought and in political behaviour. But the Young Hegelians, or the Hegelian Left, seized upon the radical and critical elements in Hegel's thought—his emphasis on change and on conflict as the essence of change—and used this anvil to forge the intellectual weapons of the rising liberal and democratic movement. At the time German political battles were philosophical battles. As Professor E. H. Carr has said: 'Hegel had been radical in his principles and his methods, conservative or even reactionary in his conclusions. The Right clung to his conclusions and ignored his principles. The Left clung to his principles and used his methods to overthrow his conclusions.'

Marx's first contact with Hegel's writings had repelled him with what he called their 'grotesque and rough-hewn melody'. But more exhaustive reading, during a bout of illness, won his respect; and the respect was quickly to ripen into admiration. Before his first year at Berlin was over, he had joined a club of Young Hegelians of the Left, of which brilliant circle he was to be, though a very junior, a far-from-silent member. One of its older members, Moses Hess, wrote at the time of their new disciple as a young man who had made upon them all 'an extraordinary impression: perhaps the one genuine philosopher now alive, he combined the deepest philosophical earnestness with the most mordant wit'. But Marx's attachment to the critical method of Hegel very soon led him to turn this criticism against the master himself, especially against the idealistic setting of Hegel's philosophy. In doing so he arrived at the view that it was not the philosophy and the ideas of an epoch which determined the social and economic character of that epoch, but the converse. This notion inevitably led him towards the study of social and economic conditions, which was to be the main preoccupation of his later years. In 1845 he was to conclude some notes on the philosopher Feuerbach with the now-famous declaration: 'In the past philosophers have interpreted the world variously; the task now is to change it.'

The next stage in the transition from Marx the philosopher to Marx the economist and social historian was an essay in journalism. Marx at this time still cherished his father's ambition for him that he should have an academic career. But it was far from easy for a man of unorthodox views to secure a university appointment; and although his friend Bruno Bauer had been given a lectureship in theology at Bonn and hoped to arrange for Marx to join him as a colleague, some lectures that Bauer gave on the New Testament soon brought upon him the frown of Prussian officialdom, which did not improve Marx's chances. When, just after taking his doctorate, Marx wrote an article for the *Deutsche Jahrbücher* criticising the Prussian censorship, this was suppressed by the censor, and his chances of appointment became very small indeed. In the following January a group of liberal businessmen in Cologne—part of that Rhineland bourgeoisie of which Mehring spoke as 'living on small business and great illusions'— founded the *Rheinische Zeitung* as a rival to the conservative and ultramontane *Kölnische Zeitung*, and proceeded to staff it with leading members of the club of Young Hegelians. Marx became a regular contributor to it, and in October was made editor. The journal soon came to be regarded as 'dangerous' by the government in Berlin. His association with it finally closed the door for Marx to an academic career. It also brought him into touch with current social questions: for example, with the property law as it affected the peasant and with questions of free trade; and when his paper was accused by a rival of flirting with Communism, Marx embarked on a study of the writings of the French socialists to discover whether the charge was true. In 1843, following a series of articles on the impoverished condition of the Mosel peasants and on the stifling of their complaints by oppressive police action, official warning was given that the *Rheinische Zeitung* would be suppressed. The censor reported that Dr. Marx held 'ultra-democratic opinions in utter contradiction to the principles of the Prussian State'; and in a bid to safeguard its continued appearance Marx severed his connection with the paper.

He took advantage of the respite to marry his adored Jenny, who was soon to follow him into exile and to be his courageous companion through many years of hardship and poverty for which by birth and upbringing she was ill-fitted. When twenty years later he paid a visit to the Westphalen home—a visit which became almost a pilgrimage—Marx was enchanted to find that his wife still lived in the memory of the town as 'the most beautiful girl in Trier'. Even on his honeymoon, however, he found time to fill five large notebooks with extracts from Montesquieu, Rousseau and Machiavelli. The honeymoon was occupied also with correspondence with young Hegelian friends about the publication of a new journal. In the autumn of 1843 it was arranged that this new journal, which was intended to have something of an international character, should be launched from Paris, beyond the direct clutches of the Prussian censors; and in order to be a partner in the new venture

Marx with his wife moved to Paris in November. Although he was not yet at this date deprived of his German nationality, his days of exile had in fact begun.

This move to Paris brought Marx into closer touch with French and with English thought, and especially with the ideas of the French socialists and the writings of the classical economists. It was during these years in Paris that he began his reading of Ricardo and McCulloch, also of Adam Smith, James Mill and Say. The new journal, however, did not prosper in the climate of the French capital, and soon came to an end. But one notable result for which its short life was responsible was the start of Marx's friendship and collaboration with Friedrich Engels, who sent an article and a review to the first number of the journal. Engels came of a family which had been one of the pioneers of machine-spinning in Germany; and at the age of twenty-two, after doing his military service with a guards regiment of artillery, he was sent by his father to join a branch of the family firm that had been recently established in Manchester. Engels, who had mixed with Left Hegelians in Berlin, was soon in contact with radical and socialist circles in England. In 1843 he was writing for Robert Owen's paper, *New Moral World*, and soon afterwards became a frequent contributor to the Chartist organ, *Northern Star*. When he met Marx on a visit to Paris in the summer of 1844, he was completing his well-known study on *The Condition of the Working Class in England in 1844*, and Marx was quick to notice the affinity of Engels's ideas to his own.

When he left Germany, Marx's standpoint was summed up in his statement about the importance of 'ruthless criticism of everything that exists, ruthless in the sense that the criticism will not shrink either from its own conclusions or from conflict with the powers that be'. To this, however, he added that the task of critical philosophy was to give society a consciousness of itself—'show it why it struggles'—and that criticism should begin by 'taking part in politics, that is to say in real struggles'. His years in Paris caused these ideas to crystallise in a more definitely socialist shape—to become criticism of existing social conditions and of the economic basis of society, not merely criticism within the circle of ideas. His meeting with Engels accelerated this tendency, and led him towards a closer study of economic conditions, and in particular to a critique of capitalism as it was displayed in its classic form in England.

In 1845 pressure from the Prussian government caused Guizot, the French Minister of Foreign Affairs, to serve an expulsion order on Marx, necessitating his hasty removal to Brussels. From there he paid a six-weeks' visit to England in the company of Engels, and made the acquaintance of the English labour movement for the first time in the shape of the Chartists and some of the trade unionists. He was quick to appreciate that, while (in Engels's words) 'theoretical differences with these fellows can scarcely exist, for they have no theory', they represented a stage of historical development which had as yet no parallel on the Continent—that here was an issue, as he afterwards wrote, 'not of republic *v.* monarchy, but of the rule of the working class and the rule of the bourgeoisie'. In the winter of 1847 he travelled again to London to attend a meeting of a body known as the Fraternal Democrats; also at the same time the second congress of an international body known as the Communist League, which was meeting at the White Hart in Drury Lane. It was this congress that commissioned Marx and Engels to draft for it the manifesto which was to become the historic *Communist Manifesto* of the following year, printed by a German printer at 46 Liverpool Street.

But Brussels was not to be a resting-place for Marx for very long. During the revolutionary year 1848, he received notice from the Belgian police to quit. From Brussels he went to Paris early in March, and then with Engels to Cologne to edit a new journal, the *Neue Rheinische Zeitung*, which described itself as 'an organ of democracy' and was intended to unite the workers, the peasantry and the progressive bourgeoisie against the autocracy. In the spring of 1849 the paper was suppressed and its editor was ordered to leave Prussian soil within twenty-four hours. As a parting act of defiance the final number of the paper was printed in red, with a poem by Freiligrath on its front page. Engels went south to join an insurgent army that was being recruited in Baden. Marx, with his wife and three children, went to live in Paris under an assumed name, pawning his wife's jewellery to pay for the journey and the rent (all his slender savings having been sunk in the suppressed journal). But the Paris police soon discovered his identity and forced him to migrate once again. This time he chose London as his refuge, where with his family he was to spend (except for short journeys abroad) the remaining thirty years of his life.

In London, after a short stay in furnished lodgings (his biographer Mehring speaks of Chelsea and Liebknecht of Camberwell, and on this brief period his letters are silent), which was abruptly terminated by the entry of the bailiff, the Marx family moved into two small rooms (one of which served as a kitchen as well as a living-room) in Soho, first at 69 and then at 28 Dean Street. During this period Marx's only sources of livelihood were the proceeds of occasional newspaper articles (chiefly for the *New York Tribune*), visits to the pawnshop with the Westphalen family silver and sometimes with Marx's overcoat, and the unfailing generosity of Engels (a generosity, incidentally, that was treated by both of them impersonally, in the main, as a pooling of one's money for the sake of the common cause). The exiled family suffered serious poverty in these years, which did grave damage to his wife's health and was no doubt a contributory cause of the death during this Soho period of a daughter and two sons, including his eldest son at nine years of age, whose death affected him deeply. Marx was thus unlike most economists in knowing what poverty was from his own direct experience. When the child Franziska died he had no money to buy a coffin; and on another occasion of illness in the house he wrote to Engels that he could not fetch the doctor because he lacked the money to pay even for the medicine, and that 'for the last 8 or 10 days I have fed my family on bread and potatoes and today it is still doubtful whether I shall be able to obtain even these'.

All this time Marx worked hard, with the British Museum Reading Room as his workshop. Here he immersed himself daily from nine till seven in what he called the 'confounded ramifications of political economy'; while in the evening he would write and smoke inordinately into the small hours. As recreation, he played chess (until his wife forbade it because he was apt to lose his temper), composed a dissertation on the calculus to distract his mind from domestic worries, recited Shakespeare and read Aeschylus in the Greek. On rare and precious Sundays he would take the family to Hampstead Heath, complete with their faithful maid Lenchen and the family hamper, to picnic on the grass near Jack Straw's Castle; Marx reciting poetry (a bit theatrically) or taking the children for rides on his back in a breathless game called 'cavalry' or to amuse them solemnly riding a donkey himself. Liebknecht tells of a memorable evening when he and Marx and Bruno Bauer's brother laid a wager to visit all the public houses in Tottenham Court Road; of how they fell in with a social gathering of the Society of Oddfellows; and ended by throwing bricks at gaslamps like undergraduates and being chased through the alleys of Soho by four policemen. After six years of cramped and sordid existence in Soho a small legacy from his wife's mother enabled them to purchase some second-hand furniture, to get their linen out of pawn, and to move to the pleasanter surroundings of Haverstock Hill, first to Grafton Terrace and later to Maitland Park Road. It was here that he was living when he participated in the foundation of the First International—its full title was the International Working Men's Association—which took place on the initiative of British trade union leaders and some French socialists at an inaugural meeting at St. Martin's Hall, London, in

September 1864, with Professor Beesly in the chair. And it was at Haverstock Hill that he prepared for publication in 1859 *A Contribution to a Critique of Political Economy*, and in 1865 completed the first volume of *Capital: a Critical Analysis of Capitalist Production*, which was first published in Germany two years later in 1867.

2 What, then, was the problem as Marx saw it in his economic analysis? What kind of question was he trying to answer?

Evidently what had struck Marx as the most significant contribution of the classical economists was their demonstration that the economic affairs of men were ruled by law, just as natural science had shown this to be the case in the realm of nature—moreover, by laws which operated independently of men's wills and served ends that were different from the ends or purposes which any individual had consciously intended. This was the significance of Adam Smith's 'hidden hand', and before him of Mandeville's paradox of 'private vices, public virtues'—that the selfish actions of individuals often worked out, in the total result, to the benefit of all. (As Adam Smith once said: 'it is not from the benevolence of the butcher, the brewer or the baker that we expect our dinner, but from their regard to their own interest'.) Marx must have been struck by the affinity of these notions with a central idea of Hegel's philosophy of history: that 'out of the actions of men comes something quite different from what they intend and directly know and will'.

This ruling law, both for Marx and his predecessors, was to be found in a law of value—the law that under competitive conditions things had a long-run tendency to exchange at certain 'normal values'. The secret of these 'normal values' was to be found in what various things *cost*—not simply in their *money* expenses of production, which in turn required explanation, but in their *real* cost to society. The ratios in which things exchanged had nothing to do with what individuals designed or willed. It was not human design or dictation that determined the exchange and distribution of wealth, but the objective circumstances of their production—the amount of various things which a given amount of labour could produce. This was the Labour Theory of Value: at least, the variant of it that was used by Ricardo and Marx. It was a conception specially congenial to Marx's mind, since the conception of history associated with his name was that the general character of society at any stage of history was determined in the final analysis by the mode of production—and in particular by the relations into which men entered in the course of production. If you looked only at men's ideas and volitions, or even if you looked at events as they appeared on the face of the market and no further than this, you were unlikely to see the real forces at work—in fact, you would probably be misled by superficial appearances. For the essence of the matter one must look deeper.

From the laws they enunciated, however, the classical economists drew two important conclusions—at any rate, the successors of Ricardo did with growing emphasis; and it was here that Marx parted company from them. Firstly, these laws came to be endowed, not only with an eternally inevitable, but also (in the main) a beneficent character. The 'invisible hand' was an instrument by which harmony emerged and the general good triumphed. Secondly, since values were established by a process of free contract on the market, constantly guarded by the watchdog of competition, there could be no question of one party to an exchange getting something for nothing, or outwitting or exploiting the other, save as a temporary or exceptional occurrence. This was generally held to apply to the wage-contract as well as to any other (despite Adam Smith's celebrated passage about combination among masters). Labour could have no permanent grievances against capital because the master was as necessary to the labourer as the labourer was to his master, and each must have his purchase-price.

With this view Marx vehemently joined issue. He was far from denying that the capitalist system marked an advance on its predecessors and was responsible for great economic achievements: on the contrary, he stressed this even in a political work like *The Communist Manifesto*. But in common with previous systems it held within it a basic contradiction (or potential antagonism) which would be the historical motive-force destined eventually to disrupt it and to transform it into a socialist system. For Marx it was evident (as an empirical fact, not as a proposition relying on some *a priori* argument for its validity) that the capitalist class, drawing an income by virtue of property-rights, lived off the surplus labour of wage-workers in the same sense as the medieval lord lived off the surplus labour of his serfs or the slave-owner off his slaves; and that this was the real crux of the matter. The difference was that today relationships between classes did not take the form, as in former times, of obligatory services imposed by *extra*-economic factors such as law or social custom, but took an exclusively value-form as a wage-contract made between two freely contracting parties.

In drawing this parallel with earlier class-systems Marx did not stand alone. In some of the classical economists there are passages which hint at it or are open to such an interpretation. Writers like Sismondi, Thompson and Bray had sought to explain capitalist income by the fact that the capitalist, through cheating or *force majeure*, underpaid his workers—paid labour *less* than its value—or alternatively sold the product for more than it cost, i.e. *above* its value. But such explanations were regarded by Marx as unsatisfactory. They were open to an easy answer from the orthodox: that if such exploitation of either consumers or workpeople occurred, this must be due to the imperfect operation of competition (otherwise the pressure of the market would cause things to exchange at their values); and the proper cure for this was more perfect competition, which was precisely what the free traders were advocating. The crucial problem for Marx was to show how the fact that one class in society drew an income without contributing any productive activity could be consistent with the prevalence of competition and the rule of economic law. He had to explain, as any theory of profit or surplus has to do, why it was that competition did not force down the value of the net product to the money expenses of production, consisting of 'wage-advances' to labourers, or alternatively force up the reward of labour until it absorbed the whole net product. Marx somewhere says:[1] 'To explain the *general nature of profits*, you must start from the theorem that, on an average, commodities are *sold at their real values*, and that *profits are derived from selling them at their values*.... If you cannot explain profit upon this supposition, you cannot explain it at all.'

The answer which Marx gave is simple enough once it has been stated: so simple that it might seem surprising that so much ink has been spilled to disprove it and to propound alternative explanations in terms of the 'services' rendered by the capitalist, in the shape of the 'abstinence' he suffers in saving up money, or in terms of the 'specific productivity' of capital. The answer amounted to an explanation in terms of the historical circumstances out of which capitalism had grown—the social conditions or relations of production which underlay exchange. Capitalist production implied, at one and at the same time, both a concentration of property in the hands of a section of society and the *dis*possession of the larger section of society. This latter class, divorced from the means of production and lacking alternative means of livelihood, were forced by the situation in which they found themselves to sell themselves to a master—to a propertied master, possessed of the means with which labour could be set to work. In other words, labour power—the working activity or physical energy of a human being for a given period of time—itself became a

[1] In *Value, Price and Profit*, ed. Eleanor Marx Aveling (London, 1899), pp. 53–4. Italics in the original.

commodity, offered on the market and trafficked in like any other; and like any other commodity, its value was determined by the labour time that its production normally cost. Labour power, according to Marx, consisted essentially of 'energy transferred to a human organism by means of nourishing matter';[1] and its production and reproduction accordingly consisted of the input of 'nourishing matter' into the human organism to replace the energy used up in work. Hence the value of labour power of, say, a week's duration was governed by the labour time required to produce the subsistence of a worker for a week. But under the conditions of modern industry, with modern technique and modern division of labour, labour power had the property, peculiar among commodities, that its consumption, or utilisation, occasioned a value *greater than its own value*—it could generally create in a given period, say a week, much *more* than its own keep. The difference, which Marx termed surplus value, was what the employer, possessing the capital to lay out in purchase of this surplus-producing commodity, could annex to himself simply by virtue of this transaction of buying labour power and selling its products, without the necessity for him to have any further connection with the act of production. It was something that he could pocket like a gentleman without resorting to shady manœuvres or soiling his hands.

This theory, of course, rested on a number of assumptions, some of which Marx set out in a letter to Engels in 1858. To make the task of analysis manageable, he had constructed a simplified 'model' of capitalist society—in order to 'disregard all phenomena that hide the play of its inner mechanism'.[2] He had taken a 'pure' capitalist society as his type form, in which there were simply capitalists, on the one hand, laying out their capital to hire labour, and workers, on the other hand, offering their labour power for sale. He was assuming, at this stage of the analysis, that the problem of rent does not exist—that land is what is sometimes termed a 'free good' ('land rent = zero').[3] He was assuming 'that all commodities including labour-power are bought and sold at their full value'.[4] To these explicit assumptions one might perhaps add that he was evidently assuming implicitly a condition of the labour market such as to exact a downward pressure on wages: in other words, something like a chronic tendency to labour surplus—men being more plentiful than jobs. The theory of the reproduction of what he termed 'the industrial reserve army' ('a

[1] *Capital*, trans. Moore and Aveling, Vol. I, p. 198, n. 1.   [2] *Ibid.*, p. 577.
[3] Letter to Engels, 2 April 1858, *Marx-Engels Correspondence*, ed. Dona Torr, (London, 1934), p. 106.
[4] *Capital*, trans. Moore and Aveling, Vol. I, p. 302.

law of population peculiar to the capitalist mode of production')[1] occupies a prominent place in Volume I. This periodic recruitment of the reserve army occurred as the result of the replacement of 'living labour' by 'stored-up labour', or of men by machines, in modern machine production. 'The labouring population produces, along with the accumulation of capital produced by it, the means by which itself is made relatively superfluous, is turned into a relative surplus population; and it does this to an always increasing extent.'[2] This process replaced that of the 'primitive accumulation' by which the ranks of the proletariat had been recruited at the dawn of capitalism through the progressive expropriation of small producers, peasant-farmers and artisans; and it was a process that operated with special force at such times as the price of labour power started to rise and in doing so threatened a contraction of surplus value. This did not mean that Marx held to a rigid 'iron law of wages': on the contrary, any such easy mechanical notion was foreign to his method, and this phrase as well as the doctrine belonged to Lassalle and not to Marx. In the first place, Marx was careful to stress that habit and custom ('an historical and social element') influenced what in any country or age was conventionally considered to be a necessary subsistence, and that trade union action was capable of raising labour above subsistence level, just as concerted or monopolistic action on the employers' part could depress wages below that level, at least for considerable periods of time. He pointed out that there might be periods of rapid capital accumulation when the price of labour power showed a rising tendency. But he emphasised that, owing to the continual tendency for technique to be revolutionised and capital to take the form of stored-up labour, while 'with the growth of the total capital, its variable constituent or the labour incorporated in it, also does increase', it does so 'in a constantly diminishing proportion'.[3] The important point was that any 'rise of wages is confined within limits that not only leave intact the foundations of the capitalistic system, but also secure its reproduction on a progressive scale'.[4]

What, then, did this explanation of the source of capitalists' income amount to, and wherein did it essentially differ from rival explanations? Firstly, as we have seen, it threw into relief the character of profit, or surplus value, as an historical category, product of a particular set of his-

[1] *Capital*, trans. Moore and Aveling, Vol. I, p. 645.   [2] *Ibid.*, p. 645.
[3] *Ibid.*, p. 643. Cf. also: 'In the measure that capitalism develops, the demand for labour diminishes relatively, even while increasing in an absolute manner.' (*Theorien über den Mehrwert*, Ed. 1921, Vol. II, Pt. 3, p. 263).
[4] *Capital*, Vol. I, p. 634.

torical conditions, of which the crucial one was the existence of a propertyless class. These historical conditions it was in the interest of one class to perpetuate at all costs and of the other class to destroy; whence arose an antagonism between them which was irreconcilable within the confines of that system. This was a qualitative statement about the contrasted character of the two classes of income, wages and profits: the one a return to a human productive activity of the equivalent of what that activity 'cost' or used up; the other a payment which was as independent of any productive activity on the recipient's part as the income of a feudal lord or a slave-owner had been. But joined with this was a quantitative statement: namely, that, given the size of the employed labour force, total surplus value, or capitalist income, depended uniquely on the proportion of that labour force which was needed to produce subsistence for the workers; or, as Marx put it more graphically, on the proportion of the working day during which (on the average) the worker was merely reproducing his own value (i.e. his own wages). This (or rather the ratio of the difference between unity and this proportion to this proportion) was the basic exploitation-ratio[1] on which the distribution of income between the classes essentially depended, and on which the constellation of exchange relationships turned.

In addition to the chapters of analysis, Volume I of Marx's best-known work is rich in historical material. This ranges from an examination of the various transitional stages between handicraft and modern machinery to quotations from the reports of factory inspectors on the wretched conditions of factory labour, and back again from contemporary blue-books to an account of the historical process—the process of 'primitive accumulation' by which a proletariat was formed. An example of his thoroughness in such matters is that when he was drafting his chapters on machinery he attended a practical course in technology at the Geological Institute in Jermyn Street, although, as he wrote to Engels, 'the simplest technical reality demanding perception is harder to me than to the biggest blockheads'.

The second and third volumes of his *opus* were never completed in his lifetime. On his death in 1883 they existed only as unfinished drafts and

[1] This is what Marx called the 'simple rate of surplus value'. Later, in Vol. II, he is careful to point out that when one comes to deal with the rate of profit (the ratio that surplus value bears, not to the wage-bill, but to total capital), it is the 'annual rate of surplus value' that is relevant, the latter being related to the former according to the number of times that a given variable capital is turned over in the course of a year (*Capital*, Vol. II, trans E. Untermann, Chicago, 1925, pp. 338–9, 349–50).

notes which Engels faithfully pieced together and published, Volume II in 1885 and Volume III in 1894. In his preface Engels speaks of this material as 'fragmentary' and 'incomplete in various places', 'not polished as to language', but 'the language in which Marx used to make his outlines, that is to say his style, was careless, full of colloquial, often rough and humorous, expressions and phrases. . . . At the conclusion of the chapters there would be only a few incoherent sentences as milestones of incomplete deductions. . . . And finally [Engels adds] there was the well-known handwriting which Marx himself was sometimes unable to decipher.'[1] But in these two volumes there is plenty of penetrating analysis and original thought, again interspersed with historical illustrations and some acute historical comment. (One would refer particularly to some notes entitled 'Historical Data concerning Merchant Capital' in Volume III, and also several chapters about types of land tenancy and rents transitional between feudal labour services and modern capitalism.) There was also to have been a fourth volume, to consist of a critical history of economic thought. But Engels did not live to complete the editing of it. It was later put together by Karl Kautsky in Germany under the title of *Theories of Surplus Value* in 1905. It has been published in a French translation in eight separate parts; but has not to date been translated into English.* The Marx-Engels-Lenin Institute in Moscow has in its possession all the manuscript material used by Kautsky; and for more than a decade this Institute has been planning to re-work and re-edit it and to publish a definitive edition.**

Volume II has as sub-title 'the process of circulation of capital', and is concerned, first of all with what Marx calls the turnover or rotation of capital—the influence of the time taken for capital invested in any particular way to emerge in the form of a final product; secondly, with the equilibrium relations between different branches of industry under conditions of 'simple reproduction' and 'expanded reproduction' (zero net investment and positive net investment). It can scarcely be disputed that in these comparatively neglected sections much of what has later been written by economists about capital and about investment is anticipated or even surpassed. Actually, the third and final part of Volume II, con-

---

[1] Preface to Vol. II of *Capital*, trans. Untermann, p. 7.

[*Since this was written an English translation of a part of this volume has been published (*Theories of Surplus Value: Selections*, trans. by G. A. Bonner and Emile Burns, London, 1951).]

[**A coming Russian edition of the first third of the work has since been announced.]

cerning the so-called 'reproduction of capital', was in a more unfinished state than the rest, being chiefly written in the years of failing health in the late 'seventies. Product of repeated revision and successive reconstructions, it represented (in Engels's words), 'merely a preliminary presentation of the subject' and 'shows traces of hard struggles against depressing physical conditions';[1] whereas Volume III was mostly drafted earlier, in his years of greater vigour in the middle 'sixties.

Volume III, which has 'Capitalist Production as a Whole' as its subtitle, comes closer to the problem of particular prices, and is concerned in the first place with the rate of profit on capital, and subsequently with the division of the *genus* surplus value into the sub-species of profit, interest and rent. This involves a closer approximation to the complex detail of reality, and a discarding of some of the assumptions made for the purpose of analysis in Volume I. The preoccupation of Volume I was with the *rate of surplus value*, defined as the ratio of surplus value to that part of the capital (called variable capital) which is laid out in the purchase of labour power. In Volume III it is with the *rate of profit*, which, by contrast, is the 'annual rate of surplus value' expressed as a ratio to the *total stock* of capital ('variable' *plus* 'constant' capital, i.e. capital laid out in purchase of living labour power *plus* capital embodied in stocks of raw material, machinery and fixed equipment). It follows that the latter ratio $\left(\frac{s}{c+v}\right)$ will be *lower* than the former $\left(\frac{s}{v}\right)$; and that it will be lower compared with the former the *higher* the ratio of 'constant' to 'variable' capital (what Marx termed the 'organic composition of capital')—the larger the sum of values embodied in stored-up labour compared to the living labour set in motion over any given period of time. It follows that as technical progress tends to substitute stored-up labour for living labour, the rate of profit yielded by a given rate of surplus value will fall—that is the rate of profit will fall *unless* the rate of exploitation of living labour is correspondingly increased. From this analysis a further important consequence is drawn. The ratio in which 'constant capital' stands to 'variable' is not uniform as between industries (as was the tacit assumption of Volume I). In agriculture or dressmaking there is much less expensive machinery and fixed equipment per man (or woman) employed than there is in iron and steel or heavy chemicals. Again, the 'period of turnover' of the capital will be different in different cases. An equal rate of surplus value in these different cases would not, therefore, yield the *same* rate of profit. But if the rate of profit were to be unequal, capital would

[1] Preface to Vol. II, pp. 10–11.

migrate from where this rate was low to where it was high; thereby contracting output and raising the price in the former case and expanding output and lowering the price in the latter case. Because of this 'competition of capitals'—that 'unconscious capitalist communism' which requires capital to earn an (approximately) equal rate of profit—it happened that commodities exchange, not at their 'values', but at what Marx termed their 'prices of production'.[1] This 'price of production' was in some cases above and in some cases below 'value' according as the 'organic composition of capital' in the industry in question was above or below the average.

It was this qualification that caused Marx's most considerable critic (Böhm-Bawerk), in his polemical essay, *Karl Marx and the Close of his System*, to speak of it as 'the great contradiction' on which the whole system foundered. It is true that at first sight the apparent incompatibility between the theory enunciated in Volume I and the analysis of prices of production in Volume III is puzzling. But the claim that the qualifications introduced in the later volume jettison the foundations of the analysis of surplus value in Volume I is based on a perverse misunderstanding of Marx's method. Marx's primary concern had been with the distribution of income between classes (as it had been Ricardo's before him): until one could explain this, one could explain nothing. For analysis of this larger problem he constructed a simplified model; proceeding by the well-tried method of successive approximations. In the first approximation he was concerned, not with the problem of relative prices of particular commodities, but with the larger problem of the exchange relationships between broad *groups* of commodities—agricultural commodities and manufactures, and these in relation to labour power treated as a whole. He was concerned to throw into relief the main basic influences which were shaping the configuration of the whole. When in the later volume he began to handle the problem of particular prices, he introduced additional features into his simplified model, and showed the difference that their introduction made. It is ridiculous to suppose that in doing so he was other than perfectly aware of what he was doing. In particular, he did not consider (which is the crucial point) that the change made any

[1] Marx defined 'price of production' as cost price *plus* a normal rate of profit on the capital employed. Cost price = expenditure on wages + constant capital *used up* (i.e. raw materials used up and depreciation of machinery, etc.). As regards the effect of the 'rate of turnover' of capital Marx wrote: 'With capitals with equal percentages of composition, equal rates of surplus value, and equal working days, the rates of profit are proportioned inversely as their periods of turnover.' (*Capital*, Vol. III, p. 87.) [See further on this 'A Note on the Transformation Problem', below, p. 273.]

significant amount of difference to his analysis of the questions with which he was occupied in Volume I. Moreover, without the theory of how *total* profit or surplus value was determined, in terms of the sort of factors thrown into relief in Volume I, he would have had no theory of profit (and hence of the *average rate* of profit) at all, and the theory of prices of production in Volume III would have been left hanging in the air (as was, indeed, the case with the Cost of Production Theory of John Stuart Mill). In other words, the analysis conducted in Volume III, despite its secondary modifications, essentially rested upon that of Volume I and would have been impossible without it. Marx regarded the *rate* of profit of which he treated in Volume III, and which was a crucial element in the formation of the 'price of production', as depending on the size of surplus value relatively to the value of the existing stock of capital; and aggregate surplus value in turn depended on the factors affecting that basic exploitation-ratio which was analysed in Volume I. It remained true that 'the law of value dominates the movements of prices, since a reduction or increase of the labour-time required for production causes the prices of production to fall or to rise', even though 'the general law of value enforces itself merely as a prevailing tendency, in a very complicated and approximate manner'; while the qualitative theory of surplus value in Volume I remained the essential kernel of the whole if one was 'to penetrate through the outward disguise into the internal essence and the inner form of the capitalist process of production'.[1]

It is also in Volume III, together with the third part of Volume II and a section in the *Theorien*,[2] that the torso of Marx's theory of economic crises is to be found. The classical economists had tended to identify the rule of economic law with an underlying stability and harmony in the economic system. There had been the famous controversy between Malthus and Ricardo as to the cause of periodic 'gluts' of commodities and as to whether it was possible for general overproduction of commodities to occur. But the view which was to become the orthodox doctrine of Ricardo's successors was that, given free trade and the removal of all obstacles to capital accumulation and the growth of industry, there was no reason for general 'gluts' to occur and no reason for the rate of profit on capital to fall.

To this optimistic view Marx opposed the notion that capitalism was not a stable but an unstable system. While he accepted (even emphasised) the view that its movements were ruled by objective law, he was at the

[1] *Capital*, Vol. III, pp. 211, 190, 199.
[2] *Theorien* (Ed. 1921), Vol. II, Pt. 2, pp. 233–332.

same time concerned to show that, as a mode of production, it rested on certain contradictions, and that the very forces which operated to yield an equilibrium of its elements generated counter-forces which periodically disrupted that equilibrium. In fact, any smooth mechanistic model, shaped in terms of equilibrium situations and smooth vectors of movement, was inappropriate. Conflict and interaction were of the essence of the system; and it was only by an appreciation of this fact that one could acquire any vision of its 'law of motion' and its historical destiny.

In the *Theorien* Marx speaks of general world crises as the succinct manifestation of 'all the contradictions of bourgeois society'; while 'particular crises (as regards both their content and their scope)' are the expression of these contradictions 'merely in a diffuse, insulated and partial form (nur zerstreut, isoliert, einseitig)'.[1] In his analysis of these contradictions he is continually concerned to rebut the optimistic theories of the Ricardian school and to demonstrate the various ways in which a rupture of equilibrium was possible, and would moreover tend periodically to occur. He did not deny that it was possible in the abstract to construct 'conditions of equilibrium development' (from which it could be deduced that crises were not necessary if only these conditions were observed): what he denied was that there was any actual tendency in capitalist society for these abstract conditions to be fulfilled—on the contrary, they were only observed 'by an accident'. Moreover, a crisis was often, not merely the expression of a rupture of equilibrium, but itself the process by which the broken equilibrium asserted itself ('For a crisis is nothing but the forcible assertion of the unity of phases in the process of production which have become independent of one another', and 'crises are always but momentary and forcible solutions of existing contradictions, violent eruptions which restore the disturbed equilibrium for a while.').[2] But the sequence of events by which a crisis originated in any particular case could not be abstractly postulated: it must be studied in the concrete circumstances of the special time and place. 'The actual crisis can only be depicted against the background of the actual movements of capitalist production.'[3] It is hardly surprising that one does not find in Marx any simple demonstration that crises are due to a single cause, or any clear-cut model to show the sequence of events by which crises always and inevitably arise. Such would have been too mechanical a procedure to have been congenial to the method of Marx. There has been a good deal of controversy in the last half-century as to which element in the situation

---

[1] *Theorien*, Vol. II, Pt. 2, p. 318. [2] *Ibid.*, p. 282, and *Capital*, Vol. III, p. 292.
[3] *Theorien*, Vol. II, Pt. 2, p. 286.

described by Marx he intended to be regarded as *the* cause of crises. Into this controversy we cannot enter here; and in the writer's opinion some of this discussion has been actuated by a search for too mechanical and over-simplified a type of answer. All we can do here is to indicate the main strands which are to be distinguished in Marx's treatment of this subject. What is quite clear at any rate is that for Marx crises were an inevitable product of capitalist society: product of the many-sided contradiction between 'the productive forces and the productive relations' of capitalism. 'The real barrier of capitalist production', he wrote, 'is capital itself. . . . The barriers, within which the preservation and self-expansion of the value of capital resting on the expropriation and pauperisation of the great mass of producers can alone move, these barriers come continually in collision with the methods of production which capital must employ for its own purposes, and which steer straight toward an unrestricted expansion of production . . . toward an unconditional development of the productive forces of society.' And again: 'The capitalist mode of production meets with barriers at a certain scale of production, which would be inadequate under other conditions. It comes to a standstill at a point determined by the production and realisation of profit, not by the satisfaction of social needs.'[1]

In the famous third part of Volume II of *Capital* Marx sets out the conditions under which capital accumulation ('expanded reproduction') can take place at a constant rate without any disturbance and breakdown of the process. But Marx was quick to indicate the numerous influences which would tend to disturb these conditions; one of them being the failure of capitalists who were accumulating depreciation reserves to spend these reserves at a steady rate on new 'constant capital', i.e. on new stocks of material and the replacement of fixed equipment. A similar breakdown of the process would occur if there was a disproportionate development of any branch of production—if one branch of production got out of step with the rest. Finding no market for its products, this industry would contract and discharge its workers, thereby tending through a spiral of declining demand to spread the contraction to other industries.

Towards the end of Volume II (in some very condensed passages) Marx introduces the case where 'expanded reproduction' occurs, not at a constant rate, but at an *increasing* rate.* He shows that in this case a special type of problem arises; and it is here that the much-discussed 'under-

---

[1] *Capital*, Vol. III, pp. 293, 303.

[*In the sense of a rise in the ratio of accumulation to net income: cf. below, p. 268.]

consumption' element in crises comes in. When in any year the rate of accumulation (as a proportion of $s + v$, or net product) increases, this means, *ceteris paribus*, that capitalists decide to spend (on their own enjoyment) a *smaller* portion and to save a larger portion of their surplus value than they did in the previous year. The rate of saving will rise and the rate of consumption will fall. When this happens, how will the capitalists in the industries producing consumption goods, who previously found a market in capitalists' luxury expenditure, be able to dispose of all their output? If they cannot dispose of all their output, how will they *realise* the surplus value embodied in this output? And if they cannot realise this surplus value in money form, how will they be able to continue the investment process? Clearly, the workers are not in a position, because of their limited incomes, to buy the wares that the capitalists no longer wish to do. In these circumstances, the process of investment must, again, break down, arrested by the failure of the *demand* for consumption goods to keep pace with their production, with the result that capitalists who have caused increased output to be produced cannot realise the anticipated surplus value or profit on this output. And if they lack the ready money with which to maintain investment, the demand for 'means of production' (machinery and raw materials, building materials, etc.) must also be curtailed.[1] 'Production without regard to the limits of the market lies in the nature of capitalist production,' says Marx.[2]

In his analysis of expanded reproduction Marx had been tacitly assuming that, as new investment takes place, the ratio in which the new investment is distributed between constant and variable capital (the organic composition of capital) remains unchanged. For this condition to be ful-

---

[1] Marx's answer to the conundrum: how then can the rate of expanded reproduction ever increase? is reserved to a few remarks in the last paragraph of Vol. II. It is that this can occur only so far as the redundant consumption goods are exported in exchange for gold from the gold producers. Evidently an export surplus for any other reason (e.g. foreign investment) would serve equally well; but a mere expansion of foreign trade—export of goods against equivalent goods imports—would not serve this end of finding an *additional* market for the goods. But an expansion of credit (i.e. of bank money) might presumably here have a parallel effect to an import of gold.

Another solution would be that prior to the change in the rate of accumulation a shift had occurred in the distribution of investment between the two main departments of industry, thereby adapting the relative outputs of capital goods and consumer goods to the change in the proportion of income spent on consumption. But Marx would have regarded this as implying too much foresight and planning to be a possible solution under Capitalism.

[2] *Theorien*, Vol. II, Pt. 2, p. 301.

filled, not only must demand for commodities, but also the supply of labour-power, be capable of a continuous and proportional expansion. In Volume III this assumption is removed, and the more likely case is considered where, along with the accumulation of capital, the technique of industry is changing, and with it the ratio of constant to variable capital is being raised. Marx shows that here a new problem arises (even if no disproportionate development occurs and the 'realisation' difficulty does not arise). This problem is the tendency, as a result of the higher composition of capital, for the *rate* of profit on capital to fall. It is clear that such a fall will tend to arrest the process of further investment and precipitate a crisis; while, operating as a long-term tendency, it will constitute a progressively increasing drag on the process of expansion of capital.

Marx is careful to add that there are a number of 'counteracting tendencies', which offset this effect. Chief of these are an increase in 'relative surplus value' due to the consequential rise in labour productivity,[1] a cheapening of machinery and raw materials (thereby lowering the value of constant capital itself) and advantageous terms of foreign trade. Moreover, what are sometimes called 'capital saving inventions' (to which Marx devotes a longish chapter), while they may increase the material volume of means of production, will not increase (and may decrease) constant capital in *value* terms (or alternatively reduce the period of turnover) and will admittedly *raise* the rate of profit. There are indications, however, that Marx considered that the tendency to decline would in general, or at least in the long run, assert itself over the counter-tendencies (although he was careful to speak of it as having 'merely the character of a tendency');[2] and it seems clear that Marx was thinking here primarily of *labour-saving* inventions and of technical change as being predominantly of this type; although the actual outcome must, of course, always depend in large part on the result of the struggle between capital and labour over the division of the product. But in determining the net effect of any given technical change, it will be evident that two ratios are of crucial importance. First, there is the ratio of the proportional change in labour productivity consequent on the improvement to the proportional change in the organic composition of capital. Save in rather exceptional periods of rapid invention (which changes our knowledge as

---

[1] It is to be noted that a rise in productivity would only raise the rate of surplus value in so far as it applied to the 'customary means of subsistence' of workers and thereby cheapened labour power. This was not an invariable consequence of higher productivity.

[2] *Capital*, Vol. III, p. 272.

distinct from our utilisation of known devices) it seems reasonable to suppose that this ratio is likely to decline as capital accumulation proceeds. Secondly, there is the ratio of this change in labour productivity to the resulting increase in relative surplus value (due to the fall in the necessary labour time and a consequent rise in the surplus labour time). In a passage which has sometimes been misinterpreted Marx points out that, as the rate of surplus value increases, each further increase in productivity (and the consequential decline in necessary labour time) must cause a progressively *smaller* proportional increase in surplus value.[1] In other words, the counter-tendency towards an increase of relative surplus value will grow weaker in its effect, and beyond a certain point will cease to arrest the tendency of the rate of profit to decline, unless, that is, the first of the two ratios we have mentioned increases progressively (which it seems extremely unlikely to do).

That in the course of expounding his own theories Marx devoted a great deal of space to the criticism of other economists has often been the subject of adverse comment. True, his criticism of others was as outspoken as it was prolific. Yet this criticism was joined with a strong respect for the leading figures of the classical school. He was remarkably well-acquainted, as his voluminous notebooks show, not only with Adam Smith, Malthus, Ricardo, Senior and John Stuart Mill, but also with the predecessors of Adam Smith and with the numerous post-Ricardian pamphleteers. In his turn Marx has been subjected to more criticism probably than any other economist; and neither understanding of him nor respect for his qualities has been characteristic of much of this criticism. To take one example: Professor Alexander Gray, in a much-used textbook, has dismissed him with references to his 'pedantic parade of learning', his 'dexterous skating on thin ice', his 'subtlety approaching perilously near to sophistry', and with the sweeping conclusion that 'nowhere is there in print such a miracle of confusion, such a supreme example of how not to reason'.[2] Into the controversy which has raged over his doctrine for three-quarters of a century we cannot enter. But one thing about which there can be little question today is the importance, at least, of the emphasis which underlay his approach. This emphasis was that the work-

[1] *Capital*, Vol. III, p. 290. This is the passage which refers to 'intensification of exploitation' as having 'certain impassable limits'. The final limit is when 'necessary labour time' is reduced to zero, when further increases of productivity can increase surplus value no further (given the amount of labour and the length of the working day): a limit approached asymptotically.
[2] *The Development of Economic Doctrine*, pp. 300–2.

ing of an economic system cannot be completely, or even mainly, explained in terms of the market—in terms of supply- and demand-schedules and of factors of production divorced from their human and social roots; and that explanation must be sought in the property-institutions and class-relations on which the system is built; a proper theory of income-distribution being the key to everything else. It is in this setting that his theory of exploitation needs to be appreciated.

Finally, before leaving his economic doctrine, one must refer to the conclusions with regard to the future to which his reading of economic events led him: a growing concentration of capital into larger masses and a growing centralisation of ownership of capital in the hands of large magnates of capital; an accentuation, not a moderation, of periodic crises as capitalism became more mature; a growing acuteness of the struggle between Capital and Labour over the division of the product, until the working-producers should demand the expropriation of capitalists and the vesting of capital in the community. It would be indeed surprising if the forecasts of economists were true in every detail; and Marx's were not. But what must, surely, strike one as remarkable today is how very much more right he was than other nineteenth-century economists and how much of his picture corresponds to leading features of our twentieth-century world. In this connection one cannot forbear to quote the verdict just before the war of a prominent American economist (who repudiates many aspects of Marx's doctrine) regarding what he calls Marx's 'brilliant analysis of the long-run tendencies of the capitalistic system'. 'The record is indeed impressive: increasing concentration of wealth, rapid elimination of small and medium-sized enterprises, progressive limitation of competition, incessant technological progress accompanied by an ever-growing importance of fixed capital, and last but not least the undiminishing amplitude of recurrent business cycles—an unsurpassed series of prognostications fulfilled, against which modern economic theory with all its refinements has little to show.' He concludes: 'If one wants to learn what profits and wages and capitalist enterprises are, he can obtain in the three volumes of *Capital* more realistic and relevant first-hand information than he could possibly hope to find in ten successive issues of the U.S. census (or) a dozen textbooks on contemporary economic institutions.'[1]

---

[1] W. Leontief in 'Proceedings of the 50th Annual Meeting of the American Economic Association, 1937', *American Economic Review Supplement*, March 1938, pp. 5 and 9.

3 If you or I had lived in 1855 and had been privileged to see a proud-looking but slightly down-at-heel man in a crookedly-buttoned frock-coat, with a commanding forehead and prominent eyebrows, deep-set black eyes and a ponderous shining-black beard, walking rather erectly between the British Museum and his shabby Soho lodgings, and if we had been told that he was destined to be the inspirer, two-thirds of a century later, of one of the major social changes in history and to found a doctrine that would be the orthodox teaching of a major world Power, we should no doubt have treated it as too fantastic to be believed. Perhaps it would even have been hard to believe for those who visited him at Grafton Terrace or Maitland Park Road, who sensed at first hand the power of his intellect and sometimes in controversy felt the lash of his tongue. When the other day a leading article in *The Times* stated of Lenin that it was he 'who first brought home to the western world the truth that a civilisation based on the antagonism of capital and labour inevitably carries within it the seeds of its own destruction', it was paying at second-hand an overdue tribute to the insight of Marx.

The last two decades of his life were less borne down by poverty than his first years in London had been. But until the end of the 'sixties he was rarely free from financial worry. His income was always uncertain, despite the constant help of Engels; and after his removal to Haverstock Hill expenses mounted—the education of his children and the illness of his wife. At one time he tried to get a clerical job with one of the railway companies, and had almost succeeded, but was finally turned down because of his handwriting. Later his own health suffered, which interrupted his work and made him irritable. 'I am plagued like Job,' he wrote, 'though not so God-fearing.' In the course of the 'sixties he became increasingly occupied with political work again, as secretary of the German section of the International. Sometimes he occupied the chair at meetings of its General Council. He was apparently an urbane chairman, successful at smoothing over the various differences that increasingly arose between the divergent elements represented on the Council; in this respect being much more successful than was Engels on his rarer appearances. Round 1870 he was increasingly involved in the detail of the struggle within the International between the General Council and the Anarchists led by Bakunin. In 1871 he wrote on behalf of this General Council his famous pamphlet in defence of the Paris Commune, entitled *Civil War in France*, one of the most eloquent and incisive of his writings, composed in English, which in his own words made him 'the best calumniated man in London' and which contained the embryo of a theory of the State and Revolution which was to inspire Lenin half a century later. Throughout these years the inevitable controversies and personal quarrels associated with *emigré* life severely exercised him; and once Engels in exasperation wrote to him: 'exile is an institution in which everyone must necessarily become a fool, a donkey and a scurvy knave.' While he had a special weakness for poets like Heine and Freiligrath, whom he thought should not be treated like ordinary men, Marx did not suffer fools gladly. He had contempt for what he called 'mutual concessions and half-measures tolerated for the sake of appearances', and he was intolerant alike of romantic revolutionaries, rich in sentiment but poor in understanding, and of those who for expediency watered down a doctrine over which he had laboured and suffered so much. He hated cant as he hated also servility; and he did not spare words in his contempt, as when he dubbed a certain colleague (half jocularly) *Deus minorum gentium, canis domesticus communismi germanici*. It is hardly surprising that he made enemies, and while the close friends he had were steadfast, they were not very numerous.

At the end of the 'sixties Engels sold out to his business partner in Manchester, settled on Marx an annual income of £350, and came himself to live nearby in London in a handsome house in Regents Park Road. About the same time two of Marx's daughters found husbands in fairly well-to-do French socialists. But no sooner had a firm income and the nearness of his greatest friend transformed the horizon for him than failing health in the early 'seventies sent him on repeated visits to take the waters successively of Harrogate, Malvern and Karlsbad. On one occasion he paid a visit to the Channel Islands; on another he was sent by the doctors to rest and breathe the sea air on Ramsgate pier. But his later years must have been clouded by other things than ill-health. After 1872 the International to which he had given so much of his energy went into disintegration; and unlike Engels, he was not to live to see the revival of socialism in the second half of the 'eighties. The publication of Volume I of *Capital* had won him considerable recognition in Russia, and a certain amount in Germany, where the book had a second edition within five years, and in France where an authorised translation appeared in 1875. But in England (beyond the circles of the International) he remained an isolated and almost unknown figure. He must have been increasingly tormented by doubt as to whether he would ever succeed in completing the other volumes. In his last few years his grandchildren were a growing source of delight to him when they were in England; and he writes to his daughter Jenny: 'It is dull since you went away. I often run to the window when I hear children's voices that sound like our children, forgetting for the moment that the little chaps are across the channel.' Their household nickname for him was 'Old Moor'. But his wife's health was failing as well as his own: she was suffering from cancer; and after returning from a visit with Marx to Paris to see their daughters she died in 1881, while Marx himself was recovering from pleurisy. He just had strength enough to be by her bedside during her last morning. This loss broke his spirit as years of adversity had never done; and he did not survive it for many months. The following year was one of slow decline. He went on a trip to Algiers and back through the south of France and the Lake of Geneva. But another blow was to fall: the sudden death of his eldest daughter, six months after the death of her mother. On his return to London Marx lingered on for a month or two, the fire gone from his eyes and the wit from his tongue. He took walks on Hampstead Heath. He started fingering his manuscripts again. He seems for a few weeks to have cherished the hope that he might be able to complete them. It was the last rally of his old indomitable will. The fogs of a London winter struck him down again—at first bronchitis and later a tumour on one lung. In March 1883 came the end. He died, a little unexpectedly, quietly in his armchair when he was not quite sixty-five years old.

He was buried in Highgate Cemetery by the side of his wife, and Engels delivered a last speech to his memory over the grave. There were not more than a dozen persons at the graveside to hear it. *The Times* printed a two-inch obituary paragraph; but it was not completely accurate (it gave Cologne as his birthplace and spoke of him as 'the acknowledged chief of the Socialist Party in Europe' since 1866), and it appeared simply as a message from 'our Paris correspondent', reporting the French socialist Press. Apart from this in England his death passed unnoticed. Today[1] he is nowhere more execrated than in the country of his birth; while his anniversaries are officially honoured in a land on which he never set foot.

[1] I.e. 1942.

X

BERNARD SHAW AND ECONOMICS
[1946]

The following was written for *G.B.S. 90: Aspects of Bernard Shaw's Life and Work*, edited by S. Winsten (Hutchinson and Co., London, 1946), and is reprinted here by kind permission of the editor and publishers.

IT IS A CURIOUS FEATURE of Mr. Shaw's writings on economic questions that, while his ideas are inspired by Henry George and Jevons as regards their form, in their forthright denunciation of capitalist property and of income from that property they continue to bear strong traces of the inspiration of Marx. 'Converted to Socialism by *Das Kapital*', but reacting against the narrow, doctrinaire Hyndman-type of Marxism which was dominant in the S.D.F. of the 'eighties, the author of the chapter on the economic basis of Socialism in the *Fabian Essays* of 1889 discarded the value theory of Ricardo and of Marx for the utility theory of Jevons, which was the latest fashion of the time. References to the class struggle disappear in favour of 'the necessity for cautious and gradual change' by 'the transfer of rent and interest to the State, not in a lump sum, but by instalments'. Revolutionary views are dismissed with a tolerant smile as the illusions of 'the young socialist [who] is apt to be catastrophic in his views'.[1] There is little here even about organising a labour movement as the instrument of the revolt against Capitalism; although a good deal is said about the extension of the franchise and about municipal politics. The keynote is appeal to reason: a demonstration that the existing system is not only unjust but absurd and unworkable, which can be made to carry conviction with rich as well as poor.

[1] These sentences are from the second essay in the collection, on *The Transition to Social Democracy*, which was a reprint of an address delivered to the Economic Section of the British Association in 1888.

Yet the generalised concept of rent upon which the economic argument is made to turn, while it is patterned upon Henry George, substantially amounts to much the same thing as Marx meant by surplus value: the product of social labour which is appropriated by a propertied class by virtue, not of any economic function they perform, but of their special position in a society divided into propertied and propertyless. This identification of what this Fabian essay calls rent with surplus value is admitted in a later work; and in the famous Maxims for Revolutionists appended to *Man and Superman* Proudhon's dictum that 'property is theft' is applauded as 'the only perfect truism uttered on the subject.'[1] One sometimes wonders why the author should have chosen to place his theory in a Ricardo-Georgian rather than a Marxian setting, unless it was with the aim of making a more ready appeal thereby to the English Radicals of the time. His denunciation of capitalist exploitation was uncompromising enough even for the taste of socialists who were proposing the 'militant organisation of the working classes' which the *Fabian Essays* treated as an infantile illusion. Private property, with its boast of 'the great accumulation of so-called "wealth" . . . as the result of its power to scourge men and women daily to prolonged and intense toil, turns out to be a simulacrum', he says in a characteristically telling passage. 'With all its energy, its Smilesian "self-help", its merchant-princely enterprise, its ferocious sweating and slave-driving, its prodigality of blood, sweat and tears, what has it heaped up, over and above the pittance of its slaves? Only a monstrous pile of frippery, some tainted class literature and class art, and not a little poison and mischief.'[2] Exposure of social abuses could scarcely be more unqualified than in those well-thumbed prefaces to *Widowers' Houses* and *Mrs. Warren's Profession*: abuses which are emphasised as products of a system and not of the immorality or inhumanity of individuals. In connection with *Mrs. Warren's Profession* he speaks of 'the alternative offered by society collectively to poor women' as being 'a miserable life, starved, overworked, fetid, ailing, ugly': 'starvation, overwork, dirt and disease are as anti-social as prostitution—they are the vices and crimes of a nation and not merely its misfortunes.'[3] The pious complacency of the Victorian bourgeoisie met no mercy from the gall of this pen. Again, he recognised that 'our present system of imperial aggression, in which, under pretext of exploration and colonisation, the flag follows the filibuster and trade follows the flag, with the missionary bringing up the rear, must collapse when the control of our military forces

[1] *Prefaces by Bernard Shaw*, p. 191.   [2] *Fabian Essays in Socialism*, 1st edn., p. 23.
[3] *Prefaces*, p. 230.

passes from the capitalist class to the people', and that 'the disappearance of a variety of classes with a variety of what is now ridiculously called "public opinions" will be accompanied by the welding of society into one class with a public opinion of inconceivable weight.' Statements like these, uttered in the penultimate decade of the nineteenth century, sound fresh and pointed more than half a century later; and Left pamphleteers of today could profit greatly from lessons in the power of such language.

It is again the inspiration of Marx rather than of nineteenth-century radicalism that one senses in his outspoken championing of the Dictatorship of the Proletariat in an early issue of *The Labour Monthly*[1] soon after the Russian Revolution; although in his dictum that 'Mr. Henderson and Mr. Clynes can no more make our political machine produce socialism than they can make a sewing machine produce fried eggs' he probably had something rather different in mind from the implication of Lenin's statement that 'the working class must *break up* the "available ready machinery of the State", and not confine itself merely to taking possession of it.' At the same time there were many who were surprised at the tributes which this Fabian gradualist paid to the achievements of the Soviet State (despite his references to the 'mistakes' of the Bolsheviks, attributable to their habit of 'despising Fabians as bourgeois');[2] and such tributes were commonly dismissed as a sign of his impish delight in the game of *épater les bourgeois* and of an undimmed flair for paradox. But most people are now sufficiently the wiser after the events of the past few years to recognise in his attitude a rare quality of realism in appraising historical situations and the process of historical change.

What some would term the eclecticism of Mr. Shaw's ideas on economic questions is responsible for much of their individual character; and his failure to adhere consistently to the Jevonian economics he espoused would be regarded by many as a saving virtue. While he accepted from Jevons (*via* the advocacy of the economist Wicksteed, I believe) the notion of 'final utility' as an explanation of exchange value, he did not adopt the so-called theory of distribution of this school.[3] Here we have

---

[1] *Labour Monthly*, Vol. I, No. 4, October 1921.

[2] *Intelligent Woman's Guide to Socialism* (1928 edn.), p. 426.

[3] One reason, apparently, why Mr. Shaw rejected Mill's cost of production or Ricardo's and Marx's quantity of embodied labour as the basis of value was because he thought that this notion could be used to deny, or at least to conceal, the fact of rent. The notion that commodities exchange 'in exact proportion to the labour they cost', he writes, 'carries the implication that the landlords cost the community nothing'. But 'so far from commodities exchanging, or tending to exchange, according to the labour expended in their production, commodities produced well within

seen that he clung to the Ricardian tradition, generalising the notion of economic rent so that it included income derived from ownership of capital as well as income derived from ownership of land. The analogy between the two he developed in a vigorous and graphic fashion; and although this exposition somewhat lacked the rigour that economists demanded if deductive argument were to carry conviction, the substantial common sense of the conclusion contrasted boldly with the sophistries about 'abstinence' and 'productivity of capital' in which the analyses of economists at the time had become enmeshed. While his view bore considerable resemblance to the well-known surplus theory of J. A. Hobson, it differed from the latter in being more unqualified. *All* income from capital was surplus (whereas Hobson had treated as 'surplus' only the excess over the 'supply price' of a factor of production, and regarded capital and 'entrepreneurship' as having at least *some* necessary supply-price; thereby walking in the footsteps of Marshall). 'Shareholders and landlords live alike,' said Mr. Shaw, 'on the produce extracted from their property by the labour of the proletariat.' Moreover, most of the incomes of the professional middle class—the so-called 'reward of ability', and especially that 'artificial rent of ability inflated by snobbery and the requirements of social status'—were part of the same *genus* of unearned surplus or rent, as were also the profits of industrial management. 'Private property, by cheapening the labourer to the utmost in order to get the greatest surplus out of him, lowers the margin of human cultivation, and so raises the rent of ability.'[1] Monopoly gains were simply the logical extension of this type of income by methods of deliberate restriction: fruit of the natural tendency in such a society to control the value of commodities by acquiring power to limit their supply. The existence of this rent in its various forms stood exposed as the flagrant injustice at the base of the present economic system, mocking the conscience of mankind. It was also the root of the system's inefficiency, since by divorcing income from labour it stultified incentive to effort and improvement, made wealth accumulate while men decayed, and simultaneously multiplied worthless luxury and ostentation among the rich and human degradation among the poor. 'By giving all the work to one class and all the leisure to another the Capitalist system disables the rich as completely as the poor.'[2]

the margin of cultivation will fetch as high a price as commodities produced at the margin with much greater labour. So far from the landlord costing nothing, he costs all the difference between the two.' (*Fabian Essays*, p. 17.)

[1] *Fabian Essays*, p. 197.   [2] *Intelligent Woman's Guide to Socialism*, p. 165.

What was essentially a social product should, in justice and reason, accrue to society as a whole; and the social appropriation of this surplus followed as a corollary which all reasonable men must accept. With regard to land, many liberals were already accepting it in their advocacy of the taxation of socially produced increment of land values (such as the rise in value of sites due to urban development around them). But what was the point of appropriating the surplus itself, if the State could not reinvest it in the development of production? The logical outcome, therefore, of the social appropriation of economic rent must be the State acquisition of the source of that rent as well: namely, the socialisation of land and capital. Thus, the case for socialism was derived primarily from a theory of distribution: as the inevitable corollary of principles of social justice to which the radicals were willing to subscribe. Socialisation would proceed by stages, and at each stage there would be full compensation to the class of owners affected. What was received by way of compensation would ultimately be taken back by the State through progressive taxation which would distribute the burden equitably over all property-owners instead of lumping it on one or a few groups alone. As a first stage the municipality would acquire land necessary for urban development and extend industries such as road-making, housing and public utilities, probably 'for the most regard(ing) their action as a mere device to meet a passing emergency'; and 'as the municipality becomes more democratic, it will find landlordism losing power, not only relatively to democracy, but absolutely.'[1] At the time of the *Fabian Essays* little was envisaged beyond this stage, except for the extension of legal minimum wages. What is here called 'the extinction of private property' by successive stages evidently rests on the belief that resistance to extinction will be strictly confined within the sphere of democratic institutions, and that the process even 'may be anticipated by sections of the proprietary class successively capitulating as the net closes about their special interests, on such terms as they may be able to stand out for before their power is entirely broken.'[2]

The writer of these words would probably admit today that subsequent events in the world at large have shown this to be an idyllic picture, probably much farther from reality than the primitive 'catastrophic' notions that in the late 'eighties he prided himself on having outgrown. In fact, in *The Intelligent Woman's Guide to Socialism*, published thirty-nine years after the *Fabian Essays*, he explicitly denies that 'the inevitability

[1] *Fabian Essays*, p. 194; cf. also *The Commonsense of Municipal Trading* (1908).
[2] *Fabian Essays*, p. 199.

of gradualness' means 'the inevitability of peacefulness'; and in the light of recent events in Ireland and in Spain and Italy he admitted the possibility of extra-constitutional resistance by the capitalists to the march of socialism. 'It may quite possibly happen that even if the most perfect set of Fabian Acts of Parliament for the constitutional completion of socialism in this country is passed through Parliament by duly elected representatives of the people; swallowed with wry faces by the House of Lords; and finally assented to by the King and placed on the statute book, the capitalists may, like Signor Mussolini, denounce Parliament as unpatriotic, pernicious and corrupt, and try to prevent by force the execution of the Fabian Acts. We should then have a state of civil war, with, no doubt, the Capitalist forces burning the co-operative stores, and the proletarians burning the country houses, as in Ireland.'[1] But he is sufficiently faithful to his earlier standpoint to be still concerned to stress two things. Firstly, such a revolution would not have the character of a class struggle. 'The line ... which separates those interested in the maintenance of Capitalism from those interested in its replacement by Socialism is a line drawn not between rich and poor, capitalist and proletarian, but right down through the middle of the proletariat to the bottom of the poorest section'; and he approves of Labour leaders who denounce extremist talk of class war: talk that 'echo[es] Shelley's very misleading couplet: "Ye are many: they are few".'[2] Secondly, the manner in which this struggle for power is fought to a conclusion in no way changes the form or the gradualness with which the constructive work of socialism must be carried through: a process in which he seems to give little place to democratic initiative, and which is apparently envisaged as essentially a civil service job, requiring considerable reorganisation of State machinery and methods at the top, but deriving very little from the impetus and activity of new types of popular organisation rising from below.

It is in *The Intelligent Woman's Guide to Socialism* that Mr. Shaw enunciates equality of income as a basic principle of socialism. Here is well exhibited the essential rationalism that has always characterised Mr. Shaw's social philosophy. Socialism is something demonstrable as the only conclusion at which pure reason, if consistently applied, can arrive. This demonstration rests primarily on a critique of capitalism as a system of distribution; and equality of income becomes the essential definition of socialism to which the demonstration necessarily leads. The argument for equality is developed by taking in turn each of the seven alternative principles of distributing income and rejecting them as meaningless or

[1] *Intelligent Woman's Guide to Socialism* (1928 edn.), p. 372.   [2] *Ibid.*, p. 373.

unworkable. Since production is a co-operative effort, the separate productivity of individuals or groups of workers cannot be estimated. Division according to the amount of work done meets practical difficulties in measuring the amount, and a difficulty of principle 'in attempting to compare the value of the work of a clever woman (or man) with that of a stupid one.' 'To each what she deserves' may mean all things to all manner of men; and 'to each what she can grab' or leaving it to the play of supply and demand represents what happens today. Hence, by a process of exclusion of alternatives, the principle of equality is left as the only satisfactory rule and as an eminently simple one. Moreover, it is the only method consistent with securing promotion purely by merit.

The simplicity of this answer unquestionably has an immediate appeal, as has also its conformity with abstract justice. But the argument by which it is reached is more summary than usual. One is left with the impression that a number of rival ninepins have been knocked over with agility without the one that is left standing being subjected to an equivalent test. In particular, the possibility that different types of work may have different 'subsistence needs' seems to be too lightly passed over (at least, in the first edition of this work); as does also the possibility that the difficulties of paying according to the amount and type of work (probably on some compromise between differences that have become conventional and what the conditions of supply dictate in a particular economic situation) may be no greater than the problems which are likely to arise in practice from an indiscriminate application of an abstract principle of equality. Later, Mr. Shaw seems to have admitted that the principle of equality is inapplicable unless production is sufficient to ensure an adequate standard of life for all, including people with special needs or accustomed to special standards, like artists and poets and mathematicians and physicists;[1] and that in the interests of raising production to the required level it may be desirable to offer the inducement of higher income to those who work harder or take the trouble to acquire skill. If it is qualified in this way, the doctrine assumes a rather different signicance. It becomes an ideal standard to work towards—'a condition essential to the stability of any association of human beings' in an ideal

[1] Cf. Penguin edition (1938) of *Intelligent Woman's Guide*, p. 441, where reference is made to Soviet experience as showing that, in view of the need in the early stages of a Socialist government to encourage persons of higher education and to encourage workers to acquire skill, 'it (the State) must fix the distribution level at a figure which will provide for the refinements and comparative seclusion and distinction which is necessary to such persons, and then work up production until that level can be attained by everybody.'

society—as the problems of production are mastered and plenty is made to replace scarcity. But then, so also, as the problem of production is mastered, should it become possible to extend the range of things whose distribution is governed by a communist principle (since, with a higher standard of life, the demand for them will have sufficiently approached satiety to become inelastic, and their scarcity will no longer require that their use be restricted, as an alternative to rationing, by charging a price for them). To the extent that this is the case, the question of money income loses its importance and recedes into the background. If the matter is viewed in this light, income-equality becomes the goal of a socialist society rather than its essential condition; and the conception does not seem to be very different from—at least, does not seem to stand in contradiction with—the distinction made by Marx (and today part of accepted tradition in the U.S.S.R.) between the 'first and lower stage of Socialism', where inequalities due to property-incomes have been banished but inequalities due to differences in the amount and type of work continue, and that 'second and higher stage of Socialism' where a higher principle of communist equality can prevail, on the basis of a greater mastery by society over the productive forces. The difference which remains between the two conceptions seems to be that between a theory of socialism fashioned as a theory of distribution and as a theory of production. With the former as one's starting-point, it seems logically necessary to define socialism in terms of some principle of distribution which will contrast it with the present order; and it is apparently this starting-point which has placed Mr. Shaw under a sense of obligation to postulate in unequivocal fashion the principle of distribution on which the society of the future will be based. But if one is willing to treat as crucial the social ownership of the means of production, and the liquidation of the old class relationships, resting on private property, then one will feel less constrained than Mr. Shaw has apparently felt to be dogmatic as to the precise pattern of income distribution that a socialist state (which may operate in a variety of historical contexts) must adopt to justify its name. Marx's well-known phrase about social justice, that it can 'never rise superior to the economic conditions of society and the cultural development conditioned by them', well illustrates the distinction between an historical approach and a purely rationalist one.

But it is probably as a mode of exposition, rather than as a systematic construction of novel economic doctrine, that Mr. Shaw's economic writings ought properly to be judged in any attempt to estimate the influence they have had on their age and their enduring importance. The brilliant lucidity of style and mastery of language, which we have all come to associate with his writing, is part, but not the whole, of the impelling quality that has fascinated the minds of three generations of readers. The unlaboured elegance of his choice of language; the gift for memorable epigram seasoned with paradox, and for the apt example; the power of denunciation and the nimble Irish wit are, again, part but not the whole of it. Even more, it is the penetration and deftness of thought, lying behind the style and the telling aphorism, which can reduce an opponent's thesis to a few terse propositions and then demolish them as self-contradictory or flagrantly untrue to reality, not by tortuous train of argument, but by adroit encirclement and by saturation with a cumulative series of pointed examples. And when one has said that, one is conscious that it is still not the whole story, and that there is some quality in the fastidiously fashioned structure of his thought and exposition which has eluded description.

Perhaps the best example of his success in polemic is his famous controversy with Mr. Mallock, which first appeared in *The Fortnightly Review* in April 1894 (when Frank Harris was its editor), and was reprinted as a Fabian Tract (No. 146) in 1909. At least, this example is one to which the present writer is particularly attached, if only because it stands out in his memory as an early formative influence on his own ideas. Here the arguments of Mr. Mallock, which only since then have been widely seen to be ridiculous as they stand and have been generally discarded by intelligent apologists of capitalism, were dissected with the touch of a master, and were severally disposed of, each in a single consuming phrase. The main claim on which Mr. Mallock had relied was that profit and interest on capital were the reward of superior ability. To this Mr. Shaw opposes 'the obvious fact that the interest on railway stock is paid mostly to people who could not invent a wheelbarrow, much less a locomotive'; and he proceeds to ridicule, as 'rustic ignorance of economic theory' and 'incredible ignorance of society', 'the notion that the people who are now spending, in week-end hotels, in motor-cars, in Switzerland, the Riviera and Algeria, the remarkable increase in unearned incomes noted by Mr. Keir Hardie, have ever invented anything, ever directed anything, ever even selected their own investments without the aid of a stockbroker or solicitor (or) ever as much as seen the industries from which their incomes derive.' To the argument that greater equality of income would leave no one willing to go into the learned professions or take positions of responsibility in industry he retorts: 'If an ordinance were issued tomorrow that every man from the highest to the lowest should have exactly equal pay, then I could quite understand difficulties arising from every man insisting on being head of his department. Why Mr. Mallock should anticipate rather that all the heads would insist on becoming subordinates is more than I can reconcile with the intelligence for which he is famous.' To the argument that socialism would abolish all incentive to production, by making the State 'an organised conspiracy' to rob men of their incomes, he replies: 'My impression hitherto has been that the whole industry of civilisation is the history of millions of men toiling to produce wealth for the express purpose of... meeting the State-enforced demands of landlords, capitalists and other masters of the sources of production.... Are not those very rents and dividends over which Mr. Mallock has so ingeniously gone astray, produced today by workers of all grades, who are compelled by the State to hand over every farthing of it to "drones"?' The long and short of it was that 'Mr. Mallock has confused the proprietary classes with the productive classes, the holders of ability with the holders of land and capital, the man about town with the man of affairs.' Was there really anything more that needed to be said?

What must have repeatedly struck those concerned with the advocacy of socialism, and contributed to a steeling of their hearts and minds, is the absence in any of Mr. Shaw's economic writings of the least trace of an apologetic note. Throughout there is the austere *hauteur* of tone which derives from a writer's supreme assurance of the rightness of his case and of his own ability to confound his opponents in verbal argument, without descent to evasions or personalities. This tone is part of the same pattern as the cogency of his exposition and the *bravura* of his polemical style. It is the invigorating language of confidence in ultimate success and of dauntless iconoclasm: language which always breathes the spirit of attack.

XI

FULL EMPLOYMENT AND CAPITALISM
[1950]

This article appeared in *The Modern Quarterly* (London), (N.S.) Vol. V, No. 2, Spring 1950, and is here reproduced by kind permission of the editor and publishers of that journal.

IT IS ONLY SINCE the world economic crisis of the early 'thirties that full employment has been seriously talked about as an objective of policy. In the nineteenth century there had been talk in labour circles of 'the right to work', and socialists had used the existence of chronic or recurrent unemployment as a leading count in the indictment of capitalism for its inhumanity and inefficiency. Meanwhile, economists of the bourgeois schools either turned a blind eye to the problem or treated it as necessary to the flexible working of an economic system that was subject to change and development. In the present century, books came to be written around the theme of 'the clash between progress and security'; and more recently the notion has been canvassed that unemployment is inevitable if consumers are to retain freedom of choice. What was lacking (at any rate explicitly) in all this talk was any appreciation of the character and imperatives of capitalism as a class system, and of the function performed for such a system by a surplus of labour in keeping that particular commodity cheap. And if this was so manifestly lacking in economists' talk until so recently, it is unlikely, to say the least, that the deficiency has been remedied now that the tune has been changed and we are told that, given the appropriate policies, a stable condition of full employment is possible under capitalism.

Talk of the possibility of full employment in a capitalist world derives from the publication in 1936 of Lord Keynes's famous theory of the factors which determine the general level of employment. There is no doubting the profound jolt which this doctrine administered to traditional notions at the time when it broke upon the world. Child of the crisis of the early 'thirties, its novel and striking feature was that it presented a system of 'crisis economics', whereas its predecessors (termed by Keynes 'classical economics') had been nurtured in what for the bourgeoisie was the more tranquil epoch of the nineteenth century, when trade depressions could be more easily ignored as temporary aberrations or incidental growing-pains of the system. The breath of fresh air which the new doctrine seemed to introduce—a novel sense of up-to-date actuality—was largely because of the fusty atmosphere surrounding the orthodoxy which it replaced: the restrictiveness of the assumptions of the older doctrine and its remoteness from a world of chronic excess-capacity and large-scale unemployment. To economists schooled in the old tradition the new theories seemed at first to move in an Alice-through-the-Looking-Glass world. Actually it was the theoretical model of a smoothly equilibrating, crisis-free world of full employment that deserved the name of 'through-the-Looking-Glass economics'; and once the conjuring trick had been exposed, it could never again pass off illusion for reality in quite the simple manner which had previously bewitched its audience.

That the new doctrine should have stirred up controversy and reawakened doubt in what for long had passed for accepted wisdom was natural enough. Like the old, the new was a theory of equilibrium; but its chief novelty was the postulate that equilibrium was possible at any level of employment; this level being dependent on the volume of effective demand (consumption *plus* investment). Hence the corollary which came as such a shock to minds reared in the nineteenth-century bourgeois tradition (with its animistic stress on the creativeness of thrift): that a high rate of saving was actually detrimental (instead of conducive) to a high level of national income and employment, and that investment, on the contrary to being limited by some pre-existent fund of saving, created its own saving (from the extra income it induced). It was this latter proposition which became the basis of policy-proposals whereby investment was to be financed by a simple expansion of bank-credit; the orthodox 'Treasury-view' being unseated in the process. A further novelty was that the rate of interest was treated as a purely monetary phenomenon, determined by the preference for holding wealth in liquid or money form (including bank balances) instead of as securities, carrying a risk of capital loss when the market-price changed. This view replaced the traditional supply-and-demand-for-real-savings theory, and carried the implication that the rate of interest could be lowered by the monetary policy of the government and the central bank.¹ This became the *rationale* of the 'cheap-money policy'. Since the current rate of investment depended jointly upon the profitability of investment and the rate of interest at which money could be borrowed in the market, this doctrine implied the corollary that the road to full employment lay in stimulating investment—by monetary policy so far as possible and where this failed by public investment by the State financed by bank-credit (the so-called 'deficit spending').

Hence the emphasis of the doctrine was upon deficiency of investment and the need to repair this lack. While consumption equally with investment was a main determinant of the level of output and employment (and the need to raise consumption, e.g. by more equal income-distribution, was stressed by Left-Keynesians), the mould in which the doctrine was cast was such as to focus attention upon investment. Investment was depicted as subject to the greater² variation, and its variation as leading other events in the trade cycle; and it was the growing deficiency of investment in the course of progress (owing to a decline in profit-expectations) that was regarded as being responsible for the chronic stagnation of a mature capitalism—that tendency towards growing stagnation in the twentieth century which was the crux of the much-debated 'stagnation thesis' associated particularly with the name of Alvin Hansen. Keynes himself said that 'the theory can be summed up by saying that, given the psychology of the public, the level of output and employment as a whole depends on the amount of investment'.³

In the immediate pre-war years this new brand of theory furnished the intellectual tools of Roosevelt's New Deal, and was hotly opposed by American 'big business' and conservative circles at the time. At the end of the war it played a rôle in the popular campaign for a liberal policy of drastic income-redistribution, low interest-rates and State expenditure on social reconstruction; echoing the popular moods and aspirations which brought a Labour majority at the polls in 1945. But the progressive

¹ By making more money (or bank balances) available to satisfy the desire to hold wealth in liquid form. The theory was that when individuals and institutions were as liquid as they wanted to be (at existing interest-rates), there would be a tendency to hold more securities until the market-price of the latter rose sufficiently to offset this preference for securities. A rise in security-prices is *ipso facto* a fall in interest-rates.

² Compared, that is, to the ratio of consumption to a *given* income.

³ In *The New Economics* (ed. Seymour Harris), p. 191. He added: 'I put it in this way, not because this is the only factor on which aggregate output depends, but because it is usual in a complex system to regard as the *causa causans* that factor which is most prone to sudden and wide fluctuation.'

rôle which a doctrine and policy of full employment played in the special situation of those years should not blind us to the fact that as a practical doctrine it was always a 'save-capitalism', or 'make-capitalism-work', doctrine, and never pretended to be more. It was in no sense a socialist doctrine; and only by contrast with the spent and decayed ideology which it supplanted could it really pose as a fundamental critique of capitalism (despite some shrewd thrusts at stock exchanges and apostles of *laissez-faire*). To fail to appreciate this may make us the victims of 'the seven devils' of new illusions about the possibilities of 'full employment under capitalism', in place of old illusions from which we had complacently begun to think ourselves free. What this doctrine can be said to have reflected as an ideology is certain tendencies towards salvage-measures of State capitalism in a situation of general crisis for capitalism; and, for all its novel features, it was an ideology which in essence stemmed from the tree of traditional bourgeois economic theory.

To elaborate this might seem unnecessary, were it not that as a doctrine and a policy full employment has been so largely adopted today as the ideology of the particular brand of State capitalism which is being passed off to the Labour movement as the true coin of 'democratic socialism'. Full employment, we are told, is not merely a product of special conditions following the war (with the large volume of pent-up demand and back-log of reconstruction needs), but can be a permanent feature of our society, given no more planning than some global steering of investment, a willingness to contemplate a large sector of public expenditure as a normal element in public finance, and some negative controls over the location of new factories. Except that the policy is not called socialism, similar claims are being made by the Truman Administration in the United States.

To speak first of what was claimed by the theory, before we come to practical application. Keynes's *General Theory* leaves us in no doubt that he considered that his theory offered an *alternative* to socialism and required no more planning than some planning *at the financial level*. He himself wrote that his theory was 'moderately conservative in its implications'. He spoke of 'the socialisation of investment' as a weapon against unemployment and economic stagnation, for the reason that 'it seems unlikely that the influence of banking policy on the rate of interest will be sufficient by itself to determine an optimum rate of investment.' But he was quick to contrast such a measure with 'socialisation of production'. 'This need not', he wrote, 'exclude all manner of compromises and of devices by which public authorities will co-operate with private initiative.' 'Beyond this no obvious case is made out for a system of State socialism which would embrace most of the economic life of the community. It is not the ownership of the instruments of production which it is important for the State to assume.'[1] He adds the surprising statement: 'I see no reason to suppose that the existing system seriously *mis*employs the factors of production which are in use. . . . It is in determining the *volume, not* the direction, of actual employment that the existing system has broken down.'[2] While he was prepared to be ruthless with the *rentier* who lived on interest, he was always favourably inclined towards the active entrepreneur or captain of industry, the recipient of profit. The famous 'euthanasia of the *rentier*' via interest-rate reduction, which he championed, was designed to leave more profit for the ambitious entrepreneur: to cut out the passive deadwood of capitalism so that the live and active part of the tree might flourish more abundantly. In other words, he thought he could separate the parasitic elements of capitalism from capitalism itself in order to save the life-blood of the system from exhaustion. One hardly needs to add that when he spoke of the rôle of State policy, he conceived of the State as an institution which not only stands above classes, but stands also above the warring interests of particular monopoly-groups: as an impartial institution which can represent the 'general interest of society as a whole' and hence steer capitalism in the social interest.

The disciples of what came to be termed 'the new economics' both in this country and in U.S.A. very soon divided into a left and a right wing. The former developed the more radical implications, such as raising mass consumption and extending the sphere of nationalisation; the latter tended to limit the significance of the theory to that of an anti-slump economics and concentrated upon financial prescriptions for giving stimulants to private enterprise. During the past ten years, however, alignments have shifted a good deal, and a stage of assimilation between the old orthodoxy and the new seems to have set in. On the one hand, there have been attempts to integrate the new ideas into the *corpus* of traditional theory; on the other hand, there have been reformulations which smoothed away the sharper edges of the new and treated its more radical corollaries as special cases. In the process there has been some blurring of frontiers between the camps; although doctrinal controversy continues to rage on special points and old battles to be re-fought with enthusiasm. Previous antagonists have 'made their peace' with the new doctrine on the theoretical plane, while abating nothing of their previous affection for

[1] *General Theory*, pp. 377-8. [2] *Ibid.*, p. 379.

uncontrolled private enterprise and a so-called 'free price system'; and there are very few academic economists who would deny that they had trimmed their sails in some degree to the new wind. This has been easier for many to do, since the plea could be made in these years that, as a system of slump-economics, the doctrine had no immediate relevance to policy in the post-war world. In conditions of post-war boom (it could be argued), most of the traditional precepts about the blessings of thrift and the dangers of rising wages and of too much governmental spending returned into their own. Indeed, at least one prominent disciple of the new school has figured during the past three years as a forthright spokesman of deflationary policy (including cuts in the building programme and in social services).

An important feature of today's situation in the capitalist world is that the fear of slump has abated since the 1930's. Memories of the acute crisis years, with their shrinking markets and empty order-books, undercapacity working and derelict plants, have grown rather dim. In its place, business circles have the more recent preoccupation with the inconveniences, even dangers (had not a Labour Government been in power to restrain the unions), of a situation where the sack had lost a good deal of its sting as a disciplinary weapon, with the virtual disappearance of the industrial reserve army. There can be little doubt that an obsession with the dangers for capitalism of too-full employment has eclipsed in recent years any sense of the hazards of the reverse situation; and that traditional policies of restoring profit-margins by wage-cuts and economising on the burdens of government expenditure have come into their own again, both among industrialists and among the economic advisers of the government. Even in the 'thirties reluctance was being shown in U.S.A. to sponsor 'full employment' as a policy-objective: the more cautious term 'high employment' being preferred even by many spokesmen of 'the new economics' and of the fashionable 'functional finance'. Today in England a journal such as *The Economist*, which a few years back gave qualified approval to the Beveridge plan for boosting effective demand, preaches the need for a margin of unemployment to 'reintroduce flexibility into the labour market' and to 'restore the force of economic incentive'. Following devaluation discussion has been focused upon the size of the cuts in government expenditure which are necessary to stave off 'inflationary pressure'. We see the wheel turned full circle to the position where right-wing Labour Party economists and their more conservative brethren differ merely as to whether half a million or a million and a half unemployed will suffice to restore the capitalist mode of production to an even keel. These are the realities of the situation of which theory and its corollaries must take account.

It commonly happens that schools of thought and movements in a class society fulfil an objective rôle which is different from (sometimes contrary to) their subjective design. This, indeed, can be said to be the element of illusion in all ideology in class society—that the aims it serves are not the aims and ideals with which it beguiles men's minds. The well-known references (in the *General Theory*) to pyramid-building and digging holes in the ground as means of raising the level of employment could always have been treated as an oblique apology for armament expenditure: as no longer a wasteful expense to be kept to a minimum, but as fulfilling a constructive function in the shape of a buoyancy-factor for industrial activity. At any rate, the fact remains that the ideas inherited from the days of New Deal economics have become an apology for the large armament expenditures in U.S.A. which are today maintaining both the activity of American heavy industry and the current American war-psychosis. Of this there had been already a foretaste before the war, when spokesmen of German fascism adopted some of the new ideas about employment-policy to defend both German war-expenditure and the gamut of Schachtian policies.

It has been frequently suggested, indeed, that armament-building is the only form of anti-slump expenditure that is at the same time adequate in scale for the purpose and stands any chance of being acceptable to capitalism. The experience of these years seems likely to show this to be true. Investment in armaments is highly profitable to various industries (e.g. to heavy industry, for which it opens a market) as well as for the firms directly involved; while, unlike ordinary investment, it does not affect adversely (by competing with them) the values of existing capital assets. Experience has shown it to be an insatiable appetite, once acquired, feeding upon the war-scare which it cumulatively generates. Today, with America's greatly enhanced productive powers, a new crisis, once it had gathered momentum, might well eclipse that of 1929–31 in its magnitude and in its repercussions on the rest of the (now shrunken) capitalist world. And the momentum of decline may well come rapidly if American business (as seems very likely) takes advantage of the reappearance of an industrial reserve army to 'settle accounts with labour', to cut wages and to call for economies in government finance. The sponsors of full employment policies anticipate that in such a situation their nostrums would be recognised as the only hope of salvation for capitalism, and that they would come into their own again. It seems probable that if State expenditure-schemes were mooted to halt the downward-spiral of a slump, it would be stock-piling of strategic reserves and the construction of atom-bomb piles and atom-bombers that would find favour.

But the utopian character of full employment under capitalism does not derive only from its political non-acceptability both as a means and as an end—unless within the framework of a policy of rearmament and war. It derives also from the diagnosis on which as a policy it is based. We have seen that it conveniently ignores the contradictions which lie within the class structure of society, and focuses attention upon measures which operate within the sphere of financial relationships and relationships of exchange. In this connection, it is a weakness, and not strength, in the new theories of employment that they operate in terms of *aggregates*—investment, consumption, income, etc., as totals. The inadequacy of this procedure is apt to pass unnoticed at the theoretical level, and only to obtrude when one comes to the detailed operation of policies which rest upon the theoretical analysis. As soon as one examines actual situations, it becomes evident that under conditions of capitalism a position of full employment (or any position in the neighbourhood of it) is a highly unstable one: unstable in the sense that a small pressure in either direction is likely to give rise to a rapid cumulative movement, uphill (into inflationary conditions and subsequent collapse) or downhill into falling production and falling demand. If this is the case, stabilisation policies framed in terms of aggregates (e.g. certain investment totals) will be too general and unselective to smother the *destabilising* tendencies at (or even near) their source. They will be too clumsy as steering instruments, and their effects too little calculable, for lack of any detailed 'feel' of the situation which they are intended to control. And be it noted that steering measures which operate purely at the financial level imply (because of their indirectness and remoteness) dealing in terms of aggregates, as well as the converse.

An example which may serve to illustrate this has been pointed out by Kaldor. It may happen that there is a large amount of excess capacity in industries producing capital goods and relatively little in consumer goods industries (or *vice versa*). Unless the increase in demand is distributed between capital goods and consumer goods in the appropriate proportions, expansion may lead to full-capacity output in one department of industry and consequential price-rises, while there still remains a substantial unemployment problem in the other department of industry. Moreover, even if full employment has been attained in both departments, any shift of expenditure between investment and consumption may upset the position and start a tendency to decline in one of the two departments, which may later communicate itself to the other. 'Full employment, therefore, not only means a certain level of real income; it also implies a real income of a certain composition . . . (it) presupposes a division of real income between real consumption and real investment in a certain proportion.'[1] If one breaks down industry into smaller segments, the same thing may apply at this level: unless there is some correspondence between the distribution of excess productive capacity and the distribution of the additional demand, expansion is likely to be arrested, and may relapse, because of the appearance of 'bottlenecks' at certain key points, long before substantial inroads have been made into excess capacity and unemployment elsewhere. If the policy were being canvassed as no more than an anti-slump measure, to be switched on when a crisis had already gathered momentum, such considerations would not have much relevance. (On the other hand, once a slump has got under way, it will be much harder, if not impossible, for financial measures to arrest its downward spiral and to put the process into reverse.) But for a policy which claims to forestall crises these are serious difficulties. In other words, without a much more comprehensive and particularised control and planning, embracing production itself and co-ordinating financial expenditures in detail with conditions of production, stable-employment policies are likely to prove unable to ride their steeds.

Connected with and enhancing this difficulty is the danger of monopolistic organisations and monopolistic practices thwarting expansionist policies by responding to increased demand with price-raising and enhanced profit-margins, instead of with expanded output. Moreover, the investment-policy of firms, especially in monopolistic sectors of industry, may well prove stubborn against all attempts to influence it in a particular direction. So long as industry remains in private hands, the bulk of investment expenditure will be controlled by individual firms, acting on the basis of profit-expectations; and State expenditure will be confined to the periphery of the economic system, where it may be too weak or too removed from the main spheres of activity to counter those strong deflationary tides which periodically arise from the depths of capitalist production. It was Sir William Beveridge who pointed out, with reference to the White Paper of the wartime coalition government on Employment Policy, that a public works policy, turned on or off like a tap when the state of trade required it, was both impracticable as a stabiliser and also undesirable in principle. He himself based his hopes on

[1] N. Kaldor in *Economic Journal*, December 1938, p. 644.

a sphere of social expenditure intermediate between public works of the traditional type and ordinary industrial investment—precisely the kind of expenditure which business circles (here and still more in America) regard with suspicion as wasteful and unproductive, and which is today being subjected to an economy-axe in the interest of 'restoring Britain's competitive position in world markets'. But even he was forced to admit that this might not suffice without direct control over industrial investment itself.

Meanwhile the tendency of post-Keynesian writing on the subject has been to play down the rôle of the rate of interest as a factor governing industrial investment. This defeatist view was already foreshadowed in the *General Theory*, where it was emphasised that, not only might there be limits in a capitalist society below which interest-rates could not be forced down, but in an acute crisis investment might fail altogether to respond to the stimulus of low interest-rates—unless interest-rates were actually *negative*. Such empirical evidence as is available indicates that changes in interest-rates (at least within what may be termed the 'practicable range') exert very little influence at all on the level of industrial activity.[1] If this be the case, there is no lever by which the investment policy of private capitalist industry can be influenced by financial policy;[2] and while high or low interest-rates may be of vital importance in determining the size of government expenditure on the service of the national debt and the size of *rentier*-incomes, they can claim no place in any causal theory of economic crises. One seems to be left with deficit-financed armament expenditure as the only item on the capitalist agenda for combating a slump.

Even if it were possible to maintain industrial investment at a boom level by various buoyancy-devices, there would be no sure ground for supposing that the crisis-tendencies inherent in capitalist economy (due to the conflict between enhanced productive power and profitability) were any more than postponed; since the very investment activity would be augmenting productive capacity and thereby undermining the profitability of existing capital equipment. This conclusion seems inescapable so long as production and investment remain in capitalist hands and are controlled by the profit-motive. To quote Kaldor again: 'As investment

[1] With the possible exception of building in normal times, and even this effect has been questioned.

[2] Investment controls through an Investment Board have often been spoken of in this connection. But these are essentially negative—instruments for restraining investment but not for expanding it.

activity continues at a high level, excess capacity of equipment is bound to make its appearance. Once redundant capacity appears, it will be almost impossible to maintain activity undiminished, unless State investment activity is extended so wide as to replace private investment.' He proceeds to liken a boom to 'a peculiar steeplechase, where the horse is bound to fall at one of four obstacles'; adding that 'it is probably a rare horse which survives until the last hurdle'.[1]

To depict capitalism as though it were a 'system of social production' (as Marx termed it), motivated by social purposes instead of by class ends, has always been an essential part of the illusionist function of bourgeois ideology. So it is no less today with the ideology of the 'third force', which depicts itself as suspended in history between the epoch of capitalism and the epoch of socialism and impartially mixing ingredients from both worlds. If capitalism could be made to operate as though it were socialism, then of course we could have full employment as a stable and permanent condition of things, and much else besides. One can recall the statement of Stalin in his 1934 talk with H. G. Wells: 'If capitalism could adapt production, not to the acquisition of maximum profits, but to the systematic improvement of the material conditions of the mass of the people . . . there would be no crisis. But then, also, capitalism would not be capitalism. To abolish crises, capitalism must be abolished.' Once economic theory is allowed to employ the *deus ex machina* of an impartial, classless state, actuated by social purposes and ironing out the conflicts of actual economic society, all manner of attractive miracles can be demonstrated, even without the aid of algebra. One might dismiss such attempts as harmless pastimes, were it not that ideas play a rôle in history, and can not only disseminate the opium of false hopes, but in the cold war of today weave dangerous illusions about the grim realities of present-day capitalism.

[1] *Op. cit.*, pp. 653, 657.

XII

HISTORICAL MATERIALISM AND THE ROLE OF THE ECONOMIC FACTOR
[1951]

This article appeared in *History*, February and June 1951, and is reproduced here by kind permission of the Editorial Board of that journal.

WHEN ONE IS trying to define a method of historical interpretation, it is usually much easier to state in brief what that method is *not* than to expound its positive claims. To define it at all completely requires that it be clothed in historical flesh and applied as a rounded interpretation of some actual period of history. Its full meaning is the historical picture which it yields. Seen apart from actual use and epitomised in a few terse propositions, it inevitably assumes the character of a lifeless *a priori schema* into which historical facts are to be fitted. In what follows, accordingly, I shall make no attempt at a comprehensive statement of the way in which historical materialism interprets the historical process; and I shall be largely concerned with stating what it is not. This may have more point than at first appears, in view of the misinterpretations of the doctrine which are current.

That historical materialism originated in antithesis to the view that history is to be interpreted in terms of the self-development of ideas is probably too familiar to need much emphasis. Hegel had stated: 'Every step in the process has its determinate peculiar principle. In History this principle is idiosyncrasy of Spirit—peculiar National Genius. . . . Its religion, its polity, its ethics, legislation, even science, art and mechanical skill, all bear its stamp.'[1] In contrast to this, Marx asserted that any given society or historical period was predominantly shaped by its 'mode of production'; the political, moral and ideal superstructure of that society being a 'reflection' of its economic base, instead of the converse. 'The premises from which we begin', said Marx and Engels in their *German Ideology*, 'are not arbitrary ones, not dogmas, but real premises. . . . They are the real individuals, their activity and the material conditions under which they live, both those which they find already existing and those produced by their activity. These premises can thus be verified in a purely empirical way.'[2] The view which they were combating they themselves described as follows. Of 'the whole conception of history up to the present' (of which the Hegelian philosophy of history was 'the last consequence, reduced to its "finest expression"') they wrote: 'The exponents of this conception of history have consequently only been able to see in history the political actions of princes and States, religious and all sorts of theoretical struggles, and in particular in each historical epoch have had to share the *illusion of that epoch*. For instance, if an epoch imagines itself to be actuated by purely "political" or "religious" motives, although "religion" and "politics" are only forms of its true motives, the historian accepts this opinion. The "idea", the "conception" of these conditioned men about their real practice, is transformed into the sole determining, active force, which controls and determines their practice.'[3]

The claim that it was the activity of men—and especially their productive activity—which determined the consciousness of an epoch was a statement, as it were, about the physiology of society—or a generalisation about the dominant lines of social causation. But this in no way implied that ideas could exert no influence, or that in historical interpretation 'economic facts are the only ones that matter' (as was suggested in a recent issue of *History*).[4] That there was an interaction between the ideal 'superstructure' and the 'base' was certainly not denied. On this the founders of the doctrine were quite explicit. Of the passages in which they refer to this question it must suffice to quote two. Towards the end of his life, in a much-quoted letter to Mehring (the biographer of Marx), Engels

[1] G. W. F. Hegel, *Lectures on the Philosophy of History* (trans. J. Sibree, 1894), pp. 66–7.
[2] *The German Ideology*, by K. Marx and F. Engels (ed. R. Pascal, 1938), pp. 6–7.
[3] *Ibid.*, p. 30.
[4] Sir J. F. Rees in *History* (February and June 1949), p. 14. Dr. Schlesinger refers to 'the assumption that it denies the power of ideas, as distinct from material forces, to influence the course of history' as being 'the most common misapprehension about Marxism' (*Marx: his Time and Ours*, p. 45).

referred to 'the fatuous notion of the ideologists that because we deny an independent historical development to the various ideological spheres which play a part in history we also deny them any effect upon history . . . these gentlemen often almost deliberately forget that once an historical element has been brought into the world by other elements, ultimately by economic facts, it also reacts in its turn and may react on its environment and even on its own causes.'[1] In emphasising this, he admitted that it was a point which 'Marx and I always failed to stress enough in our writings. . . . We all . . . laid and were bound to lay the main emphasis at first on the derivation of political, juridical and other ideological notions, and of the actions arising through the medium of these notions, from basic economic facts.'[2] A few years earlier he had written: 'According to the materialist conception of history the determining element in history is *ultimately* production and reproduction in real life. More than this neither Marx nor I has ever asserted. If therefore somebody twists this into the statement that the economic element is the *only* determining one, he transforms it into a meaningless, abstract and absurd phrase. The economic situation is the basis, but the various elements of the superstructure . . . also exercise their influence upon the course of historical struggles and in many cases preponderate in determining their *form*. There is an interaction of all these elements. . . .'[3]

What was denied was, not that ideas entered into historical interpretation both as cause and as effect, but that ideas could be explained entirely, or even mainly, in terms of a genealogy of their own, and that the influence which they exerted upon events was more than a conditional one. Within the process of reciprocal interaction between ideas and economic conditions, the two-way influence of each upon the other was not symmetrical. In the first place, events and conditions of life exercised a strongly selective and formative influence over the ideas which were dominant at a particular period, while at the same time ideas could influence events only in certain ways and subject to definite limitations. As Herbert Spencer once said: 'Ideas wholly foreign to this social state cannot be evolved, and if introduced from without, cannot get accepted, or if accepted die out. Hence the advanced ideas when once established act upon society: yet the establishment of such ideas depends on the fitness of society for receiving them. Practically the popular character and social

---

[1] Letter to Mehring, 14 July 1893, *Marx-Engels Correspondence* (trans. D. Torr, 1934), p. 512.
[2] *Ibid.*, p. 510.
[3] Letter to Bloch, 21 September 1890, *ibid.*, p. 475. Cf. also pp. 472, 477, 484.

state determine what ideas shall be current.' Even Dicey recognised that 'public opinion is itself far less the result of reasoning or of argument than of the circumstances in which men are placed.'[1] The notion of ideas as a 'reflection' of social conditions was, of course, connected with a general view of the relation between thought and the external world, according to which thought was regarded as necessarily being of and about events in the material world, and hence a product of the latter, in a sense in which the latter was not a product or creation of the former. But it did not preclude this process of reflection being complex and indirect, not just a simple mirror-image of reality, any more than it implied that the 'reflection' must be purely passive. Indeed a contention which was prominent especially in the earlier writings of Marx was that 'in all ideology men and their circumstances appear upside down as in a *camera obscura*';[2] and that this element of 'false consciousness' restricted human thought from achieving the ends which it posited by reason of this element of illusion (and hence lack of scientific realism) in all ideology.

Since ideas act upon events through the actions of men, what has been said about the influence of ideas upon events applies also to human activity. A second, and derivative, misunderstanding about historical materialism has been that history is depicted as a strange automatic march of material factors, with human beings as lifeless marionettes on the surface of the story. I shall not venture upon a discussion of the possible meanings of 'determinism' as applied to social development. But in the sense of a mechanical determinism, in which human activity can make no difference to the final outcome, the term has certainly no application to historical materialism. (If all that is meant by determinism is that human motives and human action are themselves capable of explanation in causal terms, then of course it is a quite different question.) Not only did both Marx and Engels reiterate that man makes his own history, but in opposition to the notion of an unchanging human nature as an independent historical factor Marx stated that 'by acting on the external world and changing it man at the same time changes his own nature.'[3]

It is, indeed, surprising that this misunderstanding should have arisen about a doctrine which gives central importance to the struggle of classes as the motive-force of social change. True, it treats the individual as being straitly circumscribed by his social setting: in the first place, his motivation as being causally conditioned by the social *milieu* of which he is part, and secondly the actions of individuals as being subject to the same limita-

[1] *Law and Public Opinion* (2nd edn.), p. 26. [2] *German Ideology*, p. 14.
[3] *Capital* (trans. Moore and Aveling, 1886), Vol. I, p. 157.

tions, if they are to be effective, as those to which we have referred in speaking of the influence of ideas. The individual at any given time and place finds himself conditioned by a given set of circumstances which form the *data* of his actions: 'a sum of productive forces, a historically created relation of individuals to nature and to one another, which is handed down to each generation from its predecessor.'[1] Or as Engels said in a letter: 'Men make their history themselves, only in given surroundings which condition it and on the basis of actual relations already existing.'[2] Individual acts, if they are unattuned to the social situation which they seek to influence, will represent no more than a futile tilting at windmills. But when the objective situation is of a certain kind, and action has an appropriate direction, such action can have a large, even an epoch-making effect. Not any kind of pattern can be woven from given material, however purposeful and inventive the human agent may be: on the contrary, the emphasis of Marxism is that in the conditions of a given form of production the number of possible patterns which can be woven is very limited. But this is not to say that the weaving of patterns is independent of those who weave them or to depict those who do the weaving as robots operated by inhuman historical forces.

When one speaks of the motivation of human action, one approaches a region that is, perhaps, the least adequately charted of any in the social sciences, whether on the scale of the individual, as the concern of psychologists, or on the scale of the social group or class, from the perspective of historian or sociologist. But although this is complex and obscure territory, there are some important things which can be said of it with some certainty. Firstly, the extent to which individuals are unaware of the true motivation of their actions, so that the influences which move them are largely different from the reasons which they would consciously formulate, is nowadays very widely recognised—much more so than when Marx and Engels were writing. This consideration alone makes the old debate as to whether people are actuated by 'selfish interests' or by 'higher motives' much too *simpliste* an issue, and renders even the framing of the question a more difficult matter than most participants in this rather barren discussion seem to have realised. At any rate, Marxism does not stand or fall (as some have supposed) with the postulate that individuals are always actuated by conscious and direct calculation of their own economic interests; even if it be true (to quote Dicey again) that 'in matters of legislation men are guided in the main by their real or apparent interest',

---

[1] *German Ideology*, p. 29.
[2] Letter to Starkenburg, 25 January 1894, *Marx-Engels Correspondence*, p. 517.

and that 'from the inspection of the laws of a country it is often possible to conjecture, and this without much hesitation, what is the class which holds, or has held, predominant power at a given time.'[1]

Secondly, the notion that what human actions achieve bears any simple relation to the motives which inspire those actions has long since been discarded by students of the social sciences. What in its time appeared as the shocking paradox of Mandeville's 'private vices, public virtues' was to become the commonplace of nineteenth-century political economy, that the individual entrepreneur's pursuit of maximum profit eventuated in a continual cheapening of prices such as no individual had intended. Moreover, it was Hegel (possibly inspired in this connection by Adam Smith and the classical economists) who generalised this into the well-known statement that 'out of the actions of men comes something quite different from what they intend and directly know and will'. In other words, the product of human will and action depends both on the relation in which the individual will stands to the wills of others (with the consequence, *inter alia*, that the so-called 'composition of causes' does not here apply), and upon the total character of the objective situation which human action seeks to influence. Indeed, to such an extent have assumptions changed that it often happens nowadays that those situations in which outcome conforms to design—where an historical movement corresponds in its objective tendency to what subjectively it conceives its own rôle to be—cause surprise and call for explanation, rather than the converse cases. In this connection it is worth recalling the remark of Engels, the revolutionary, about 'people who boasted they had *made* a revolution': they 'have always seen the next day that they had no idea what they were doing, that the revolution *made* did not in the least resemble the one they would have liked to make.'[2]

Thirdly, there is plenty of evidence that when one is dealing with large numbers—at the level of the group or class—there is much greater uniformity in the response of human beings to various situations and to various stimuli than can be noticed when one is observing individuals. If this be the case, it follows that social tendencies and historical movements are much more capable of being subjected to causal analysis than those who make much of 'historical irrationalism', of 'the unique quality of the historical event' or 'the intricacy of the world of time' have been willing to allow. Once this is granted, the claim of economic factors to exercise

---

[1] *Op. cit.*, pp. 12-13. Dicey goes on to comment that 'a man's interest gives a bias to his judgment far oftener than it corrupts his heart.' (*Ibid.*, p. 15.)
[2] Letter to Vera Zasulich, 23 April 1885, *Correspondence*, pp. 437-8.

a predominant influence in shaping the actions of social groups and classes is an extraordinarily high one: not on the spurious ground that 'man lives by bread alone', but because so much in the mode of life of man in society —his nurture, his habits and conventions, his prejudices and sense of values, his cultural opportunities and pursuits, and his relations with other members of society—is dependent on the source and nature of his income.

That the shaping of individuals by their social *milieu* and of social groups by their relations to the mode of production is a simple formula which can yield a direct answer to every historical problem, no serious Marxist has ever maintained. Still less can he be accused of deducing from a proposition about the primacy of the mode of production an abstract *schema* of historical development into which historical facts are to be cunningly fitted. Such a proposition plays the rôle which a scientific hypothesis plays in any other branch of study: a method of investigation by which research into the multiform complexity of actual phenomena (and moreover political action to change the world, as well as research into the past) can be illuminated and guided. What a leading economic historian of our day has said of the rationalist's approach to history could be said also, *mutatis mutandis*, of the historical materialist's: 'He cannot be accused of trying to solve by syllogism or by laboratory experiment every problem of the universe and to base on them every rule of conduct. The history of rational thought, as distinct from the history of rationalist claims, is a record of study which reason proved capable of understanding, not a history of attempts to pack the entire universe into a technical formula. The rationalist admits that there are questions to which he cannot give a complete and final answer, but he also claims that there are few questions to the understandings of which he cannot make some contribution however small.'[1] To this one may add the well-known passage from Marx in which, with reference to an historical problem, he says: 'By studying each of these forms of evolution separately and then comparing them one can easily find a clue; but one will never arrive there by the universal *passe-partout* of a general historico-philosophical theory, which explains everything because it explains nothing, the supreme virtue of which consists in being super-historical.'[2] 'Our conception of history', said Engels, 'is above all a guide to study, not a lever for construction after the manner of the Hegelians. All history must be studied afresh, the

---

[1] Professor M. Postan in *The Cambridge Journal*, Vol. I, No. 7, pp. 407–8.

[2] Letter to the Editor of *Otechestvennie Zapiski* (no date, probably end 1877), *Correspondence*, p. 355. Cf. the translation of this passage in I. Berlin, *Karl Marx* (1939) p. 117, which has been followed here.

conditions of existence of the different formations of society must be individually examined.'[1]

But because historical materialism lays emphasis upon the derivation of ideas from a given social environment, this is no reason for identifying it with a mere 'sociology of knowledge' or for classifying it as yet another doctrine of historical relativism. True, justification for such an interpretation can be found in the writings of some who have derived inspiration from the works of Marx. These writers have sometimes been so occupied with exploring the social origin of ideas as to imply that no question as to the truth or falsehood of those ideas could, or need be, entertained. Some vulgarisers have certainly implied, even if they have not explicitly stated, that there is 'bourgeois truth' about history and 'proletarian truth', and that what is truth and what falsehood simply depends on the side to which you belong. But such an interpretation does not, I believe, derive any justification from the work of the founders of historical materialism themselves. It is true that for them an ideology represented the 'world view' of a particular class, standing at a particular point in the historical process and viewing things from the perspective of a particular position in a prevailing system of social relations. Thus, a class ideology was inevitably relative and contingent: subjectively biased by the perspective from which the world was viewed, and objectively limited by the limitations of social and historical experience of the epoch. Yet ideologies were not pure illusion (as Mannheim, for example, seems to have held). Certainly there was a large, even predominating, element of 'false consciousness', especially in the ideology of an established ruling class which clung to power when already faced with a revolutionary challenge. But at the same time an ideology, especially in its revolutionary and formative phase, could contain an important 'scientific' and realistic element, which could be treated according to the objective criterion of human experience as an addition to human knowledge. Absolute truth was not a Kantian unknowable, even if it could never be reached at any finite point in the historical process: it could be approached asymptotically, and criteria existed by which one could speak about being nearer to it or more remote.

In conclusion, a word is perhaps needed about the sense in which the term 'mode of production' is employed, since its connotation in the writings of Marx and Engels was a good deal wider than many of their 'interpreters' and critics have taken it to be. The notion that this term

[1] Letter to Conrad Schmidt, 5 August 1890, *Correspondence*, p. 473. Cf. also *German Ideology*, p. 15.

refers only to the technique of production (and hence implies a purely technological interpretation of history)¹ may well have contributed to the view, which we have discussed, that historical materialism dethrones men as makers of history and puts some mechanistic demiurge in their place. For Marx, however, the mode of production was evidently a more precise development of Hegel's 'civil society' (of which he once spoke as 'the true source and theatre of all history')²; and although not coterminous with the latter, it constituted the kernel of 'civil society', or (to change the metaphor) this society's structural foundation. It embraced two categories of things: the 'forces of production' and also the 'social relations of production', by which he meant the social relations between men which arose from their diverse relations to the productive process. The conflicts between men which arose from antagonistic relations of production were regarded by Marx as the main motive-force of history (these by contrast with Hegel's conflict of national cultures or spirit, and with the positivists' conflict between certain basic human traits and the environment). In such conflicts in a class society the battle of ideas and of human passions, of politics and of political institutions, held the centre of the stage. They were, indeed, the outward forms of the fundamental conflict itself; the latter, to the extent of its dominant influence, shaping political and ideal alignments. In this sense divisions between political groups or parties and between ideologies were derivative from the tension within the social relations of production.

This emphasis upon class conflict, epitomised in the famous phrase of the *Communist Manifesto* of 1848 that 'the history of all human society, past and present, has been the history of class struggles', rests, of course, upon an analysis of society since primitive times as *class society*, depending upon various forms of exploitation (i.e. appropriation of surplus labour, surplus product or surplus value) of the direct producers by a dominant class. Whence derives Marx's pregnant statement that 'the specific economic form in which unpaid surplus labour is pumped out of the direct producers determines the relations of rulers and ruled. . . . It is always the direct relation of the owners of the conditions of production to the direct producers which reveals the innermost secret, the hidden foundation of the entire social structure.'³

---

¹ E.g. Lionel Robbins, *Essay on the Nature and Significance of Economic Science*, p. 42; R. N. Carew Hunt, *Theory and Practice of Communism*, p. 46: 'Marx's economic interpretation of history explains all major events by changes in the *technique of production*.'

² *German Ideology*, p. 26.   ³ *Capital*, Vol. III, p. 919.

The test of such a view for historians will naturally lie in its power of illuminating the historical process. Like most general theories of this kind, it is not capable of proof in any simple or direct manner. No more was the Copernican hypothesis, on its introduction, as against its Ptolemaic rival: its justification lay in its effectiveness as an instrument of investigation and enquiry. That direct proof of this kind is lacking can be no justification for the attitude of some empiricists who claim that general theories of this type hamper rather than aid the researcher's groping after truth, and should be discarded as useless baggage for the scientist. On the contrary, such general hypotheses may not only be extraordinarily fruitful (as the analogy from cosmology shows), but also be essential as scaffolding to thought, or as signpost to the facts and relationships to be looked for in the selection and interpretation of data—to the relevant questions which must be put to reality. Regarding historical verification in our present case all that can be briefly said is this: that the emphasis upon economic factors and class relations which historical materialism has introduced into historical thought and writing has already done much to enrich research. As examples of periods of development upon which by common admission it has shed considerable light, one need mention only the close of the middle ages, the seventeenth-century struggle in England, 1789 in France and the whole epoch of the industrial revolution in Europe. Professor Tawney has remarked that 'an author is unlikely to make much of the history of Europe during the last three centuries' without the concept of capitalism as an economic system: a concept which (though it may be differently defined by different writers) mainly derives from Marx. Can we not likewise say of our own time and of the past half-century, dominated as these years have been by such phenomena as economic imperialism, the so-called capital-labour problem, the growing concentration of economic power, and the issue of capitalism versus socialism, that little if any sense can be made of events by an interpreter who does not use the categories of historical materialism?

Part Three

XIII

ECONOMISTS AND THE ECONOMICS OF SOCIALISM

Reprinted from *The Modern Quarterly*, Vol. II, No. 2, April 1939, by kind permission of the editor and publishers.

THIS BOOK[1] DEALS WITH a narrower subject than its title implies: with what has been termed the problem of pricing or of economic calculation under socialism; and the fact that this should be described as 'the economic problem' is a good example of the modern limitation of the field of economic study to the realm of the market (pushing production and production-relations into the background). To many economists this has come to mean the problem of socialism *par excellence*; and to most economists its solution has appeared to be a matter of crucial importance. Yet to the non-economist (not unnaturally) the controversy has generally seemed a meaningless one—a pseudo-problem created by the peculiar notions that economists are wont to use.

Is the layman's scepticism justified, and is the whole matter, about which Dr. Lange writes so elaborately and so skilfully, a pseudo-problem that has no counterpart in the actual world? Put in so extreme a form as this, the sceptic's disposal of the matter is clearly wrong. Some problem of economic calculation and of allocating productive resources between different uses clearly exists for a socialist economy, and its existence has been indicated by the leading theorists of socialism, as Dr. Lange shows by several apt quotations. (Marx spoke of 'this necessity of distributing social labour in definite proportions (which) cannot be done away with by the *particular form* of social production, but can only change the *form it assumes*'; while Engels, speaking of socialism, said: 'the utility yielded by

[1] *The Economic Theory of Socialism*, by Oskar Lange and Fred. M. Taylor (University of Minnesota Press and Oxford University Press, 8s. net).

the various consumption goods, weighted against each other and against the amount of labour required to produce them, will ultimately determine the plan.') At the same time it can quite justly be said that the problem has been assigned an exaggerated importance, and made to assume a distorted complexity, by the highly abstract setting that economists have given it.

The first stage of the discussion was concerned essentially with a very practical point: was the existence of a market, not only for consumers' goods, but for producers' goods (machines, raw material, etc.) as well, an essential condition of any economic calculation at all? The critics of socialism (most notably Mises of Vienna, and more recently Hayek and Robbins in London) maintained that this was the case. On the market the play of consumers' demand against the scarcity of various resources assigned certain relative values to commodities and agents of production; and it was these values, assigned by the market, that constituted the economic criterion as to what it was economic to produce and what was a more, compared with a less, 'economic' method of production. Without a market no such economic criterion (as distinct from technical criteria) could exist: the essential basis of rationality in economic decisions—a scale of valuations—would disappear, and decisions would be purely arbitrary. Since there could be no market under socialism—at least, no market in any sense in which values were determined by the play of competitive bidding—socialism was *ex natura* irrational, if not impossible as a working system.

Socialist economists (e.g. H. D. Dickinson) who took up this challenge at first admitted the theoretical basis of the Mises-case. They agreed that only a market could provide that system of valuations on which economic calculation must depend. What they denied was that a market system was incompatible with socialism. There was no question, of course, that a market for consumers' goods (i.e. a retail market) could and would prevail, at least under what Marx termed 'the first period of socialism'. What was in question was a market for intermediate goods and factors of production—for raw materials and machines, for capital and for land. Mr. Dickinson's contention was that it was perfectly possible for such a market to exist under socialism (as to a limited extent it did in U.S.S.R. under N.E.P.). All that was necessary was that the managements of industries, or of sections of industry (e.g. State trusts), should be made financially autonomous, and should purchase one another's products at flexible prices under ordinary market conditions, and should compete with one another in the process. State industry could 'play at competition', as a means of keeping a market and market valuations alive. The State Bank could let out loans (both short- and long-term) at a competitive rate, allowing each industry to take up as much of the loan as it calculated that it could profitably use at the ruling interest-rate and at the ruling prices of its products. With the motive of monopoly profit removed, and with the abolition of income-inequalities characteristic of capitalism, the resulting allocation of resources would be much more, and not less, rational than under capitalism. Market valuations would cease to be distorted as they are today and would become a much surer criterion of social utility.

Within the limited context of debate between professional economists this argument can be said to have had importance as a refutation of the *a priori* impossibility of socialism that the Mises-school had tried to establish. But since the argument had adopted common ground with this school in admitting the need for a competitive market, it refuted the *a priori* argument only to replace it by a modified one of its own: namely, the categorical imperative for a socialist economy to make use of this particular mechanism. And if this mechanism is essential, a serious limitation is imposed on the potentialities of planning. Planning would be almost entirely limited to fixing the aggregate *amount* of investment in any year: the allocation of this capital between various industries, and *a fortiori* its utilisation, must be left to competitive bidding by industrial managements to determine. It would seem as though much of the uncertainty that is characteristic of a system of 'anarchy of production' (arising from atomistic diffusion of decisions and from competition) would still remain, and with it the possibility of similar maladjustments as occur today (for example, between the demand for capital goods, dependent on the aggregate volume of investment, and the demand for consumption goods, dependent on the size of the total wages-bill). If such maladjustments occurred, they could be corrected, of course, by *post facto* readjustments at the behest of the planning authority; but only by readjustments carried into effect by compulsory planning decisions, overriding the decentralised autonomy that had been the sinew of the competitive system. It might well be the case that the need for co-ordination of the various parts of the economy would very soon result in centralised encroachments on this autonomy of a very substantial kind. This would be specially likely to occur at times of rapid industrial change: in particular, at times when the maintenance of a high rate of investment was the dominant consideration, as under the First and Second Five-Year Plans; and it seems highly probable that in any country embarking on socialism the achievement of an unusually high rate of investment in order to raise the productive power of the economy in the shortest possible time would be the dominant motive of policy for several decades.

There was a simple answer to those who maintained the necessity of a market for intermediate goods and for capital, to which surprisingly little attention was paid. It was that on their own showing the prices of such goods were derived from those of the finished goods that the former helped to make. If there was a retail market for consumption goods, why have a market for intermediate goods as well? If the latter could anyhow only acquire a price by an elaborate process of imputation, after they had been allocated in a certain way, why not allocate them according to the principle of directing them to the use where their productivity (at the margin) was greatest, without the added complication of pricing them? One reason advanced for rejecting this simple solution was the alleged complexity of the decisions involved. The present reviewer has never been convinced that the complexity would be as great as is alleged, provided that scope were given for decentralisation of *particular* decisions inside the limits set by the shape of a *general* plan (as apparently occurs in U.S.S.R.). One reason why its complexity has been apparently so exaggerated may be because the problem has been abstractly pictured as being one of taking all decisions *de novo*, whereas decisions about allocation would always in fact concern the *direction* of change from an existing situation, and the criterion of shifting from a position of lesser to one of greater productivity would suffice in each situation to determine the direction in which movement should take place. In other words, the principle of the maximum would be directly, instead of indirectly, applied. Even should this method involve difficulty, it is unlikely that this difficulty would be as great as that involved in the unco-ordinated character of decisions taken under a 'market system'.

What is important in Dr. Lange's essay is that he takes a further step in rejecting, not only the conclusions of the Mises-argument, but also part of its assumptions. Previously there had been tacit agreement that if things were to be priced, a market must exist to do the pricing. This assumption Dr. Lange rejects, at least so far as intermediate goods and capital are concerned. His contention is that the prices which form the basis of economic calculation need be no more than 'accounting prices', which do not require a market to create them and need not be represented in any actual transactions. These prices can figure simply in the books of accountants and be fixed by a process of 'trial and error', on the simple principle that all things of which there is at any time a surplus should have their accounting-prices lowered, and those of which there is a deficit should have their prices raised. This shifting of prices would continue until the thing in question was neither in surplus nor deficit supply, but the current supply was exactly carried off by the current demand. Then the correct, or 'equilibrium' price, would have been reached. Two simple rules would then be laid down to govern the conduct of all industrial managers: (1) that in choosing between various industrial methods they should choose that which, on the basis of the given accounting-prices, involved the lowest average cost, (2) that they should fix that scale of output at which, on the basis of the given accounting-price, 'the marginal cost is equal to the price of the product'. It is claimed that this technique, in addition to the attraction of simplicity, would have the advantage that the accounting-prices which formed the basis of an industrial management's estimates and of its actions need have nothing to do with any payments actually made to it or from it, e.g. in its account with the State Bank, and need have nothing to do with whether it showed a profit or a loss on the total of its operations. The accounting record and the financial record could, if necessary, be kept entirely distinct.[1]

This ingenious solution, which is developed by Dr. Lange with great cogency and lucidity, was suggested by the late Professor F. M. Taylor ten years ago, but at the time attracted little notice. For this reason the original article of Professor Taylor is reprinted here as a preface to Dr. Lange's more elaborate exposition, together with a rather long and repetitive introduction by the editor.

That this is worthy of serious consideration as a possible accounting device in a socialist economy can hardly be denied. Whether or not it is practicable can only be decided by the test of experience, and no general answer in advance of such experience seems possible. At the same time there is no valid reason to maintain that it must necessarily be the solution adopted—to deduce it, Mises-like, from the 'nature of the economic problem' as the imperative solution (Dr. Lange nowhere says this; and it is not clear whether he intends this to be implied or not). The scheme is subject to the objection that it would involve a lack of co-ordination between the various decisions being concurrently made by various parts of the economic system (a co-ordination which it is the prime object of centralised planning to obtain). True, the central authority could quickly correct any maladjustments that arose by appropriate changes in the accounting-prices. But it could do this only as *post facto* corrections of

[1] The possibility of such a separation had previously been suggested by Mr. Dickinson (to whom Dr. Lange seems to pay too little attention) but had not been developed.

mistaken decisions already made (e.g. decisions to start such-and-such a construction job); and in the case of investment in durable plant the previous decisions might have committed industry too far and on too large a scale for the corrective effect of changed accounting-prices to produce any speedy adjustment. After all, changes in these prices could not be made every month, or no manager would ever dare to take any decisions at all. One can, therefore, imagine fluctuations of over- and underinvestment developing, with resultant fluctuations in accounting-prices, reminiscent of the fluctuations under capitalism. An important advantage to be expected of a planned economy is that it could plan its investment through time on the basis of a much greater degree of foresight; but to take advantage of this would require that there should be central planning, not only of the *amount* of investment, but of the nature and direction of investment as well. No amount of grading of interest-rates for loans of different durations, under Dr. Lange's scheme, would achieve this; since, what is 'correct' investment-policy for five or seven years hence will depend on the investment-policy of the next twelve months, and of the whole of the intervening period, and *vice versa*. In Dr. Lange's scheme of things these factors, on which decision depends, are unknowns. Indeed, it seems to be a misnomer to speak of an accounting price for capital as a 'trial and error' price, when the events that are to test it always lie in the future. An alternative method (advocated elsewhere by the reviewer) of deciding questions of long-term investment (construction-work and large-scale replacement of plant) 'arbitrarily' through a centralised plan, and assessing current operating costs in terms of labour alone, seems likely on balance to have more to recommend it and to represent the most practicable compromise between the rival merits of centralisation and decentralisation. This, indeed, appears to be the method adopted in the Soviet system of planning: a fact which furnishes a strong empirical argument in support of it.

But to discuss technical questions of accounting in the abstract in this way, as though they constituted the economic problem of socialism *par excellence*, is to ignore the essence of the matter. And there is no doubt that the whole debate has set the question in an entirely wrong perspective. That it should have done so is a result of that narrowing of the focus of study to problems of exchange-relations, and to exchange-relations as reflections of states of minds of consumers, for which economics for more than half a century has been responsible. It should be clear that the question of socialism is primarily one of *production*; and that the principal energies of a socialist economy will be directed towards increasing the productive power of labour by planned construction on a scale never previously achieved, towards rationalising production by greater standardisation both of products and of equipment, towards eliminating the huge wastage of resources that occurs under capitalism in the shape of recurrent crises and the chronic tendency for the economic machine to operate at less than full capacity. Along these lines it is evident that the signal triumphs of a socialist economy will be achieved. This Dr. Lange seems to admit when he comes to speak of 'the Economists' Case for Socialism'. To exploit the possibilities of increased productive power in all directions, and to maintain a correct balance between capital-goods production and consumption-goods production (which Dr. Lange agrees must rest on an 'arbitrary' decision) will take precedence over the question of securing a theoretically perfect adjustment between the output of various types of consumption goods. Moreover, this latter problem may well prove to be, not merely secondary, but of a quite minor order of importance. Even in countries of Western Europe and America the early years of a socialist economy will be preoccupied with the abolition of poverty—with increasing the supply of primary necessities for the mass of the people. Here no complex problem of adjusting supply to demand arises: to decide in what proportions houses or boots or bread must be increased in order to augment welfare does not require any elaborate mechanism of 'consumers' voting' to decide. True, once this first stage is over, and the standard of life has been raised to that of, say, the average lower middle class family today, industry will become increasingly preoccupied with the supply of luxury products of growing variety; and here more subtle adaptation of varieties to tastes will become an important consideration. But at the same time, at the other end of the scale, the very problem of scarcity will be disappearing as saturation of demand is approached in a number of directions. With the disappearance of competitive multiplication of varieties as well as of the conventional emulation in consumption which derives from a class society, this saturation might be reached, not only in the case of necessities but also of minor luxuries, more rapidly than we are accustomed to think.

Dr. Lange's essay concludes with some interesting, if brief, remarks on 'The Policy of the Transition'. He offers some cogent economic reasons why the transition to socialism cannot come by a process of 'economic gradualism'—why 'a socialist government really intent upon socialism has to decide to carry out its socialisation programme at one stroke, or to give it up altogether'; why the 'one economic policy which (an economist) can commend to a socialist government as likely to lead to success' is 'a policy of *revolutionary courage*'. At the same time he indicates the value, if not the necessity, of a transitional 'labour plan' to attack unemployment and the depression, to be operated by a socialist government (he does not mention a people's front) prior to complete socialisation. Thereby such a government could rally mass support behind it and strengthen its position. 'Thus a labour plan, or a series of labour plans, may prove an important link in the evolution which finally must issue in the emergence of an anti-capitalist mass movement of irresistible power and impetus enforcing a wholesale reconstruction of the economic and social order'. At the same time Dr. Lange adds the warning that 'even a socialist government whose purposes are confined within the limits of such a labour plan needs boldness and decision in carrying out its programme; otherwise it degenerates into a mere administrator of the existing capitalist society'.

XIV

COMMENT ON SOVIET ECONOMIC STATISTICS

Reprinted from *Soviet Studies*, Vol. I, No. 1, June 1949, by kind permission of the editors.

THE VIEW THAT ALL Soviet figures are naturally suspect, designed as propaganda-instruments to deceive the unwary, is no longer seriously held, and scarcely merits attention here. Though commonly met with in uninformed circles before the war, it was seldom if ever accepted, at any rate in its crude form, by anyone with much experience of handling Soviet statistics and submitting them to normal tests of consistency.[1] Gaps there were, of course (which grew larger towards the end of the 'thirties for security reasons), and continuous series were difficult to construct in many cases owing to changes of base and of definition. A notable post-war gap has been the absence of regular annual output figures of particular industries (although these can to some extent be deduced from the published index-figures which have 1945 as a base, and from information as to the relationship of post-war output to 1940 output). But such difficulties are met with in varying degrees in the handling and interpretation of the published data of all nations. And although in some respects Soviet published data before the war were deficient by comparison with this country, in other directions they were more plentiful.[2]

[1] Cf. Dr. A. Baykov: 'I do not share the view that Soviet statistical and other sources are less reliable than those published in other countries. On the contrary, systematic study over a number of years has convinced me that they can be used to analyse the economic processes ... of the U.S.S.R. with the same degree of confidence as similar sources published in other countries.' (*The Development of the Soviet Economic System*, p. xiv.)

[2] The fullest collection of quantitative data is the 500-page *Socialist Construction: a Statistical Abstract* (in both Russian and English) of 1936. For the years subsequent to 1936 nothing of the kind was published; and one had to rely on particular sets of published figures (e.g. of output of selected industries).

COMMENT ON SOVIET ECONOMIC STATISTICS

One deficiency that aroused much comment in the West during the 'thirties and was often cited as a reason for suspicion, was the absence of any index number of general prices; the publication of such indices having been discontinued in the early years of the first Five-Year Plan. This deficiency is qualified, however, by two considerations. Firstly, we have now learnt from our own experience of recent years that price-indices have very restricted meaning and limited use in conditions of rationing and controlled prices and wide dispersion of price-movements,[1] and that they may be positively misleading at a time when consumption-habits are subject to considerable change. Secondly, value-data concerning production were generally given in 'constant prices of 1926-7', and accordingly did not depend on the use of a price-index for conversion from money into real terms when comparing the value-data for different years. What this meant was that the constituent items of the total in question (e.g. for some branch of industry) for any year were valued at the prices ruling in the base year; 1926-7 being chosen as this base year on the ground that it was the first 'normal' year after the reconstruction-period following the war and civil war, when prices had been restored to some kind of normal relationship with one another. This practice of valuing output in different years in the prices of a single year is now familiar to us in this country; seeing that it has become the practice since the war in our own official statistics to express the gross value of consumer goods and services (i.e. consumers' expenditure) 'in 1938 prices'.

This particular method of valuation has been the subject of a more serious, if less sweeping, criticism of Soviet statistics, of which a good deal has been heard in the past ten years. The use of 1926-7 prices as a basis of valuation is said to be defective as a measure of output over a period during which considerable price-changes have occurred—moreover, price changes involving a considerable dispersion of particular prices. The effect of using it was to introduce a serious 'upward bias' into the measurement of industrial output between 1928 and the war. This was the onus of Colin Clark's criticism of Soviet claims about the growth of industrial output in his *Critique of Russian Statistics*; and it was repeated in a recent

[1] In the U.S.S.R. between 1929 and 1934, there was not only a spread between the price-movements of rationed and unrationed commodities, but multiple prices for the *same* commodity according to whether it was bought 'on the ration' or 'off the ration' (the Soviet ration-system taking the form of a minimum quota to which one was entitled at a fixed 'ration price'; additional amounts being purchasable, if available, at a much higher price) and in the case of the latter according to the market in which it was purchased (e.g. in the 'closed co-operative', the State 'commercial stores' or on the free market).

248

symposium in the American *Review of Economic Statistics* for November 1947, entitled 'Appraisals of Russian Statistics'.

This criticism is essentially concerned with the comparative 'weighting' of different items in an output-total. The contention is that, since products like tractors and certain types of machinery, which expanded rapidly under the first two Five-Year Plans, had a relatively high cost of production in the middle 'twenties, valuation in 1926–7 prices assigned to them an undue weight. Any general index of production represents a summation of numerous dissimilar items: tons of steel and of coal, yards of cloth, numbers of motor vehicles (of diverse types), of railway locomotives, of machine-tools, etc. The total (and changes in the total) will depend on how the summation is made—on the basis upon which these dissimilar items are added together. The only common property in terms of which they can be measured and added together is their value at some given time and place; and the result will vary according to which of various possible sets of relative values is taken. Evidently the relative values of motor cars, locomotives, textile products and wheat will be very different in U.S.A. in the year 1938 from what they will be in, say, Russia or Italy or Scandinavia or India in the same year, or from what they were in U.S.A. at the beginning of the century. If one is trying to measure the output-change of a total comprising these items over a period when the percentage changes in output of motors, textiles and wheat differ appreciably, it will clearly make a difference whether one chooses a set of prices which allots much weight or importance to motors and little weight to wheat and textiles, or the converse. A fundamental and insuperable problem confronting all such computations is that there will inevitably be an arbitrary element in the selection of this system of weights. One can, of course, exclude the more obvious cases of abnormality, such as the choice of a year when some prices are subsidised and others are inflated. But there is no criterion by which one can decide (except for some purpose within a specially defined context) whether the structure of relative prices in a country in the early stages of industrialisation or in a country at a late stage of industrialisation gives a more 'accurate' or 'true' result.

That measurement in prices of the earlier period will (in the case considered) yield a higher rate of growth than measurement in prices of some later year is not, I think, to be disputed; although the extent of the divergence is probably less than is commonly suggested (one recent American computation[1] indicating that the limits of such divergence are

[1] Paul A. Baran in *The Review of Economic Statistics*, November 1947, pp. 232–3.

about 35 per cent). What can be disputed is the claim that the former measurement is biased in the sense of being *wrong* according to some objective criterion as to what is the 'correct' weighting of different products for the purpose of comparing an output total at one date with an output-total (differently constituted) at another date. An American writer has put the matter in this way: 'In a country in the first stages of industrialisation the spread between prices of industrial goods of a low degree of fabrication and prices of highly fabricated goods is relatively larger than in a well-developed industrial country. . . . As the country progresses on the road of industrialisation, the spread tends to become more narrow. At the same time the share of relatively highly fabricated goods in total output increases. If prices of the first year of the period are used as weights, the increase in output over the whole period appears greater than it would if prices of the last year of the period were employed.' This he refers to as 'a specific case of a general index problem', and admits that 'the choice between the two methods is in general arbitrary'.[1]

From the tone of some Western critics one might have supposed that Soviet statisticians were quite innocent of such difficulties and limitations inherent in the choice of 1926-7 prices as a base. This, however, they are very far from being; and there has been, in fact, considerable discussion of the matter in Soviet economic literature.[2] As a result of this, valuations of fixed capital and of investment are made in the prices of later years, owing to the large changes in constructional costs which have occurred. For example, all investment-expenditures in the second Five-Year Plan were expressed in prices of the year 1933; and for the two subsequent quinquennial plans the prices of the years 1936 and 1945 were respectively chosen as a basis. Moreover, a recent article in a Soviet economic journal contains a hint that a change from 1926-7 prices to present-day prices as a basis for valuing gross industrial output is now contemplated.[3]

A particular difficulty attaches to new products introduced since the base year. In some cases these could be treated by analogy with similar pre-existing products. But in many cases it would be impossible, or at any

---

[1] Alexander Gerschenkron in *The Review of Economic Statistics*, November 1947, p. 220.

[2] For examples cf. the present writer's *Soviet Economic Development since 1917*, pp. 261-2; also V. Sobol, 'On the Question of the Valuation of Fixed Capital', *Planovoye Khozyaistvo*, 1947, No. 4, pp. 54-62, which criticised existing 'motley' methods of valuing fixed capital and argued that 'only valuation of fixed capital in replacement prices' could afford a 'firm basis'.

[3] P. Vladimirov in *Voprosi Ekonomiki*, 1948, No. 8, p. 32.

rate misleading, to do this. The method was at first introduced of valuing these new products in the prices of the first year in which they were put into full and normal production. This has been made the ground of a second criticism: namely, that owing to price-inflation in the 'thirties it had the effect of inflating the output-total of later years (and hence exaggerating the growth of output), since the part of output consisting of new products was valued at much enhanced prices. For example, if in the year 1932 some new type of combine-harvester or machine-tool was introduced for the first time, and if the general level of costs had risen between 1926–7 and 1932, the addition to output which these combines or machine-tools represented in 1932 and subsequent years would be unduly inflated (since they were valued at the higher 1932 prices) compared with older types produced both in 1932 and in preceding years (which were valued at 1926–7 prices).

It may be that there is some weight in this criticism for the years of the First Five-Year Plan, during which money-wages and prime costs exhibited a marked rise. But any upward bias thereby introduced into the total figure of industrial output is, I believe, much smaller than the critics imply, for the following reasons. The majority of cases in point were capital goods (since consumer goods were not subject to much diversification and novelty during the First Five-Year Plan, which was predominantly a plan for the development of heavy industry). Now heavy industry continued to receive subsidies up to 1936, with the object of stabilising the prices of capital goods. The original reason for this was that in the middle and late 'twenties heavy industry was relatively backward in recovery from the effects of war and civil war and many plants were old and high cost plants. Subsequently the policy of subsidising their products no doubt had the effect of preventing the prices of capital goods from rising as much as other prices and costs. Moreover, the extensive replacements of older equipment in these years with modern equipment and the opening of new plants must have had the effect of substantially lowering real costs as compared with 1926–7; as must the extension of standardisation of products and specialisation of plants.[1] Hence, despite the rise in the wage-level in the interim, the disparity between the prices of new capital goods introduced in the later years of the Plan and of their prototypes in

[1] For example, in the engineering industry (according to the *Summary of the Fulfilment of the First Five-Year Plan*, Gosplan, 1933, p. 68) 'in 1932, the mass production works, which played an insignificant role in the beginning of the Five-Year Plan period, produced 48·6 per cent of the total output'. In 1937 four-fifths of total industrial output came from plants newly built or totally reconstructed since 1928.

1926–7 was probably much smaller than is commonly assumed. At any rate, this method of dealing with new products was abandoned in 1936; and therefore did not influence any output totals subsequent to that date. It may well be significant that the year of its discontinuance saw also the termination of subsidies to heavy industry. The defects of the method have been stressed by Soviet writers: for example, the statement in a well-known textbook published in the same year that under it ' "constant" prices lose the notion of an internally linked system of weights in the base period', and that it produces 'an inevitable distortion of the weights of heterogeneous articles in a general total of production constructed on the calculation of individual articles according to the prices of various years'.[1] According to the new method items which were introduced into production after 1926–7 were to be valued at their 1935 prices, which were then to be converted to a 1926–7 level by means of an index of price-changes since that date in the branch of industry in question or in some analogous product.[2]

A number of critics in the West (including Professor Prokopovicz) have pointed to the discrepancy between the percentage growth of basic metal production (in *quantity* terms: e.g. pig-iron and steel tonnage) and the percentage growth of output in the engineering industry (expressed in *value* terms at 1926–7 prices), and hence in the total for heavy industry, as presumptive evidence that the latter contains an 'upward bias'. Between 1928 and 1938 the output of steel and of pig-iron increased rather more than four times (that of coal by rather less than four times and of electrical power eight times), whereas the value of output of machinery increased over the same period sixteen times, and the value of output of industry in general six times.

But such a divergence between the two series (basic metal production and value of final output), on the contrary to being surprising, is precisely what one would expect. Particularly would one expect to find it in a period of rapid industrial transformation, such as the Soviet Union witnessed in the pre-war decade. Industrial progress, especially at an early stage of development, consists in a shift from simpler to more complex products; and hence in a steady increase in the ratio of 'value added by

[1] A. I. Rotstein, *Problemi Promishlennoi Statistiki S.S.S.R.*, Vol. I, pp. 242–4; also cf. Vol. III (1947), pp. 65–9.
[2] Rotstein, *op. cit.*, Vol. I, pp. 248–9. In the case of industrial co-operatives 1932 prices were chosen; these being converted to the level of 1926–7 by the co-operative centre before being submitted to Gosplan ('Instructions for the Composition of the Plan for 1937', *Plan*, 1936, No. 18, p. 29).

manufacture' to basic materials. Not only was there a shift in the proportion of metal put into steel rails and the proportion put into tractors, motor cars and machinery in the years of the Five-Year Plans (a shift in favour of the latter group of products), but there was also a shift towards the production of the more complex and intricate types of machine-tools, scientific instruments, etc., which previously had been imported or else had been manufactured on no more than an experimental scale. An influence in the same direction would also be exerted by economies in the utilisation of raw materials (e.g. improved utilisation of steel scrap and fuel economies). The same divergence between the two series is in fact found in the statistics of other countries. Nor is the divergence in the case of the U.S.S.R. any greater than could reasonably be expected. The surprising thing is, rather, the close correspondence in the relationship between the two series in the case of U.S.S.R. and of the U.S.A. In the American case one has, of course, to take a longer period to find any comparable degrees of growth. For the period between 1899 and 1929 one finds that the index of American blast-furnace products increased by approximately *three* times, while the index of value added by the American machinery industry (adjusted for changes in wholesale metal prices) showed an increase of approximately *eight* times. This compares with a figure of five-and-a-half times[1] for the value-index of ferrous metals and sixteen times for machinery in U.S.S.R. between 1928 and 1938.[2] This particular criticism of Soviet statistics of industrial output seems to have no validity at all.

A final matter which has aroused a good deal of comment is the definition of national income in Soviet statistics. This definition is a more restricted one than that employed in Britain and America, and adheres fairly closely to the concept of 'material production'. By a distinction, familiar enough to the classical economists, services supplied directly to a consumer and unconnected with the creation of an actual commodity are not classed as part of current production, and the valuation of them (either directly or *via* the incomes of those who supply them) is not included in estimates of the national income. The incomes accruing to those who supply such services are treated as belonging to the category of 'redistribution of the national income': to a second stage at which the

---

[1] The divergence between this value-index and the quantity (tonnage) increase referred to above is evidently due to the more rapid increase over the period in the higher grade metal products.

[2] Cf. the present writer in *The Review of Economics and Statistics*, February 1948, pp. 36–7.

primary constituents of real income (the 'real values created in production') are exchanged against such services and supplied as 'derivative' incomes for the maintenance of those responsible for these services. It should be explained that such a dividing line between what is 'productive' and what is 'non-productive' is not endowed with any moral significance and is by no means intended to be identical with the distinction between what is socially useful and useless. It is intended merely as a dividing line between what are treated as distinct economic categories, to one of which the notion of a product and of per-man productivity can be tangibly applied and to the other of which it cannot be so applied, at any rate with anything approaching precision.

This definition has, again, been the subject of considerable discussion in Soviet economic literature; and a number of Soviet economists have maintained the view that no satisfactory line can be drawn between intangible services and material products. Evidently such a line is hard to draw, like all dividing-lines in both the natural and the social sciences, and when drawn contains elements of illogicality. But these difficulties are not any greater (and may well prove, I think, to be much less) than those involved in the Anglo-Saxon definition, which includes the armed forces and policemen and advertising agents as well as educationists and doctors and public health administrators (on the ground that all such services are paid for) while excluding the unpaid services of housewives. In the Soviet classification not all services are excluded. The public catering services appear as a constituent part of the national income, and industrial medical services which are financed by industrial enterprises (and which accordingly figure in industrial costs) are apparently included. So also is industrial administration up to the level of industrial enterprises or trusts (but excluding the industrial Ministries and their sub-departments—admittedly an arbitrary demarcation line) and both transport and the commercial distribution of commodities. But a dividing line is drawn between the transport of goods and the transport of passengers; the latter being omitted from computations of the national income, as are also the services of administrators in State departments concerned with such things as health and education, defence and social welfare, and the services of the armed forces, most doctors, teachers and artists. It has been estimated that the items which are excluded by the Soviet definition and included in the American and British definitions of national income amount in American conditions to about a third of the American national income and in Soviet conditions (where such services have a proportionately smaller weight) to slightly more than one-tenth of the Soviet national

COMMENT ON SOVIET ECONOMIC STATISTICS

income.[1] This affords a rough indication, at any rate, of the magnitude of the adjustment which has to be made in any comparison of the national income totals of this country or the U.S.A. and of the U.S.S.R.

The national income is designed to measure 'the values newly created within a given year'. In Marx's terminology the gross production of a period consists of (1) that part of the value of constant capital which has entered into production during the period (current wear and tear of machinery and plant, raw materials and components and fuel and power used up in production, etc.), *plus* (2) the total wage- and salary-bill of the labour force, *plus* (3) the surplus-value created (which in a capitalist economy goes as profit, interest and rent to owners of property in the means of production). National income, by contrast, includes only the second and third of these items. Alternatively, the national income can be regarded as the sum total of the *net* production of all the various branches of the national economy. A Soviet handbook of statistics contains this description: 'National income, considered from the aspect of its material-real composition, represents a compound-total of consumable material wealth, consisting of a fund of unproductive consumption and a fund of accumulation [i.e. new investment]. . . . The size of the national income can be calculated: (1) as the sum of the net production of the branches of the national economy in which national income is created; (2) as the volume of means of production and articles of consumption utilised for accumulation and for unproductive consumption; (3) as the total of individual incomes of the population occupied in the productive sphere and of incomes of productive enterprises; (4) as the size of the final income of the population and of enterprises. In correspondence with these are distinguished the real (productional) or personal (distributional) methods of calculating national income.'[2]

The published output-figures for Soviet industry are, of course, figures of gross production, since they consist of quantities of final output of all enterprises multiplied by price (whether the current price or the equivalent 1926–7 price).[3] The method of calculating net production (by con-

[1] Paul A. Baran in *The Review of Economic Statistics*, November 1947, p. 230; Paul Studenski in *Studies in Income and Wealth* (National Bureau of Economic Research, New York), Vol. VIII, p. 205.

[2] *Slovar-Spravochnik po Sotsialno-Ekonomicheskoi Statistike* (2nd, revised edition, Gosplanizdat, 1948), p. 82.

[3] Since the values of components and semi-finished goods *produced within the accounting unit in question* are deducted from output of the final stage of production in estimates of gross production, the result will depend on a number of factors such as the definition of the accounting unit, the degree of vertical integration in industry,

trast with gross production) is defined in a pre-war Soviet textbook on the national income as follows: 'One can arrive at the total of net production of industry by subtracting from the total of gross production (with increment of goods in process) expenditure on materials used up (including that on materials used in the increase of goods in process). This quantity should consequently include that net product which is included in the increment of goods in process and of partly finished products.'[1] But in addition to the subtraction of materials and fuel, etc., used up in the course of production, the amortisation (or depreciation) of fixed capital is also deducted. This amortisation is customarily expressed as a given percentage (varying with the particular case) of the value of the fixed capital.[2] It is in this connection that questions of the method of valuation of fixed capital, which were referred to above, have a special importance. Whether fixed capital is valued at its original value or at its replacement cost will clearly make a significant difference to the result if building costs or the cost of equipment have changed in the interim. Moreover, if the former method is used (which has been the practice) fixed capital brought into existence prior to 1936, when products of heavy industry were subsidised and hence were often supplied by a factory at less than their prime cost, may be valued at a lower figure than fixed capital of a later date, despite a fall of real costs in the capital goods industries in the interim.[3] And if fixed capital is valued at an unduly low or an unduly high figure, the amortisation-charge will be equivalently low or high as a percentage of the value of current output, and the estimate of net production, and hence of national income, will to this extent be inflated or underestimated. It is to problems in national accountancy such as this[4]—the strict relating of all such estimates to real pheno-

etc. For variations of practice and definition, cf. the writer's *Soviet Economic Development since 1917*, pp. 262–4.

[1] *Narodny Dokhod S.S.S.R.* (ed. Chernomordik, 1939), p. 58.

[2] In agriculture allowance is made for depreciation of buildings, machinery and livestock and for expenditures on such things as current repairs, seed, feeding-stuffs, fertilisers, fuel and oil, in the calculation of net agricultural production from gross production.

[3] V. Sobol, *loc. cit.*, p. 60.

[4] Another example is the problem of railway rates, about which there has been discussion. The tendency of recent changes has been towards basing freight-rates upon the estimated cost of transport, in place of the traditional system under which rates were related to the prices of the goods transported (cf. a paper read to the Institute of Economics on 'Railway Tariffs in U.S.S.R.' by Professor D. J. Chernomordik summarised in *Izvestia Akademii Nauk S.S.S.R.*, Econ. and Law Section, 1949, No. 1, pp. 55–6).

mena of production lying behind the price-structure—that recent Soviet discussions about the relationship of price to value and the rôle of the concept of value in a socialist economy seem very largely to refer.

The statement of national income in terms of 'constant prices of 1926–7' meets special difficulties owing to changes since that date in the ratio which the items needing to be deducted from gross production bear to the value of the gross product. This ratio will alter as a result of changes in productivity, of changes in relative prices, and also of shifts in the relative importance of different products and industries. To make the kind of deductions of which we have spoken above, both final output and the subtracted items have initially to be valued in terms of *current* prices. The problem is then to reduce the net product thus reached to the basis of 1926–7. A method which was put forward in the middle 'thirties was to reduce this net product in current prices to 1926–7 prices by using the price-index appropriate to gross production; the result being defined as 'net production calculated in constant prices'. This method clearly has defects which have been pointed out by Soviet statisticians; one textbook, to which we have already referred, speaking of it as 'conditional and approximate' only, and 'the more approximate ... the more distant the base year from the year in question'.[1] But the defects of this method are only likely to be considerable over a period in which the prices of raw materials or of capital equipment have moved differently, in a marked degree, from the prices of final output. To some extent this may have been the case in the pre-war decade, owing to the more rapid development of the machine-making industries (and hence of productivity in them) as compared with consumer goods industries: an influence which would have given to this method a 'downward bias' in measuring the growth of the national income. But it seems probable that this influence was to a large extent overlaid by other factors (e.g. the subsidisation of capital goods prior to 1936, to which we referred above, and possibly offsetting movements of raw material prices); and one cannot think that any such bias could have been very considerable, especially in view of the relatively small proportion which costs of amortisation bore to total costs in most industries.

[1] A. I. Rotstein, *op. cit.*, Vol. I, pp. 309–10.

XV

A NOTE ON THE DISCUSSION OF THE PROBLEM OF CHOICE BETWEEN ALTERNATIVE INVESTMENT PROJECTS

Reprinted from *Soviet Studies*, Vol. II, No. 3, January 1951, by kind permission of the editors. The proposals of Academician S. G. Strumilin referred to below were contained in an article by him on 'The Time Factor in Planning Capital Investment' in *Izvestia Akademii Nauk S.S.S.R.*, Economics and Law Series, 1946, No. 3.

IN THE DISCUSSION about the details of Academician Strumilin's calculations too little attention seems to have been given to the central problem which he raises, to which his solution is, I believe, both original and important. This problem is a very real problem for economic planning, and not a purely formal one (whether it can be solved by any simple economic criterion is another matter; but at least such a criterion, if it could be found, would help, at least as a first approximation). Both Professor Bettelheim and Dr. Meek have referred to this. But in case its significance may not have been made plain to the general reader (and even have escaped some of the participants in the discussion), a few words more on the subject may not be altogether otiose. Although much of what I am going to say will be commonplace to professional economists, its repetition may serve to give the non-economist reader some idea of the general setting of what has been to-date a distinctly technical discussion.

First to clear away a possible misunderstanding (to which economists rather than non-economists are likely to be prone). A theory by which the payment of interest in a capitalist society has been traditionally defended is that, because human nature is wont to 'discount the future' (i.e. treat a given amount of goods next year, or ten years hence, as less worthwhile than the same amount of goods available today), it is reasonable for consumption to be foregone (or 'saving' to take place) only when a *greater* amount can thereby be gained in the future. It has been contended that a similar principle must rule in a socialist economy, if its investment policy is to be rationally determined. Since future goods of a certain kind and amount have (allegedly) a lower utility than present goods of the same kind and amount (given that the total income to be expected at both dates is the same and there is no uncertainty about that income), it would not be rational to carry investment beyond the point where the 'yield' (in terms of future annual additions to income) on invested capital compensates for this rate at which the utility of future goods is 'discounted'.

I think it can be shown fairly easily that this would not be a rational principle for any socialist economy to adopt, and that consequently it is irrelevant to discussion of investment problems in the Soviet Union. To discount the future may or may not be a common defect of human nature; but that it is a *defect* seems certain—an irrational defect due to weakness of will or of imagination. For the community as a whole to discount the future (i.e. to give less weight in its planning to income or output *merely* because it accrues at some future date) would be an irrational and short-sighted procedure. To provide food for tomorrow should be no less and no more important, other things being equal, than to provide food for today in any rational planning-policy. As we shall see below, there may well be *other* reasons (especially a difference in total national income in the future from the present) why planners should attach a different weight to an addition to (or subtraction from) income in the present and income in the future. But such reasons have nothing to do with 'time discount' as such, in the sense in which we have been speaking of it, and should not be confused with it.

It might seem, therefore, that we could adopt 'zero time discount' (i.e. equal regard for income whatever the year in which it accrues) as our postulate and leave the matter at that. Such a postulate, however, though it has negative value, in excluding irrelevant considerations, does not in fact get us very far. It does not give any positive criterion as to the amount that should be invested out of the national income of any year in order to increase the productivity of labour, and hence output, in the future. That it cannot do so becomes clear if we take an extreme case. It might appear to follow that, if additions to future income are to be treated as exactly on a par with additions to (or subtractions from) present income, the present generation should starve itself in order to devote all its productive forces to investment, as long as additions to the community's stock of capital equipment, or 'stored-up labour', promise *any* net[1] addition to the productivity of labour in future years. This would be a *reductio ad absurdum* of the postulate. Obviously it cannot be so interpreted, for the simple reason that in the case we have supposed (as in most other conceivable cases) the national income would be more easily produced in the future than in the present, and the disposable income of the future would be much in excess of the consumable income of today. The crux of the investment problem is that the income of the future is always likely to be different from present income through the very fact that current investment and technical change are increasing the productivity of labour over time. Hence it would seem impossible, for *this* reason alone, to treat income (and additions to it) on a par irrespective of the date at which that income accrues. But this reason, let it be emphasised again, has nothing to do with the 'time discount' of which we spoke a moment ago.

Economists of the Utility School have here introduced another principle: that of the so-called 'diminishing marginal utility of income'. Since the utility at the margin (or the utility of an increment of income) will be smaller, the larger is total income, it follows that a given addition to the (larger) income of a future year will be equivalently less worthwhile than a given addition to (or subtraction from) the (smaller) income of the present. If this ratio (i.e. of the utility of future income to that of present income) were known, it would supposedly afford a criterion for investment policy. Such a ratio could be used by planners in making the following decisions:

(*a*) the *total amount* of investment to be made out of current income;

(*b*) the *distribution of this total* among different industries, etc., in such wise that the 'yields' are equal to this ratio (and hence equal to one another) at the margin of all industries;

(*c*) the *technical form* that investment should take in any particular case — whether a very expensive mechanical structure and layout which will increase productivity in the future by a large amount, or a less expensive one which will increase productivity in the future by a smaller amount (i.e. smaller absolutely, but larger as a ratio to the initial expenditure).[2]

---

[1] I.e. 'net' after allowing for amortisation (or depreciation).

[2] This is commonly called by economists in this country a decision as to the degree of 'capital intensity' of investment. It is analogous to the Marxian 'organic composition of capital'. Of course, there might be some technical projects which were

This is not the place to enter upon a general discussion of this solution in terms of Utility. It must suffice to point out a crucial difficulty of this notion as a practical criterion of investment policy. Quite apart from any question of the adequacy or inadequacy of the notion of the Utility of income, there is the difficulty that the relation between Utility and income cannot in practice be determined. The most that advocates of the theory have been able to do is to postulate such a relation *a priori*. Some would say that the notion cannot be given any precise meaning; and that, even if it could be given a meaning, the relation would not be independent of historical change (with changing social relations and social standards, changed products and changed wants), and hence could not be deduced for any future period by extrapolation from the past.

If we accept the view that Utility can provide us with no adequate criterion, then it follows that in a socialist economy decision (*a*) has necessarily to be taken as a policy-decision by the government. In taking a decision as to the proportion of present productive resources to devote to capital-construction for the future, it will *ipso facto* be deciding, on behalf of the community, what sacrifice of present consumption a given increase of future income is worth. No 'automatic' criterion can afford an answer, to be read off as from a slide-rule. There remains, however, the question of co-ordinating decisions (*b*) and (*c*) with it, so that all aspects of investment policy are internally consistent.

It is at this point that Strumilin's solution takes the stage. He is primarily interested in decision (*c*), and the examples he cites fall under this head. What gives his contribution a unique interest is that it is the first attempt to furnish an answer to this question in Marxian terms. Unlike the subjective value theorists, he seeks a criterion, not in consumption (i.e., Utility), but in conditions of production: namely, the governing ratio between future income and present income depends upon the relative amounts that can be produced by a given quantity of labour in the future as compared with the present. In planning calculations more weight is to be attached to income at a date when it costs more labour to obtain it than at a later date when that same income can be more easily obtained. This ratio is his 'rate of devaluation of fixed capital' with the increase of labour-productivity (and hence fall of values) over time. To be worth while, a given investment-project must suffice to yield a net addition to annual output of this amount (as a ratio to its original cost), as well as

cheaper initially *and* also increased productivity by a larger absolute amount than other projects. But then no question of choice between them and more expensive ones would arise, since the latter would not be worth considering at all.

enough to allow for its eventual replacement (or perpetual maintenance). The *greater* the rate at which productivity (and hence future output) grows over time, the *smaller* (*ceteris paribus*) should be the amount of present labour invested as stored-up labour, and the *less expensive* (relatively to their future yield) should be the investment-projects that are chosen.[1]

Since this is essentially a *social* concept (i.e. from the nature of the problem it is conceived in terms of some kind of social average), I cannot see the relevance of the criticisms which have been made of him (e.g. by Mstislavsky and Bettelheim) on the ground that this rate of change of labour productivity will be different in different industries. Since the problem essentially consists in making investment-decisions in different industries consistent with one another and with the overall rate of investment for the economy as a whole, I cannot understand Professor Bettelheim's statement: 'to the extent that the calculations which are made concern one particular branch of industry, it is the rate of increase appropriate to that branch or to associated branches which should be used as the basis of the calculations, and not the average national rate'.[2]

If what has been said above is a correct interpretation of Strumilin's approach, then I think it affords an answer to another objection made by Professor Bettelheim: namely that Strumilin's method of debiting investment *both* with amortisation (the cost of replacing the original investment when it wears out, or of 'keeping the capital intact' by periodic maintenance) *and* with the 'devaluation of fixed capital' 'over-estimates the expenditure of labour which should properly be so debited.'[3]

At first sight this objection seems a plausible one. If the calculation is done in terms of labour, as in the examples which Professor Bettelheim cites, comparing the original cost of the investment in labour and the subsequent cost in 'living labour' of operating the capital equipment, it might seem as though the factor of growing productivity over time was already allowed for, and that to allow for it again by debiting the original cost with the 'devaluation of fixed capital' was double-counting. But reflection shows, I think, that the factor of growing productivity is *not* in fact included, *unless* some additional allowance such as Strumilin

[1] As we shall see below, Strumilin does not put it in this way. But if I have understood him rightly, I think that his basic principle is equivalent to this; and the above way of expressing it may be clearer to English readers.

[2] *Soviet Studies*, Vol. II, No. 1, p. 28 footnote. Professor Khachaturov seems to hint at a similar view in the paper summarised in the present issue of *Soviet Studies* below, p. 322.

[3] *Ibid.*, p. 36.

makes is introduced; and that accordingly Strumilin's method does not involve any double-counting. The examples used by Strumilin and cited by Professor Bettelheim assume that the *product* of the plants in question is a *given* quantity: what is in question is the varying cost of producing that given quantity by various methods. If I understand Professor Bettelheim correctly, his principle of maximum saving of labour (both original or embodied and living labour for current operation of the plant) does not give us the answer we need. It might be held to afford a principle of choice between investment-projects in the limiting case where no growth of productivity over time was to be expected and future income was likely to be no greater than present income (or if greater, its greater size was held to be irrelevant). But it does not seem to give us a criterion of choice which varies with the future rate of growth of productivity and income: i.e. which results in a choice of less capital-intensive investment projects the greater the size of future income relatively to present income. To do this one has to include some factor of bias against the more capital-intensive projects which varies in weight with the rate of growth of productivity over time. This is what Strumilin's 'devaluation' factor seems to me to do.[1]

What may make Strumilin's method of calculation appear strange to Western economists, schooled in the Utility-approach, is that he allows for the future rise of productivity and income, not as a discount to be applied to the future 'yield', but in the form of an addition to the cost of an investment-project. Consistently with this, in the examples he uses for comparing different technical projects, he assumes that the gross product over a given period will be the same in all cases, and that they differ merely in the cost (in labour expended) which they severally involve. In this way he is able to discard the notion of a 'yield' of an investment altogether; and uses simply the criterion of least total cost in labour.

There remains the question whether a criterion of this kind could furnish an 'automatic' rule for what we have called above decision (*a*), concerning the total amount of investment. Apart from the various non-economic considerations which inevitably enter into a decision of this kind, one is confronted with what looks like a crucial difficulty in

[1] Whether Strumilin is right in calculating amortisation in terms of replacement cost instead of original cost is a separate question into which I shall not enter. Professor Bettelheim advances cogent reasons against his method. It is to be noted, however, that Strumilin's use of replacement-cost acts as a partial offset to what Professor Bettelheim regards as his 'over-estimation' of the expenditure of labour to be debited against investment projects.

regarding it as an economic criterion for this type of decision: namely, that the future trend of productivity will itself be affected by the current rate of investment. Thus we would appear to be involved in a circle. There is the further difficulty that it is quite possible that the criterion, used as an instrument of choice among technical projects, might yield so many and so expensive projects as to swallow up the whole national income of the present if all of them were to be satisfied—a difficulty to which Professor Bettelheim's alternative criterion would seem to be even more prone. This is, of course, an extreme case; but it serves to illustrate that the criterion could not suffice of itself to determine the amount by which consumption in any year ought to be reduced in order to satisfy the needs of investment. As was said above, this must inevitably involve a policy-decision which cannot be submitted to any automatic rule.

It is possible, however, to conceive of decision (*a*) and decision (*c*) being co-ordinated (as in practice they would have to be by some means or other) by a process of mutual adjustment between them. For example, decisions about the capital-intensity of various projects (according to the criterion we are considering) might result in a total investment (as the aggregate of all the separate decisions of each industry) larger than had been originally decided upon. Either the latter would have to be raised or the former pruned.[1] If total investment were raised, then presumably the rate of increase of productivity to be expected in the future would be raised also; and the effect of this upon the criterion used by the industrial project-makers would be to reduce the capital-intensity (and hence the expensiveness) of the projects chosen, and thereby reduce the aggregate demand of industries for capital goods. This reduction might be a large one or a small one according to circumstances; and in some circumstances might not be enough to reduce the demand for capital goods within the limits of what the government had decided to be the maximum possible size of the investment programme. But at any rate the two sets of decision would have a tendency to converge towards a point where the capital-

[1] In the short-period (which might well extend over a quinquennium or even a decade) the projects would almost certainly have to be pruned in this case, since the possibility of satisfying all the projects would be limited by the existing productive capacity of the capital goods industries. (Alternatively, the period of construction of the projects might be lengthened, which would be equivalent to postponing the date in the future at which the stored-up labour would come into action and hence bear fruit.) But in the long run it would be possible for adaptation to take the form of stepping-up total investment—a likely outcome if there were numerous 'economic' (according to current criteria) projects waiting in the queue.

intensity of the projects chosen was consistent with the size of the general investment programme.

[An interim summing-up of the Soviet discussion since Strumilin's article, appearing in the journal *Voprosi Ekonomiki*, 1954, No. 3, pp. 99-113, emphasises the importance of this problem of calculating 'the effectiveness of capital investments'—'a problem at present quite neglected in political economy'. 'Recognition that comparison of economy in current expenses with additional capital investments has a scientific basis must put an end to the vacillations in the theory and practice of "project-making", which in recent years have brought it no little damage.' The relation of additional capital investments to the resulting reduction of prime cost, while it cannot be treated 'as a decisive index of effectiveness of capital investment', can be used as one of its indices, which in certain circumstances 'can acquire great importance when the projects compared do not substantially differ' in other (e.g. social) respects. However, the view advanced by some participants in the discussion that this ratio could serve as regulator of the distribution of investment between whole economic sectors is rejected. No agreement has yet been reached, apparently, as to how such a uniform index of effectiveness should be determined, whether according to Strumilin's principle or some other.]

[Since the above was written there have been considerable developments with regard to the use of coefficients of effectiveness of investment both in the U.S.S.R. and in other socialist economies of Eastern Europe. In 1960 there was officially issued, jointly by Gosplan and the Academy of Sciences, a small handbook of 'standard methods' for calculating the effectiveness of investment (*Tipovaia Metodika Opredelenia Ekonomicheskoi Effektivnosti Kapitalnikh Vlozhenii i Novoi Tekhniki v Narodom Khozyaistve S.S.S.R.*, Gosplanizdat, Moscow, 1960). Instead of a uniform coefficient being adopted for all industries, however, differentiated coefficients were established for different branches, varying between 0·1 in transport and electricity generation and 0·15 and even as high as 0·3 in some branches of industry. In Poland, by contrast, (also in Hungary), a uniform coefficient is adopted. The specific proposals of the *Tipovaia Metodika*, and their relation to contemporary proposals regarding price-policy, have been discussed by the present writer in an article in *Soviet Studies* for April 1961 ('Notes on Recent Economic Discussion', Vol. XII, No. 4, pp. 342-352)].

XVI

THE ACCUMULATION OF CAPITAL

Reprinted from *The Modern Quarterly*, Spring 1952, by kind permission of the editor and publishers.

ROSA LUXEMBURG will go down to history as a great socialist, who fought to keep alive the revolutionary traditions of the working class in the years when the tide of revisionism was setting strongly in German Marxism, with its corrupting influence over the Labour movement. Her writing had a compelling vigour and freshness; in polemic she was both trenchant and unusually skilful; at the same time the thought behind her writing was impressive in its range and insight. Many will find an interest in this English translation of her well-known work[1] as their first introduction to this figure of international socialism and to her much-debated theory.

Her *Accumulation of Capital* (first published in 1913) was both a study in the Marxian theory of crises and a preliminary sketch for a theory of imperialism. Its outstanding quality is the distrust which it shows for theories tending to demonstrate that a smooth and harmonious development of capitalism is possible, whether via universal free trade or via some kind of 'planned capitalism'. A large part of the work (some 150 pages) consists of a polemic against such views, from J.-B. Say to Tugan Baranovsky. She is even critical of Marx's formulae when they seem to her capable of such an implication. In particular, she is concerned to stress that capital accumulation necessarily, from its essential nature, involves an unsold surplus of commodities, which can only be marketed *outside* capitalist society *per se*. This is her famous theory of the 'external (or third) market': that

---

[1] Rosa Luxemburg, *The Accumulation of Capital*, translated by Dr. A. F. Schwarzschild, with an Introduction by Joan V. Robinson, M.A. (London, Routledge and Kegan Paul, 1951).

capital accumulation can only proceed at all if new demands are continually tapped in non-capitalist strata (small commodity-producers, etc.). Thus 'colonies' are not incidental adjuncts of capitalism, but essential to its very being; and predatory expansion, battening on petty commodity production and eventually destroying it, is part of capitalism's very nature. As she puts it in her powerful concluding paragraphs: 'It (capitalism) is . . . the first mode of economy which is unable to exist by itself, which needs other economic systems as a medium and soil. Although it strives to become universal . . . it must break down—because it is immanently incapable of becoming a universal form of production' (p. 467). For many readers the most interesting will be those chapters in the third and final section of the work, in which she describes the methods of capitalist expansion into colonial territories, including her richly factual accounts of the British in India, China, Egypt and South Africa, the French in Algeria, and American capital penetrating its own hinterland.

In the more strictly theoretical core of her work her intuition has much more to commend it than her analysis. She has the virtue of emphasising that the process of accumulation requires, not merely certain proportions (or 'equilibrium conditions') between different sectors of production (as economists from Say and Ricardo to Tugan Baranovsky had stated), but also certain proportions between productive power and consumption; and that moreover under capitalism production has a tendency to proceed faster than consumption. In other words, her emphasis was upon the reality of a problem of so-called 'realisation' of surplus-value, as well as of production of surplus-value; and upon the fact that the conditions of the one were apt to stand in contradiction with the conditions favourable to the other. But her analysis of why this was so, and in particular her critique of Marx's formulae of 'expanded reproduction', shows a good deal of misunderstanding and confusion. The result is not only of formal interest: as we shall see, it had the effect of giving certain misleading twists and emphases to the practical implications of the theory.

The first misunderstanding (if the reviewer has grasped her rather prolix argument correctly) relates to Marx's arithmetical examples in Volume 2 of *Capital*, which she takes as her starting point. These examples were designed to show the relations which would need to hold for expanded reproduction (i.e. a process of annual net investment) to take place and continue of its own momentum. Marx's 'Second Illustration,' which she quotes on page 333, represented expanded reproduction *at a constant rate*: all the main quantities growing in the same proportion (as Mrs. Robinson points out in her Introduction, and illustrates in a commendably simplified example). In this case expansion was assumed to occur without any change in composition of capital or in the rate of surplus value; while the proportion of capitalist income saved remained constant, and consequently both saved income (or accumulation) as a proportion of net income ($=V+S$) and the relation between the two departments of production (means of production and means of consumption) also remained constant. This model is criticised by Rosa Luxemburg as quite unreal. (It is of course abstract, but not unreal in the sense that it could not correspond to reality even as an approximation. She does not seem to appreciate that development *can* at times occur on the basis of the same organic composition, provided there are sufficient reserves of labour-power available.) She accordingly substitutes for this model one (p. 337) in which *both* the composition of capital is changing *and* the rate of surplus value is rising due to rising productivity of labour. (It is to be noted incidentally that in the example she chooses the rate of profit would actually be rising, as she herself points out on page 338.) She then shows that in such conditions there will always be a problem of unsaleable surplus of consumer goods in Department 2. Unless these can be sold outside the system, the capitalists in this group of industries will be unable to realise their surplus value in money form, and the process of capital accumulation must break down.

Corresponding to this surplus of consumer goods is an actual deficit of means of production (the one being the obverse side of the other). Curiously enough, having pointed out this deficit, she seems to forget it on the very next page (and at some stages of the subsequent argument), and to speak as though the problem were one of a surplus of means of production also. This apparent confusion is not, however, of major significance. More significant is an apparent failure to see that the result, to which she attaches so much importance, depends, not on the change in the organic composition, but on the rise in the rate of surplus value, which (on the assumption that capitalists save a constant proportion of their surplus value) means that the *saved part of the income must grow as a ratio to newly created value, or net income* (total $V+S$). Hence it is, not *any kind* of expanded reproduction, but expansion involving *this* kind of change that creates a problem of 'realisation', owing to productive power in Department 2 running ahead of consuming power. As Lenin said, disproportion between productive power and consuming power is only one, if a very important one, of the many-sided contradictions of capitalist development; and to a considerable extent accumulation *can* (and does) take place on the basis of an expanding 'internal market'.¹

As a matter of fact, it is possible even for the above-mentioned ratio to rise, *provided* that this is sufficiently offset by a simultaneous rise (due to technical change) in the average composition of both departments and (as the necessary corollary of the latter) an expansion of Department 1 at a *faster* rate than Department 2. Then, and only then, will the increased saving be prevented from being abortive (to use a modern way of expressing it). This is illustrated in another of Marx's examples: his 'First Illustration' (first stage, pages 596–8); and indicates that Rosa Luxemburg was wrong in suggesting that the realisation difficulty arose necessarily and directly from a rise in the composition of capital. (It is to be noted that in her own example, on page 337, Department 1 is *not* made to expand faster than Department 2, and it is therefore hardly surprising that her model should run into difficulties.)

Actually Marx had himself drawn attention to this 'realisation' difficulty in a still earlier example (page 591 of Volume 2) where examination of his figures shows that reproduction must have been taking place *at an increasing rate* (in the sense of a rise in the ratio of accumulation to net income) without any change in composition of capital. (Alternatively one can put it that Marx's 'conditions' are not fulfilled in this case, and the ratio of accumulation is too high for the size of the consumer goods industries as compared with the size of Department 1.) For this case he himself poses the question: how in these circumstances do the capitalists in the consumer goods industries realise (by sale) their surplus value in the form of money—money which they can invest in new means of production? This is equivalent to asking how accumulation can ever proceed at an increasing rate, or for that matter ever have got going at all. Marx reserved his answer to this riddle until the very end of Volume 2; where the answer he gave was that the capitalists of Department 2 sell their products *against gold* to the gold producers (who are implicitly included in Department 1). The point of this answer is not I think that money thereby comes into the system, but the fact that an exchange with gold producers represents a one-sided exchange of goods against money, and not of goods against goods.

This leads us directly to the second misunderstanding. Rosa Luxem-

¹ Cf. for Marx's statement of these conditions, p. 604 of Vol. II. Cf. also Sweezy's analysis in *Theory of Capitalist Development*, p. 164. Incidentally the reviewer's own statement of the conditions in a footnote to p. 107 of his *Political Economy and Capitalism*, 1940 edition, is wrong, since it fails to allow for the increase of variable capital.

burg, having posed this problem of markets, goes on to speak of *foreign trade* as the solution which capitalism finds for its crucial difficulty. (See especially page 359: 'international trade is a prime necessity for the historical existence of capitalism'.) But foreign trade is normally a two-way-traffic: it is an exchange of goods against goods; export of goods is matched by import.[1] What is needed to assuage a crisis of over-production is an *export surplus* from the capitalist world.* Since goods are never given away, this implies an export on loan, i.e. an export of *capital*.

That this point should not have been appreciated, apparently, by Rosa Luxemburg is strange. It leads to an over-emphasis, when she comes to imperialism, upon the search for markets and a tendency to neglect the central rôle of export of capital. While she devotes a chapter to international loans and refers to the need for new proletarian strata in the colonies to exploit, she seems to treat capital export, not as an essential element, but as incidental to the subjection of colonial areas and the breakup of pre-existing 'natural economy'. Moreover, her notion that accumulation is *never* possible without an external market leads to a treatment of colonial exploitation as a product of capitalism at all stages (since the days when it thrived on primitive accumulation) rather than of capitalism at a relatively mature stage. It also carries the implication that the 'collapse of capitalism follows inevitably as an objective historical necessity' when there are no more 'third markets' left to conquer (page 417); even if 'a string of political and social disasters and convulsions' (page 467) is likely to bring about its downfall before that point of final mechanical breakdown is reached.

It is interesting to note that the standpoint of Rosa Luxemburg bears a striking analogy with that of the Russian Narodniks whom Lenin had criticised nearly fifteen years earlier in the first chapter of his *Development of Capitalism in Russia*. The Narodnik writers also had spoken of the impossibility of realising surplus value without the aid of an external market, and had identified this problem with that of an unsaleable surplus of consumer goods. (From this they had drawn the conclusion that Rus-

[1] True the problem implied in her particular example could be met by an export of consumer goods against imports of producer goods; but this is not the universal pattern of foreign trade, least of all in the most mature capitalist countries where heavy industry exports play an increasing rôle.

[*To this criticism Mrs. Robinson has replied in a letter to the present writer that, *provided* exports are continually expanding, this expansion will act as a stimulus to investment in the export trades (more cotton exports, more looms), and it will be this additional investment which will keep income and expenditure at a higher level than they would otherwise be.]

sian capitalism was an alien and artificial growth and had no future.) Lenin's statement has already been quoted that the 'striving towards unlimited expansion of production and limited consumption' is 'not the only contradiction of capitalism' (Lenin, *Sochinenia*, 4th edition, Vol. 3, p. 36). This was one form in which disproportion between the various branches of production might be expressed; and such disproportion could create difficulties 'not only in the realisation of surplus value, but also in the realisation of variable and constant capital; not only in the realisation of products in means of consumption, but also in means of production' (*ibid.*, p. 25). He went on to emphasise that the growth of capitalism is invariably associated with a faster rate of growth of capital goods than of consumer goods: since 'according to the general law of capitalist production constant capital grows more quickly than variable', it follows that 'the department turning out means of production must grow more quickly than that which turns out means of consumption. Thus the growth of an internal market for capitalism is to a certain extent "independent" of the growth of personal consumption, being accomplished rather at the expense of productive consumption' (i.e. investment in constant capital). This might seem paradoxical, since it involved ' "production for production"—an extension of production without a corresponding extension of consumption'. But this, he declared, was 'a contradiction not of doctrine, but of real life', pertaining to the essential nature of capitalism (*ibid.*, pp. 32, 34). Indeed, it was precisely in this expansion of production without a corresponding expansion of consumption that the historical mission of capitalism consisted. Such a contradiction was the very stuff of development of capitalism; and while it contained the germ of periodic crises, it in no wise implied the mechanical 'impossibility' of development without an external market.

Mrs. Robinson in her Introduction summarises the main points of Marx's and Rosa Luxemburg's analyses, which she does with her usual lucidity of exposition and with an eye to translation of their ideas into terms familiar to academic economists. Translation, however, is apt to be a slippery business when it is not merely a question of finding equivalent symbols for the same notion, but where the notions themselves are different. Naturally interpretations of a doctrine such as Rosa Luxemburg's (which is often far from rigorous in its exposition) must be expected to differ. (Compare, for example, the interpretation given in this Introduction with that given by Sweezy.) All the same, one cannot help feeling that the attempt of the Introduction to show Rosa Luxemburg as a forerunner (if primitive and in some respects misguided) of Keynesian doctrine, and to treat her analysis in this setting, has resulted in her argument perhaps suffering a misleading gloss in places, and in her being given both too little credit as a critic of capitalism and too much credit as a reviser of Marx. But one can wholeheartedly agree with the conclusion that 'this book shows more prescience than any orthodox contemporary could claim'.

XVII

A NOTE ON THE TRANSFORMATION PROBLEM

THIS PROBLEM IS ESSENTIALLY whether or not the Prices of Production of Marx are deducible from the Value-positions (as determined by quantities of embodied labour) once the Compositions of Capital (ratio of Marx's Constant Capital to Variable Capital) are known. If they are not deducible completely, then there is a logical flaw in the theory so far as the explanation of Prices (= Cost *plus* average profit-rate on capital employed) is concerned when the Composition of Capital is different in different industries. In other words, is a Cost of Production Theory of Price reducible to terms of the Labour Theory of Value, or not?

What makes the problem of deriving prices from values more complex than might appear at first sight is that, if outputs are expressed in Prices of Production, so also have inputs to be (e.g. labour-power and capital goods); so that the transformation from values into prices involves a mutual interaction between output-prices and input-prices.

In what follows the letters S, V and C are used to denote Surplus-value (or Profit), Variable Capital (or Wage-fund) and Constant Capital respectively.[1] We shall call Prices of Production prices for short, and the situation where exchange occurs at such prices the price-situation (by contrast with the value-situation of Marx's first approximation in Volume I of *Capital*).

---

[1] It should be noted that Marx in his treatment of Prices of Production avoided the complication of a difference between the *stock* of fixed capital and the currently *used-up* part of it by the simplifying assumption that the whole of C is used-up in each 'turnover-period' of production. This convention is followed here. There is also the tacit assumption that turnover-periods of V are uniform.

A NOTE ON THE TRANSFORMATION PROBLEM

There have been several answers supplied in algebraic form,[1] which show that the problem (of which Marx was aware but which he left uncompleted[2]) is capable of solution. This Note is an attempt to describe in ordinary language the main relationships involved, with special reference to two particular questions that have arisen in the course of propounding a solution. Firstly, Bortkievicz and Sweezy have argued (whereas Winternitz and May disagree) that Marx's equilibrium-conditions of 'Simple Reproduction' (defining the relationship between the categories S, V and C, as sources of expenditure by workers or capitalists, and the outputs of the three main departments of production: capital goods, wage goods and luxury goods) must form part of the conditions for a solution (if I understand them rightly) as well as a test of consistency by which to judge the validity of any solution. Secondly, Bortkievicz and Sweezy have emphasised (and here Winternitz concurs, although May apparently dissents) that a solution is independent of the composition of capital in Department III: in other words, that the rate of profit is determined exclusively by the situation of Departments I and II, producing capital goods and wage-goods respectively.

In an earlier version of this Note I argued that, since the equation determining the rate of profit in the price-situation involved the *quantities* produced in each of these three departments, as well as their productprices, and since these quantities would be different in the price-situation from the value-situation,[3] the equations of Simple Reproduction would

[1] L. von Bortkievicz, 'Marx's Fundamental Theoretical Construction in the Third Volume of *Capital*', Eng. trans. as Appendix to *Karl Marx and the Close of his System by E. von Böhm-Bawerk and Böhm-Bawerk's Criticism of Marx by R. Hilferding*, ed. Paul M. Sweezy (New York, 1949), and 'Value and Price in the Marxian System', Eng. trans. in *International Economic Papers*, No. 2, pp. 5–60; Paul Sweezy, *Theory of Capitalist Development* (New York, 1942), pp. 109–25; J. Winternitz, 'Values and Prices: a Solution of the so-called Transformation Problem', in *Economic Journal*, June 1948, pp. 276–80; cf. also Kenneth May in *Economic Journal*, December 1948, pp. 596–9. Bortkievicz's two articles appeared originally in 1907, in the *Jahrbücher für Nationalökonomie* and the *Archiv für Sozialwissenschaft* respectively. Kenneth May describes the solution as 'trivial mathematically'.

[2] *Capital*, Vol. III, pp. 190, 194 ('the price of production of a certain commodity is its cost-price for the buyer, and this price may pass into other commodities and become an element of their prices'); also *Theorien über den Mehrwert*, Vol. III, pp. 200–1 and 212.

[3] My reason for supposing this was that I had mistakenly presumed that the process of establishing Prices of Production must involve a migration of capital and labour, and consequently shifts of output, between industries; in which case the average rate of profit would have depended, *inter alia*, upon the sum of the new quantities multiplied in each case by the appropriate Price of Production.

have to be explicitly introduced to determine these quantities. I now realise that this argument was wrong, and that on the assumption of a constant quantity of labour in the system (also a given level of real wages, given labour productivities and given quantities and compositions of capital) the output-quantities of the three departments must necessarily remain constant. Indeed, the solution of the late Dr. Winternitz (which derives the deviations of prices from values and the rate of profit from the assumption of an equal rate of profit in Departments I and II) does not explicitly introduce the equations of Simple Reproduction.

The reason why output-quantities will be the same in the two situations can be quite simply expressed as follows. With a given level of real wages and size of total labour-force (both assumed as unchanged by the transformation from value-situation to price-situation), the output of wage-goods must obviously be constant. Given the quantity of C in the system, the output of Department I, producing capital goods, must also be constant. With a constant labour-force, this means that the quantity of labour in Department III, treated as a residual, must also be constant, and hence the output in this department. The transformation problem, accordingly, remains a matter merely of a change in *prices*; and we have as the four unknowns to be determined the product prices of the three departments and the rate of profit. The latter depends in any department on the surplus of its net output over the cost of its labour-power as a ratio to its capital $(C + V)$, all these quantities being expressed in *price*-terms. In equilibrium, prices must be such as to make this ratio the same in all three departments.

Returning to Department II, producing wage-goods: it will be clear that if there were no constant capital here the *rate of surplus-value* (ratio of S to V), expressible as this is in product-terms, would be invariant to changes in the price-relationships between the departments: i.e. it would be the *same* in the price-situation as in the value-situation. Moreover, if capital consisted only of 'advances to labourers', the rate of profit (since it would be identical with the rate of surplus-value) would be unaffected by the transformation from values into prices. This was, indeed, Ricardo's theory: in it the rate of profits was uniquely determined by the ratio of corn produced at the margin of agriculture (the wage-goods industry) to corn consumed by labourers as subsistence: prices in non-wage-goods industry being adjusted to the level at which the same rate of profit was earned there as in agriculture.[1]

[1] Cf. Introduction to *Principles* in Vol. I of *The Works and Correspondence of David Ricardo*, ed. Sraffa, p. xxxi.

A NOTE ON THE TRANSFORMATION PROBLEM

But with constant capital in the picture, it is clear that the rate of profit in Department II $\left(\dfrac{S}{V+C}\right)$ will be influenced by the rate of exchange between Department I (producing capital goods) and Department II, and hence will no longer remain unaffected by a change from value-relationships to price-relationships. The rate of profit in Department II can still be expressed in terms of its own product; but that part of its capital which is C will have to be expressed as the quantity of its own product which it must exchange with Department I to procure the requisite capital goods; and this quantity will vary with the rate of exchange between the two departments. Moreover, a change in this quantity will influence the size of its net product and hence of S. (The same will be true, *mutatis mutandis*, in the case of Department I; but here the V-part of its capital will have to be procured from outside, and when expressed in terms of its *own* product will be affected by the rate of exchange between the two departments.) The effect on the profit-rate of a transformation from values to prices will be as follows. If Department I has a higher organic composition (C/V) than Department II, prices in the former will tend to rise relatively to those in the latter.[1] This raising of the price of the constituents of C relatively to V will *lower* the profit-rate in Department II (and conversely raise it in Department I by cheapening the constituents of V). The change in price-ratio will continue until the profit-rate is the *same* in the two departments. This new equilibrium-profit-rate will be *lower* than the profit-rate of Department II in the value-situation (and conversely in the case of Department I). If, however, the composition in Department I were the lower of the two, instead of higher, a reverse change in the price-ratio would occur, and the profit-rate would end up in the price-situation at a higher level than it had been in Department II in the value-situation. This, I gather, is putting into words what the Winternitz-solution amounts to.

It remains true, therefore, that the conditions of Simple Reproduction remain implicit in the assumptions of the initial value-situation (as Dr. May pointed out); and it is true that they are necessary to determine the output-quantities of the three departments—moreover to establish the *constancy* of these outputs in the two situations. But they do not need to be introduced to derive prices and the (new) rate of profit from the original value-situation: these can be derived simply from the assumption

---

[1] Since initially, with equal rates of surplus-value, the profit-rate in Dept. I would have been *lower* than in Dept. II.

of an equal profit-rate in Departments I and II, and are independent of output-quantities.[1]

What of the alleged independence of this result from the situation of Department III? Here again the composition of capital in Department III will, of course, help to determine the *outputs*: the larger its C relative to its V, the larger will be the output of Department I relative to that of Department II, *ceteris paribus*. But this is not to say that it can influence the rate of profit or prices in the other two departments. We have seen that, just as when capital consists only of V the rate of profit is determined solely by relations internal to Department II, so when capital is composed of V and C the rate of profit is determined by the conditions of the two departments which produce respectively capital goods and wage goods, and by them alone. This may seem a strange conclusion in view of the fact that surplus-value is also created in Department III.[2] What will happen, however, is that the price of luxury goods will be adjusted to the level which yields a rate of profit equal to that at which Departments I and II have been brought into equilibrium. The degree of this price-adjustment (i.e. its deviation from value) will depend, of course, on the composition of capital in Department III; but since this price-adjustment cannot affect any of the components of the rate of profit in the other two departments (affecting neither the ratio of S to V in them nor the ratio of V to C), it cannot alter the rate of profit, however large the shift of price in III has to be. Since it cannot reciprocally influence the others, it can only adapt itself to them.

Bortkievicz illustrates this with some arithmetical examples.[3] Let us

[1] Except in the sense that *both* the prices *and* the output quantities are dependent upon the initial data as to the magnitudes of S, V and C.

[2] When Dr. May speaks (*loc. cit.*, p. 599) of the conditions of Simple Reproduction being implicit in the original values, he concludes from this that the profit-rate in the *value*-situation is 'not independent of division three'. But in the value-situation profit-rates are unequal, and those in Depts. I and II are severally dependent solely on the composition of capital prevailing in them. Perhaps Dr. May has in mind the average of the three profit-rates; but since these rates are unequal in the value-situation, an average of them is without significance, and at any rate need bear no definite relationship to the average (equal) profit-rate in the price-situation. I should hasten to explain, perhaps, that my view on this point also has shifted between the first draft of this Note (when my position was much the same as that expressed by Dr. May) and the present draft.

[3] In 'Marx's Fundamental Theoretical Construction in the Third Volume of *Capital*', Appendix to Sweezy edn., pp. 208–12; including the intriguing example on p. 211 where Dept. II has no constant capital, only variable, and the rate of profit in the price-situation remains equal to the rate of surplus-value in Dept. II in the value-situation.

illustrate it here with a simple example of a *change* in the composition of capital in Department III. We will suppose that this rises, so that more C is used in production for each unit of V. The change will involve as its consequence *either* a larger output from Department I *or* a decrease of employment in Department III, or some mixture of both. On the assumption of a fixed labour-force a larger output of capital goods can only come about if there is a transfer of labour from Department III to Department I, so that both employment and output are increased in the latter, and employment in the former (and possibly its output, temporarily at least) reduced.[1] The increased need for C in Department III will accordingly be accompanied by an absolute as well as a relative decrease in V. Labour productivity here will presumably have risen as a result of technical innovation, and the price of the product (luxury goods) will have to be adjusted until the same rate of profit as before is being earned. But neither a change in the price of luxury products nor the increase in output and employment in Department I will affect any of the determinants of the rate of profit in Departments I and II (namely, in each case the price of its own output and the price-ratio of capital goods and wage-goods).

So far we have spoken of relative prices only, and of changes in price-ratios from an initial position. How the price-level is affected absolutely in the process of transformation from value-relations to price-relations (i.e. whether some prices will rise and others remain constant or some rise and some fall) will depend on what the conditions of production of gold (as the money-commodity) are assumed to be. This is equivalent to Ricardo's problem of choosing an invariable standard—whether to take this as being produced without fixed capital (as in edition 1) or under average conditions as regards the proportion of fixed capital and the turnover period of circulating capital (as in edition 3).[2] Here the Bortkievicz-Sweezy solution assumed the product-price of Department III to remain unchanged in the process of transformation, which is equivalent to assuming that gold is a product of this department (or produced under conditions identical with it). Things produced with a higher composition of capital than Department III will then rise in price in the course of

---

[1] If the assumption of a fixed labour-force is dropped, then the output of Dept. I can be increased by drawing upon previously unemployed labour (after a temporary period in which its own stock of C is being built up from its own output), and no transfer of labour from Dept. III or reduction in the latter's output (except possibly quite temporarily) need occur.

[2] Introduction to *Principles* (ed. Sraffa), pp. xlii–xlv.

transformation from values to prices, and things produced with a lower composition will fall in price. Winternitz, however, by postulating that 'total prices equal total values', in effect assumes that gold is produced under *average* conditions as regards composition of capital. Some prices will then rise and some fall, according as they are of things produced with above-average or below-average compositions of capital. So far as the transformation problem is concerned, the difference of assumption is purely formal: as Sweezy says, any such assumption is significant only as a way of establishing a *numéraire* linking Prices with Labour-Values.

Postscript

The above Note was privately circulated, but not published. While the question discussed is mainly of formal interest,[1] as showing that what had been regarded as a difficulty in Marx's theory is really no difficulty, it has given rise to some discussion over the method of solution and over implications which solution has disclosed. Of more substantial interest is the emphasis which analysis of the problem has laid on the rôle played by the rate of surplus-value in the group of industries producing wage-goods as a fundamental determinant—a fact of which Ricardo seems already to have been aware at the time of his earliest formulation of a theory of profit.[2] The implication was underlined by Bortkievicz (for all his show of battling with Marx) as follows: 'This result [that only quantities from Departments I and II are involved in the solution] is hardly surprising from the point of view of the theory of profit which sees the origin of profit in "surplus labour". Ricardo had already taught that a change in the relations of production which touches only such goods as do not enter into the consumption of the working class cannot affect the height of the rate of profit.'[3] This, he suggests, is much more in accordance with a 'deduction' theory of profits (as he prefers to call it, instead of Marx's term 'exploitation'), and elsewhere writes: 'If it is indeed true that the level of the rate of profit in no way depends on the conditions of production of those goods which do not enter into real wages, then the origin of profit must clearly be sought in the wage-relationships and not in the ability of capital to increase production. For

[1] Mrs. Robinson dismisses it as 'purely formal and of no importance', like 'the "adding-up problem" in "bourgeois" economics' (*Collected Economic Papers*, p. 149).
[2] Cf. Introduction to *Principles*, ed. Sraffa, pp. xxxi–xxxii.
[3] Appendix to *Karl Marx and the Close of his System by Eugen von Böhm-Bawerk and Böhm-Bawerk's Criticism of Marx by Rudolf Hilferding*, ed. Paul M. Sweezy, p. 209.

if this ability were relevant here, then it would be inexplicable why certain spheres of production should become irrelevant for the question of the level of profit.'[1]

It is to be noted that Marx, while agreeing with Ricardo so far as the rate of surplus-value is concerned, criticised him for supposing that the rate of profit was similarly determined by the conditions of production of wage-goods alone—this he declared was a sign of Ricardo's neglect of constant capital (i.e. in his theory of profit as distinct from his theory of exchangeable value). The rate of profit, by contrast with the rate of surplus-value, depended upon the total social capital in all spheres of production.[2] As we have seen above, the rate of profit cannot be deduced from the ratio of net output to wages in wage-goods industry alone, but is dependent on the circumstances of production of capital goods as well as wage-goods. Marx, however, operated with two departments only, in order to emphasise the relation between production of capital goods and of consumer goods; and since he did not break down the latter (at any rate in his schematic representations) into goods consumed by workers and by capitalists, the question of the possible irrelevance of the latter to the determination of the rate of profit did not directly arise.[3]

Another aspect from which this problem can be viewed is the effect on Prices of Production of a rise of wages (sometimes spoken of as the 'Ricardo-effect' since this was the way in which Ricardo always posed the problem). A general rise of wages will have the result (1) in each industry, or group of industries, of increasing one of the elements of Cost-price (in Marx's sense), (2) of reducing the rate of surplus-value and hence the rate of profit. This latter effect is one that operates on a *social* scale, and is not apparent if one looks at an industry, or group of industries, in isolation. It will follow that in industries of high organic composition of capital (relatively to that of gold production) the influence of (2) will tend to be stronger than the influence of (1), and the Price of Production will actually *fall*.

The objection has been made against Marx's presentation that his contention is purely arbitrary when he speaks of the rate of surplus-value remaining unaltered (save for the price-adjustments referred to above) and of a given total of surplus-value being merely redistributed among

---

[1] 'Value and Price in the Marxian System', Eng. trans. in *International Economic Papers*, No. 2, p. 33.

[2] *Capital*, Vol. III, p. 192; *Theorien*, Vol. II, Pt. 1, pp. 104–5, 147–8 (in Bonner and Burns trans., pp. 289, 325–6).

[3] See, however, *Theorien*, Vol. II, Pt. 1, p. 147.

industries in the transformation-process. Would it not have been more reasonable to say that, since labour-productivity is higher where there is more fixed capital, more surplus-value is produced by labour in those industries and hence the rate of surplus-value there is higher?[1] If, however, this latter way of putting the matter were valid, it would be inexplicable if a rise of wages *lowered* the price in industries of high organic composition. Indeed, on this view there would be no ground for prices to change at all: a wage-rise would simply lower the rate of surplus-value to the extent that wages had risen, and, since the productivity of labour remained unaffected, there would be no reason for the price to change.[2] Still less would this way of presenting the matter be capable of explaining why the rate of profit should be determined by the conditions of production in Departments I and II alone (nor, indeed, would it be consistent with the profit-rate being determined in this way).

[1] See Joan Robinson, *An Essay on Marxian Economics*, p. 18: 'productivity per man is greater where capital per man is greater. . . . Thus the rate of exploitation tends to vary with capital per man employed.' Also cf. the views of J. Wolf, *cit.* in the Preface to *Capital*, Vol. III, pp. 26–7.

[2] Such a result would involve the contradiction that profit-rates were now *un*equal. If the answer were to be made that competition would equalise profit-rates again by lowering some prices and raising others, then this answer would be inconsistent with the initial assumption that each industry produced surplus-value in proportion to the productivity of its labour appropriate to its own composition of capital.

INDEX

Abstinence, 188, 208
'Accounting-price', of factors of production, 41, 57, 242–3; of capital, 42 n., 44–6, 47 and n., 52–4; fixed by trial and error, 54, 57, 243; as a possible planning technique, 51 n., 58
Accumulation of Capital, problems of, 196–7, 266 seq. (See also Investment, Capital)
Accumulation, primitive, 191
Advertising, economic effects of, 37–8; significance of, for economic theory, 113, 114
Allocation, of economic resources in an 'ideal' way, 6–8, 36 seq., 105; problem of, 55, 75, 79–80, 239 seq. (See also Calculation, Welfare, Optimum)
America, United States of, rate of industrial growth of, compared with that in U.S.S.R., 119, 124, 125 n., 126 n., 129, 253; New Deal in, 217, 221; 'New Economics' in, 219; opposition to full employment in, 220; armament expenditure in, 221; danger of a new crisis in, 221
Amortisation, 40, 197, 250 n., 256, 263 n.
Anarchists, 167, 202
'Anarchy of Production', 56, 241
Arrow, Dr. Kenneth J., 63–4 n., 65–6 n., 72 n.
Austrian School of economists, 6, 15
Aveling, Dr. Edward, 189 n., 190 n.
Aveling, Eleanor Marx, 188 n.

Bakunin, Michael, 202
Balances, method of, 91
Baran, Professor Paul A., 82, 118 n., 138, 152 n., 249 n., 255 n.

Barter, 26
Bauer, Bruno, 182
Baumol, Professor William J., 63, 67, 68 n.
Baykov, Dr. Alexander, 123 n., 247 n.
Beesly, Professor Edward Spencer, 186
Bergson, Professor Abram, 56, 59 n., 69, 120 n., 125 n.
Beria, Lavrenti P., 128
Berlin, Isaiah, 232 n.
Bettelheim, Professor Charles, 258, 262, 263, 264 and n.
Beveridge, Lord William, 220, 223–4
Birck, Dr. L. V., 11
Blackman, J. H., 120 n.
Bogdanov, A., 168
Böhm-Bawerk, Eugen von, 15, 194
Bonner, E. A., 192, 280 n.
Bortkievicz, Ladislaus von, 274, 277, 279–80
Bray, John Francis, 188
Brutzkus, Boris, 35
Bücher, Karl, 5 n.
Burns, Émile, 192 n., 280 n.

Cairncross, Professor Alec, 79
Calculation, rational economic, 33 seq., 239 seq.
Cambridge School of economists, 6, 7
Cannan, Professor Edwin, 11
Capital, defects of treating it as a factor of production, 138–9; treated as a stock, 140, 149; Composition of, effect of differences in, 111, 193–5, 273, 276–278, 281; Constant C., 193, 197, 273, 276–8, 280; turnover of, 191 n., 193, 194 n.; price of, 42 n., 45–6; 'productivity' of, 188, 208; 'deepening'

283

INDEX

and 'widening', 46, 49 n., 55, 127 n., 150; 'c.-saturation', 47–8 n.; 'c.-intensity', 46, 52, 55, 89 n., 138 seq., 260 seq.; c.-output ratio, 87–8, 131 n., 135; export of, 101, 198 n., 270; difficulty of measuring, 115, 138–9; process of circulation of, 192–3; valuation of fixed c., 250; 'rate of devaluation of fixed c.', 261–3; replacement of fixed c., 197. (See also Marginal Net Product, Investment)

Capital goods, production of, 14, 77, 245, 276, 278; market for, 56; as the limit on rate of investment, 85, 150; rate of growth of, under Soviet Five Year Plans, 120–5, 128–32, 134, 251; investment in expanding, determinant of future rate of economic growth, 130–1, 150–1; faster rate of growth of, than of consumer goods a 'general law of capitalist production', 271

Capitalism, 3, 4–6, 9–10, 107; instability of, 43, 195–9, 245, 266 seq.; and its need for a 'third market', 266 seq.; 'ideal', 51; and class conflict, 98–9; and employment, 215 seq.; economic theory as an apologetic of, 105; Marx's analysis of, 187 seq.; Keynesianism as a 'save-c.' doctrine, 218; State C., 218; 'planned', 266

Carr, Edward Hallett, 181
Carr-Saunders, Professor A. C., 93 n., 100
Cassel, Gustav, 34 n., 35
Causal-genetic sequence, 116
Change, economic, 74 seq. (See also Growth, Development)
Chartism, 183, 184
Chernomordik, Professor D. J., 256 n.
Clapham, Dr. J. H., 179
Clark, Colin, 248
Class; -differentiation and historical development, 8, 10; and income-distribution and 'rent', 12; division of product between classes, 97, 190–1, 194; -struggle, 93 seq., 201, 229, 234; problems of defining a, 94–101; c.-consciousness, 103; in Classical Political Economy, 110

Classical Political Economy; its treatment of exchange relationships and their determination, 109 seq.; and the objectivity of economic laws, 110; and Marx, 183, 200; and Hegel, 231
Classless Society, 11, 15, 29; international relations in a world of classless states, 101–2
'Cobweb theorem', 105
Coefficients; technical, of production, whether fixed or variable, 81 seq.; input-output, 68, 91; of fabrication, 120, 253
Colonies, 267, 270. (See also Imperialism, Under-developed countries)
Communism; conditions for transition to, 129–30, 131; Marx and, 182, 184; 'capitalist c.', 194; as 'second stage of socialism', 212
Communist League, 184
Communist Manifesto, of 1848, 94, 184, 187, 234
Compensation-principle, 62–3 and n.
Competition; effects of, in causing fluctuations of output, 13–14; playing at, under socialism, 57, 240–1; 'freely competitive capitalism', 86; imperfect, 98, 105; theory of, in relation to increasing returns, 112; whether surplus value is consistent with, 188
Complementarity; in consumers' wants, 81, 84–5
'Compounding-effect', 146–8
Consumer goods, production of; under Soviet Five Year Plans, 122–3, 129–32; also 245
Consumers; charge of sacrificing their welfare to arbitrary judgements of dictators, 58, 70 n., 73; preferences, 36–8, 69 seq., 79, 87–8, 113–14, 245; 'sovereignty', 36, 69, 70, 71, 73, 109; indices available to a planning authority for estimating consumers' demands and comparing these with the relative costs of meeting these demands, 87–8; the myth of c. as isolated individuals, 79
Consumption; conventional standards

284

INDEX

of, 27–9; 'communal' and 'individual' distinguished, 58, 71–2, 87; 'Gresham's law' of, 73; complementarity in, 81, 84–5; level of in U.S.S.R., 129–32; under-c., 197–8, 267 seq.
'Contract Curve', 26, 62 n.
Convention, social; and habits in relation to standards of consumption, 27–9, 245; in relation to demand, 71–3, 79, 114
Cost; 'capacity-c.', 90 n.; prime c., 42, 44, 45, 54–5, 87, 88, 91 and n., 265; 'planned c.', 91 n.; constant c., 112; total or average, 64, 82–3, 243; relation of, to selling price, 88–9, 105; and value in economic theory, 110–2. (See also Marginal Cost)
Crises, economic; and over-expansion of constructional trades, 13–14; Marx on, 195 seq.; and 'full employment' policies, 221–5; Rosa Luxemburg on, 266 seq.

Dalton, Dr. Hugh, 11, 13 n.
Decentralisation; of economic decisions under socialism, 42–3, 53–4, 57–8, 77, 81, 242, 244
Demand-curve; condition of independence of, 23; for labour, 27, 29; for a commodity: is it independent of market price?, 31, 114; kinked, 85; what does it represent?, 113–14
Demand, Joint, 84, 151 n.
Demand situation, under socialism, 85
Democracy; of the market, 36–7, 69 seq., 245; Parliamentary, 101, 172–3, 210. (See also Consumers, Price-system, Social Democracy)
Depreciation. (See Amortisation)
Determinism, 229
Deutsche Jahrbücher, 182
Development, economic; nature of economic problem under, and how it differs from the problem of static equilibrium, 74 seq., 116; under Soviet Five Year Plans, 118 seq.; in under-developed countries, 138 seq.
Dicey, A. V., 229, 230–1 and 231 n.

Dickinson, Professor H. D., 12 n., 13 n., 35, 37, 39, 50 n., 57–8, 68 n., 71, 87, 240, 243 n.,
Distribution of Income, 11–12, 29–30, 31, 97, 210–12; theory of, 16, 17n.,23, 94, 106, 108; interest of Ricardo and Marx in, 194; and so-called *optimum* conditions for allocating resources, 60 seq.; separation of problem of, from production, 61; logically prior to question of 'ideal output', 63–4; and nature of market-demand, 85; taken as given in modern theory of exchange, 108
Dividend, Social; as a stabiliser, 49–50
Dupuit, Jules, 82 and n., 89

Economica, 3
Economie Appliquée, 138
Economic Journal, The, 17, 20, 23, 33, 34, 35, 112
Economies; of scale, 45–6, 64, 112; external, in consumption, 71–2; external, in production, 45–6, 64, 75, 89 n., 112
'Economism', 162–4, 166
Economist, The, 220
Edgeworth, Francis Ysidro; and 're-contracting', 18; and 'indeterminateness', 22; and 'Contract Curve', 27
Efficiency; varying types of, 67, 79–80, 91–2
Ellis, Howard S., 56 n.
Empiricism; traditional in Anglo-Saxon countries, 20
Employment; 'full e.', 44, 49 and n., 50, 55, 98, 215 seq.; increase of, in U.S.S.R. and U.S.A., 125–7; expansion of, said to be greater if investment takes labour-using form, 140; this view criticised, 141 seq.
Encyclopaedia of the Social Sciences, 94
Engels, Friedrich; his relations with Marx, 183, 184, 185, 191, 202–4; on the rôle of ideas in history, 228; 'men make their history themselves, only in given surroundings', 229–30; on people boasting they have *made* a

285

INDEX

revolution, 231; on historical materialism as 'a guide to study, not a lever for construction', 232–3; utility of goods and cost in labour will determine the economic plan, 239–40; on the manuscript of *Capital*, 192–3; also 227

Entrepreneur, 3 *seq.*, 219

Equality, economic, 11, 60, 64 n., 66, 210–2

Equilibrium; nature of, 17 n., 18, 19, 35; 'neutral', 18; 'determinate', 19, 22–3, 26; multiple, 36, 62; in development, 91–2; static e. contrasted with problems of development, 74 *seq.*; at various levels of employment, 105; reached by trial and error, 54, 57, 243; e. conditions between departments of production, 267–8

Erlich, A., 120 n.

Excess capacity, 82–3, 83 n., 89, 99, 105, 124 n., 216, 225

Excise Tax; varying with the rate of investment as a stabilising mechanism, 46 n., 50, 55,

Expansion-Factor, The, 147

Exploitation; as used by Marx, 98, 187, 189, 191, 279; colonial, 94; referred to by G. B. Shaw, 206, 208

Fabians, 4, 205 *seq.*; *F. Essays*, 205, 206, 209

Fabricant, S., 124 n., 126 n.

Factors of Production; pricing of, 42 n., 56, 57, 59 n., 106 n.; market bidding for, 57; definition of, 110; difficulty of treating capital as one of the, 138–9; proportions of, not relevant to choice of capital intensity of investment, 142, 149

Farber, Professor Martin, 104

Fascism, 100–1, 169, 210

Feuerbach, Ludwig, 181

Fitzgerald, Edward, 178

Fluctuations, economic, 105, 241. (*See also* Trade Cycle, Crises)

Foreign Trade, 154, 199, 270

Foresight; effect of, on investment-decisions, 55. (*See* Uncertainty, Investment)

Formalism, 108–9, 114, 138

Fortnightly Review, The, 213

Foxwell, Professor H. S., 93 n.

Friction, economic, 7, 15

Galenson, Walter, 126 n.

Gapon, Father, 167

George, Henry, 206

Gerschenkron, Professor Alexander, 118–119 n., 120 n., 121 n., 124 n., 250

Gold; as money-commodity, 278–9; exchange of unsold consumer goods against gold, 198 n., 269

Gorky, Maxim, 159, 168, 175–6

Gosplan, 120 n., 123 n., 132, 251 n., 252 n.

Gradualism, economic, 245

Gray, Professor Sir Alexander, 200

'Gresham's Law'; of consumers' taste, 73

Gross and Net Production (or Income), 255–6

Growth, economic; and economic theory, 74 *seq.*; under Soviet Five Year Plans, 118 *seq.*; significance of distribution of investment between capital goods industries and others for rate of, 130–1, 150–1

Haley, Professor B. F., 82 n.

Hall, Sir Robert L., 41, 42 n., 44, 77

Handicraft industry, 153, 191

Hansen, Professor Alvin H., 217

Harris, Frank, 213

Harris, Professor Seymour E., 217 n.

Hawtrey, Professor R. G., 46

Hayek, Professor Friedrich August von, 56 n., 70 and n., 107, 240

Hegel, Georg Wilhelm Friedrich; on objectivity, 110, 231; his influence on Marx, 108–1, 186; the Young Hegelians, 181, 182; on history, 226–7, 231, 232; 'civil society', 234; also 161

Heimann, Eduard, 110

Henderson, Sir Hubert D., 11, 34 n.

Hess, Moses, 181

Hicks, Professor J. R., 17–18 and n., 62–3 n.

INDEX

History, 226, 227
Hobson, John A., 208
Hotelling, Professor Harold, 89
Housing; in U.S.S.R., 129, 136 and n.; in under-developed countries, 152 n.
Hunt, R.N. Carew, 234 n.
Hutchison, T. W., 16 n., 17 n., 53 n.
Hyndman, Henry Mayers, 205

Ideology; rôle of, in emphasising social unity and concealing social conflict, 97–8, 225; element of illusion in, 221, 227, 229, 233; as 'reflection' of social conditions, 229; not wholly illusory, 233; its rôle in history, 228–9, 234; bourgeois, illusionist function of, 225
Imperialism, 101–2, 168–9, 267, 270
Income; money and real, 62 n., 63–4, 65, 65–6 n. (*See also* Distribution, National Income)
Increasing Returns, 112. (*See also* Economies, Marginal Cost)
Independence; condition of, for supply and demand, 23
'Indeterminate'; applied to wage-level, 18–19, 25–6
Index-numbers; of output, problems of, 118–19, 249 *seq.*; of prices, in U.S.S.R., 118 n., 247, 248, 252; of output, in U.S.S.R., 118–20, 122–3, 133, 248 *seq.*; of labour productivity in U.S.S.R., 126 n.
Indian Economic Review (University of Delhi), 33
Indifference; -curves, 26, 29, 62 n.; -map 75, 79, 92
Indivisibility; of capital equipment, 82–4, 90
Iktisat Fakültesi Mecmuasi (University of Istanbul), 33
Inequality, economic, 9–10, 11–13, 96–7. (*See also* Distribution, Class)
Institutional rent, or revenue 12. (*See also* Rent, Surplus-value)
Interest, Rate of; under socialism, 38, 39, 40, 42–3, 52–4, 241, 259; long-term and short-term, 47; criterion of choice between investment-alternatives, 148,
258–9; as a monetary phenomenon, 216; as a determinant of investment, 217, 224; and capital intensity of investment, 148
International, First, 185, 202, 203
Investment; rate of, under socialism, 41 *seq.*; rate of, in U.S.S.R., 125, 129–32; policy concerning, in U.S.S.R., 89, 91, 125 *seq.*; 'ratio of effectiveness' of, 89 and n., 265; 'socialisation of', 218; *ex ante* co-ordination of, by planning, 40–1, 53–4, 76–7, 244; total social benefit as a criterion of, and not the covering of total cost, 82–8; whether decisions about, require the inclusion of capital-costs in the current price, 90 and n.; factor-proportions not relevant to choice of capital-intensity of, 142, 149; distribution of, between capital goods industries and others a determinant of future rate of economic growth, 130–1, 150–1; appropriate form and rate of, in under-developed countries, 140–1, 149–50; social i., 152 n.; as a determinant of level of employment under capitalism, 217; criteria for deciding the amount and technical form of, 258 *seq.*
Iskra, 164–5
Izvestia Akademii Nauk S.S.S.R., 258

Japan; rate of industrial growth, in, compared with that in U.S.S.R., 124
Jasny, Naum, 118 n.
Jay, Douglas, 58 n.
Johnson, Harry G., 138
Jevons, William Stanley, 104, 111, 205, 207
Jones, D.C., 93 n.

Kahn, Professor R.F., 50 n.
Kaldor, Nicholas, 35–6, 62 n., 62–3 n., 222–3, 224–5
Kalečki, Dr. Michal, 48
Kant, Immanuel, 41, 72, 107, 161, 168, 233
Kaplan, Dora, 172, 176
Kautsky, Karl, 192

INDEX

Kerensky, A. F., 158, 171
Keynes, Lord John Maynard, 7, 93 n., 104, 215–17, 218–19, 221, 224, 271
Khachaturov, Professor T. S., 262 n.
Krassin, L.B., 160, 167
Krupskaya, Nadezhda K. (Lenin's wife), 160, 165, 166, 167, 174, 176
Krzhyzhanovsky, G. M., 160

Labour, Division of, 5–6, 8, 9, 94, 112 n.
Labour; long-period supply-curve of, 18; supply-price of, affected by wages, 18, 25; demand for, 27, 29; theory of value, 110–12, 115, 117, 186 seq., 273; reserve army of, 189–90, 221; productivity, 126, 141 seq., 199 and n., 261–2; l.-saving technical change, 127, 141 seq., 199; Government, 210, 220, 246
Labour Monthly, 207
Laissez-faire, 4, 41, 76, 218
Lange, Dr. Oskar, 37 n., 41, 44, 48 n., 49, 50 and n., 51 and n., 54, 56, 57, 58, 62 n., 68, 77, 78, 114 n., 239 seq.
Lassalle, Ferdinand, 190
Lausanne School of Economists, 23
Law, economic, 11, 15; of socialism, 70; its objective character, 110, 195; as a 'synthetic *a priori* proposition', 107
Law, Natural, 4
League of Nations, 124
Lenin, Vladimir Ilyich; his quality of greatness, 157–8; his birth and parentage, 158; education, 157–8; expulsion from the university, 158; early revolutionary activity, 159–60; his exile and marriage, 160; controversy with the Narodniks, 159, 161–2, 270–1; controversy with 'Economists', 162–4; split between Mensheviks and Bolsheviks, 164–6; in London, 164, 173; in Switzerland, 165, 166–7, 169–70, 173; on the rôle of the working class in the revolution, 165–6; on State and Revolution, 172–3, 203; in 1905, 166–7; on imperialism and war, 168–9; in 1917, 169–72; attempted assassination of, 172; his personality, 173–6; on the Party, 162–4; his views about democracy, 163, 172–3; his views on the internal and external market and the causation of crises, 270–1; his zest for controversy, 174; his rejection of dogmatism, 174; Gorky's account of him, 175–6; his death and burial, 176
Leontief, Professor W. W., 68, 201
Lerner, Professor Abba P., 41, 42 n., 45, 54, 59–60 n., 60, 66, 70 n., 78, 89
Liebknecht, Karl, 157, 171
Liebknecht, Wilhelm, 184
Little, I. M. D., 60 n., 63, 65–6 n., 66
Location of industry, 78
Lorimer, Frank, 127 n.
Lunacharsky, Anatol V., 166, 168
Luxemburg, Rosa, 157, 266–72

Mach, Ernst, 168
Madge, Professor Charles, 136 n.
Malenkov, G., 122 n., 127, 136 n.
Mallett, Miss S. Y., 119 n.
Mallock, W. H., 213–14
Malthus, Rev. Thomas Robert, 6, 195, 200
Mandeville, Bernard de, 186, 231
Mannheim, Professor Karl, 98, 233
Marginal Cost; and marginal utility, 6; and price, 42 n., 43–4, 45, 46 n., 50, 55, 58 n., 59 and n., 64–5, 75 n., 89, 243; in decreasing cost industries, 59, 64, 75 n.
Marginal net product; of labour, 17; of factors and factor-prices, 42 n., 59 n., 61 n.; of the existing stock of capital, 48 n., 138; of investment, 74, 138; of capital, 115, 151
Marginal Productivity, Theory of, 16–17, 106 n., 138
Market; labour-m. compared with other markets, 25; retail, as way of registering consumers' demand, 70, 87–8, 240; 'free m.' said to be necessary if consumers' welfare is to sway production, 69 seq., 109, 240; 'external', or third, m. 266 *seq*; 'internal' m., 269, 271
Marshall, Dr. Alfred, 3, 9, 18, 94, 98 n., 208; and 'indeterminateness', 22, 26; on wages 'not a fund but a flow', 24; and

INDEX

barter, 26; and identification of desire with satisfaction, 36 n., 72
Marshall, Professor T. H., 93, 96
Martov, L., 164-5, 170, 174
Marx, Karl: *his ideas*; and 'German Socialist School', 5 n.; his theory of surplus value, 12, 187-91; and consumption as guiding aim of production, 70; and definition of class, 93, 103; his schema of reproduction, 77, 192-3, 267-9, 275-8; and departments of industry, 77, 130-2, 151, 198 n.; and rate of profit, 111, 193-5, 199, 280; and exploitation, 98, 138, 187 *seq*.; and value, 109, 110-12, 186 *seq*.; and Prices of Production, 194-5, 273, 280; and tendency of profit-rate to fall, 193, 199-200; and Transformation Problem (of values into prices), 279-80; and separation of production and distribution, 61; and objectivity of economic laws, 110; and mode of production, 116, 233-4; and stored-up labour, 139; Lenin on his theories, 174; and economic crises, 195 *seq*., 266 *seq*.; and 'realisation of surplus value', 198-9, 267-9; on 'first stage of socialism', 212; on history, 226 *seq*.; on ideology, 227-9; on rôle of individuals, 229-30; on problem, common to any society, of distributing social labour in definite proportions, 239; on gross and net values created, 255; also, 159, 161, 205, 206, 207 and n., 261

his life; his parentage and birth, 178-9; his father-in-law, 180; at the University, 179-81; his doctoral dissertation, 180; his study of Hegel, 180-1; marriage and honeymoon, 182; essay in journalism, 182; his study of economists, 183; exile, 183 *seq*.; friendship with Engels, 183, 185, 202; poverty and family life in London, 184-6; writing of *Capital*, 186; criticism of other economists, 200; studies technology at Geological Institute in Jermyn Street, 191; his failing health, 203-4; his wife's death, 204; his death and burial, 204

Marxism; and the consumer, 70; of Hyndman and the S.D.F., 205; in Russia, 159 *seq*.; and history, 226 *seq*.; 'Vulgar M.', 233; in Germany, 266
Marxists, 'legal', 160, 162
Materialism, Historical, 110, 181, 226 *seq*.
Materialism, Philosophical, 168
May, Dr. Kenneth, 274, 276, 277 n.
Maximum, economic, 6-7, 35, 39, 61-2, 65-6. (*See also Optimum*)
McGill, Dr. V. J., 104
Meade, Professor J. E., 71
Meek, Dr. Ronald L., 258
Mehring, Franz, 178, 182, 184, 227, 228 n.
Mensheviks, 165, 166, 168
Mercantilism, 10
Mercantilists, 110
Mikoyan, A. I., 130 n.
Mill, James, 94, 183
Mill, John Stuart, 20, 61, 104, 195, 200, 207 n.
Mises, Professor Ludwig von, 35, 56-7, 58, 59, 65, 67, 70, 71, 86, 240, 241, 242, 243
Modern Quarterly, The, 215, 239, 266
Molotov, V., 123 n., 130
Money; Quantity Theory of, 16; 'neutralising', 50; rôle of, under socialism, 56
Monopoly; and the growth of capitalism, 9-10; and class interests, 100; modern predominance of, 99; theory of 104, 115-16; and exploitation, 208
Moore, Samuel, 189 n., 190 n.
Mstislavsky, P., 262
Multiplier, The, 47 n.
Myrdal, Gunnar, 63-4 n.

Narodniks, 158-9 161-2, 270
Narodny Dokhod S.S.S.R., 256
National Income, proportion of, invested in U.S.S.R. and America, 125 n.; growth of, in Fifth Five Year Plan, 132; Soviet definition of, and valuation of, 253-7
Nationalisation, 172. (*See also* Socialism)
Nationalised industries; price-policy of, 55

INDEX

Neo-Classical Economists, 6
Neue Rheinische Zeitung, 184
New Moral World, 183
New York Tribune, 184
Northern Star, 183
Numéraire, problem of, 278–9
Nurkse, R., 139 n.

Optimum; conditions for allocating resources, 59 and n., 105; conditions and income-distribution, 60 seq. (See Welfare, Maximum)
Owen, Robert, 183

Pareto, Vilfredo, 22, 23, 34 n., 62 n.
Pascal, Professor Roy, 227
Pawley, Walter H., 129 n.
Peasantry; whether a class, 103; and the marketed surplus of agriculture, 152; Lenin's attitude towards, 166
Perroux, Professor François, 138
Petrov, A., 125 n.
Petty, Sir William, 139 n.
Pierson, N. G., 56 n.
Pigou, Professor A. C., 14, 30, 42 n., 53 n., 68 n., 73, 77, 97, 98 n., 108
Planning; nature of problem in conditions of development, 81 seq.; 'Central P. Board', 42 n., 58 n.; central p. authority, 42–3; superiority of, 53–4; financial, 218–19; 'democratic', 58; and the consumer, 87–9, 122–3, 129–32, 134; said to be 'a possible rather than necessary' element of socialism, 58 n.; limited by decentralised price-system, 241; investment over time, 40–1, 53–4, 76–7, 258 seq.; horizon of, 85–6; Soviet, 59, 89, 90–2, 118 seq., 242, 244 (See also 'Project-making', Soviet economy)
Plant, industrial; size of, 45; number of plants in an industry, conditions determining, 45–6, 47–8 n.
Plekhanov, G. V., 159, 160, 165, 174
Population; growth of, 127; urban and rural, 127–8
Positivists, 61, 63, 234
Postan, Professor M. M., 232

Pravda, 171
Price, 'parametric function of', 114 n.; 'P. of Production', 111, 194–5, 273 seq.; multiple prices in U.S.S.R., 248 n. (See also Value, Index-numbers, Accounting-price)
Price-system; its rôle, 6–7; and fluctuations, 14, 43, 46–9, 53–4; and socialism, 33 seq., 239 seq.; and income-distribution, 60–5; difficulties of, where indivisible units prevail, 82–3, 90
Priority list; of investment projects based on a net productivity-ratio, 52, 88
Production; as the primary problem under socialism, 244–5; gross and net, 255–6; 'productive' and 'unproductive', 253–4
Production, Mode of, 110, 116, 233–4
Production, Period of, 145–8
Production, Rates of Growth of, 118–25
Production, Social Relations of, 116
Productivity; of labour in U.S.S.R. and elsewhere, 126 and n.; of labour, as affected by technical change, 141 seq., 199; of labour, growth in, over time, 261–2; of labour, effect of change in upon surplus value, 199 n.
Profit; Ricardo's theory of, 275, 279; Marx's theory of, 111, 188, 190–1, 199–200; 'deduction' theory of, 279; rate of, 193–5, 199, 273 seq; as creation of and motive for uneconomic practices, 105; profits of State industry under socialism a function of the rate of investment, 44–5, 46–8; lack of modern theory of, 106 n.
'Project-making', 91 n., 265
Prokopovicz, Professor S.N., 252
Proletariat, 94, 160, 162–4, 188, 190–1, 208; its rôle in the bourgeois-democratic revolution, as viewed by Lenin, 166; dictatorship of, 173, 207
Property, income from, 13 n., 96–7; power and political influence as consequence of ownership of, 99; abuses of private p., 206
Proudhon, Pierre Joseph, 206
'Pursuit Curve', 40–1

INDEX

Rationalists, 232
Rationality; in allocating resources, 56–7, 240; in consumers' choice, 72
Rearmament; in U.S.S.R., 135 n.; in U.S.A., 221; and employment-policy, 221
'Re-contracting', 18
Reder, M. W., 91 n.
Rees, Sir J. F., 227
Reilly, Captain, 172
Relativism, historical, 233
Rent, 12, 206, 207 n., 208–9
Rentier, euthanasia of, 219
Reproduction, Simple and Expanded, 197–9, 267–9, 274–6
Review of Economic Statistics, 249
Revolution, Bourgeois, 161, 165–6, 170–1
Revolution, French, 94, 179, 235
Revolution, Industrial, 3–4, 9, 10, 40
Revolution, Jevonian (*See* Jevons)
Revolution, Russian; 1905, 166–7;1 917, 169–72, 207
Revolution, social, 100, 166, 209–10, 231
Rheinische Zeitung, 182
Ricardo, David, 6, 110, 183, 200, 205, 207 n., 208, 267; his theory of value, 110–11, 186; and theory of distribution, 108, 194; theory of profits as determined by production-situation in wage-goods industry, 275; and choice of invariable standard, 278; 'R.-effect', 280; Marx's criticism of, for neglecting constant capital, 280; criticised as author of heresy about conflict between Capital and Labour, 93 n.; on labour employed for a certain duration of time, 139; his treatment of wages as consisting of corn, 141; and effect of machinery on net and gross product, 143 n.; and 'gluts' of commodities, 195
Robbins, Professor Lionel, 35, 68, 100–1, 107, 234 n., 240
Robertson, Professor Sir Dennis H., 17n., 18–20
Robinson, Mrs. Joan Violet, 16 n., 106 n., 140, 266 n., 268, 270 n., 271, 272, 279 n., 281 n.

Rodbertus, Johann Karl, 5 n.
Ropner, W. C., 35 n.
Rostas, Dr. L., 126 n.
Rothstein, F. A., 167
Rotstein, A. I., 252 n.
Ruggles, Nancy, 64 n.

Saburov, M. Z., 132, 135 n., 137
Samuelson, Prof. P. A., 62 n., 64 n., 71 n.
Saving; principle governing, in socialist economy, 259 *seq.*; conditions in which industrial profits under socialism would measure the community's s. and correspond to the amount of investment, 47; 's. equals investment', 48; and employment and interest, 216; Pigou on 'telescopic faculty' in individuals towards the future, 73; 'forced s.', 101 n.; 'saved-up labour and land', 139
Say, Jean-Baptiste, 183, 266, 267
'Say's Law', 14 n.
Schlesinger, Dr. Rudolph, 227 n.
Schwarzschild, Dr. A. F., 266 n.
Scitovsky, Professor Tibor de, 62–3 n.
Seton, Francis, 118–19 n.
Sellars, Professor Roy Wood, 104
Senior, Nassau, 200
Shaw, George Bernard, 205 *seq.*; and Marx, 205; and Henry George, 206; and the dictatorship of the proletariat, 207; on gradualism, 207, 209–10; on rent, monopoly and exploitation, 208; on equality of income as essential to socialism, 210–12; on the U.S.S.R., 211 n., 212; his style 213, 214; his reply to Mallock, 213–14
Sidgwick, Henry, 4 n.
Sismondi, J.C.L. Simonde, 187
Slavonic Review, 157
Slovar-Spravochnik po Sotsialno-Ekonomicheskoi Statistike, 255
Smiles, Samuel, 206
Smith, Adam, 3, 6, 10, 94, 110, 183, 186, 187, 200, 231
Sobol, V., 250 n., 256 n.
Social-Democracy; and anti-planning, 58; S. D. Party of Russia, 164 *seq.*;

INDEX

S.D. Federation in England, 205; and full employment, 218; in Germany, 266 (*See also* Socialists, Fabians, Mensheviks)

Socialism; Sidgwick's view of, 4 n.; economic calculation under, 33 *seq.*; transition to, 161–2, 173, 209–10, 245–246; whether equality is essential to, 210–12; 'first-stage of', 212; whether it would destroy incentive, 214; 'socialisation of investment', 218

Socialists; versus individualists, 3–6; German School of, 5; revisionist, 161, 266

Social Revolutionaries, Left, 172

Sorel, Georges, 103 n.

Sombart, Werner, 5n.

Soviet economy, 35, 50 n., 80 n., 88–9, 91, 118 *seq.*, 140, 242, 244, 247 *seq.*

Soviet Union, 40; economic discussion in, 34, 89, 250, 254, 265; Five Year Plans in, 50 n., 80, 118 *seq.*, 241, 249–253

Soviets, in Russian Revolution, 167, 170–172

Soviet Studies, 118, 247, 258

Spencer, Herbert, 228–9

Sraffa, Piero, 23–4, 39, 112, 275 n., 278 n., 279 n.

Stagnation, economic, 98, 217

Stalin, Joseph; and basic economic law of socialism, 70, 130; and constraints of economic laws, 85 n.; on Soviet long-term industrial targets, 129; on preliminary conditions for transition to communism, 129–30; on capitalism and crises, 225

State; and revolution, 172–3; Bernard Shaw on the, 207; regarded as an impartial body standing above classes, 219; S. capitalism, 218

Statistics; Soviet, 118, 247 *seq.* (*See also* Index-numbers, National Income)

Streeten, Paul, 63–4 n.

Strumilin, Academician S. G., 127 n., 258–65

Struve, Peter, 160

Studensky, Paul, 255 n.

Substitution; between factors of production, 19, 59 n.; marginal rates of, 59 n., 61 n.

Supply; joint, 84

Surplus; of corn (assumed to be synonymous with wage-goods), 141 *seq.*; marketed s. of agriculture, its significance, 152

Surplus value, 12, 117, 188 *seq.*, 206, 208, 234; analogy with surplus product of previous forms of society, 187; rate of, 191, 193, 199 n., 275 *seq.*; 'relative s.v.', 199; 'realisation' of, 198–9, 266 *seq.*

Sweden; rate of industrial growth in, compared with that in U.S.S.R., 124, 125 n., 129

Sweezy, Dr. Paul M., 58 n., 115–16, 269 n., 271, 274, 277 n., 278, 279 and n.

Swingler, Randall, 177

Taussig, Professor F. W., 12

Tawney, Professor R. H., 235

Taylor, Professor F. M., 57 n., 239 n., 243

Terms of trade, 154

Thompson, William, 187–8

Time; choices extending over, irrationality of, 38–9, 73, 77, 259; t.-preference or -discount, 39, 148, 258–60; t. and labour as measures of capital, 115, 139; co-ordinating investment-decisions over t., 40–1, 53–4, 76–7, 244–5 (*See also* Production, Period of)

Times, The, 202, 204

'Tolerances', or 'limits'; within which precision is possible in defining an 'ideal' allocation of resources, 65–6

Torr, Dona, 189 n., 228 n.

Tractors, in agriculture, 128, 141 *seq.*

Trade Cycle, 13–14, 215 *seq.* (*See also* Crises)

Trade Unions, and wages, 20; and referendum, 73

Transformation Problem, 273–81

Trotsky, Leon, 166

Tugan-Baranovsky, M., 160, 266, 267

Turnover Tax; varying with rate of investment as stabilising mechanism, 50; in Soviet Union, 50 n., 88

INDEX

Uncertainty; its effect on investment decisions under a decentralised pricing-system, 53–4, 77, 243–4; and over-production, 13–14

Under-developed countries, 138 seq.

Unemployment, 49, 99, 101 n., 246; and equation of price to marginal cost, 55; rural overpopulation in Russia, 127; disguised, 140; and capitalism, 215 seq.

United States (See America)

Untermann, Ernest, 191, 192 n.

Usher, Professor A. P., 5–6, 8, 9.

U.S.S.R. (See Soviet Union)

Utility; maximisation of, 6, 60 seq.; measurement in money depends on amount of money income, 11; meaning of, 31; index of, disturbed by inequality, 12, 60 seq.; marginal u. of income, 24 seq., 260; interpersonal comparisons of, 60; marginal u. and marginal cost, 6, 59 n.; modern theory of, 110, 113–14; G. B. Shaw and, 207; comparing future and present, 258–61 (See also Welfare, Consumers, Demand, Value)

Value; subjective, or psychological, theory of, 31, 69, 106, 108–9, 110, 113–116, 117, 205, 207; cost of production and, 195, 207 n., 273; Labour Theory of, 110–12, 115, 117, 186 seq., 207 n., 273; and Price, 273 seq.; significance of a theory of v. as a method of analysis, not as a basic premise for *a priori* deduction, 117 (See also Surplus-value)

'Value-judgements', 58, 61

van Dorp, Dr. E. C., 48 n.

Variation, Principle of, 18–20, 81 seq.

Veblen, Thorstein, 28, 72, 84, 99

Vladimirov, P., 250 n.

Volodarsky, L., 127 n.

Voprosi Ekonomiki, 89 n., 265

Wages, Theory of, 16 seq.

Wages-Fund, doctrine of, 24

Wages; effect of rise in, on Prices of Production, 280–1; differences in, which correspond to differences in disutilities of work and which do not, 37 n.; treated as an independent variable, 151; iron law of, 190

Wage-earners, 97, 98–100

Wage-goods; supply of, as determinant of investment, 141, 150; decisive rôle played by conditions of production in industries producing w.-g., 275, 279–280

Wagner, Adolf, 5 n.

Wants; new, 38, 78, 84; modified in course of economic development, 75, 79 (See also Consumer, Consumption, Utility)

War; socialist attitude towards, 169

Webb, Sidney (Lord Passfield) and Beatrice, 3, 73, 160, 163

Weber, Max, 56 n., 107

Welfare, social; conditions for maximising, 59 n., 60 seq.; dividing w.-economics into two parts, 62 n.; treated as a summation of individual satisfactions, 69; defined in terms of consumers' market-behaviour, 73 (See also Optimum, Maximum, Consumers)

Wells, H. G., 158, 225

Westphalen, Baron Ludwig von, 180

Westphalen, Jenny von (Karl Marx's wife), 180, 182, 185, 204

Wicksell, Knut, 43, 62 n., 139

Wicksteed, Philip Henry, 207

Wieser, Friedrich von, 4 n., 15, 34 n.

Wiles, P. J. D., 80–1 n.

Wilson, P. A., 100

Winsten, S., 205

Winternitz, Dr. J., 274, 275, 276, 279

Wolf, Julius, 281 n.

Wright, Professor D. McCord, 118 n.